Tudor Victims

For Linda, Angela and Hannah, for being such good friends, and for Jan, for being my sister

'Sono enormamente grata'

Tudor Victims

Lynda Telford

First published in Great Britain in 2016 by
Pen & Sword History
an imprint of
Pen & Sword Books Ltd
47 Church Street
Barnsley
South Yorkshire
S70 2AS

Copyright © Lynda Telford 2016

ISBN 978 1 47383 403 3

The right of Lynda Telford to be identified as the Author of this Work has been asserted by her in accordance with the Copyright, Designs and Patents Act 1988.

A CIP catalogue record for this book is available from the British Library

All rights reserved. No part of this book may be reproduced or transmitted in any form or by any means, electronic or mechanical including photocopying, recording or by any information storage and retrieval system, without permission from the Publisher in writing.

Typeset in Ehrhardt by
Mac Style Ltd, Bridlington, East Yorkshire
Printed and bound in the UK by CPI Group (UK) Ltd,
Croydon, CR0 4YY

Pen & Sword Books Ltd incorporates the imprints of Pen & Sword Archaeology, Atlas, Aviation, Battleground, Discovery, Family History, History, Maritime, Military, Naval, Politics, Railways, Select, Transport, True Crime, and Fiction, Frontline Books, Leo Cooper, Praetorian Press, Seaforth Publishing and Wharncliffe.

For a complete list of Pen & Sword titles please contact
PEN & SWORD BOOKS LIMITED
47 Church Street, Barnsley, South Yorkshire, S70 2AS, England
E-mail: enquiries@pen-and-sword.co.uk
Website: www.pen-and-sword.co.uk

Contents

Chapter 1	1
Chapter 2	13
Chapter 3	24
Chapter 4	37
Chapter 5	51
Chapter 6	63
Chapter 7	77
Chapter 8	89
Chapter 9	101
Chapter 10	121
Chapter 11	136
Chapter 12	152
Chapter 13	166
Chapter 14	177
Chapter 15	188
Chapter 16	203
Chapter 17	219
Chapter 18	235
Epilogue	253
Notes	257
Select Bibliography	288
Index	292

Cardinal Thomas Wolsey. (*Bridgeman Images*)

Chapter One

During the early 1470s, in the reign of King Edward IV, Robert and Joan Wolsey celebrated the birth of a son. We cannot be sure of the exact date on which this extraordinary child first saw the light of day, but that was common enough. Births often went unrecorded, or the records were subsequently lost. Historians vary slightly in their estimates of the appropriate date, ranging from the March of 1471 to the winter of 1472/3.[1] The slightly earlier date was recommended to coincide with the feast date of St Thomas Aquinas on 7 March.

One of the many events considered to be prophetic was the appearance of a comet. At around the time of Wolsey's birth a comet appeared in the sky over England. It was quite a large one, now known to have been a magnitude 4 (Halley's Comet is magnitude 7), so the event was easily seen and lasted for some time. It first appeared on 25 December 1471 and was clearly visible until 21 February 1472. For those readers with an interest in such phenomena, it is registered as 'C/1471-Y1'. Whether it was indeed to foretell unusual happenings ahead, or not, is open to interpretation.

The son born to Robert and Joan (née Daundy) probably had no siblings, but it was obvious that, contrary to custom, this apparently gifted child could be spared from the family business. However, Robert aimed high for his son. The parents of this child were in a comfortable situation. The epithet often applied to Wolsey by detractors during his later life was 'son of an Ipswich butcher'. However, the prosperous Robert Wolsey was actually rather more than that. The family had moved to Ipswich from Combe near Stowmarket.[2] This meant that the newcomer would have to deal with competition and even resentment from already established businesses within Ipswich. However, Robert did succeed in making a suitable living for his family. Perhaps this accounts for the suggestions that his dealings were not always entirely within the law. He appears to have had difficulties with the town authorities on several occasions, involving offences such as selling for excessive gain, selling bad meat at Ipswich market and not exhibiting the skins of slain beasts, in accordance with the rules. By the time Thomas was around 9 years old, his father was known to be something of a shady character, in fact he is referred to as 'the worst offender before the leet'.[3] There was even at one time a suggestion that he had allowed his house to be used for immoral purposes, although no details are given.

However, despite a certain loss of good name, his machinations paid off. The family began to do very well, regardless of the difficulties still lingering from the effects of the catastrophic plague of the previous century. These were still evident in a lack of manpower, along with a new and disturbing line of thought among people who had realised that they finally had worth in the labour market. There were also echoes of remaining instability from the civil wars, which had taken King

Edward IV to the throne. Great changes had come about since the Hundred Years War, which had also leeched England of manpower and prosperity. But change and upheaval was good for men such as Robert Wolsey. They were the very ones eager to grasp at any opportunity and were able to thrive on change which could bring them some advantage. Robert Wolsey was officially a grazier, making his living from sheep and cattle. By 1480 he was actually referred to as a 'squire' by a monk of Ipswich, who spoke of the 'fat cattle he saw grazing on the lands of Maister Wolci'.[4]

Not only meat would be produced by such a livestock business, but also hides and other by-products, most particularly the all-important fleeces for the wool trade at Calais. 'Maister Wolci' was obviously in a fair way to becoming comfortably well off.

Such people as these, rising in a world that opened new horizons, were the ones most likely to appreciate the benefits of good education. It must quickly have become obvious to the father of young Thomas that he had produced a boy of unusual intelligence, whose ability could be better used to further the family's good than merely to make another grazier out of him. Children were always considered a source of revenue in one way or another, but in this case there would be far more gained by sending him away to acquire a proper education.

By 1479 Robert Wolsey had purchased for £8 a certain amount of land, along with a house, near Rosemary Lane. It was a respectable address and close also to the Ipswich Grammar School, although by the age of 11 the young Thomas had already taken what he could from the educational facilities of Ipswich. He moved to Oxford, a good three years ahead of the usual time for finishing an education there. Peter Gwyn in *The King's Cardinal* states that for a young man in Wolsey's situation, given the new social and financial standing of his family, it would have been perfectly normal for him to expect to be sent to Oxford. He attended the new College of St Mary Magdalen. This was in the process of erection when he arrived, the foundation of Bishop William Waynflete. In the new colleges attempts were being made to compel the students to accept some form of discipline as well as regulate their otherwise very erratic learning patterns.

Thomas Wolsey was at Magdalen, moving towards his batchelor's degree, in 1483 when King Edward IV died. This early and unexpected death was to lead to the further upheaval of the reign of King Richard III, after the marriage of the late king, his brother, had been declared bigamous and its offspring illegitimate.[5] Richard III spent some of his first year of kingship moving around the country, culminating in a triumphant visit to York in August of 1483. However, we know that he also paid a visit to Oxford just prior to that, in July, using Magdalen College as his headquarters, and was honourably received there.

Wolsey would certainly have seen King Richard on that occasion. Did he have any premonition that he too was destined for great things? He was certainly a young man full of confidence, willing to take chances, proud of his achievements, so he may have been determined to make something of himself, quite apart from the expectations of business and modest prosperity.

Richard III's brief reign was to come to an untimely end due to the Tudor claimant and his ferocious mother Margaret Beaufort, but during his term of kingship Richard did make genuine attempts to bring order to the country. In many parts, including the north where he was known and respected, there was grief and resentment at his passing. This feeling was to make the throne uncomfortable for his successor in the years to come. Although these upheavals need not have concerned Thomas Wolsey, he would by that time have been casting his eyes towards his future prospects.

His own testimony tells us that he received his degree 'at the age of fifteen years, which was a rare thing, and seldom seen!' (the usual age was 17). The ceremony during which the degree was actually attained was a difficult one and known as a 'determiner'. This involved the student standing, for nine days, being obliged to defend his level of learning against all comers. This gave an opportunity to show off the oratorical skills of the student, his ability to work a crowd and sway opinions, in something akin to the old Roman tradition of rhetoric. It must have been stressful, but when successful also uplifting, and was accepted as being the high point of any young man's college career.[6]

Wolsey remained at college and later became a Fellow of Magdalen. He also earned for himself the title of 'boy bachelor' in reference to his scholastic achievements at such a young age.

While Thomas was advancing in his studies, his father was advancing also. He had bought another house in the south ward of the town. He was still often at odds with the authorities, due to his dubious methods of conducting business, but on the whole such problems were small and did him no real harm. He began to enjoy a different sort of reputation in the Parish of St Nicholas, one of respectability and social acceptance, no doubt greatly bolstered by his now substantial income. He had moved quite rapidly into the emergent merchant and business class. These people, though without any claims to gentle birth or good family connections, could still find themselves in a position to gather serious wealth, and even helped to finance the 'enterprises' of their social superiors. Any merchant who had the shrewdness to see openings in the new markets would have realised the good sense in producing cloth at home, from the fleeces of his own flocks. Rather than sending bales of fleeces abroad, as was the custom formerly, it was by then increasingly effective to export the finished woollen cloth. By managing the whole process in this way, it showed not only an eye for the main chance, but also the ability to read the changes in the wind prevalent throughout Europe. It was this concern for market forces and the accompanying willingness to adapt that was to produce the great merchant princes of the future.

By 1485, when the Tudor opposition to Richard III had flared into real conflict, the Plantagenet dynasty came to an end at Bosworth Field. The new victor, calling himself King Henry VII, would always be conscious that there were several people alive in the kingdom who had a better right to the throne than himself.[7] He was to pass on this sense of insecurity to his successor Henry VIII and it would eventually prove to be the catalyst that was to change the face of England forever.

For Wolsey, the rise and fall of kings may still have seemed something outside his concern. The difficulties at the start of the reign of Henry VII, with its discontents and pretenders, would hardly have touched him. But Henry VII was to visit Oxford just after the Battle of Stoke in 1487, which demolished the attempts of Lambert Simnel to press forward a claim to the throne. There were to be other pretenders ahead, and Henry must have realised the need to canvass the approval of men of the College. These were to be the very men the new king would favour in the future. Not the members of the old noble families, with their divided allegiances and proud sense of self-worth, but men of the people who had risen by their own efforts. These were the men he liked, ones more likely to be able to appreciate a businesslike, rather than a warlike, king. One who was determined to build his dynasty on solid foundations of prosperity at home and abroad. One, also, who was determined to eradicate (ruthlessly where necessary) all those proud nobles who still opposed the new regime and were capable of considering themselves his equal, if not his superior, in birth. Henry VII intended to build on the approval of men of like minds, and to begin to amass a huge fortune for himself, which alone could make him feel truly secure.[8]

Henry VII was successfully to establish a solid base for those men, who loved money for its own sake. He was also to bring to life the new Court of Star Chamber (so named because of the star-painted ceiling of the room in which it met) within the Palace of Westminster. This court was specifically designed to deal with 'difficult' cases, which were the ones that might prove unpopular. These were aimed at the people who might be reluctant to accept the King's reforming zeal and his determination to be the sole arbiter of their behaviour. The old days were certainly gone when a man could consider himself a prince on his own estates. Matters both large and small would now be dealt with in the new court, all with an equally ruthless intent to make the country in general bend to Henry's will.

But what he had created was not merely a court designed to enforce his laws, but a new ruling class. These men would be administrators, rather than the soldierly nobles who had previously held sway. Those nobles were to find themselves gradually pushed aside, their privileges curtailed, by a new generation of men who were preferred by a king whose own antecedents were doubtful. He would always prefer the money-men, with their usefully flexible consciences. They could provide what he needed, making money to provide stability, which in turn would produce more money.

By 1496 Wolsey's father's wealth had been increasing steadily and he had already made arrangements in his will to bequeath funds to his local parish church.

Thomas had by this time become Bursar of Magdalen, involved in administrative duties but he also had under his care the three sons of Thomas Grey, the Marquess of Dorset. He quickly gained the approval of this gentleman, making the most of the connection, to the extent that he stayed with the family at Christmas at their manor of Bradgate Park, Leicester.

By the will made by Robert Wolsey before his death in 1496, Thomas was to receive a bequest from his father *if* Thomas had already become a priest and sung Masses for him. Thomas was by this time around 23 years old, and canon law decreed that no man could be ordained as a priest before the age of 24 years. However, obtaining a dispensation for that would not present many difficulties. Surprisingly, Thomas missed the deadline for receiving the Mass money, as he did not take holy orders until five months after the expiration time stated in his father's will.[9] However, on 10 March 1498 he was finally ordained by the Bishop of Lydda (the Bishop of Salisbury's suffragan). Was Wolsey actually hesitating about taking the final step towards holy orders? There is some suggestion that Wolsey's father may have been attempting to apply gentle pressure to his son. If so, why? The young man would surely have been aware that it was the only really secure door through which he could rise to higher office. Was there a woman involved? What is certain is that after Thomas was ordained at Marlborough he read nothing for a year afterwards. He was undoubtedly going through some personal turmoil. He was given a rural deanship in the county of Norwich, then later in 1498 was appointed Junior Bursar of his College, in the following year becoming the Senior.[10]

In his role of Bursar he was responsible for the completion of the Magdalen Tower. There was later to be an accusation that he had misappropriated the funds for this when they were in his charge. The Register of the University of Oxford confirms his appointment, but there is certainly no mention of any offence in the records. This matter is often quoted to Wolsey's detriment, but the accusation cannot be proved. Any such wrongdoing would be punished by immediate dismissal, and we know from the existing records that this did not happen.[11]

When Wolsey became a priest he was still an unknown young man without any of the useful connections that would help him to advance, but the world was changing. It was now ready to use men like himself, who had much intelligence and ability. Such men were beginning to step forward into the new order created by the King. John Morton, Archbishop of Canterbury and Chancellor of England, Bray the Lord Treasurer and Foxe the Bishop of Exeter were all to be examples of this trend, the finest example of which would one day be Wolsey himself.

For a man such as Thomas, the Church would always be a career, rather than a vocation, but he could not be said to be unusual in this. The Church had also changed. Administrators of ability had always been needed, both in monastic establishments and as the servants of great men whose reliance on chaplains and clerical secretaries could be total. But now a whole new 'civil service' was coming into being, and Wolsey's priesthood, like that of many another, would become merely a means to an end.

Although it was still correct form to have a show of piety, and to be fair many people were still genuinely pious, a feeling had certainly grown that the 'real' religious were still those who lived apart from the world, in enclosed communities. The world held far too many temptations to allow the lay clergy to escape entirely from its influences and this was shown by the temperate, even faintly amused, attitude shown towards the peccadilloes of priests and even higher clergy. Wolsey, when in office, would certainly provide for the two children he sired in his relationship with one Mistress Joan Larke, the daughter of a respectable family.[12] As long as a certain amount of discretion was observed, this was considered to be tolerable behaviour.

It is often not realised that the members of the priesthood had to be celibate since Pope Gregory VII introduced the rule in the eleventh century, but by the fifteenth century the vow was not always taken by members of the secular clergy. This created a significant distinction. Monks and nuns took the vow of celibacy at their ordination, and were obliged to keep it. The secular priests were obliged to follow that rule only because it was a regulation imposed by the Pope. This was responsible for the way in which the various kinds of clergy were viewed by the laity. It began to be seen as a far more heinous offence for a monk to break his vow, than for a member of the secular clergy to commit fornication or even openly keep a mistress. It gradually became so common an offence that by the time Wolsey had achieved high office, many priests lived more or less openly with women, and the Church had tacitly accepted the practice by turning a blind eye to it. When a situation became scandalous, it was often dealt with by recourse to fines. This of course influenced the laity to consider the secular clergy to not be 'real' religious in the same way as those who lived away from the world. It also gradually eroded the idea of a man being forced to do without normal life, and it proved less of a sin, and therefore less of a bar to a man rising through the ranks.

The erosion of the old traditions of allegiance led to the Church beginning to lose its monopoly over the careers of men who wished to rise in the world. There was naturally corruption in all walks of life. Even within the confines of the Church it had been endemic in its control of licences, passports and permits of all kinds. The receipt of tithes and bribes and the saying of Masses, the marrying and burying and christening of the people, and the payments for absolution had all begun to eat away at the respect felt for it. The common practice of holding multiple beneficies, in paying another priest to perform the duties for a small sum while the holder often never saw his parishioners, was increasingly felt to be wrong, although the practice would continue for some time and Wolsey would benefit from it. There was a strong feeling of competition between the members of the secular clergy to gain as many benefits as they could. Such pluralities were very common, even though they did require a dispensation which would again entail the use of a bribe, which ensured the passing of money from hand to hand and the spreading of financial benefits from every position gained.[13]

Wolsey was a clever man, able to make use of his learning, but he had made his choice. Whatever the temptations of the world – and he was always to enjoy extravagance and display – he had thrown in his lot with the Church. It needs to be remembered that obtaining his degrees of B.Th. and D.Th. shows enough level of learning during his residence at the College for him to be able to expect that his future held an interesting and financially rewarding career. Also it is a matter of record that he had the Mastership of the School and the post of Dean of Divinity just prior to his resignation from the College.[14]

When his college days finally came to an end he had made enough of a friendship with the Marquess of Dorset for that gentleman to arrange for him to become the Rector of Limington in Somerset. Having accepted this post, with its useful income of £21 per annum, the rules of the College made it necessary for Wolsey to resign his appointments.[15]

Why was it, then, that Wolsey left Magdalen when things were going so well for him? He naturally had hopes of preferment in the wider world, and a friend to recommend him, but he was to find it more difficult than he expected to make his mark. The life of the College had benefits, together with comfort and security, despite its claustrophobic atmosphere. It provided an almost cloistered existence, safe from the world, which many men appreciated. We know that Wolsey was ambitious, eager to experience the greater things that the world might offer, but 'might' is the operative word. He was giving up a great deal, and stepping out into a more precarious existence. Certainly the new promised income of £21 per year was not to be lightly refused, but it would not be enough in itself.

We know that he shortly accepted the post of chaplain to the then Archbishop of Canterbury, Henry Deane, who had been appointed in 1501. Perhaps it seemed to Wolsey at that point that the world was opening up for him and providing him with opportunities. When he became chaplain to the new Archbishop of Canterbury he did not relinquish the income that he was receiving from the parish of Limington. He had already received permission to accept the revenue from more than one benefice and had begun the common practice of farming out the actual work to a curate, while he kept the bulk of the income. In fact, for the last eight years during which he drew the income of Limington, he never went there at all.[16]

Interestingly for later on in Wolsey's life, the thing for which Archbishop Henry Deane was to be most remembered was that during his Archbishopric he had, in 1501, married the King's heir, Prince Arthur, to Princess Katherine of Aragon, the daughter of Ferdinand and Isabella of Spain.

Unfortunately, what had seemed to be a new beginning and a new prosperity, was not to last. By 1503 both Wolsey's patron the Marquess of Dorset and the new Archbishop of Canterbury were dead. Henry Deane had followed the Queen, Elizabeth of York to the grave. She had died at the age of 37 in a futile attempt to produce another heir to reduce the pain and disappointment of the death of Prince Arthur, who had died only six months after his marriage to the Spanish princess.

Wolsey was responsible for dealing with the arrangements for the funeral of the Archbishop, taking the body by water to Faversham for burial. Despite the acknowledgment that he had performed his duties well, it must have been a period of worry for him. He would immediately have to look about for a new employer.

He found what he needed in Sir Richard Nanfan, the Governor of Calais, in whose household he was to stay until Sir Richard's own death in 1507. Sir Richard Nanfan is popularly supposed to have recommended Wolsey to the King, praising his abilities, but he showed his true confidence in him by making him the executor of his will. Naturally, the court would be Wolsey's aim, where preferment was to be found, so the recommendation from Nanfan would be valued. Only there could a man like Wolsey be able to show his true worth. It is to be remembered that he had already lived out more than half of his allotted life's span![17] He could not know that his years would be cut short, but he must by then have been feeling some concern that he had not already made his mark. It had never been his intention to leave the security of Magdalen to be a mere clerk. He had little time to waste and must have been always looking about him for better opportunities.

Following the death of Sir Richard Nanfan, Wolsey was transferred to the royal household, after being offered the post of chaplain to King Henry VII. Henry was by that time nearing the end of his reign. He had lost both his heir and his queen within a year of each other. He had another promising boy, but seemed to be dissatisfied. He had already arranged a betrothal between his widowed daughter-in-law and the remaining prince, Henry, despite there being a rather worrying six-year age gap between them, on the wrong side, the Prince being his proposed bride's junior. This boy had originally been intended for the Church, the regular fate of younger sons when their elder brothers succeeded. However, this 'spare' son was now destined to step forward into his brother's place, taking over not only his future crown, but also the bride.

Despite this advance in status, young Henry was to suffer a considerable amount of confinement during his waiting time. The King did not seem to have a great deal of confidence in his younger son's ability to grow into the part now intended for him without a struggle. The King kept him within his own chambers, ordered his activities and his friends, and insisted on his continuing education. He was not even allowed to take part in the sports of the court, for which he would have seemed to be ideally suited. Perhaps the King was concerned that there was a possibility not only of injury to the only surviving prince but the opportunity to make the sort of friends the King did not approve of, and the contacts he did not wish his heir to pursue. Henry, once freed from his father's restraint, was to blossom out into everything his cautious father would have preferred him not to be. Extravagant, pleasure loving, sport loving, bombastic, attention seeking, open to making indiscreet friendships with the other young men of the court, and eager to become a devil with the ladies. Perhaps these were the very character flaws that his father saw in him while he was a prince, and the real reason why Henry VII was so concerned to keep his son occupied with tutors. It is usual to assume that Prince Henry had, since the death of his brother, become too precious to be put at risk, but perhaps there was rather more to it than that. Henry VII had carefully trained Prince Arthur, arranging for him a separate household and tutors, and there is good reason to believe that the eldest son was showing the signs of being all that his father wanted him to be – sensible, serious minded and willing to soak up all the knowledge his father laid out for him.[18] The younger son, now the heir, was very different and it is fair to assume that there was no real meeting of minds between the two men. All the solid foundation-building, the money-collecting, the suspicion of courtiers and the hesitation to allow anyone to know what he was thinking was to be casually thrown aside when Henry VII died. His son would remake the court in his own image, with the abandon of a man throwing open a window and letting the fresh air in. His late father would have shuddered at the draught he created.

Perhaps this is one of the reasons why Henry VII actually considered a new marriage for himself prior to his death, to none other than the sister of the Princess

Katherine of Aragon. Her sister, Juana, had been married to Philip the Fair of the Netherlands and had already proved her fertility as the mother of a son who would one day be the Emperor Charles V. But she was far more than just a mother. After the death of Isabella of Spain the great union of the Spanish kingdoms was broken. Ferdinand had no jurisdiction over the lands of his deceased wife, which were inherited by her daughter Juana. (Castile did not recognise a Salic law, unlike Aragon, and therefore Juana became the heir of Castile, although it would be her son who would inherit the whole kingdom when Ferdinand died.)

Henry VII now briefly contemplated marrying the widowed Juana himself. What were his motives? It is usually considered that he wanted to get his ever-greedy hands on Castile, as husband of the heiress. Ferdinand countered the proposals by declaring that his daughter was mad, and about to be locked up. She had, in fact, shown some signs of instability after the death of her husband, when she had refused to allow his body to be buried. However, it is just possible that she was not quite as mad as her father liked to pretend. He, too, was concerned to keep Castile under his own control, at least until his grandson was old enough to take over.[19] Is it also possible that Henry VII still had some hope of another son? He had sired a child on his late wife not too long before, so he cannot have been so infirm as many liked to imagine. Did he have concerns about the pleasure-loving son who would succeed him?

Was the suggested marriage to Juana a last-ditch attempt to produce another heir, as well as being a wonderful opportunity for England to acquire her extensive lands?

However, the negotiations came to nothing and Henry VII actually went on to propose marriage to the Queen of Naples, and then Margaret of Savoy.

Whatever Henry VII's true intentions at that time, it must have been a gloomy court that Wolsey entered after Nanfan's death. Becoming chaplain did not necessarily mean that he would spend much time with the King, nor would he confine himself to Henry's religious needs. Here again, duties involved with day to day administration would have taken up a great deal of his time, but ability always shows itself. Richard Foxe and Sir Thomas Lovell, the King's advisors, recommended Wolsey to start the negotiations with Savoy, although Wolsey ended up going to Scotland instead on the King's behalf. He did later visit the Netherlands, but to take a message to the Emperor, rather than to arrange a marriage. The King certainly used his servants widely and any man wishing for advancement needed to have a good deal of flexibility and to make himself available for whatever duty arose.

Living at court would not provide Wolsey with a luxurious life. Not only was the King known to be a miser, and oblivious to his own comfort or anyone else's, but space and privacy were at a premium in all large households at that time, and it was a rare courtier who merited a room to himself. Often not even a private bed could be expected. We know that Wolsey was obliged to share a bed with Lord Darcy of Templehurst, and this gentleman was actually a member of the Privy Council. However, the arrangement did not seem to disturb either man, and they remained on friendly terms for many years. Wolsey was by now in his mid-30s and although he had been fortunate to have one or two influential patrons, he seemed to have once more reached an impasse. He was not alone in wondering what the future held when Henry VII died.

Katherine of Aragon had been sidelined, despite her supposed marriage to the new heir, who had actually been obliged to reject their betrothal officially. After several years of being a poor relation at court, living in penury because her father and father-in-law differed in opinion as to which of them ought to support her, she had seen her followers either drift home or suffer poverty with her. She saw very little of the prince to whom she was supposed to be betrothed, and suffered at the death of her mother, knowing that her father had far too many other concerns to give her any support. He was, moreover, a slippery character, with an eye to his own affairs, who was not to be relied upon. Katherine, too, must have wondered if the future would ever hold anything better. Henry VII no longer seemed to need an alliance with her father. Indeed, he was to go on to suggest that not only could he marry the Archduchess Margaret himself, but that his daughter, the young Princess Mary, would make a suitable wife for the Archduke Charles. Katherine was surplus to requirements.

Cardinal Morton and Reginald Bray were dead by this time, but Wolsey was able to form a friendship with Richard Foxe, who was then Bishop of Winchester, a contact that would be useful. Henry VII had also noticed that Wolsey had carried out his mission to the Emperor with great despatch and efficiency. It was remarked upon that he had travelled to the Netherlands with his message and managed to return to England within 70 hours! It was worthy of catching the King's attention.

Wolsey was made Dean of Lincoln in 1508, received the vicarage of Lydd in Kent around the same time, and then was appointed Royal Almoner.[20] At that point he let the Limington living go to another priest in early 1509. But by the spring of 1509 the King was ailing and Wolsey, as Almoner, had taken over the work of dealing with his charities. Henry VII had always seemed a miser, putting the collecting of money before anything else. But at the end of his life he spent a great deal of money on charities, but not even making a dent in the large (indeed huge) sums that were later to be found in his coffers at Richmond. He expended the money freely, attempting to gain God's approval and save his soul. Many alms, hospitals and charities were to benefit from his last illness in this way, although it was not so altruistic as it appeared.[21] The money used for these came from the closure of a few small religious houses, falling into decay and not paying their way. No doubt he thought their failing revenues could be put to better use. It was a good lesson, which Wolsey himself would use in later years, but one that Prince Henry, waiting for his turn to come, also filed away in his mind for future reference.

Nothing could prevent the natural march of time. The King died in April of 1509 at his favourite Palace of Richmond. He left directions that he should be buried beside his late wife, Elizabeth of York, and this was a duty to be undertaken by Wolsey. The funeral took place on 10 May 1509. Henry VII was to share a magnificent tomb with Elizabeth, and their effigies were to be worked in gilded bronze by that master craftsman Torregiano. A chapter of history, which had begun with plots, treachery and the death of the white rose royal line, ended with an embittered king, trying to keep a grip both on the country, and on the next generation.

It was a new spring, a new king and a new start. Although shrewd enough, and very eager to start on his new life, King Henry VIII was only 18 years old when he succeeded to the throne. But he intended to be a very different sort of king. He would be free of the restrictions imposed on him, and he would grasp the opportunity to prove himself a man and a ruler, but he would need advice and help. Furthermore, he intended to enjoy life. He must already have noticed and approved the efficient and capable Almoner, trusted even by Henry VII. Henry VIII wanted an advisor who could not only help him, but a man who understood his needs and had the diplomatic skills and sophistication to stand as his representative abroad.

Thomas Wolsey was to be that man. He was very willing to step into the position assigned to him. It would give him an unprecedented opportunity to rise. He knew he was capable of earning the respect of those people whose opinions counted. Popes, kings and princes would become his equals and he would make a career like no other. It must have been a thrilling time for him, seeing himself against the backdrop of Europe. He could not only assist the new king, taking from him the more boring responsibilities of kingship and holding them in his own hands. He could influence the young king, turning him into a figurehead to impress, yet a man who would be prepared to ask and take advice. He could use his diplomatic skills at home and abroad, gaining the respect and even reverence that was his due.

Wolsey was by then around 38 years old and his long wait was over. He was in his prime, willing and ambitious, eager to get on. His time of greatness was beginning.

Anne Boleyn as Queen, from a drawing by Hans Holbein. (*British Museum Images*)

Chapter Two

The woman who would sweep through the centre of Henry VIII's reign like a comet, glittering briefly though brilliantly, had her birth unrecorded. Anne's date of birth has been the subject of argument for over a century and ranges from a date of 1500 to almost a decade after that. The most respected authorities have settled, in the absence of any conclusive documentary evidence, on the year 1501 as being the most likely time.[1]

Sir Thomas Boleyn and his wife, Lady Elizabeth Howard, had five children we know of. There may, of course, have been more children whose short lives remain unrecorded. In the early days of his marriage, Sir Thomas had remarked that his wife 'brings me every year a child!'.[2] This was not normally a cause for complaint, indeed many men would have been delighted. However, in the early days of the marriage the pair were relatively poor, and not only the regular babies would be a problem, but even more the prospect of suitable education for boys and future dowries for girls would have proved a strain.

There had been two other sons, Thomas and Edmund. Both these children died young, their brief lives being recorded only in the brasses of the churches of Hever and Penshurst. The three surviving children were Mary, Anne and George.

For Mary, there is no birth date at all, though we do have strong clues to the fact that she was the elder of the girls. Her grandson, George Carey, 2nd Lord Hunsdon, was quite specific that his grandmother had been the elder daughter of the Boleyn family. In 1597 he was attempting to acquire the title of Earl of Ormonde, which had formed part of the Boleyn/Butler inheritance. The title had been held by his great-grandfather, Thomas Boleyn, as Earl of Wiltshire and Ormonde. After the death of Thomas Boleyn and the earlier death of his heir, George, Lord Rochford, in 1536, the title should have devolved upon the heirs of the eldest daughter. This, he claimed, was Mary Carey (née Boleyn), hence his claim. If Anne had been the elder girl, as some have erroneously claimed, then the title (and more to the point, the lands), would have devolved upon Queen Elizabeth herself, as heiress to her mother Anne.

Also relevant is the fact that Mary Boleyn was chosen to be sent abroad some time before her sister Anne. She was to be part of the escort of the Princess Mary Tudor, on her marriage to Louis XII of France in 1513. Anne had been sent to the Netherlands in order to complete her education along with other fortunate youngsters, at the court of the Archduchess Margaret, and would have by then been only 12 years old! There was, in fact, a strict court rule that the earliest age for acceptance for court service was 12 years, which fits nicely for Anne being born in 1501.[3] She was, in fact, chosen merely as a replacement for another lady, probably because of her grasp of the French language, which was necessary for the attendants of the English Princess.

George, the only surviving boy and therefore the heir, received his first court grant in 1524. In 1529 Jean du Bellay was reported to have remarked that he then considered George to still be too young for the post of Ambassador when he was sent to France. He would at that time have been around 25 years old, if he had been born in 1504/5 as is suggested by Professor Ives. This would make him the youngest of the three surviving children of the Boleyns.

Other facts corroborate the belief that Mary was the elder sister. After both daughters had gone to France, Mary had begun to acquire something of an unsavoury reputation. We know that she was, at least for a short time, one of the mistresses of King Francis I. He did at one point refer to her as his 'English mare'. This might, of course, have been a play on words, given the French pronunciation of the word 'Mary' but it can also be taken to be a derogatory and insulting way to refer to a young woman. When Mary returned to England (to quickly become one of the mistresses of King Henry VIII), her sister Anne stayed in France, completing her education at the court of Queen Claude. Also, Mary was actually married before 1520 while marriage plans for Anne were not seriously discussed until the end of 1521.

The Boleyns were not merely an up-and-coming family, desperately treading on toes in their efforts to advance themselves. Although there was a distant connection with trade, on her father's side of the family, Anne certainly had enough noble relatives on both sides to be able to claim that she was indeed a great lady.

Her father's grandfather, Geoffrey Boleyn, had left Norfolk in the 1420s, made a fortune as a mercer in London, served as an alderman and had become Lord Mayor in 1457/8. This rise to wealth and status from relatively small beginnings was not exactly a new thing. The old families were looking around for an infusion of money, which was hardly unusual after all the upheavals and expenses of the previous decades, and newer families were always eager to improve their social standing. Therefore, it was not such a surprise that Geoffrey Boleyn married one of the daughters of a 'real' nobleman, Thomas Lord Hoo. Their eldest surviving son, William, made a very good match with Margaret Butler, daughter (and co-heiress) of the Anglo-Irish Earl of Ormonde.[4] Anne's father, Thomas Boleyn, merely continued the family's tradition of 'improving' marriages by going one better still, in securing a daughter of the Earl of Surrey, Lady Elizabeth Howard. This meant that the young Boleyn siblings, very far from being stained by connections with middle-class trade, actually came from very much the same sort of background as any other family at court. They could, in fact, claim in their immediate family tree a duke, an earl, an earl's granddaughter, the daughters of two barons and an esquire and his wife.[5] Anne, as it turned out, would be better by birth than any of the other three English wives of King Henry VIII.

Geoffrey Boleyn's wealth had allowed him to make a substantial Norfolk gentleman of himself. His son Thomas was the prospective heir to great wealth, even if a little hard-up while his family was young. He stood to inherit not only the Boleyn and Hoo estates, but also the half share of the Ormonde fortune, and half of the lands of the Hankford family, which would come down to him through his Butler grandmother.

However, for the time being he was obliged to try to run his household on the sum of £50 per year, living at Hever in Kent, which had been bought and rebuilt by his grandfather. He was also grateful for any money that could be extracted from his wife's Howard connections, to keep the young family afloat. Unfortunately, Elizabeth's father had only recently completed his repurchase of the Howard lands, which had been lost after his support of Richard III at Bosworth, and he was not in a position to give them financial assistance. The sum of £50 per year would not be sufficient to maintain a large and growing household, let alone provide that high profile so necessary at court.

Nonetheless, good family connections could be counted on for a great deal and Thomas Boleyn could certainly lay claim to those. The all-important Howard match had given him the chance to enter the King's service in 1501 (the probable year of Anne's birth). Thomas attended the marriage of Henry VII's elder son and heir, Prince Arthur, to Princess Katherine of Aragon. Later he was given the sadder duty of carrying the canopy at the funeral of that same Prince, who died of the sweating sickness shortly after, taking the King's dearest hopes with him.[6] Later, in 1503, he escorted the King's elder daughter, Princess Margaret, over the northern border to her marriage with James IV of Scotland.

By the time of the death of King Henry VII in April of 1509, Thomas Boleyn was squire to the body to the King, and walked in the funeral procession. Prospects must have seemed to be glowing. He had not only made a very advantageous marriage, his children were growing and the Earl of Ormonde was ageing, with the certainty of a substantial inheritance to come.

It is probably not easy for many to understand the importance of a career at court at that time. In the sixteenth century, court access was considered absolutely vital. The ability to become known and respected, one who was likely to catch the eye of the King, and be selected for personal service to the monarch, was the only way to achieve any real movement up the ladder. It was the centre of real power, without which mere wealth was impotent. It was also the only way to rise to further wealth, titles and estates, which were in the gift of the King. It was the only way in which a man could take a part in the decision and policy making which would mean that he was helping the sovereign to rule the country.

In this aim, children were important. A man alone was working for nothing. Any sensible man was working for the advancement of his family, for his sons and daughters and the welfare and future careers of their children, each generation hopefully achieving more than the one before it. In this aim, not only sons were important, daughters could also play their part. A presentable daughter could obtain a post at court, in attendance upon the Queen or one of the princesses, where she could be seen and bid for on the marriage market. Her aim would be to acquire a husband of wealth and position, who would add to the family's widening social connections. A son, embodying all his father's hopes for the future, would not only be expected to make a grand marriage and provide a further generation of children, but also to make an impression at court in his own right. He would need to gather offices, honours and titles as they became available, as well as the financial incentives that went with them.

There was no shame in the most personal form of service, either to the monarch or his immediate family. No sense of humiliation in performing or supervising the most humble or distasteful of tasks, involving the most intimate functions. Even the highest in the land were grateful for a chance to become close to the royal family. In the reign of Henry VII the position of Chamberlain to the Queen (Elizabeth of York) was taken by the Earl of Ossory (later of Ormonde), Piers Butler.[7] Many another would have envied him his close connection to the Queen.

These forces, powerful and all-inviting, were to shape the lives of Anne and her siblings. Naturally, the marriage of the surviving son, George, would have been discussed at some length, perhaps even arranged while he was still a child. The girls, too, would go to court when properly educated, to catch the royal eye (dangerously so in Mary's case), and also catch rich and noble husbands. The treadmill would go on, and if the futile round of court service ever bored, or the nature of the job galled, there could be no open sign of it. Ever willing, ever smiling, ever quick to recognise and grasp at every opportunity that came their way, which might put them a step or two ahead of their companions.

Such self-seeking was not confined to the lower levels of court life. Even the highest placed, seemingly most fortunate families, must always be aware that their position could easily be lost without constant striving on their part. There could be no qualms of conscience, no squeamish reluctance to perform an unpleasant duty, or even to accept an unattractive marriage partner. A fall from favour could be as quick as a rise, but a fall from favour could mean the failure of the entire family, not merely one individual. Girls like Mary and Anne Boleyn would be trained, educated to take their places with the correct display of grace and charm, courtesy and accomplishments.

Once the girls had completed the first part of their education, usually at home, they would be expected to move out into the world, at an age that to us would seem appallingly young and inexperienced. However, wherever they moved, in the household of another noble family, or in the court itself, they would doubtless have many family connections around them. These people would be very interested in keeping the youngster not only to their early, humble, place, but also as far as possible on the straight and narrow, to ensure that the newcomer always represented the family correctly.

By the time of the accession of Henry VIII in 1501 the court was changing. The old ways were no longer quite enough and the new king was conscious of a need to make his mark. His late father had been ill for some time, a widower and a man happier to save than to spend. Henry VIII was to prove to be the opposite. Still young, freed from constraint and finding himself suddenly immensely rich, he was determined to enjoy everything that his deceased elder brother would have had.[8] This was to include the widowed Princess Katherine, who had also had her share of confinement since Arthur's death, and who was also eager to step into sunshine again, even if her new husband was almost six years her junior and rather immature. The alliance originally arranged between England and Spain could be revived, and the Princess could become Queen of England after all.[9] Henry had already decided that now he was king he would do as he pleased. He already had Wolsey in mind, to be his advisor. Wolsey, eager for his own rise, smilingly agreed to Henry's proposals. Even to the marriage with the widowed sister-in-law, which caused some muttering. But dispensations could be arranged, and the Princess was still young enough to bear the all-important children.

By the time that Henry VII was buried, he could hardly have been mourned. The future was too bright to allow for much grief over a king who must have seemed to have been a relic of an earlier time.

That first summer of Henry VIII's reign must have been a time of great promise.[10] Wolsey was already moving forward to take advantage of the new King's need for freedom, yet guidance. He would be able to work hard yet enjoy the pleasures of life. That very contradiction would have appealed to Henry. He, too, considered himself a man of many parts, able to appreciate the finer things, while still keeping control of the mundane. Yet, he was not employing just anyone, he was not a lightweight. Wolsey would certainly earn his keep, and if the rewards of such an elevated and favoured position were to be substantial, they would certainly be paid for in full.

Thomas Boleyn must also have felt that things were improving. He was ready for the changes ahead. His wife Elizabeth had already been appointed to the household of the new Queen, Katherine of Aragon, and Thomas was determined to hold what position he had, as well as becoming one of the group of new young men around the King. Gradually, Henry VIII would build himself a nucleus of companions, capable of hunting and hawking, encouraging him in his rightful pleasures, yet still able to give sensible advice, or be sent on an embassy. Experienced men of the world would be valued, education would be appreciated, but the arts and religion would also have a place.

Thomas Wolsey was aware that the King's group of cronies could one day grow in power and rival his own influence. At that stage, Henry was still young enough to leave the trivia of everyday ruling to Wolsey, while still feeling that he had his own hands on the reins. In the meantime Wolsey could instruct him in the diplomatic niceties, hopefully at the same time consolidating his own position, so that he would be unassailable when Henry grew mature enough to begin to take full control for himself.

Henry and Katherine had been married the summer of the accession, 1501, at the Oratory of the Franciscan Observant Friars at Greenwich.[11] It would remain to be seen whether the new Queen would successfully perform her most important task, that of producing heirs to the throne. At first, things boded well. Katherine was pregnant quickly, but it ended with a miscarriage. This was the first of many such disappointments the couple were to face, but at the time it seemed a fairly small thing. All women miscarried from time to time. They would try again and they did, successfully. Katherine was to produce the eagerly awaited son in the New Year of

1511. The country and the succession seemed safe. Henry had done the right thing in marrying the girl who had waited so long to become queen. Unfortunately, the Prince died within six weeks, and the real world asserted itself. Although Katherine was to prove herself an able queen, a loyal wife and a competent and kindly mistress to those in her household, she was not to produce another child for many years.

Thomas Wolsey was to use these formative years to build on, he had used the Church as a ladder to climb by, but that was not unusual, and he was a most able climber. But other men liked to climb. He had suspicions of them, particularly of Thomas Boleyn. They were both in pursuit of similar aims, but they could never become friends. Wolsey's purpose was to represent the Church. Boleyn represented himself, and his family. But he also represented a new train of thought, very dangerous and divisive. He was interested in the new religion, which was taking hold abroad. That alone would always forge a deep division between Boleyn and Wolsey. He was a useful servant to the King, a useful man abroad, with his education and gift for languages, but it was this skill that had led to him becoming contaminated by the new learning. He must not be allowed too great an intimacy with the King, must not progress so far as to become an open opponent of Wolsey.

Boleyn's gifts had become apparent to other men than Wolsey. This emergent courtier had intelligence, the ability to work hard and an obvious loyalty to the King. Between 1519 and 1523 Thomas Boleyn was to be Henry VIII's Ambassador to France, and an attendee of the meeting with the Emperor Charles V at Gravelines after the Field of the Cloth of Gold. He was a member of the Calais Conference of 1511 and an Ambassador to Spain.[12]

But in 1512 he was in Brussels on his first embassy, meeting with Margaret of Austria, the Regent of the Netherlands. He was to establish friendly relations with this lady, and they were to result in the first appointment of Boleyn's daughter Anne. She was accepted by the Regent Margaret, as a member of her household, at her court at Mechelin in 1513, when Anne would be 12 years old. Margaret of Austria's court was known for its culture and learning, and Anne would not be the only young person sent there to complete an education that had begun at home.

Margaret was the paternal aunt of the future Emperor Charles V and one-time sister-in-law of Katherine of Aragon herself.[13] She had been married to Katherine's only surviving brother, the Infante Juan. He had died quickly, leaving the bride a widow within a year. After three marriages, but no children, Margaret based her court at Mechelin where a new palace had been built for her. It was centrally situated, modern and possessed every comfort and luxury available. It has been suggested that Anne remembered the glories of Mechelin and in later years was to remodel part of White Hall in its image.[14]

The Burgundian ducal court had for a long time been the glittering centre of Europe, but was gradually being drawn into the larger state that would eventually comprise Spain, Austria, the Empire including the Netherlands and even part of the Americas when Charles V was grown. In Anne's time, it was a very cultured centre for a lady of impeccable tastes, from which she could reach out to control the growing lands of her 13-year-old nephew.

While in Margaret's care Anne received glowing opinions, and on her arrival Margaret had written to Thomas Boleyn:

> I have received your letter by the esquire Bouton who has presented your daughter to me, who is very welcome.... I am confident of being able to deal with her in a way which will give you satisfaction. So that on her return the two of us will need no intermediary other than she. I find her so bright and pleasant for her young age that I am more beholden to you for sending her to me, than you are to me.[15]

Later, the French poet de Carles also praised the young Anne during her time there. He said of her that she had 'listened carefully to honourable ladies, setting herself to bend all her endeavours to imitating them to perfection, and made good use of her wits, that in no time at all she had command of the language'.

Thomas Boleyn had indeed been fortunate in managing to place his daughter with Margaret of Austria, for everyone was clamouring to find a place for a relative at such an important and cultured court. Unfortunately for Anne, events that had been shaping in England were to cut short her residence there, and finish her education untimely.

Queen Katherine of Aragon had for some time been working as Ambassadress for her father Ferdinand of Aragon. While this might at first seem a good idea, it did prove to have one grave disadvantage. This was due to the slippery and unreliable character of Ferdinand himself. Any unreliability of her father was bound to rebound on how Katherine was perceived. As with many English kings, it had long been the dream of Henry VIII to conquer France. Ferdinand had his own similar agenda towards Italy, and appeared to support his son-in-law, but his support turned out to be illusory.

The English had travelled to San Sebastian in 1512, believing that they would meet there with Ferdinand's own troops, in order to make an assault on France together. Yet in the three months they spent there, the English did nothing but wait for Ferdinand. Ferdinand, eagerly expected, did not appear.[16] The English soldiers finally demanded a return home, and their commanders had no choice but to agree. Ferdinand had done well out of their presence. Simply by being there, they had kept the French at bay on his behalf. Henry VIII was furious at the waste of time and money and Katherine was obliged to use all her influence to intercede on behalf of the leaders (particularly Dorset), whom Henry was inclined to blame. The Venetian Ambassador, Sebastiano Giustiniani, was aware of the extent of Katherine's influence with Henry, but also of her constant contact with her father. Ferdinand had been working only for himself, which was confirmed by the fact that he then signed a truce with the French in April of 1513.

When Henry heard of the truce he was angry, although Ferdinand managed to convince him that it had all been a misunderstanding. It makes one wonder what Wolsey thought of it all. Always privately anti-Spanish, he must have been disgusted by Ferdinand's perfidy and also by Henry's gullibility.

It must have seemed a great boon to Ferdinand to have such an easily manipulated son-in-law, but events were soon to enable Henry VIII to grow up and realise that his father-in-law was not his friend. One wonders how much Wolsey had to do with this change of heart and mind. He was a powerful figure, whose support and advice was of great value, but even the closest friend cannot compete with a wife who still holds her husband's trust, as Katherine did. She had an intimacy with the King which was impossible for anyone to compete with. However, times were beginning to change. Wolsey's influence over Henry was to increase exactly in proportion to the decrease of Katherine's. Her seniority over her husband, her lack of an heir and her father's known shiftiness would work against her, depriving her of the influence over her young husband that had once been absolute.

Again, preparations were made to go into France with an army, at further great expense. But this time Wolsey would be at Henry's side, to encourage and support him. Katherine was pregnant again and would be left at home. Henry was eager to be off, particularly as he was due to meet the Emperor Maximilian in France. This gentleman had actually 'hired' himself out to Henry. He was chronically short of money, and rather overplayed the deference he gave to the King, but Henry lapped it up, rejoicing in the idea that he was becoming a leader of men.

Naturally enough, but unfortunately for Henry's (and Wolsey's) peace of mind, as soon as the English were across the Channel, the Scots then came over the border to the north, led by their King James. A treaty was still in force at the time between England and Scotland but it was easily discarded when such an opportunity, far too good to miss, dropped into James' hands.

Katherine moved quickly and well. Supported by old soldiers who had been considered a little past it for the trip to France, she swept into action against Scotland, while Henry busied himself in France enjoying the comforts of his gold-embroidered tents, playing at being in a war. He was proud that he had actually fired a cannon with his own hand outside Therouanne!

This was very different from the conflict Katherine was engaged in back home in England. Her efforts, hugely successful, were to result in the Battle of Flodden, with the death of the King of Scotland and the flower of his army fallen around him.

Henry's efforts were to culminate in the Battle of the Spurs, where he was able to claim a victory of sorts due to 'defeating' the French. He was not actually present in person on the day, and in any case the French had been ordered to avoid a pitched battle at all costs, retreating rather than being defeated.

Henry was exultant at his apparent victory and Katherine, knowing her husband's character well enough, was obliged to play down her own real one. She had more to concern herself with than having to deal with a sulky husband. For one thing, she had lost the child she had been carrying when Henry went away. Whether it was the stress of the situation in which she found herself – which she had dealt with magnificently – or merely another of the failures of her reproductive system, the result was the same. Whatever successes she had achieved in the absence of her husband, the most important one would have been to present him with a son on his return, and in that she had failed again.

She was as aware of the passing years as any woman, even though in public she put on a brave face and kept her dignity. At this point the age gap began to stretch to its widest, Henry was reaching his prime, while hers was almost past.

Furthermore, Ferdinand's repeated betrayals of Henry had begun to affect the way he viewed his wife. Was Wolsey responsible for this? It would have been an easy thing at this point for a few well-chosen words to stick in the King's mind, a persuasive reminder that both father and daughter had failed him repeatedly.

Henry was beginning to enjoy the company of other women, and was leaving more of the responsibility of ruling on Wolsey's shoulders. He had by this time begun to turn to Wolsey for the advice and support he had once requested from Katherine.

Katherine's inability to carry her children to term was not unusual, even though it could prove disastrous. Henry VII and Elizabeth of York had had seven children, of whom only three survived to adulthood.[17] Isabella and Ferdinand of Spain had reared five, but lost easily as many to miscarriages, stillbirths and infant deaths. Margaret of Austria, despite three marriages, was childless. A grave misfortune for any family, but for a king and queen, with the responsibility of continuing a royal line, it could be catastrophic.

Henry in that year took a new mistress, Elizabeth Blount. Like all Henry's preferred ladies, she was of good birth, being a relative of Lord Mountjoy. She was to give Henry what he wanted most, a healthy living son, whose birth and thriving childhood could justify his pride in his manhood, and convince himself that he was capable of producing healthy male children. The event was to provide Henry with a source of pride and joy throughout the boy's life but was to alter Katherine's life irrevocably. She must have felt the first twinges of unease at the news that her husband was at last the father of a living and apparently healthy son.

There was another more immediate result of the seemingly endless problems of that year. Henry VIII and Louis XII of France had formed an alliance, which would be bonded by the marriage of that elderly King with Henry's younger sister Mary. His sister Margaret was already in Scotland. The recent Battle of Flodden should have been enough to teach anyone that formal treaties did nothing to advance real friendship between the countries concerned. In fact, they usually resulted in the isolation of some princess, sent from her home to become a member of an alien court, where she might forever be considered to be a spy.[18]

However, in this case Henry's hopes were running high. The King had no son and due to France's Salic law the throne would go to his daughter's husband, Francis of Angoulême. For both countries there must have been some hope that the King was still able to produce a son for the throne, even though his age might prevent him. If this happened, it would knock Francis off his perch and destroy his expectation of becoming King of France. For Henry it just might prove the way in which he could control France. If his sister were lucky enough to bear a son, then when Louis died Henry could step in to help her rule. Whatever Katherine thought of this new alliance with France, she would have been obliged to put up with it. Wolsey, on the other hand, would have been pleased enough for both of them. Always pro-French, he would have been glad to see that this new venture could open up possibilities, enough to replace the old, uneasy relationship with Spain.

The Princess herself, the younger, livelier and prettier of Henry's sisters, was most unwilling. Like any girl, she had pictured a husband and, despite his crown, Louis XII in no way fitted the picture. She had already been betrothed to the Archduke Charles, but this match had suddenly been abandoned, to the great annoyance of Margaret of Austria. It would have been a scintillating match, the best in the world on the face of it. Rumours abounded that Maximilian had decided against it, on behalf of the young Charles, and the Venetian Ambassador, always quick to send in his reports, had recorded Henry's annoyance when he proudly exclaimed, 'There is no faith in the world, save in me only. Therefore, God Almighty, who also knows this, prospers my affairs!'[19] The Princess would not have been consulted regarding that or any other arrangement made for her.

Not only was Princess Mary Tudor unwilling to marry the ageing Louis, she had her own ideas of the man she did want. She had set her heart on her brother's friend, Charles Brandon, Duke of Suffolk. This man already had a very shady matrimonial record, but he encouraged her infatuation.[20] However, none of this mattered. Henry would be the one to decide his sister's husband.

It has been reported that Mary extracted a promise from Henry prior to her distasteful marriage to Louis. This was to the effect that when he died (assuming that he would not live long), she could choose her next husband for herself. If Henry ever gave her such a promise, he would not have taken it too seriously and could not have intended to be bound by it, although it might have served to persuade a recalcitrant princess to accept her fate without fuss.

Mary might have realised this. It shows in the light of her subsequent hasty and secret marriage to Brandon after the death of the King of France. She would have known better than to trust her brother on a matter of policy. But her desperate act was yet to come. In 1514 her marriage was arranged and the preparations for the selection of her suite were beginning.

Mary Boleyn was already on the list to go, but Anne was still with Margaret of Austria.

The Princess had put forward her own candidates, wanting to have congenial company around her. One of her favourites, Jane Poppincourt, had been in her household since she was 5 years old. However, when the list of prospective attendants was passed on to France, the King crossed off Poppincourt's name. He had heard that the lady was involved in an affair with a married man, and declared that he did not want such persons in attendance on his queen.[21] This left a vacancy on the list, and the new person chosen would need to be fluent in the French language. Thomas Boleyn grasped the opportunity of putting forward the name of his younger daughter. Despite her still being at the court of Margaret of Austria, and well settled there, Anne's residence at Mechelin, which barely lasted a year, was to be cut short. This was one of the realities of court life, that opportunities were to be watched for and grasped when they appeared.

Margaret of Austria did not look favourably on Thomas Boleyn's request to allow Anne to leave her household, particularly to join the household of Mary Tudor. Margaret still had resentments regarding the broken match with her nephew. It is known that the Archduchess showed some reluctance to allow Anne to leave, which delayed her journey. This probably accounts for the fact that when the list of attendants for the Princess was finally drawn up, Anne Boleyn's name was not on it.[22] It may have been that, due to her being already in Europe, she went directly to France, rather than joining the other ladies for their journey across the Channel. This would be the logical step to take, but would mean that she only joined her new mistress's household when it had already reached France.

If Anne was unsettled by the sudden change, she could console herself that she was now serving where her knowledge of French would be most useful. In any case, she was bound to obey her father.

She was by then just 13 years old.

Chapter Three

Despite Katherine's continued failure to become the mother of an heir, Henry had reason to feel optimistic. He was finally growing up. The early years, characterised by reliance on Catherine, and her slippery father, were almost over. Henry now had another mentor, far more reliable. He had Wolsey.

He may have had time to reflect that the marriage to his queen, initially full of promise for the future, had not been plain sailing. Some churchmen had agreed with the late king, Henry VII, expressing doubts about the suitability of the match at the last minute, but Richard Foxe, Bishop of Winchester, had approved it. Wolsey had gone along with the opinions of his friend, whatever his private reservations may have been.[1] Their objections were religious. Whether it was advisable to marry brother and sister-in-law together, even if the first marriage had been very brief. On a more prosaic level, there was a consideration that was not alluded to.

The Tudors were not good breeders of boys. The Trastamaras, the Spanish royal family, also, despite large families, did not find that their sons lived long enough to breed heirs in their own right. To match together two families with the same difficulty in producing male heirs who lived beyond adolescence was asking for trouble in the future.

However, Henry's illegitimate son by Elizabeth Blount, Lord Mountjoy's relative, would thrive, and that would give him confidence as a sire, despite Katherine's lack as a provider of healthy children. He would not see that neither of his sons would live long, therefore the blame was as much his as Katherine's.

Wolsey had slipped easily into the position vacated by the wife, becoming the King's closest advisor. He was able to give the impression of dealing with everything with ease. He was already adept at concealing difficulties and followed a lucrative policy of smoothing the King's path, taking upon his shoulders any tedious work or unpleasant duty. He allowed him to believe that the final decision was his and gave him space to play the king. Henry, enjoying this regime, had already begun to make inroads into the huge fortune left by his father.[2] This was a process that he would continue until the mid-1530s, when he would need to institute desperate measures in an attempt to restore it.

Wolsey's hard work had begun to pay off. Henry was beginning to find in him exactly what he needed. He was also prepared to offer rewards commensurate with the efforts of that man, and gradually left aside everything in the way of real work, in the knowledge that all would be dealt with competently and with discretion. Wolsey must have been in his element.

Wolsey was not only fiercely ambitious, but had the ability to cover at least some of that competitiveness with a smooth veneer of culture. That is not to say that the veneer was pretence. He was multi-faceted, and could move in any circle. At first carefully and unobtrusively, but eventually openly and magnificently, glorying in his position and the power it gave him, not only to rule, but to enjoy all the luxuries that defined such a position. He was very soon to become the master statesman of Europe, capable, calculating, able to carry with him almost an aura of royalty, but with the all-encompassing power of the Church. Yet Europe was not peopled by fools. There were plenty of other able men, and they would not have been taken in by a sham. Wolsey was all that he appeared to be. He was not a vulgarian, as some have claimed. A vulgarian could never have become Henry's friend, as Wolsey did.

Eventually, a pupil of Wolsey's, Thomas Cromwell, would try to emulate his huge success. Although he gathered wealth and titles, and for a time enjoyed a powerful position, he remained essentially a common man, unable to deal with the greatest people in Europe as Wolsey had done effortlessly. Despite his usefulness to his royal master, he stayed a servant to be used, never achieving the position of a friend to be enjoyed.

Four months after Henry VIII's wedding to Katherine of Aragon, Wolsey became Almoner to the new king. Later that same year he was granted one of the homes of Sir Richard Empson, who, along with his colleague Dudley, paid with his life for the exactions they had performed at the orders of Henry VII. The grant was dated January of 1510 and refers to 'Le Maison Curiale. With 12 gardens and orchards, between the Thames and St. Bride's gardens, in Fleet Street.'[3]

It sounds a most substantial property and it was probably here that Wolsey first began his association with the woman Joan Larke. This relationship was not such a scandal as might at first appear. The edict of total celibacy for all clergy was not an idea that ever fully gained ground in England. Many clergymen kept 'housekeepers' without losing their livings. Sometimes fines were imposed if the association became too flagrant. Wolsey's mistress was described as the daughter of one Peter Larke, 'a gentleman of Huntingdonshire'. In the mid-1460s the family were associated with Thetford, near Ipswich, and a Peter Larke had twice been Lord Mayor of that town. One of Joan's father's kinsmen was Thomas Larke, a surveyor of the King's works, and later a confessor to Wolsey himself.[4] It seems that the lady who became the mother of Wolsey's children was from a perfectly respectable, even prosperous family. But respectability on this level was not really an issue. Even the apparently impeccable Archbishop William Warham was said to have had a 'wife' while in office. Joan Larke's presence in Wolsey's life was to prove no obstacle to his meteoric rise. Later he found a decent husband for her. He had already provided properly for their two children. Joan Larke was eventually married to a George Legh of Aldington in Cheshire. He was a wealthy landowner, who remained on good terms with Wolsey, as did Joan's family, who had never been disturbed by her irregular relationship with such a powerful figure. Indeed, many respectable families would have been flattered by it, and hopeful that it might bring them advantage.[5]

Wolsey was then a landowner in his own right. He may have taken pleasure in his commodious house by the Thames and its pleasant gardens and orchards, but any pleasure would be on the understanding that he intended to do better.

The King had summoned Parliament to meet on 10 January 1510. This was the first time in six years that there had been any Parliament called. It was to last merely twenty-nine days, and Wolsey, though still officially only the King's Almoner, was busy. He had written to the Bishop of Winchester, Richard Foxe, that Thomas Howard, Earl of Surrey, had had a frosty reception at court and had left the following day. Wolsey gloated that 'with a little help, he may be utterly excluded therefrom'.[6]

He was obviously exulting in the rush of power he enjoyed due to the confidence the new king had in him. He was soon to become a member of the Council and immediately began to transact business on the King's behalf. He also began the process of encouraging Henry to enjoy himself. Cavendish was to later report that 'he loved nothing worse than to be constrained to do anything contrary to his royal will and pleasure'.[7] Why should he, with a man like Wolsey present willing to shoulder the burdens? Wolsey understood Henry very well, and his understanding and acceptance of a young man's need for pleasure endeared him to the King. However, even Henry was not completely pleasure-seeking, he was power-seeking too. He was able to see himself in a kingly light, ready to go to war to achieve personal glory, though it would mean providing himself with all comforts while doing so. Henry's idea of warfare would be to drag along behind him a great train of baggage with all his dignity required. He intended to attempt to extend the boundaries of his Kingdom. Hence the attempts at war with France, always a sore point with English kings, who had ambitions in that direction since the days of King Henry V. The conflict would be known as 'Wolsey's War'. If it was a failure, it did show how far Wolsey had advanced in his influence over the King.

Wolsey had gone far and fast, but he was still only the King's Almoner. That would soon change. On 16 January 1512 he was made a Prebendary of York Minster. This was at the instigation of Christopher Bainbridge, the Archbishop of York, who had been made a Cardinal by the Pope. A year later, Wolsey was made Dean of York, and when Henry left for France in June of 1513 Wolsey was already very much in charge.

He had arranged everything for the campaign, from biscuits to bedding, tents to 'the very colour and satin of the King's doublet'. He had not neglected even tiny details, sending a message to Sir Gilbert Talbot, Deputy of the Port of Calais, to 'have a tun of a certain wine ready against the King's coming, to the house wherein he is to lodge'.[8] It was the intention that war should be dealt with in a courtly manner, not only under the rules of chivalry, but without undue discomfort! Despite his ambitions of empire, Henry did not intend to go without every possible convenience.

Despite all the careful preparations, the ending was to be a damp squib. Quite overwhelmed by the real triumph of Queen Katherine over the Scots, who had taken the opportunity to cross the border while Henry and his courtiers were playing at war in France. Henry was an innocent still. Not only had Ferdinand used him, but Maximilian too. The Pope's idea of a Holy League between the great leaders had also effectively come to nothing. The leaders had proved that they could not work together, and that France was not so easily taken as expected. It had been expensive and wasteful while Katherine dealt with a real conflict at home, and very successfully. Like a true wife, she played down her own triumph, while allowing

Henry to believe that he had done well. But the reality was different. Heavy taxes would again have to be imposed, and Wolsey would see the price he would have to pay for his newly dangerous intimacy with kings. He would be blamed for leading Henry into a war that had solved nothing.

Nonetheless, he would have the benefits as well as the disadvantages of great responsibility. After the war he was given no less than three bishoprics in one year. First, he was made Bishop of Tournai. Henry considered that as he had 'captured' the town in his phony war, so that gave him the right to bestow its bishopric where he pleased.

Secondly, the diocese of Lincoln fell vacant through the death of its incumbent, and Wolsey became Bishop of Lincoln. There was, however, some slight 'blip' about his acceptance of this honour. Sylvester de Gigli (the English Agent in Rome) was in correspondence with Wolsey regarding the reduction of the Pope's fee, which was payable by Wolsey for the right to take up the see. Wolsey wanted the payment to be less, and after negotiation the fee was reduced. But the correspondence on the subject had become known, and caused unfavourable comment in England.

Best of all, Cardinal Bainbridge, Archbishop of York, died while in Rome. Wolsey rapidly succeeded him too. All of these honours were in Henry's gift to bestow on the man of his choice, sanctioned by the Pope, but still within the King's power. Not satisfied with such elevations, Wolsey began to yearn for the one honour that Henry was incapable of giving him. The Cardinal's Hat. Shortly after becoming Bishop of Lincoln, Wolsey had begun to angle for it, and had sent Polydore Vergil to Rome, to pay his respects to Cardinal Hadrian. This was more than a respectful visit. It was intended to refresh Hadrian's memory of the support Wolsey had given him, two years earlier, when it had appeared that Pope Julius II (Giuliano della Rovere) was about to die. Now Wolsey was calling in favours.

The mission went well, and Cardinal Hadrian recommended Wolsey to Pope Leo X (Giovanni de' Medici) who decided that, in the light of the Protestant threat in Europe, it would be wise to bolster this capable churchman's position by elevation to the Cardinalate.[9] It was not intended to be an honour for Wolsey alone. Since the death of Cardinal Bainbridge, England no longer had a Cardinal. What it did have was a young king, and pleasing him was more important than another honour for a pushy man. Bolstering Rome's authority in England was more important still.

The Protestants in Europe were then rather gaining ground and serious division had opened up in England over the matter of one Richard Hunne. He had been a wealthy merchant taylor in London, who had differences of opinion with his parish priest over a burial cloth which had covered the coffin of his recently deceased infant son. The priest had claimed the item as his 'mortuary' or fee, which Hunne resisted. He said that the deceased, being only a few weeks old, owned no property, therefore there was nothing for the priest to claim. Hunne had then been sued for the item, in a spiritual court, and had countered by a suit against the priest in the Court of King's Bench, claiming any purely spiritual court was a 'foreign tribunal' and any persons using it were guilty of 'Praemunire'. This was the act of putting a foreign power over the authority of England's King and therefore treason. The Bishop of

London had exacerbated the situation by having Hunne arrested for heresy and imprisoned.

The already inflammatory situation was made worse when Hunne was found dead in his prison cell and the Church claimed that he had committed suicide. A Coroner's Court found against that accusation, and charged one Dr Horsey (the Bishop's Chancellor) with organising a murder. The matter raised public indignation to a dangerous level, particularly when Hunne's corpse was tried for heresy and subsequently ceremonially burned at Smithfield.[10] The Church had triumphed in the matter, but it left a bad impression and harm had been done to its credibility. Some damage limitation was necessary, with reinforcement of papal power over those people who were encouraging the new ideas.

This useful new honour was not enough for Wolsey. Even as a Cardinal in the English hierarchy he still held second place, as Archbishop of York, under the authority of Warham, who as Archbishop of Canterbury was senior. He was blocked by Warham's presence from achieving the highest English position. He was to look once again to Rome to give him the edge. Warham was, by virtue of his position, the Papal Legate 'Natus'. Wolsey did not wish to be awarded any temporary 'nuncio' status. He intended to be Legate Latere, i.e. for life. This would make him the Pope's permanent representative in England. Henry VIII was to send the Pope, on 12 August 1514, a letter singing Wolsey's praises, and declaring him to be indispensible. It seemed to do the trick, although even then Wolsey did not get quite all he had wanted. The message came back through Sylvester de Gigli that the Pope was prepared to grant almost all of his demands. Not 'for life', but a compromise. Wolsey could be granted the status for successive periods of a few years each, renewable when the terms expired. This arrangement was agreed and put Wolsey technically ahead of Warham, who should have been his superior.[11]

It may be ironic to note that the recommendation from Henry to the Pope on Wolsey's behalf had not touched on his 'spiritual' abilities at all. The King had informed the Pope that Wolsey was his 'secret counsellor' and of importance to him. It was in this advisory capacity that he was being honoured.

There was another reason suggested for Leo X's reluctance to advance Wolsey to the highest honour, and it was nothing to do with any failing as a religious man. It was due to scandal arising out of the death of Cardinal Bainbridge. It had been rumoured that the death was not natural, and that the Cardinal had been poisoned. It must be remembered that almost any death of a prominent person, if not completely obvious of cause, could be attributed to poison. It is not wise to pay too much credence to this accusation. Wolsey could have done better – had he had murder in mind – removing William Warham, the senior, rather than Bainbridge. That would have opened Wolsey's way to the higher position, also Warham was in England and certainly easier to attack. He would have saved himself having to negotiate titles or terms with Rome, and would simply have stepped into the senior position automatically.

It is far more likely that Leo X's reluctance had more to do with Wolsey's rather too rapid rise to power, which worried the Pope. Not to mention the aggressive campaign Wolsey had instigated. Leo's Master of Ceremonies (de Grassis) wrote, 'men say an English Cardinalate should not be granted too lightly, because the English already behave so insolently!'. There were fears in Rome that Wolsey, backed by Henry, would be a nuisance. While the Cardinalate was granted in September 1515, the much-desired hat, symbol of power and authority, did not arrive in England until 15 November of that year, carried by a courier as though it were any ordinary piece of merchandise. This was not enough for Wolsey. He ordered celebrations to take place in London to welcome the hat, which was to be carried on a cushion, taken to Westminster Abbey and left there for two nights of public reverence on the altar. This was done the following Sunday, 18 November, after which a High Mass was celebrated, and a state procession formed to escort the hat back to York Place, led by the Dukes of Norfolk and Suffolk and accompanied by eighteen other temporal lords.

It was not the only incident to arouse adverse comment. There was talk in England that in the previous year Wolsey had accepted a substantial annuity from Lady Margaret Pole as payment for handling her financial affairs. It was clear that he was not prepared to be dependent on his income from the Church for making his fortune. He was famous for his ability to work hard and deliver the goods. It may be argued that he had every right to charge for work done, particularly as he was a most capable man of business. Many other people would find it useful to pay him to take their side in a serious dispute, or look over their financial affairs, to the increase of his own fortunes in recompense.

Despite the usual papal delays along with slightly squalid skirmishing, the matter had been settled to everyone's apparent satisfaction. If the Pope had voiced concerns over Wolsey's meteoric rise, it must be considered that any power given to him would be used for Rome's benefit also.

Eventually, Leo had made a prophetic decision. He decided that Wolsey was throwing in his lot with Rome. That if ever push came to shove with divided loyalties, he would opt for Rome. He was right in his estimation. Although Wolsey had been awarded both the positions of Archbishop and Cardinal Legate, it would be some years before Henry was made to realise what Leo had seen in his new Cardinal back in 1514.

While the negotiations were going on between England and Rome, Wolsey had been busy at home. He was a natural administrator and a diligent man prepared to take infinite pains. He was also as greedy as the next man for money, let alone the power it represented, but he certainly worked for it. George Cavendish reported that Wolsey had once 'sat down at four of the clock in the morning, to write letters, with his chaplain vested and waiting to say Mass, until four that afternoon, without once rising to piss, nor yet to eat any meat, but all that time wrote with his own hand, having his nightcap still on his head'.[12]

Lesser men, unwilling to put in the amount of sheer work that Wolsey got through, would never understand the drive behind his rise, the real reason why he went so far and so fast, and why Henry valued him so much. Yet his other side was there too, ready to peep out when the pressure of work slackened, or any display was called for.

Wolsey's love of luxury and pleasure was still there, and this was something he could share with Henry. While the King leaned on him for sound advice and a clear head for business he also took pleasure in his company. Wolsey had efficiently taken over Katherine's role at Henry's side. Her only real function now was to bear a child, and she still hadn't managed to provide one. This was the situation in England in 1514, when Henry's younger sister, the Princess Mary, was gathering her household to go across to France to become Queen to its King Louis XII.

The first view the very young Anne Boleyn would have had of the French court was as a humble maid of honour to the Princess Mary. Wolsey had arranged everything perfectly. First, Mary's proxy marriage, then the journey to France for the real thing, all with an eye to England's standing when the Princess arrived in her new country.

It was designed to be impressive. The King, Louis XII, more accustomed to living quietly, had also pushed the boat out. In welcoming Mary he was as determined as the English to appear to do the right thing. Mary Tudor was acknowledged to be one of the best-looking princesses in Europe, and was also lively, charming and determined to get pleasure out of life. Such people have the gift of taking pleasure with them and Mary was popular from the first. As Henry VIII's favourite relative, Mary had been a bright and cheerful, if rather spoiled, presence at court. She was used to getting her own way, and being the centre of attention. In this one thing she had been obliged to obey her brother, but had her private hopes.

She may have been dismayed at the first sight of her husband. She knew he was an older man, but not that, at the age of 51, he had already embraced old age with enthusiasm. She knew he had children from his first wife and that his now-only-living child, Princess Claude, not far from her own age, had just married her cousin, Francis of Angoulême. This young man was ostensibly the heir to the Crown of France, provided that Mary could not produce a son.

This left Francis in an ambivalent position regarding Mary. She should have been an opponent, standing between him and the throne, potentially reducing his position to nothing. His desire was to succeed. But Mary was such a charming presence, a tempting prospect for any young man, that he was attracted to her, despite intentions to stay aloof. His marriage to the King's daughter had brought him a fertile and placid wife, but without physical attractions. She, too, was old before her time, and slightly lame, a condition mirroring that of her late mother, Anne of Britanny, whose title she inherited.

Claude would bear Francis seven children in ten years of marriage, before dying at the age of 25. But her portrait shows a woman of more maturity. Perhaps knowledge that her husband regarded her as a step to the throne, and a brood mare, contributed to her melancholy appearance. But this was the woman into whose household Anne Boleyn would come, to be trained as the epitome of the court lady. Both Claude and Francis may have looked with disapproval on King Louis' rash entry into matrimony, at a time when he should have been preparing his soul for death.

Before the wedding party had left England, Louis XII had begun to shower Princess Mary with jewels. The Sieur de Marigny had been entrusted with a gift for her so extravagant, and extensive, that even the coffer in which it was packed had to be borne into the presence chamber on a white horse![13] Mary was also presented with the famous pearl and diamond pendant known as the 'Mirror of Naples'. This item was immediately valued by Henry at Jewellers Row, and Lorenzo Pasqualigo, an Italian merchant resident in London, described it as 'a diamond as large as a person's finger, with a pearl beneath it as big as a pigeon's egg!'. Its value was estimated at 60,000 crowns.[14]

Diplomatic activity was as busy as Mary's women, and Wolsey would have been in his element again. The Earl of Worcester, the Dean of Windsor and Sir Thomas Docwra (Prior of the Order of St John) had been sent to France in September of that year to finalise the peace treaty that formed an important part of the marriage negotiations. The arrangements for the Princess' reception on her arrival in France, and the wedding, were in their charge. Mary's dowry had been agreed at 400,000 gold crowns. This was to include her jewels and plate, although the poor state of health of the bridegroom was so well known that it raised concern in England. A clause had been inserted in the treaty, ensuring the return of all the Princess' personal belongings, including jewels and plate, if Louis died quickly. It is tempting to credit Wolsey with so pragmatic a clause, assuring that there would be no financial loss to England in the event of the early death of the King of France. There would be no point spending vast sums of money if all were to be wasted.

In return for all this largesse, Mary would receive the usual revenues of a Queen of France. According to the Venetians, Henry was hoping to have the Duchy of Milan included in the new Queen's possessions – but even the besotted Louis was not prepared to go that far. Mary's formal proxy betrothal was performed in Paris, and the matter was definite.

Henry had paid lavishly for Mary's trousseau. It included sixteen gowns of cloth of gold and silver, made in the French fashion. She also had various items of jewellery representing roses and fleurs-de-lis, symbolising the union. However, an inventory ordered by the French King paints a different picture. It itemises eighteen dresses made in the English style and five in the Milanese style. These all had matching headdresses. Everything was cloth of gold, silk or brocade, with one gown of crimson velvet also mentioned. However, it appears Henry was trying to cut corners a little, particularly when his expenditure is compared to the Mirror of Naples. Probably the French King's poor health, and the prospect of a short marriage for the Princess, were troubling him. There were, however, many other items fit for a queen that Mary would need. Chapel hangings were mentioned, along with bed hangings, and even embroidered saddle-cloths were accounted for.[15]

Lady Jane Guildford had been appointed Mary's chief attendant and had known Mary since childhood. However, she was also an interfering creature, and Louis disliked her immediately. He complained that he could not be intimate with Mary in the presence of that woman, and it must have been embarrassing for an ageing man to flirt with his bride under Lady Guildford's sardonic eye.

Henry VIII and Katherine of Aragon saw Mary off from Dover, although the party had to await the end of stormy weather for several days before it was safe to embark. There was an extravagant procession at Abbeville for the Princess, when the Venetians said that the English were 'positively shackled by the weight of their gold chains'.

We know that Mary Boleyn was in the new Queen's procession, but little Anne was delayed by Margaret of Austria. She did not arrive in France to take part in the initial rejoicing. The wedding took place quickly, and Francis of Angoulême admitted to his intimates that he 'was struck through the heart' – not at the loveliness of the bride, but at the idea that she might produce an heir to blight his hopes. He still hoped that the King was incapable in that direction, despite the allure of the new Queen.[16]

Anne Boleyn's name does not appear on the lists made up at Mary's wedding, which were intended to include all the members of her household. As we know of her delay in the Netherlands, it is possible that she did not arrive until after the wedding had taken place. So it is understandable that the lists were drawn up without her name.[17]

Despite the hopes of the parties concerned (except Francis), Louis was soon worn out by trying to keep up appearances with his Queen, and was to die only three months after the wedding, on New Year's Day 1515. Henry's and Wolsey's fears had been realised and they must have been relieved that they had been forward-thinking with regard to the treaty.

There was the usual waiting period, to ensure that the Queen was not with child, before the Crown was presented to the successor. Francis, having seen Louis' attempts to keep up with his teenaged queen, might have been sweating at this time. Mary had to wait in seclusion for forty days, and her household – and the king-in-waiting – would have to be patient.

She must have been anxious. Whatever promises she had extracted from her brother before leaving England, she could not enforce them. He would exercise his rights over her, for a future marriage, despite any affection he felt for her – it was a princess's duty to obey. There was a suggestion that Charles of Castile was being considered for her, the rumour carried by two friars who visited her at Cluny while she was in retirement.[18] Whether there was any truth in the suggestion, she could find herself spoken for before she had even finished her mourning period.

There is a contradictory opinion that Henry VIII intended to honour his promise to his sister, but that in view of the political situation he did not wish to rock the boat by any hasty arrangement. That is presumably why, before sending Brandon to France to collect the widowed Princess, he extracted another promise from him. This was that he would not make any proposal to Mary while escorting her home.

Brandon arrived in France and he and Mary married secretly. Brandon later claimed that as soon as he saw Mary, she began to cry and confessed to him her fears of another arranged marriage. His later letter to Wolsey included the words, 'Sir, I never saw a woman so weep!' He also was to claim that he recommended writing to Henry, as he did not dare to marry himself to the King's sister without consent. He believed that he took 'the only course open to him' and 'so she and I were married' with only ten witnesses in attendance.[19]

There has been some suggestion that the future dislike shown between Mary Tudor, then Duchess of Suffolk, and Anne Boleyn in her later career was due to the distaste shown by a young and idealistic Anne. The idea of the royal Princess, a one-time queen, throwing herself away on Brandon, was shocking. The hurried wedding to a man of lower degree, one known to be an adventurer with a shady background, was a let-down after all the glory of the recent royal marriage.

It was not unlikely that an impressionable and haughty teenager had shown too clearly that she thought her mistress had been foolish and too hasty. If that were so, Anne Boleyn was not the only one to believe that the Dowager Queen of France had married beneath her. Many were quick to express disgust that a lovely princess, so valuable to England, 'should be wasted on a mere love match' when she might have been more usefully placed where she could ensure a good alliance. There were many men on the King's Council eager to use the situation as an excuse to demand the Duke of Suffolk's ruin as a punishment for presumption.

This is the only reference to Anne Boleyn at this time. But another clue to the truth of the matter may well come from the fact that, whereas Mary Boleyn was to return home to England with the new Duchess of Suffolk and her husband, Anne did not. Perhaps due to her disapproving attitude towards the marriage, she made herself unwanted. She stayed in France, entering the household of the new Queen, Claude, wife of the new King, Francis I.

This would be no hardship for Anne. The household of the daughter of Louis XII was to prove a perfect training ground, giving her that extra polish and sophistication that marked her out on her return home. But it gave more. Claude was known for her piety, strictness and close management of her household, with care for the good reputation of the ladies. These things Anne was to learn from her. She was to mature while in France, in a way the ladies in England often did not. She acquired grace and a sense of style, together with an ability to express herself, which would set her apart. Her time to shine was not yet, but during her life in France the foundations were laid.

Back in England, Wolsey had an important job to do. Henry VIII had been furious that Brandon had 'betrayed' his confidence and broken his promise. Or was he enjoying the situation, playing one of his many parts? It could have been a way of allowing his sister leeway to do as she wished, without taking responsibility for it. That would have been in character. His sister had the husband she wanted, and his boon companion was his brother-in-law but Henry would never let him forget how beholden he was. He could extract from them whatever he liked by way of recompense.

That was Wolsey's domain. He was in a good position. Working for Henry and eager to please, but being cast as negotiator for and champion of the abject Suffolks. Henry would eventually forgive them, that was understood. But he would require a very high price for his forgiveness and magnanimity. Even the newly-weds would be surprised at exactly what his exactions would be.

Initially, the Duke was to pay to Henry the huge sum of £4,000 per annum during Mary's lifetime. He was also to hand over to Henry all the gold plate and jewels she had taken with her into France. Plus Henry wanted the 200,000 gold crowns forming the main part of Mary's settlement as Queen. Francis wrote in support of Mary. Probably relieved that she was no longer a problem to him, he could be more open with friendship. Even his wife, Queen Claude, was to write to Henry begging forgiveness for the Suffolks.

On their first arrival back in England, 2 May 1515, Wolsey met them both and escorted them to Lord Abergavenny's house at Birling, where Henry was waiting. They must have faced him with trepidation, but he was inclined to show kindness. Another financial settlement was thrashed out by 11 May but it was slightly less fearsome. Mary was required to pay to her brother the sum of £2,000 per year, for the next twelve years – until the total sum of £24,000 had been paid off. Suffolk was obliged to forfeit the lucrative wardship of Lady Lisle (nothing further being said about the betrothal with her, which would have constituted an impediment to any further marriage; Wolsey would deal with that too). Mary had also to give Henry all the jewels and plate she had been given at her marriage to Louis, or forfeit a further £100,000.[20] Some of these items were to cause future problems with France.

After these serious matters were dealt with, they were put aside. It was time for rejoicing. The Suffolks went through another marriage ceremony, to confirm the first, at Greenwich on 13 May 1515. All the court was present. Sir William Sidney, who had been present as one of the ten witnesses to their first nuptials in France, was obliged to sign a document binding him to secrecy.[21]

Wolsey may well have enjoyed the situation as Henry did. The negotiations confirmed him Henry VIII's most trusted man, which he cherished even while he acknowledged the truth of it. It also placed him in an unprecedented position at the heart of Henry's family, entrusted with confidences. It was flattering to have the King relying on him, while the king's favourite sister, one-time queen, pleaded with him to intercede for her. No man could have hoped for better confirmation that he had risen to the highest level. That he was able to placate Henry and do the Suffolks a favour must have resulted in great satisfaction.

The relationship between England and France broke down after the death of Louis XII. Resentments between the two kings, natural rivals, were very real. They were too much of an age, too much competitors, to expect anything else. Henry may have considered that Francis had encouraged the Suffolk business, but Francis had plenty to say about the King's sister, particularly about the disappearance of the jewel the Mirror of Naples which she had no right to purloin. Henry VIII had the arrogance to remind Francis that the French jointure, due to Mary as a widowed Queen of France on 1 May of that year, had not been paid. Francis replied with a sharp retort about missing jewels, pointing out that they had been given to Mary to wear while Queen, not to keep. Henry could not see Francis' point of view, though in the future would prove quick enough at recovering jewels from wives who fell from favour. The French jewels were not returned, and it led to a permanent resentment. For many years afterward the French considered Mary Tudor little better than a thief.[22]

These problems may seem trivial, but they were the cover for real rivalries between the two, which never ceased. Despite treaties, friendships and enmities, and the passing of years, they were always present. They simply did not like each other.

This feeling prompted Henry to make one final effort with his father-in-law, Ferdinand of Aragon. Katherine was delighted at the idea of Henry turning towards Spain after so long a dalliance with France. Ferdinand, eager for Henry's friendship again, made every effort to reciprocate.

During that summer Wolsey was busy with a new treaty between England and Spain. Ferdinand flatteringly consulted his son-in-law on the best way to invade France, as though Henry's limited experience fitted him for the role of instructor. Henry blustered, confident that France would not dare to march into Italy. He directed De Mesa, Ferdinand's envoy, to tell Ferdinand that 'the French will not attack Milan without my leave!'.[23]

It was another example of the braggadocio that Henry should by then have been growing out of. When Francis did promptly march into Italy, occupied Milan and easily acquired dominance over all of Northern Italy, Henry looked like a fool. Panic in England ensued and Katherine was obliged to reassure her father that the English (on whom she now considered herself an expert) were generally of unequal temperament and very easily swayed by events. She encouraged him to continue with the treaty with England, and must have felt confident in her position as mediator.

She was pregnant again and had hopes that this time it would be different and that she could perform a different kind of service for her country of adoption. Miraculously, it was. Katherine carried her child full term, and on 18 February 1516 gave birth to a healthy child, Princess Mary. Henry was elated, declaring excitedly that 'the Queen and I are both still young, and if it is a girl this time, the next will be a boy!'.

The little Princess was christened at the Church of the Observant Friars at Greenwich on 20 February 1516. The ceremony was magnificent and even though Henry had hoped for a son, he was determined to show that he was satisfied with his daughter.

Cardinal Archbishop Thomas Wolsey stood Godfather to the Princess and the canopy was held over her by Sir Thomas Parr, Sir Thomas Boleyn and two other knights. Catherine Plantagenet, the daughter of Edward IV, and the Duchess of Norfolk were Godmothers. Margaret Pole stood sponsor for the Princess at her confirmation, which took place immediately after the christening. All the ladies involved were Katherine of Aragon's personal friends, so Wolsey, in his elevated position as Godfather, stood at the centre of the royal family. By now, he would probably have expected no less.

Henry was then 25 years old, but Katherine was already 31. Her success with the birth of the Princess Mary was becoming less likely to be repeated with every passing month, and her new position as a mother was to take up more of her time. She was soon to begin that process of gradual retirement, from active ambassadress to queen consort, obsessed by the child she had always yearned for.

But it was also to be the final admission that Henry had replaced her with other women. She knew that Wolsey had taken her place as confidant and counsellor, but she had turned a blind eye to Henry's eye for the ladies. Mistresses had always been a part of his life. It has become common to claim that he was 'abstemious' because he only had 'two or three' known mistresses, Elizabeth Blount, mother of his little son (who would be born three years after the Princess Mary), and Mary Boleyn. Mary's son's paternity would always be discussed with relation to Henry (though he bore the surname of her new husband William Carey). They are quoted as being the sum of his transgressions in that respect. But we know that not to have been the case.

His close friends, Bryan, Carewe and Compton, were his panders, arranging assignations with the wives of other courtiers at their London houses.[24] It was not a secret that Henry had many affairs, albeit mostly of short duration. Catherine had ignored such unpleasantness, confident that it meant nothing. She had her father's example in her memory. All men did such things, particularly kings, whose temptations were greater and more easily fulfilled.

Katherine took refuge with her child, her religion and her close circle of friends, mainly middle-aged. That was one of the problems, that Katherine, in her thirties, was to age rapidly. This was easily put down to all those years of attempted pregnancies, and not her fault that she lost her figure and became tired of the struggle. But it was a pity. Reports from various ambassadors were unflattering, struggling to say something pleasant about the appearance of the English Queen. She had a queenly presence, never forgetting her Spanish reserve. She dressed magnificently, bejewelled and dignified. But she also became plump and homely, hardly the subject of a young man's fancy, and Henry considered himself a young man.

Katherine was increasingly to distance herself from the rowdier elements at court, concentrating on her daughter, her hopes for that child's future and her intentions for her education in the meantime. She had her contribution to make, in the upbringing of the Princess Mary, but the days of her ascendency with Henry seemed to be over.

Fortunately for Katherine, happy with her child, content in her seemingly unassailable position as Queen of England, the storm clouds had not yet begun to gather.

Chapter Four

Even before the Cardinal's hat, which meant so much to Wolsey, had arrived in England, he had started work on the project that would be his most abiding legacy – Hampton Court Palace. This was to be the place into which he poured his heart; his desire for grandeur, his collections of beautiful things, his centre for the entertainment of the court and the reception of distinguished foreigners, and his masterpiece.

It was begun in 1514 when the Archbishop of York leased a house on the site of the Knights Hospitallers. He needed a property that would express his personality and satisfy his need for glory. For other men there were family manors and estates, passed down from generation to generation. Wolsey had no such background to lean on, but he could make his own. Not for him would be the steady building for the family's eventual benefit. For Wolsey, the greatness had to be immediate. By then, its loveliness of setting, its beauty of form, its cohesion of design was second to none – which of course is precisely why Henry wanted it. Wolsey would be obliged to give it, pretending an act of supreme generosity, but it must have nearly broken his heart to part with it. But, in the sunnier days of the early years, Wolsey was free to plan, and to build, the most glorious house in the country. This is still there, despite Henry's later alterations and the still greater depredations of the William and Mary era in a future century.[1]

His quasi-paternal eye missed nothing in making the place as perfect as it was possible to be. Spring water was brought to the site from 3 miles away at Coombe Hill, stone came from Caen and Reigate, and timber from Weybridge and Reading. The red and purple bricks were baked locally.[2] Inside, carpets, tapestries, furniture and *objects d'art* abounded, even glassed windows, indoor lavatories and baths. It became a rich, comfortable, luxurious – even dangerously 'royal' – setting for this non-royal man who had risen to such unimaginable eminence.

The building boasted the usual inner and outer courts, hall, chapel and spacious kitchens. Its chambers were splendid enough to entertain anyone. There was ample space for the households of royalty and of the Cardinal himself. Ambassadors and their suites could be easily and impressively accommodated, and they were intended to return with tales of the grandeur he had created.

Outside, there was everything provided to give pleasure – gardens, orchards and gravelled paths to keep the feet dry when walking alongside the river. The proximity of the water also gave easy access to transport, boats taking the smoothest way to London when required. Later, when Henry took over the place, he would add tennis courts, bowling alleys and a tiltyard.

In Wolsey's private apartments, the great statesman could conduct his diplomatic duties surrounded by every convenience. It was still not fully completed in 1525, but it had already become famous, featuring in the poet laureate John Skelton's cheeky rhyme:

> Why come ye not to Court?
> To which court – the King's court, or to Hampton Court?
> The King's court should have the excellence,
> But Hampton Court hath the pre-eminence!

While the rhyme may have been amusing, it marked a dangerous achievement. Henry was beginning to show himself as the kind of man who wanted not only the best of everything for himself, but all of the best. The idea that a man like Wolsey could have produced something so special would cause envy in the man Henry was becoming.

It is difficult to know where Wolsey acquired his great ability as an architect and builder. His desire to show the world how far he had risen cannot account for the skill and taste he showed as the property developed under his guidance. He had already built York Place in London, but that was the official residence for the Archbishops of York. Hampton Court was intended to be his own. Into it he poured not only vast sums of money, but also his considerable creative abilities. He must have loved the place. As the centuries passed, other people were to find it enchanting, so for its instigator it must have touched his appreciation of beauty. The King and Queen were to visit him there on 20 March 1514. On 11 January 1515 a ninety-nine-year lease was signed between the Knights of the Hospital of St John of Jerusalem and 'the most Reverend Father in God, Thomas Wolsey, Archbishop of York'.[3]

Along with the manor house went 2,000 acres of pasture, which was converted into 2 parks. It was to be fenced off 'partly with paling and partly with a stout red-brick buttressed wall' into which were inserted blackened bricks in the form of crosses at intervals. One of the last moats to be dug in England was also made, indicative of Wolsey's desire for some privacy in his new home and his need to make it into a residence, rather than a merely official property like York Place.

Incidentally, although so busy at this time, he was also keeping in touch with his former mistress, Joan Larke, and the man she had subsequently married, one George Legh. The couple went on to have four further children of their own (one son and three daughters – Thomas, Isabel, Margaret and Mary Legh).[4]

That Wolsey intended to try to enjoy some privacy at Hampton Court is shown by the report of one Sir Thomas Alen, an agent of the Earl of Shrewsbury and Land Steward to the royal household. This man had been trying to get an audience with Wolsey for some time, and finally followed him to Hampton Court. There he found the Cardinal walking in his gardens. Wolsey showed his great displeasure at being disturbed at home in such a way that the despairing agent later told the Earl that he 'would rather be commanded to Rome' than be obliged to approach the Cardinal there again.[5] It would develop into a regular complaint, as even members of his own household sometimes found him hard to pin down when he did not want to be disturbed.

Though things seemed outwardly settled, in the years following the birth of the Princess Mary the balance of power in Europe was certainly changing.

Henry and Wolsey had already become aware that Francis I could be a slippery character to deal with, untrustworthy as an ally. Henry liked to boost his confidence with anyone who would listen, by assuring them that the King of France still looked up to him, and would do nothing of any importance without his leave. Not only had he told De Mesa, Bishop of Elne, that Francis would not attack Milan without his permission, but he went on to say as much again to the Venetian Ambassador, making an even more foolhardy assertion that 'The French King will not go into Italy this year. I believe that he is afraid of me, and that will prevent him from crossing the Alps!' Henry could not expect such wild claims to remain confidential, but perhaps intended them to be taken as a warning. Whatever reason he had for making foolish assertions in public, his arrogance meant that he was riding for another humiliating fall. Along with other European leaders, he was amazed at the speed with which Francis moved, perhaps more amazed that he had dared to defy Henry by moving at all. Francis had no intention of ruling France as any man's puppet and was determined to make his own decisions.[6]

Despite heavy losses, Francis' attempt was eventually successful. He fought bravely at the Battle of Marignano, and Europe was stunned to realise that Francis was suddenly in command of Italy.

While Henry was making a fool of himself, Wolsey seemed to be rising higher, finding new ways to display his greatness to the nobles at court who must have been beginning to hate him. His reception of the Cardinal's hat had been excessive, and humility had no place. He rode a mule, as a good churchman should, but his was no humble animal. It was as sleek and costly as any nobleman's charger. He wore clergyman's dress, but it was of silk, in the vivid colour that denoted his rank. But before anyone saw Wolsey, they would see his escort.

The Cardinal could not move anywhere without his retainers. They held aloft gold and silver crosses, and pillars of silver, to make everyone aware of the status of the man who followed. But it was the possession of the Cardinalate, the one thing that Henry could not have given him, that showed he was not entirely subject to England's King. He had a separate allegiance to the one ruler to whom all others must defer; the Pope. While Henry was a ruling prince, Wolsey also was now a prince, of the Church, and was able to demand respect from all men, even kings. Along with that special power came the possibility – remote perhaps, but still tantalising – that he might rise to the supreme power himself. That would be his defence, for any possibility of achieving the papal crown would benefit Henry even more than Wolsey himself.

It was all a far cry from the modest way of life of William Warham, the Archbishop of Canterbury. He was still the senior churchman in the country, but would very soon be superseded in all real powers by Wolsey. John Colet, the Dean of St Paul's, was also beloved of the common people for his simplicity of living and his frugal modesty. This man had preached before Cardinal Wolsey and had stressed the importance of the spiritual side of the Cardinalate. He had bidden Wolsey to use his position to 'execute righteousness to rich and poor alike, and mercy with truth'.[7] Such an exhortation must have fallen on deaf ears. Modest simplicity was not Wolsey's style. There was a tradition in Rome of exhibiting power by the display of luxury and the considered used of ostentation. There seemed little point in hiding one's wealth, what else were jewels, silks, tapestries, gold and silver for? The idea had always found favour with kings and princes, particularly Henry. A modest, economical churchman may well have been respected, but he would hardly have appealed to Henry as a colleague and a close friend, he would have made an uncomfortable companion. But the intellectual, cultured, luxury loving Cardinal, with his aura of power, was not only an ornament to the court, but someone who confirmed and enhanced the King's own status.

But such considerations could not be allowed to detract from the real problems the Church was facing at that time. Men were not only demanding the right to think for themselves in their everyday lives, but were expecting to make their own decisions on religious questions. There was no longer automatic respect for a churchman. The new ideas seeping in from Europe had begun to erode that natural order and the Hunne case had sparked a flame impossible to extinguish. Why should any clergyman be allowed to demand a stiff fee for every occasion? Surely the service they rendered to the laity was paid for already? Revolt was in the air long before Henry VIII decided to use it for his own purposes.

The rights of the secular courts to have any clear jurisdiction over men in orders were to be debated again. This question had once fanned the flame leading to the death of Thomas à Becket in 1170. But nobody wanted that sort of nonsense now. Blind obedience to the Church was no longer acceptable, or offered.[8]

The Abbot of Winchcombe appeared to state the case for the clergy, who were trying to defend their ancient rights. Dr Henry Standish spoke for the state. A favourite preacher of Henry VIII's court and Warden of the Greyfriars, he refuted the claim of the Abbot of Winchcombe that the papal decree forbade the calling of criminous clerks before any secular court, by pointing out that the decree had never been accepted in England. The outcome was that the clergy who supported the right of any papal decree to have jurisdiction in England were themselves accused of Praemunire, with its suggestion that the Convocation was acting under the influence of a foreign power. Times had certainly changed, and too quickly for many people, but progress, once admitted, is always very difficult to halt.

One of the positions Wolsey took seriously was the office of Lord Chancellor. The Chancellor was supposed to be placed between the King and the people, a go-between, joining two extremes. Wolsey intended to inspect and regulate the lives of the common people, to organise and control the unruly and disturbing mob they could so easily become. They needed to be guided and governed, and Wolsey could be entrusted with the responsibility of ensuring that the King's peace was kept. This often meant that those quarrelsome people had to be kept in subjection, ruled firmly, but turned into useful and loyal subjects. To help him do this, Wolsey had a network of Justices of the Peace, law courts and regulations stretching like a web over the country. At the head was the King himself, who was intended to be the 'centre and focus of the whole life of the people'.[9]

Wolsey also reinstituted the Court of Star Chamber at Westminster Palace. This court had been established during the days of Henry VII, but Wolsey would empower and extend it, to deal with cases of riots, perjury or appeals in criminal cases. It was also to include usury, enclosures and all business overseas.[10]

Wolsey was in the habit of presiding personally in Star Chamber every Monday, Tuesday, Thursday and Saturday. This is a credit to his insatiable appetite for work, but also his ability to keep a finger in every pie. At times, many of the nobles of the court were called before him. In 1516 the Earl of Northumberland appeared. In the same year, the Marquess of Dorset, Lord Bergavenny, Lord Hastings and Sir Richard Sechaverell. In 1517 it was Thomas Pygot and Sir Andrew Windsor. In 1518 Sir Robert Sheffield. In 1519 Lord Edmund Howard was called, and Sir William Bulmer (for wearing the livery of the Duke of Buckingham).[11] Also Sir William Brereton, Sir William Compton, Sir Henry Grey, Sir John Hussey and Sir Christopher Willoughby.

In 1524 and 1525 Sir Robert Constable and Thomas Dacre had to appear, and in 1521 the court was to try the Duke of Buckingham himself in a landmark case.[12] By that time, Wolsey had grown to believe that he was the equal of those gentlemen, but also that he had a duty to chastise them. In taking these people down a peg or two he was following the pattern he had created, by giving the greater justice to the humbler people. The nobles who were obliged to appear would find the scales were definitely not weighed in their favour. They would prefer to believe that it was due to desire to show power over them and rub their noses in it, rather than being able to admit that he had a sympathetic nature.

Wolsey would have been aware of the distaste he aroused in some of them, and perhaps it amused him. It certainly did not frighten him. He had worked very hard for his position and he went on working very hard to maintain it. He may have had some contempt for people whose precedence was the result of a fortunate accident of birth. He was human after all!

To his credit, he never pretended to a sainthood which he knew he could not attain. His position was based on his ability to understand problems and be prepared to put in the sheer effort necessary to deal with them, particularly in smoothing the King's path. If he had an excessive taste for display – and he certainly did – surely he had earned those signs of his achievement? Few men in his position would consider that enjoying the fruits of success was wrong. Only his position as a churchman made his love of luxury and display inappropriate. Wolsey may have felt these contradictions irksome, and decided to ignore them. Due to his supreme value to the king, it might be thought to be a perfectly reasonable attitude. Few other men in history have proved to be so vital to their country's well-being. He drew the King out, he encouraged him in a love of pleasure, partly for its own sake, but also because he believed that in the extravagance of kingship lay an important part of Henry's status.

Wolsey was an admirable administrator, a diplomat, a statesman par excellence, and that should never be taken away from him. He was not a fool. He knew perfectly well that the young man he had taken pride in teaching would stretch his wings and need him no more. But Wolsey would have hoped that there was to be some recognition, some respect shown to him for all that he had done. He had a genuine fondness for Henry, behaving towards him almost like an indulgent father. He had no reason not to believe that he would be equally valued in return. Unfortunately it was not to be.

An event, happening in May of 1517, shows how far Wolsey had risen. The situation in London had become dangerous due to riots started by the apprentices. These were ostensibly against the numbers of prosperous foreigners who thrived there at that time. The disaffected young men were resentful of the success of the incomers. The court felt differently, knowing the value of the successful businesses run by the foreign residents, who lived under the protection of the King. One Dr Beal, a Canon of St Mary's in Spitalfields, had already preached a very inflammatory sermon, which did more harm than good. In it he claimed that the common artificers of the city could get no work to feed their wives and children on account of the large number of foreigners in London. He claimed that these people took away 'all their living'.

Thomas Howard, by then Duke of Norfolk (raised to the higher title due to his great success at Flodden), put the city under military occupation and began to punish the rioters. Thirteen of these people, some of them still very young, were convicted of high treason. Lord Edmund Howard (Norfolk's son) was given the task of organising the executions, which he then performed with a cruelty that caused outrage. There were still another 400 rioters in prison, waiting their own turns to be hanged, drawn and quartered, but at that point the Queen intervened. She decided to beg publicly for pardons for the remaining rioters.[13]

Henry, with his love of play-acting, decided to make a show of pardoning them. They were all taken to Westminster Hall, wearing halters around their necks, on 7 May. Wolsey, in his position of Lord Chancellor, opened the proceedings with a speech, in which he not only reproved the rioters, but also laid blame upon the city authorities for failing to keep order.

The King was present, intending to awe with magnificence, haughty and unapproachable. But it went according to the script prepared. First Wolsey and then Queen Katherine were obliged to kneel to Henry, 'with tears in their eyes', to beg him to forgive and release the prisoners. Although there were also cries of 'mercy, mercy' coming from those who were condemned, he still appeared unmoved.[14] Wolsey was to kneel before Henry a second time, before he showed signs of relenting. Finally, he thawed, then graciously agreed to pardon the wrongdoers, ordering them all to be released.[15]

Some people had been obliged to suffer the full horror of the sentence passed on them, but the majority were freed. Henry, delighting in his power, probably took pleasure from the sight of his noble Queen and his powerful statesman showing humility before he allowed them to cease and declared himself satisfied enough to accede to their request.

It must be remembered that Wolsey was not alone in his abasement on that occasion. Katherine, with her hair hanging loose as a supplicant, was also to kneel before her husband and beg for the lives of the prisoners.[16] In this instance, she and Wolsey were forced to work together. The incident tells us a great deal about Henry and his need for adoration. It also tells us great deal about Thomas Wolsey. Not only that he was still prepared to pander to Henry's childish side, which cannot really have suited such a man. But it shows something more important. That he was working in tandem with the Queen, placing Wolsey at the heart of the source of power. The implication would have been apparent to all the people who watched the display, and would have gone a long way in recompensing Wolsey for having to submit to it.

Over the next few years, Wolsey would continue at the centre of events. With his ability to guide Henry, he was able to help place England under the eyes of Europe, more than it would have been, for Henry could be tactless. He cannot have been easy to work with, yet Wolsey, despite all his other responsibilities, made England into a real player on the international stage.

Perhaps it was at this point that the glory of Wolsey's achievements, initially such a source of pride for Henry, began to rankle? Henry would not be able or willing to put in the agonisingly long hours of work. Such an effort would have been incomprehensible to him. But had he any idea of the strain under which Wolsey was living? Was this not the real reason for Wolsey's need for Hampton Court, and also the reason for his displays of temper if followed there, when he needed rest. To be fair, he loved celebrity almost as much as Henry did, but even for the most status conscious man, there is a point where the years begin to show and slow him down. Sheer tiredness creeps in, and a need for solitude. All the more since any sign of advancing age must be ruthlessly hidden.

To any outsider Wolsey's power and abilities must have seemed still absolute. In May of 1519 several of the King's personal friends and companions were dismissed from court. These included Francis Bryan, Nicholas Carewe, Edward Neville, Arthur Pole, Henry Norris and William Coffin. It was said that they had been sent away because they had become 'too familiar' with the King, although the action was not considered to be at the King's instigation – but Wolsey's. It was claimed to be another manifestation of Wolsey's desire to exercise power over the court. The truth was that many of the young men who were temporarily banished had proved to be a nuisance for some time. They were considered to encourage the King in foolish extravagance, as when Edward Stafford, Duke of Buckingham, lost the sum of £14 in a bet with the King over a game of tennis.[17]

Wolsey still had the influence to mastermind and arrange the greatest show, to take place the following year. It is quite likely that he was already bogged down with the logistics for it and had little time to spare for bothering with the antics of a group of high-spirited young men. The political situation had swung round again, and now Francis I and Henry VIII had been persuaded that the time had come for them to indulge in a show of friendship towards each other.

The situation had partly been brought about by the Pope, Leo X, requiring all Christian monarchs to unite in a crusade against the Turks, who were again ravaging Eastern Europe. Henry had no intention of going personally on such a crusade, although he was wary of declaring any open refusal in case his great rival, Francis, should then declare himself willing. Despite all the discord, it was still important to give an appearance of amity, and this is what the second part of Leo's decree was about. He demanded that there should be a Treaty of Lasting Peace between all the Christian Kings of Europe, ensuring that they cleave together in friendship, in the face of the threats from outside the European centre.[18] As this effectively meant Francis I, Charles V and Henry VIII (with Henry being the least influential of the three), it would be easier to deal with than any real crusade. Meetings could be arranged in which the rulers would discuss any differences, creating an appearance of unity to satisfy the Pope.

Wolsey had been straining every nerve to arrange for the meeting with Francis, but first would come the event to which Katherine of Aragon was very much looking forward. A meeting with her nephew, Charles V, had been scheduled to take place before Henry and his court went to France. Wolsey knew that a treaty between England and one other of the superpowers would not be enough. He had to broker a deal with both to please the Pope. He could delegate the actual work involved in the forthcoming meeting with Francis to others, but he needed to keep overall control. As to the meeting with Charles, which was to take place in England, he may have felt less in control than he might have liked.

This was Katherine's project. This meeting between actual blood relatives was to be a far more private affair than the French one. Wolsey would know that a betrothal between the Princess Mary and Charles V himself was being suggested, and may have caused him some concern. But even that meeting was delayed (consequently delaying everything else) because there first had to be the contest of the election to the Imperial title. The Holy Roman Emperor Maximilian I had died in 1519. King Francis fancied himself taking on the role. It also greatly appealed to Henry, but he was less of a front runner and there was subsequently little chance of him getting the accolade. The Pope was only too well aware that Charles, in his enviable position as ruler of so many lands, was the obvious successor. Not only would it be most suitable for him to have the title, with his powerful influence it was more important to conciliate him. His favour must therefore be sought, and he certainly could not afford to fall out with the young man who would rule so much of the known world. Charles must have the honour.[19] Whatever the feelings of the other two, it would have to be accepted.

Charles was travelling from Spain to his lands in Germany in early 1520. Therefore, he would be relatively close to England, and the opportunity to visit his aunt and uncle could not be missed. Katherine must have had far more than the usual feelings about it. This was not just the visit of another king. This was her own nephew, her sister Juana's son. She must have had the most eager anticipations, particularly as she had the desire to see her daughter betrothed to Spain. The Emperor's powerful and influential aunt, Margaret of Austria, had also declared that a meeting between Charles and Henry was desirable. Because of the new show of friendship between England and France some rapprochement was needed. The Imperial ambassadors, aware of the difficulties due to his Francophilia, had tried hard with Wolsey, and plans had been finalised for Charles to arrive in England by 15 May. Unfortunately, he was then delayed again, not arriving until 26 May.[20] Katherine must have been on tenterhooks during that waiting time. Henry was impatient to be off. For Katherine, though, this meeting was the more important of the two. It was her opportunity to show herself as a major player, being able to greet that most important of young men in her adopted country, but those precious hopes for Mary's future must also have been at the forefront of her mind. It seemed that Henry would not be prepared to wait, but in the end common sense prevailed.

Charles was able to stay with his relatives in England until 30 May only, a short visit considering the importance of the meeting. Wolsey must have been dismayed to realise that Katherine had taken over. It was the best excuse to make the talks very private indeed. Wolsey was excluded as he had feared he would be. He must have been seething, knowing that the secret talks might undo all his meticulous work. There was absolutely nothing he could do about it.

However, he was correct in one thing. He had assumed that Henry was playing a double game, and he was even then plotting behind Wolsey's back. Wolsey heartily disliked this sudden new closeness with Spain, whatever the Pope had demanded. Charles was keen to replace Francis in his control of Italy, notably in Milan and Genoa. He would also probably want back Burgundy, which had lapsed by then to the French Crown. That could result in the destabilisation of all the hard work, making the treaty worthless. Everything hung in the balance.

Katherine was working hard. The greatest wish of her heart was a proper alliance between her husband and nephew and this seemed to be a real possibility. It would also be in Katherine's interest to foster some of Henry's natural jealousy regarding Francis, which would not have been difficult. The handsome and charming French King would always be more of a rival than the unprepossessing Charles. Charles was sensible enough, while in England, to defer to Henry and make a respectful fuss of his aunt. Flattering them would bring dividends, though despite his correct behaviour he was always careful to keep his private thoughts to himself.

Katherine must have been ecstatic at the idea that her daughter might be Queen of Spain. But there was one serious problem, which, in her enthusiasm, she preferred to overlook. The question was one of age. Charles was sixteen years older than Mary, who was still a child. It would be a long time before he could take her as a wife. While Katherine might be happy to ignore the facts, they were a serious obstacle. Charles would have to marry, and produce children of his own, long before Mary grew up. He simply would not have the time to wait for her. Katherine may have consoled herself that the age gap was on the right side, a woman's fertile years being so much shorter than a man's, as she knew to her own cost. She may even, in the joy of the moment, not really have considered it at all, hoping that the benefits of the match might outweigh everything else.

Charles had barely left, when the English court had to set sail for France.

Wolsey was determined to pull out all the stops to prevent his carefully orchestrated efforts being destroyed by that previous unfortunate meeting.

Though concerned with the larger issues, Wolsey had directed the French arrangements with such thoroughness that nothing – surely – could go wrong. The meeting between the two kings and their queens, with nobles, clerics and thousands of hangers-on providing a supporting cast to the main players, who would move like marionettes through a setting of make-believe chivalry, has gone down in history as the 'Field of the Cloth of Gold'.

Interestingly, the previous year the Venetian ambassador, Giustiniani, had reported that Wolsey's greatest desire was to be considered as the 'arbiter of Christendom'. Giustiniani thought this was shown by his work behind the peace attempts. He also claimed that Wolsey was 'intoxicated' by his power in England and had already begun to use the phrase 'the King's Grace and I' which could be easily Latinised into its reverse form of '*Ego et Rex Meus*'. Wolsey had, he said, gone so far as to mention to him that he should not 'heed any words spoken on a sudden, or in any way inadvisedly, by the King'. Giustiniani remarked that he already well knew that it was Wolsey who 'led the dance'.

Holinshed also wrote that the French knew perfectly well that Wolsey ought to be flattered by them, and that Francis I had granted to Wolsey a pension of £2,800 of Tours, plus £12,000 of Tours as compensation for the loss of the Bishopric of Tournai, after 1518. (The currency 'of Tours' was approximately £10 of Tours equivalent to £1 sterling.) However, being in receipt of such pensions was certainly not exclusive to Wolsey. The Dukes of Norfolk and Suffolk, and several other nobles besides, received French pensions.

However, Wolsey's unique position was acknowledged by the Doge of Venice (at that time Leonardo Loredano) when he said that the Cardinal should be considered to be the King of England's 'second self'. Before leaving England in 1519, Giustiniani promised the Cardinal sixty Damascene carpets from Cairo as a gift. These did not arrive until 1520, and Wolsey had been obliged to enquire about their delivery date. When they did arrive, he thanked the Signory officially, promising to send them 'all the important news'. One item of news for the year 1519 might have concerned a smaller and more personal service, which Wolsey had offered Henry.

Henry's mistress, Elizabeth Blount, had retired to a priory in Essex, where she had given birth to a healthy son. Wolsey would stand as Godfather to that much-wanted child, just as he had done to Henry's legitimate daughter Mary only three years previously.

Elizabeth Blount was to marry Gilbert Tailboys and live discreetly with him, and her son, in Lincolnshire for the next few years, but Henry would not be content to leave the matter there. The thriving son, whom he would be delighted to acknowledge as his own, meant far more to him than merely proof that he could sire a healthy male child. The boy would eventually give Henry the idea that if his Queen could not provide such an heir, then perhaps somebody else could. In a few years time Henry VIII would bring that precious, albeit illegitimate, son to court and cover him with titles and honours, much to Katherine's anguish. For the time being, his father's delight in him was to ignite a bonfire, which would eventually change everything.

For Katherine it meant little, except the lingering regret that she could not have provided her husband with the same. However, she could console herself with her recent achievements, providing for her daughter the most important husband in the world, who could help bolster England's position in the future.

For Wolsey, there might have been a feeling of tension as the all-important French meeting got under way. There had been so much work involved, not only in arrangements, which were extravagant in the extreme, but also with the characters of the two main protagonists. He could only hope that those two young men would play their parts sufficiently well so as not to undermine all the efforts made. The end result would, however, be out of his hands. Henry's behaviour was the one thing that Wolsey was unable to control.

The Field of the Cloth of Gold was intended, on the face of it, to demonstrate the power, sophistication, culture and luxury available to the participating countries. It was to be little more than an opportunity for two men to show off and outdo each other in pointless extravagance. Members of the nobility and gentry from all over the country, many still bearing grudges from the last conflict with France, very nearly bankrupted themselves in order to attend.

The sheer logistics of the event, another example of Wolsey's brilliant organisational ability, are staggering. There are some wonderful illustrations of vast tents, designed for the nobility, and these were the most costly single items made. But then there were the 'enrichments' freely indulged in by both sides. Yards upon yards of cloth of gold and silver, velvets and satins were used freely by the bale or cut into 'devices' to be sewn onto canvas. One official on the French side was obliged to journey no less than seven times to Florence for cloth of gold, with three other journeys made to Milan for the same purpose. The French party was as eager as the English to buy up every luxury within reach. The Queen Mother of France was allowed one huge tent and several small 'pavilions' also, and had these covered in crimson satin and purple velvet, strewn with fleur-de-lis, and enriched with the white crosses of Savoy, made of silver.

For Henry, the Lord Chamberlain (the Earl of Worcester) and three other commissioners (Sir Nicholas Vaux, Sir William Sands and Sir Edward Belknap) were appointed to construct 'an honourable lodging'. Their difficulties were heightened by the chronic shortage of timber near to Guisnes, to provide the more solid accommodation Henry wanted. It had to be brought from Holland to Calais by sea. The wooden framed buildings were to be roofed with canvas, then decorated with paint, gilt and other 'devices' to make them look as real as possible. The temporary palace, designed for Henry's comfort, was built on a stone foundation, with brick walls up to a height of 8ft above ground. Timber walls then rose another 30ft, all painted to look like brick. The roof of 'seared canvas' was also painted to represent slate. There were also stone chimneys. The whole building stood in a large square, 60 paces long, surrounded by a moat, its effect of solidity being completed by its glass windows, for which the King's Glazier, Galyon Hone, had been responsible.

Inside, everything was thought of. From the obvious comforts of hangings and cushions, to the spicery, scullery and saucery, and a large cellar holding 3,000 butts of the choicest wines. The state apartments were on the first floor, allowing three large rooms each for the King, the Queen, the King's sister, Mary of Suffolk, and Cardinal Wolsey. Three rooms each may sound modest, but the 'large chamber' intended for Henry was 124ft long, 42ft wide and 30ft high.

There was the usual panic about things not having been delivered on time, or not delivered at all. A chapel and banqueting house, originally planned, had to be cancelled as time ran out. People of lesser status could be expected to 'make do' with less spacious and comfortable accommodation. The royal librarian, Bude, complained that in his lodgings he had no room even for writing materials, and Benvenuto Cellini remarked that even in normal times the travelling court was so crowded that the courtiers had to set up small canvas tents like gypsies.

At the lower end of the scale it was probably a most uncomfortable business, expensive and irritating. Many were obliged to attend in clothing not paid for, while parading about with firm instructions to be polite to their enemies. Many could be forgiven for remarking that they would far rather have stayed at home.

Once everything was in place, the time was intended to be taken up with religious devotions, elegant ceremonials, extravagant feasts and feats of arms. Many taking part had, in the not too distant past, been fighting each other for real.

For the ladies time must have hung on their hands. Attending to superiors, changing clothes, overeating and eyeing the men, all in an atmosphere of cramped discomfort and boredom, hidden under a polite facade, just as their menfolk hid their own resentments. Even the missing jewel, the Mirror of Naples, was not forgotten. Did the Princess Mary so far forget diplomacy as to actually wear it? Or did Henry? There were plenty of people present with good reason to dislike their opposite numbers, despite all Wolsey's careful arrangements.

The two queens played their parts to perfection. Katherine may well have been cheerful, hugging to herself the secret betrothal of her daughter to Charles. Queen Claude, always obedient, might have been surprised to realise that she actually liked the older, Spanish-born Queen of England.

It was, however, still a slightly uneasy time for Wolsey. The earlier meeting must have niggled, and despite all the glory around him, he must have been eyeing Henry warily. His behaviour could be unpredictable and he had never seen the need to keep his temper in check. The whole thing was dependent on the two kings at the centre of the proceedings, and the fact that they did not really like each other added tension. Francis was too witty, too clever by half, to ever please Henry. His elegant sophistication must have made Henry feel like a country bumpkin. He had only his bombast, his self-regard and his over ornate and essentially tasteless ostentation with which to combat Francis' effortless charm. Katherine of Aragon could afford to be gracious but Henry, true to form, very nearly spoiled it all by allowing his insecurity to get the better of him.

Henry tried to force Francis into a physical competition between them, in which he did not show well. This was not England, where people would pretend to be charmingly surprised at Henry's boyish enthusiasms. He must have been a rather tiring companion for Katherine by that time. She was not only his senior by several years, she was also his superior in diplomacy, and may have looked on him slightly more as a wayward son than as a husband.

Wolsey, also, after years of nurturing and training, might have sometimes despaired at how easily Henry's desire to show himself top dog might risk wrecking someone else's hard work. The French King had no interest in pandering to Henry's childish streak, and despite all the efforts the mutual suspicion was still there. On one occasion Francis had ridden early to see Henry. His courtiers, fearing he had been kidnapped, made a fuss that almost sparked a riot, until he reappeared safely. Such was the tension underneath the surface of politeness.

The tents, the feasts, the glorious clothing, mock feats of arms, chanting religious ceremonies and fountains of free wine all amounted to nothing more than a prodigious waste of money and a strain. Wolsey had checked every list, covered every possible eventuality, in vain.[21]

The delicate process was demonstrated one day when Henry, at dinner with Francis, suddenly jumped to his feet, grabbed the French King by the collar, and to the horror of everyone present cried, 'let us wrestle!'. There was a short, rather embarrassed struggle between them. They were seemingly well matched, before Henry, to his own amazement, found himself stretched on the carpet! Francis made some politely deprecating remark about Henry's strength, but Henry was humiliated. The two queens intervened, along with the Cardinal, who must have been cursing Henry's stupidity.[22] The matter was smoothed over, but everyone knew the truth. Any really lasting, reliable friendship between them was impossible.

It had all been a tiring, expensive waste of time, which had achieved nothing. Wolsey was certainly no fool, although he might by then have been feeling his age. He was suspicious of Katherine's sudden step forward, as well as being aware that Francis was still determined to attack the Emperor. His sense of dissatisfaction would have been heightened by the fact that, on the way home, Katherine and Henry had another brief meeting with Charles at Gravelines. There the diplomats formalised the agreements they had made informally on the previous meeting with Charles at Canterbury.

There was another person who had probably attended the Field of the Cloth of Gold, but it was a person of no importance at all to Wolsey. In 1520 Anne Boleyn was around 19 years old. She had lived for some time in France, serving in the train of Queen Claude and probably was quite indistinguishable from any noble French lady. She was fluent in the language, elegant and probably enjoyed the Cloth of Gold, which gave her a chance to meet with her family, who also attended.[23]

Queen Claude was only 21 years old, but was already the mother of three children and expecting a fourth (one other had already died). She was completely overshadowed in her own court by Francis' mother, Louise of Savoy, sister of the reigning Duke, and by her sister-in-law, Margaret of Angoulême, then Duchess of Alençon. These two were at the centre of Francis' life, and the Queen could not compete with them. To be fair, she was far too sensible to attempt it.

She was to die young, but while in her household Anne Boleyn had acquired not only that polish that would soon set her apart in the English court. She also acquired a slightly prudish nature, and a certain reserve, a natural exclusivity, which was later to attract rather than repel.

She could enjoy herself and was as eager as any young woman for admiration and attention, but she kept her sense of independence and self-worth, which would prove all important. She was very different to her sister, who had spoiled her good name in France, and was now busy doing the same in England. It was a situation that Anne could only deplore and from which she would be determined to dissociate herself.[24]

Anne was described at that time as being 'beautiful and graceful'. Her attractions were remarked upon in the rather staid presence of Queen Claude, she was aware of herself and determined not to sell herself cheaply. She would have a good marriage before long, and her future seemed pleasant and assured, with the normal aristocratic marriage in which she would live quite unknown by the wider world.

Who would have believed that the daughter of Thomas Boleyn would soon begin to acquire fame, even as great as that of Henry VIII himself?

Chapter Five

The year 1521 opened for Wolsey on 6 January when Pope Leo X granted an extension to his term as Papal Legate, as promised in the agreement made between them when Wolsey was created a Cardinal. The increased term was intended to run for a further two years. This was done largely in response to the new threat posed by Martin Luther who had, in the previous year, been excommunicated by the Pope (on 15 June), unless he recanted of his heretical opinions within sixty days. The Bull against him was finally published in Cologne on 22 September 1520 and his books began to be publicly burned. The Pope had expected Henry VIII and Wolsey to take similar steps in England against the threat of heresy, but Wolsey was aware that his term as Legate was due to end in the summer of 1521. He refused to move against the heretics unless Leo granted him the extension that he wanted.

Wolsey had issued a decree banning the importation of books of Lutheran content, but would go no further. Once his Legatine powers were confirmed by Rome, he showed himself happy enough to comply with the Pope's request and the first burning ceremony was held at St Paul's Cross on 12 May 1521. Wolsey made an occasion of it. He processed in state to the cathedral, under a golden canopy held by four doctors of divinity. Fisher preached a sermon, then the offending books were burned, while the decree was read out condemning Luther as an excommunicated heretic.[1]

By the summer of that year, Henry also waded in. He had decided to write a book in support of the Church, refuting Luther's arguments. But there was an ulterior motive. The election of Charles V as Holy Roman Emperor made him envious, even though he had never been a serious candidate for the honour himself. Francis I of France was known as the 'Most Christian King' and even the King of Castile was blessed with the title 'the King Catholic'. For Henry there was nothing and it was in the hope of remedying this omission that he prepared his book. He wrote it (with help from More and Fisher) with the intention of impressing Leo X with his religious fervour. By August of that year the book was ready and twenty-eight copies were despatched to Rome, one of which was covered in cloth of gold for personal presentation to His Holiness, who was then duty bound to make some show of recognition of the work. When Leo read it he issued a Bull bestowing on Henry the title of 'Fidei Defensor'. When the Bull arrived in England it was greeted with more ceremony, being read out aloud with a full court assembled at Greenwich. Leo declared that Henry was 'his friend and brother, doing the Lord's work' and added, 'we likewise command all Christians that they name Your Majesty by this title, and that in their writings to Your Majesty, immediately after the word 'King' they should add 'Defender of the Faith'.[2]

At that time the Pope was leaving more business in the hands of Cardinal Giulio de' Medici who was a favourite. This man was already talked of as being a future Pope, but Charles V had made some suggestion that he would back Wolsey for the supreme office if a papal election came soon. Whatever he had gained thus far, it was as nothing compared with that glittering prize.

Quite early in the year, something else happened which would emphasise Wolsey's power but also add to the opprobrium surrounding his name and reputation.

It would be attributed to Wolsey's determination to humiliate the members of the higher nobility. Whether Wolsey intended to conduct a war of attrition against these people is debatable. But the resentment against his elevation was still strong, albeit under the surface. Certainly Wolsey's predilection for show did nothing to lessen his public profile, so he added fuel to the fire of their dislike.

George Stafford, Duke of Buckingham, was one of the few nobles elevated enough to dare to show scorn to the Cardinal. He was the Lord High Constable of England, and due to his descent from Thomas of Woodstock, the sixth son of Edward III he could boast his own strain of royal blood. He was also secure enough not to need the Cardinal's approval.

As a young man, Buckingham had been high in the favour of King Henry VII. He became a companion to Prince Henry. In those days, he was the only Duke England had and was a 'great gentleman' despite being slightly slow-witted.[3] He grew up to be one of Henry VIII's closest friends, but the privileges of his high birth made him less able than most to tolerate the promotion to power of a man like Wolsey. The world was moving on, attitudes were changing, men of ability were sliding into positions of authority, but George Stafford found it impossible to accept. Friction was inevitable. On one occasion, when the Duke was holding a basin of water for the King to wash his hands, Wolsey rinsed his own in the same water. Buckingham considered such a liberty a personal insult. Holding water for the King was one thing, but performing the same service for Wolsey was insupportable. It was said that the Duke responded by splashing the water over Wolsey's shoes.[4]

Such was the situation when Henry was told that the Duke had uttered treason against the Crown. In such a charged atmosphere it would not be difficult for any remark made to be reported back, with embellishments. Whatever remarks Buckingham made, it is unlikely that he was actually plotting treason. However, it was the King – not the Cardinal – who made the next move.

The Duke was at his estate in the west of England when he was summoned to return to court immediately. On the journey it was noticed that an escort had appeared, who 'hovered in the distance at every winding of the road, as if to cut off all hope of escape, real or imaginary, they drew more closely upon him'.[5] These people took lodgings where the Duke did, and the next morning the Duke questioned a man who was loitering suspiciously, who told him that he was 'there by the King's commandment'. It was recorded that the Duke's face turned 'ashy pale' as he realised that there was a serious situation awaiting him in the city.

The charges against him were based on the testimony of a servant, one Robert Gilbert. He said that he had heard the Duke declare that the Cardinal was an idolator, and that he ministered to the King's vices. Gilbert had gone on to claim that the Duke had complained that he had done the King as good service as any man, yet he gave 'offices and fees to boys, rather than noblemen'. There were individuals at court who might fit the description, one of whom was George Boleyn, Sir Thomas' heir. He had been at court as a child page, and by the early 1520s the family had risen to prominence. Despite their noble connections, the Boleyns may well have been one of the families Buckingham looked down on. Henry VIII had shown himself impressed by the young George Boleyn, which may have been another spur for the spite of the remark.[6]

Despite the matter being nothing much to make a trial, tensions were at work and other, more damaging, claims began to be made. On 13 May 1521 the Duke of Buckingham was taken to Westminster Hall to be tried for treason. The Duke of Norfolk was his Chief Judge. Buckingham hotly denied having any treasonable intent and declared that all the charges against him were false. He was allowed no counsel to help defend him, while witnesses could make whatever accusations they liked. When they had finished, the Duke of Norfolk pronounced the sentence of death on him. The matter was certainly a foregone conclusion and the Duke was condemned almost unheard and certainly without much evidence of any weight.

He retained his dignity to the end, refusing to sue the King for mercy (he was aware it was useless and would be a humiliation for nothing). He declared that he would pray to none but God. He said he was amazed that he was so suddenly to die. Four days before the execution the King graciously allowed the sentence to be commuted to beheading, in recognition of the Duke's status. Buckingham was beheaded on 17 May 1521.

Katherine of Aragon is known to have begged Henry to spare the man who had been her friend, but there was no mercy.[7] One of the remarks attributed to Buckingham and passed on to Henry had been that 'God would not suffer his [Henry's] issue to prosper', which was a statement guaranteed to rankle with Henry, given his lack of a male heir. Whether such a comment was actually made it is perfectly possible that he did allow himself to make indiscreet remarks during confidential conversations with friends. Absolutely nobody could be trusted in the court the Tudors had created. Any remark might have an uncomfortable basis of truth.

Wolsey had stayed well away from the proceedings, but did not stop rumours that he had played a central role. Suspicions against him reached such a pitch that he was even believed to have dabbled in the black arts. Later, a man claimed that he had been approached by Sir William Neville, who wanted a ring made which would bring him into favour with the King. He claimed he wanted one because the Cardinal had had such a ring, and 'seeing that the Lord Cardinal had such a ring, and that whatsoever he asked of the King's Grace, that he had!'. Another case referred to a man who had tried to have a spirit summoned up, but without success. He was told that the spirit refused to speak with him as he was 'bound unto my Lord Cardinal'.[8] This kind of ridiculous accusation shows how amazing his continued hold over the King's confidence appeared to be. People were happier attributing such success to occult means than to Henry's awareness of Wolsey's value to him. Also, the ability of the Cardinal to bring down such a nobleman as Buckingham must have been equally incomprehensible. Wolsey was blamed for it, despite his care to keep in the background.

Wolsey's regular duties were such as to make any far younger man consider himself overworked. One of his concerns was the treasury of the King's Household, known as 'The Chamber'. From this funds would be drawn for the King's personal expenditure. Given Henry's love of pomp and ostentation, which resulted in lavish spending, it is no wonder that Wolsey felt there was a desperate need to retrench. He made attempts to reform the system stretching from 1515 to 1525.

In 1519 payments made to the Chamber had dropped to £50,000 a year (still a vast sum, but in 1515 they had been over £74,000). Wolsey complained of the way that 'the King's money goes out in every corner'. He was to bring in extensive reforms, including a quarterly audit of the books, with one of the books being submitted to the King, and another kept in the Chamber, which was to be made available for inspection at all times. He was trying desperately to control the severe loss of money from the household accounts, but such extravagances were practically impossible to prevent, when the system allowed for withdrawals merely under the heading 'for the King's business' without further details being given. Wolsey, no miser himself, must have been frustrated, seeing all the money slipping through Henry's fingers like water.[9]

But there were important matters coming to a head in Europe and Wolsey had more to concern himself than Henry's spendthrift habits.

Francis I was fully aware that Henry and Charles V had agreed to work together against France. Pope Leo wanted to unite the Italian states against Francis, bringing in Charles V as the champion of the Papacy. Francis was surrounded by opponents and his only defence was to invoke the Treaty of London, which had been signed in October 1518. It had been one of Wolsey's own projects, a natural follow-on to his preference for France over Spain. The treaty had provided that the three powers would defend each other, if ever attacked. In the strained situation surrounding France, it was a courageous move on Francis' part to invoke it, knowing Henry's involvement with Spain, but he had no choice. Pretending to be unaware of the agreements made behind his back, he held Henry to the bargain they had made three years before. Despite the fact that France was already busily engaged with defence, Francis brazened it out. He also took a dig at Charles, by allowing Henry d'Albret to repossess Navarre. This was, of course, designed to make Charles move against him, in which case he could oblige Henry to aid him. Charles was furious to hear that d'Albret had Navarre, and in his turn demanded aid from England, again under the Treaty of London. Francis insisted that he was the victim of Spanish aggression. Henry VIII, stuck in the middle, could only suggest that Wolsey should mediate between the two. It was eventually agreed that Wolsey would go to Calais, to meet with representatives of both sides.

This meeting would be known as the Calais Conference and, despite the pomp with which the protagonists met (Wolsey being accompanied by several nobles, including Sir Thomas Boleyn), it was ultimately destined to achieve very little.

Wolsey reached Calais on 2 August, but along with his commission, supposed to guarantee impartiality, he had private instructions from Henry to complete the treaty of marriage between Charles V and the Princess Mary. He even held a commission to arrange for military co-operation between England and Spain against France – so much for neutrality. Wolsey listened to both sides, but he did not have free power to decide between them, as he was still under instructions from Henry. Wolsey refused to proceed without assurances that the Emperor's agents would accept his decisions, and decided to visit the Emperor personally in Bruges. Amazingly, the agents of France agreed to this.

Wolsey was received like royalty by the Emperor and after two weeks the marriage of Princess Mary and Charles V was finally agreed on terms advantageous to Henry. By the time he returned to Calais, Margaret of Austria reported that Charles seemed to be changing his mind again. Charles said, 'I see that the Cardinal asks for things that are unreasonable and affect my honour'.[10] He then went on to say, 'I shall have no difficulty in finding a bride and he cannot sell me his princess so dearly!'

Why Francis allowed the talks to drag on is incomprehensible. Even after being with Charles for two weeks, he still seemed to think that Wolsey would make a fair decision. Unfortunately for France, on 24 November he signed agreements drawn up at Bruges, which included the terms that if Francis did not immediately make peace with the Emperor, Henry VIII would make war on France. It is hard to see that Francis had gained anything, except time itself.

Four days later, Wolsey sailed for home, taking fifteen days to cross the Channel in terrible weather.

While Wolsey had been away, the Boleyns had been reaping the rewards of royal favour, having been recipients of part of the confiscated estates of the executed Duke of Buckingham. It was usual for interested parties to sue for estates before the previous owner was dead. We have no evidence whether the Boleyns asked for anything from the King in this instance, or whether their rise made them automatically in line for such gifts. George Boleyn had not only served as a page as a child, taking part in the Christmas revels, but as soon as he was old enough he became a gentleman of the Privy Chamber.

As Buckingham had been rich enough to be able to afford to pay 20*d.* for a haircut (which was then about five times the daily wage of an average servant), it was understood that the pickings after his death would be worth angling for. The Boleyns were given several offices, centring around Tonbridge in Kent, close to the family property at Hever.[11] Later more would be added, when George's marriage was arranged. His financial position was secure with his position in the King's favour. It was at about this time that Sir Thomas Boleyn started looking around for a bride for his heir.

The Cardinal could not be pleased at these signs of favour being given to a family he could never approve of. The discord with France was to cause the young Anne Boleyn to return home. She may well have remained in the household of Queen Claude, but the family requested her return, since she was of marriageable age, and negotiations had begun on her behalf.

A proposal had been made whereby Anne was to marry James Butler, heir to Piers Butler, the Earl of Ormonde. This was the Irish peerage to which the Boleyns had a claim through the co-heiresses who had earlier married a Boleyn and a St Leger. The disputes between Butlers and Boleyns had gone on for years and Henry VIII (with Wolsey's agreement) had considered that a marriage joining the two families could settle the dispute without costing him anything. James Butler had already been living at the English court for some time. It partly suggested a mark of honour for the Butlers, but was also a way of keeping a hold on the heir, as the Irish could be less than reliable in their allegiance. Anne would not have been consulted about the arrangements. She would be expected to comply, to understand the advantage to her family and see that the match would one day ensure that Sir Thomas' grandson would be the Earl.

Returning to England would have been an opportunity for Anne to renew her acquaintance with her brother George. He had spent his growing years learning statecraft and diplomacy at court, while Anne had acquired her polish abroad. When they met again it was with recognition that they were soulmates. They developed a deep friendship such as few people are fortunate to enjoy. That it would be fairly short-lived, with Anne destined to live in Ireland while George stayed in England, must have made it all the more poignant. The girl would marry where she was bid, and Sir Thomas was quite enough of a sycophant of Henry's to keep his future son-in-law in check.

Pope Leo X was dying. This would not only cause upheaval in the policies he had made, but would mark the beginning of the usual race for the papal tiara, which Charles V had once promised to Wolsey. But did Wolsey really want to be Pope – or was it more of a case of Henry wanting it for him? Would Charles actually give the promised support if Wolsey should make a bid for the supreme office? Leo had been Pope since 1513, long enough to provide some stability of policy. By December of 1521 all would be to do again, with a new man at the helm. It has been generally supposed that it was Wolsey's greatest wish eventually to reach the position of Pope. Probably the dream of any man newly made a Cardinal was that he might one day hold the supreme power.

It must be remembered that all of Wolsey's power was based in England. Henry VIII was his centre. Naturally, he was very proud of his Cardinalate, and his Legateship, who wouldn't be? But he had not really considered what it would mean to leave all that he had achieved to take part in the heady infighting, which made up the real life of the Vatican. Since Cardinal Bainbridge had died, Wolsey was the only Cardinal England had, and even Bainbridge had died in Rome, where Wolsey had never been. He had always had his hands full in England. His roots were in England. A.F. Pollard quoted that 'the Papal tiara hovered in Wolsey's eyes over his own uplifted brow'. This, in his opinion, emphasised that Wolsey had a great yearning to be Pope.[12] That is an unfortunate simplification, which has become accepted as being the truth. It is not evident that Wolsey's foreign policy was essentially based on the desire for the Papacy, or that he ever made any attempt to achieve it.

Polydore Virgil's comment in 1521 was that Wolsey's 'diplomatic situation exceeded his true ambition'. Similarly, the Venetian Ambassador, Sebastiano Giustiniani, had remarked in 1519 that 'Wolsey was already in very great repute, seven times more so than if he were Pope!'[13]

The Vatican was, in reality, a bear garden where the Pope was supposedly 'advised' by the College of Cardinals. The Vatican's famous predilection for delay was often caused by the opposing opinions of these factions and this was dealt with by many of the Popes by bringing into the College as many of their family members and political supporters as they could manage. Not only for the initial election, where a strong following would make all the difference between success and failure, but also for later on, when a Pope without the necessary backing would never get anything done at all.

This extension of the College was always opposed, as the Cardinals were not paid individually, but as a group. Therefore, the more Cardinals there were, the less in solid funds each one could expect to receive. This situation led to a great increase in pluralities as each one tried to bump up his income. Not only that, but any great increase in the numbers of the College would threaten the power of the 'papal families' in Rome. This had been the way since the thireenth century, and by the fifteenth century the Popes had generally managed to strip the College of much of its real power by putting so many family members into it. This nepotism resulted in situations such as the one in 1492 when, of the twenty-three Cardinals attending the Conclave after the death of Pope Innocent VIII, nine of them were relatives of previous Popes.[14]

Wolsey had never shown any sign of angling for the honour. If he had done so (as has usually been taken for granted), then he would have needed to be far more active in buying support in Rome. Contrary to normal practice, Wolsey made no attempt at all to sustain real friendships with the other Cardinals who would be in a position to help him. The few letters sent between them were merely courtesies and consequently his real influence in Rome was negligible. He had never attempted to make it otherwise. He seemed actually to dissociate himself from Rome, except in the matter of his Legateship (which he valued because it gave him precedence over the Archbishop of Canterbury). Earlier it had been reported that 'he ignored those who had tried to encourage him to come to Rome'.[15] He had even ignored the fact that his revenues for the Church of St Cecilia in Rome were being embezzled, after the Ambassador, Thomas Hannibal, warned him of the fact during 1522 and 1523.[16]

This all shows clearly that keeping a high profile in Rome (which would be necessary for anyone eager to become Pope) was not important to him. Also, that all his energies were reserved for his English interests. Strangely enough, for such an ambitious man, it seems that he was satisfied with what he had.

Or did he fear to lose the supreme power he did have in England, knowing that even if he did fight for the Papacy, he would never have the solid base under him in Rome that he had forged for himself in England? Any such attempt would be sacrificing a firm reality for a mirage, and that he would be, at best, a Pope on sufferance, totally dependent on Charles V for his position. Lacking the backing of the College, he could not secure his position and advance his policies. In realising the limitations of his personal ambition, Wolsey was showing himself to be a far more realistic and judicious man than he has often been given credit for.

In 1522 the new Pope was elected, and it was a surprise choice. It was Pope Adrian VI (Adrian Dedel), who was a Fleming, and had formerly been the tutor of the young Charles V. He was still in Spain, where he was Cardinal of Tortosa. He seemed very reluctant to move into the spotlight in Rome, taking almost six months to arrive there, despite his almost unanimous election. He was obviously going to be a Pope beholden to Spain, but with his close personal ties to Charles it would be less of an imposition on him than it would have been on Wolsey. However, Wolsey would gain something from the new Pope's election. The Abbot of St Albans had recently died and the monks had applied for permission to elect his successor. With Adrian's agreement (together with a little backing from Henry VIII) Wolsey was given the office, along with the usual dispensations regarding the holding of pluralities and being non-resident. As St Albans was known to be one of the richest abbeys in England, Wolsey was no doubt quite happy to take the money and be spared further stress.

Henry, as usual, attempted to take all the credit for Wolsey's newly bestowed abbacy, saying that he would 'rather give unto you the Abbey of St. Alban's, than to any monk'.[17]

Incidentally, due to the growing Italianisation of the College of Cardinals, which as far as possible prevented the election of non-Italian Popes, Adrian VI was to be the last non-Italian Pope to be elected for the next 450 years. Not until the Polish Pope Karol Josef Wajtyla became Pope John Paul II in 1978 would there be another.

Wolsey may have been relieved that it was over. He had not travelled to Rome for the election and he appeared to show little interest in it. Matters at home were still engaging his attention. War with France was simmering and would be officially declared by May of 1522, a bare six months since the abortive Calais Conference.

Despite his international concerns, Wolsey held a revel at York Place on 4 March 1522. This marked the first recorded appearance of Anne Boleyn in the household of Queen Katherine. There is a detailed description of this event and her personal appearance at that time is described. Brewer uses contemporary documents to describe Anne as a 'lithe, sparkling brunette' with long black hair, going on to say that 'the beauty of her hair and eyes struck all beholders alike'. Her manner was described as being 'passing sweet and cheerful'.[18]

Wolsey would have been disappointed at the new conflict with France, which went against his preferred policies. He was perfectly sincere in his preference for France, though he was often obliged to obey the dictates of his master. There were also intimations that Henry was thinking ahead, in a way that would cause Wolsey some unease. It was at this time that Henry sent a letter to Wolsey, telling him that he wanted 'new young men' to be trained up into diplomacy, saying rather hurtfully, 'whereas old men do greatly decay within this realm'. He also said that his mind was 'to acquaint other young men with his great affairs'.[19] As Wolsey had always had the handling of those affairs, it must have seemed like a cold warning from the future. Wolsey must have felt the reins of control slipping from his fingers, knowing that Henry was already looking ahead to replacing him.

Also, in that spring of 1522, Charles V made another visit to England. He met Wolsey at Dover on 27 May, and with great cordiality they went together to Dover Castle, where Henry met with them the following day. Shortly after, they moved to Greenwich, where Katherine of Aragon and her daughter welcomed them. It must have been a particularly proud moment for Katherine, even if it was a sour one for Wolsey. She must have been convinced that her own standing was improved since the new rapprochement with Spain.

But Henry was still ill prepared for war. Money was again the problem. Despite the vast fortune he had inherited (and squandered) he was now obliged to send officials around the country to enquire into the land, property and moveable assets available. He intended to impose a property tax on his most prosperous subjects, in order to finance his side of the bargain made with Charles V. This was to cause so much dissatisfaction among the people that he would be obliged to instruct Wolsey to abate his original demands, allowing people to make 'their own declarations' of what could be afforded.[20]

Even then it was obvious that it would be nowhere near enough and he was obliged to then summon a Parliament in early 1523. As the House had not assembled for the past eight years it shows how desperate he was. The Cardinal was given the task of addressing the members, convincing them of the necessity for the approaching war, and all the grievances against the French over the past years. These stretched from the withholding of the French Queen's (Mary Tudor's) dowry payments, to the non-payment of money after Tournai. Henry had recommended that Parliament would grant to him a sum of 'not less than £800,000'.[21]

The members asked the King to accept a lower sum. Talks went on for so long that the Cardinal became annoyed by the delay and said that the 'matter was being blown abroad in every alehouse!'. The final agreement was for some form of graduated income tax, which pleased nobody, and, due to his efforts on the King's behalf, Wolsey was then criticised for being a tax gatherer as well.

With all this on his mind, as well as the worry about his own future as Henry's closest advisor, Wolsey could have done without the irritation of another matter, relatively minor, and closer to home.

The households of the Queen and the Cardinal met together from time to time, and Anne Boleyn, in the service of the Queen, had met a young man in the service of the Cardinal. He was Henry Percy, heir to the Earl of Northumberland. That these two young people fell in love is not in dispute. Anne has been accused of social climbing, but her own proposed match to James Butler would have made her a countess, so mere social position cannot have been an issue. Henry Percy was also betrothed elsewhere, to Mary Talbot, a daughter of the Earl of Shrewsbury. None of this mattered to the two young people involved. When the King heard of the association, he was furious. Two carefully arranged marriages were in jeopardy. He ordered Wolsey to break it up.

This Wolsey did, with a rough lack of sympathy which may only have been evidence that he had more on his mind. It may have also afforded him an opportunity to humiliate the Boleyns. Percy was called to see him at York Place, and there was berated by the Cardinal in public. The Cardinal declared him lacking in common sense to so 'tangle and ensure himself with a foolish girl about the court ... I mean Anne Boleyn!' He went on to remind Percy that he would 'be most like to inherit one of the most worthiest earldoms in the realm'.[22] To his credit, the young man did try to defend his lady and his intentions towards her. He claimed that he had done no wrong, and that he considered his chosen lady his equal saying, 'though she is but a simple maid with but a knight to her father, yet she is descended from right noble parentage.... her estate and descent is equivalent to mine when I shall be in most dignity'.[23]

Wolsey was unimpressed. The Earl of Northumberland was sent for and eventually his chastened son was sent home, to his unwanted marriage to Mary Talbot. Anne was also sent home in disgrace. She believed that Wolsey had acted on his own initiative and was said to have held a resentment over the matter. Whether or not she did blame Wolsey, she certainly was deeply upset about it. It was reported that 'she smoked'. It would not be fair to suggest that their romance was only a passing thing. Anne showed every sign of being deeply attached to Henry Percy and of having been wounded by the experience. Percy's own arranged marriage took place, but was a dismal failure. He made no attempt to play the husband with his young wife and showed every sign of being an embittered man. He was gradually to form hatreds against his family, deliberately and arbitrarily disposing of family powers and properties to spite his brothers, and allowing his sense of loss to take over his life. Knowing that there would be no children from his detested marriage, he refused to leave his patrimony to his brothers, and in February 1535 he made the King his heir instead. He was to die a broken man in June 1537.[24]

Anne had plenty of time for her anger to fester. She was old enough to be aware that arranged marriages were the norm, and she already knew what had been arranged for her benefit and that of her family, as indeed had Henry Percy. It was an area in which romance had no place. But personal feelings are not so easily controlled, and Anne was to later become a person whose personal feelings would sometimes swamp her. Anne's early successes and level of popularity had not fitted her for rejection and humiliation. The King, through his mouthpiece the Cardinal, had made his intentions clear. Anne's personal hopes and plans were worth nothing in the face of that authority.

There can be no suggestion that Henry was already infatuated by Anne at that point. In fact, he was probably still seeing her sister Mary, although it does seem that he was not quite so committed to the idea of the Butler/Boleyn match as Wolsey was. Cavendish records the haste with which the Earl of Northumberland did Wolsey's bidding in the matter, but it was not unusual for the Cardinal to have this effect on courtiers.[25] But if Wolsey, worried about the future, with the French matter on his mind, spoke harshly about Anne, it merely reflects his irritation with the Boleyns. Henry seemed to like them well enough, and to have been satisfied with their services (of all kinds) but it does not mean that he was already emotionally involved with Anne at that time.

Wolsey was struggling with the fallout from the tax he had been forced to impose. Incidentally, by this new tax, he was personally to pay £4,000 towards the war. Even the raising of the necessary money could not guarantee a good outcome.

In July 1522 the Earl of Surrey crossed the Channel and captured Morlaix before running desperately short of supplies. The whole campaign was poorly organised and, after a few weeks of inflicting brutality on the French peasants, by October 1522 the force was back in Calais. Plans were made for the following year's campaigning season, which took place under the command of the Duke of Suffolk, with no more success than the Earl of Surrey had had.

The only thing of any real moment to happen in 1523 was the death in Rome of the Flemish Pope, Adrian VI. He was already 64 years old and had been in power for only eighteen months. He had done his best to institute reforms of the corruption at the Vatican but was not given the time to see them through.

Again, Wolsey made no attempt to go to Rome, seeming as reluctant then as he had been when Adrian was elected. Henry, though, seemed quite keen on the idea of Wolsey becoming Pope. Perhaps by now he felt that it was time for the two of them to part, and if Wolsey could possibly by elected it would be of inestimable value. There was, however, still no sign of the promised help from Charles V in the papal elections.

The Conclave was to be a long one, running from 1 October to 23 November and the Cardinals were determined to make sure that their votes were not wasted. It has been suggested that Wolsey received no votes at all, but this is very easily refuted.[26] Cardinal Campeggio wrote that Wolsey had in each scrutiny received several votes, but that it was his continued absence from Rome, together with strong opposition from Cardinal Colonna, that went against him. Thomas Hannibal sent back very full details of the proceedings on 24 October, as well as an early letter, 'the 16th day of this month of October, a friend of mine sent to me a secret servant and told me that Your Grace had XXII votes in the scrutiny. I beseech God send you IIII more.'[27]

A long, flattering letter sent to Wolsey on 24 October 1523 explained that the powerful Cardinal Colonna's objections to Wolsey were due to his absence. He also objected to Giulio de' Medici, who was a front runner, but when that objection was removed (probably for a consideration), the de' Medici Cardinal was elected, becoming Pope Clement VII.

Wolsey was to send a letter of congratulation via his agents in Rome, which seems to show a good deal of relief that the matter was finalised. 'I cannot with my tongue or my pen explain the inward joy which I have taken, and do take, to see him, whom I so much loved, honoured and have been so entirely dedicated unto, thus called by God to the supreme place and governance of Christ's religion.'[28]

The new Pope was 45 years old, having been born in 1478. He was already a very experienced and worldly diplomat, although young for such a high position.

He was also the cousin of Pope Leo X who had died in 1521, emphasising yet again the inter-relationships that formed the backbone of the Vatican, usually effectively excluding those who did not become a part of it.

Clement VII would unfortunately, in the future, prove to be a catalyst when Henry's growing dissatisfaction with his marriage to Katherine of Aragon would prompt him to make a desperate bid for change, within the Church if possible, but without it if necessary.

Chapter Six

The year 1524 was to see an addition to the Boleyn family in the form of a wife for the heir, George. Talks were begun and considerable thought had been given to the choice of a daughter-in-law for Thomas and Elizabeth.

They had decided on Jane Parker. She was daughter to Lord and Lady Morley, otherwise known as Sir Henry Parker and his wife Alice, who was a daughter of Sir John St John of Bletsoe. The prospective bride's father drew his wealth and lands from his mother, Alice Lovel, who had died in 1518. The young bride to be had been at court for several years, but their family home was considered by them to be their property at Great Hallingbury in Essex. This was sometimes known as Hallingbury Morley.[1]

The Boleyn and Parker families had things in common. They were both of the humanist persuasion and were equally well educated. Lord Morley was a noted scholar, and an Oxford trained classicist. His mother Alice had been born into a respected Bedfordshire family and her own marriage had been arranged by no less a figure than Lady Margaret Beaufort, mother of Henry VII. She was a relative of the St Johns and a patroness of the family, despite the Parkers having fought for King Richard at Bosworth.

The legal pre-nuptial contract for the Boleyn-Parker marriage was signed on the 4 October 1524, as soon as the financial side was agreed to ensure the security of the bride. One of the contributors to her 'jointure' was Henry VIII himself. This was not unusual, but it was a sign that the families were in high regard with the King. Thomas Boleyn had already proved himself as an ambassador, where his fluent French proved useful and he was by then Treasurer of the King's Household. He was made a Knight of the Garter just before the talks with Lord Morley began.

George also benefited from a generous gesture from the King. He received the grant of the manor of Grimstone during that summer of 1524. Jane's father had also served the King as an ambassador, having been sent to present the Order of the Garter to the Archduke Ferdinand of Austria (Charles V's younger brother) in December of 1523.

The young betrothed couple were similar in age (both around 20 years old). George and his bride would also be given the manors of Aylesbury and Bierton in Buckinghamshire, and other manors in Norfolk, including West Laxham.[2] The young couple would have no reason to fear a lack of funds blighting their future.

The date of the actual wedding is lost to us. However, a note of Cardinal Wolsey's, listing the personnel of the Privy Chamber, refers to 'George Boleyn and his wife' so it is likely that the marriage took place before the Lenten Season of 1525 started. During Lent marriages would be prohibited, and there would be no grounds for the families to delay any further, once the arrangements were made. Also, as there is no record of any special licence being sought, it is probable that Jane Parker was married at her local church of St Giles. They would have no reason to expect any other than a satisfactory and fruitful life together, but the clouds were already gathering.

This would be the year Cardinal Wolsey gave up the most incomparable of all his possessions, Hampton Court Palace. He would be obliged to make a 'gift' of it to his king. Henry was aware that Wolsey's great residence was joked about as being far more impressive than any property of his own. For a man of Henry's nature such knowledge, and its resentment, could prove dangerous to Wolsey. He had already had a warning from Henry, when disapproval had been shown. He knew that his grip on Henry was beginning to loosen since the King had made it clear to him that he was thinking of replacing him. Or, at the very least, intended diluting his power and influence by introducing younger men to take over the workings of England's diplomacy. Wolsey knew that his days of monopoly were numbered, therefore the 'gift' of the most precious thing he owned, in an effort to keep the king's favour.

Hampton Court's loss could be taken as a desperate throw to show the King what a devoted servant he had in Wolsey. He gave up his masterpiece. Henry accepted the gift eagerly and immediately began to rebuild it, adding to its grounds and enlarging its buildings to form an even greater setting, fit for a king.

If Queen Katherine of Aragon had an opinion on the matter, it might have been that is was suitable for a servant to give to his King the best there was to give. But then, her opinion of her lord and husband had always had a slightly maternal flavour. If she took any personal pleasure in the transference of such a gift of property, and the wrench it must have been for Wolsey to make it, she was soon to receive her own jolt from Henry. She, too, would be reminded that Henry was not entirely satisfied with the status quo, and that changes would be made.

In her own case the worrying reminder came when Henry brought to court his illegitimate son by Elizabeth Blount. This precious child had been living with his mother and stepfather in Lincolnshire, provided for liberally by his biological father. By 1525 he decided that the time had come for the 6-year-old boy to be more prominent at court. Being acknowledged as the son of the King was no longer enough. He now wanted an open, more formal acknowledgment of the child's unique status, and if Katherine were to be hurt by the parade of this boy, it was too bad.

While other men were content to provide for any illegitimate offspring, making up as far as they could for the inauspicious circumstances of their birth by giving them education and whatever future prospects they could manage, Henry intended to go very much further. He had been pondering the situation for some considerable time, holding the boy almost in reserve. He had possibly entertained some faint hope that Katherine might still produce a late child, many women did before their childbearing years were over. This last brief flowering of fertility was not unusual, and the children born of it were sometimes known as 'Tail Ends' and often became great favourites in their families. But Katherine had shown no sign of producing one last child, and by then all hope of a legitimate son born of his Spanish wife was dead.

Henry intended to make his feelings about that clear, not only to acknowledge the child, but to raise him higher than any bastard child had been raised since William of Normandy became his father's heir. He was to be given not only titles, but royal titles, by which Henry would betray his deepest and most secret aims for the boy.

Other men would be invested with honours at the same time as the child, including Sir Thomas Boleyn who became Viscount Rochford on that occasion. But his elevation, and that of other men, would not be allowed to detract from the centrepiece. It was to take place at the Palace of Bridewell and all the court were to attend.

Well-behaved for a child of 6, Henry Fitzroy is recorded as having gone through the long day of ceremonies with dignity. He was escorted by the Dukes of Norfolk and Suffolk, who would in future be obliged to step down one place in the pecking order. By the day's end, the apple of his father's eye was transformed into His Grace the Duke of Richmond and Somerset, and Earl of Nottingham. He was also proclaimed Lord Admiral of England, Wales and Ireland; of Normandy, Gascony and Aquitaine. He became a Knight of the Garter, Keeper of the City and Castle of Carlisle, and indubitably the first peer in England.[3]

Henry had done everything he could for the boy, and more than many people thought suitable. The only thing he had omitted was actually to make the child his heir – but the threat was there. Queen Katherine was as capable of reading such signs as anyone else. Henry didn't care, and made it clear he didn't. This was his son! If he had his way, the boy would one day be Henry IX.

Queen Katherine's furiously outspoken indignation at the insult to her and to her daughter the Princess Mary, with the threat implied by the raising of a bastard to royal titles, has come down to us. So has Henry's reaction – he sent Princess Mary away from court. She went to Ludlow as Princess of Wales, and this acknowledgment of her status must have been some consolation to her mother. She was accompanied by a suitable train of household retainers, which correctly included her Lady Governess, Lady Margaret Salisbury. The Countess of Salisbury was of the old Yorkist royal line, being the daughter of George, Duke of Clarence, brother of Edward IV. She was also a close personal friend of Katherine of Aragon. But however suitable Princess Mary's removal might have appeared, it must have still worried Katherine. The boy Fitzroy, was only a child, but in his growing would bring a serious threat to the right of the Princess Mary to succeed to her father's throne. Did Henry really consider the male line so much better, even if it was not legitimate? He had already made it publicly, painfully, obvious that he did not consider a daughter to be enough in herself, despite her legitimacy and her impeccable lineage. Katherine's failure as a queen was also being made perfectly clear. Although she was forced to put a brave, calm face on the matter of her beloved daughter's removal from court, she would have plenty of time to brood and try to estimate just how far her husband would be prepared to go.

Although Thomas Boleyn had by then risen to the peerage, he was not actually a member of the King's Privy Chamber. His son, George, was, as was his son-in-law, William Carey. Also Henry Norris, Sir Francis Bryan, Sir William Compton,

Sir Nicholas Carewe and several other young men who were the personal favourites of the King. These 'minions' of the King's, his closest male companions, had always played an important part in his life. Katherine may well have disapproved of them, knowing that their dissolute lifestyle encouraged his, and drew him away from her even more than did the difference in their ages. It had graduated into being a slightly 'young' crowd, intended to keep Henry's own youthfulness and eagerness for life well to the fore.

William Carey, husband of Mary Boleyn, was a pleasant-faced young man, easy-going and cheerful. He was from a Wiltshire family, the son of Eleanor Beaufort, and therefore distantly related to the King. He was also an eminently sensible young man, quite prepared to overlook the fact that his pretty wife was the King's mistress.

While she was still in France, King Francis had openly called Mary '*una grandissima ribalda et infame sopra tutte*', or 'a very great bawd and infamous above all'. Hardly the kindest way to describe the sweet-faced young woman he had used. Once back in England, she had transferred easily to the bed of Henry VIII and it was to William Carey's advantage to turn a blind eye to the goings-on between his wife and his king. Even when her son was born, and was not acknowledged as a king's bastard (therefore Carey was expected to accept the child as his own, which to be fair, it may have been), speculation was rife at court whether or not the child was the King's or Carey's.[4]

Henry VIII was, by this time, beginning to consider a completely fresh start, and hopefully a new family. The elevation of his bastard had met with ambivalent reactions and he still had hopes with regard to France, so perhaps the time for such upheaval was not yet. However, time was not on his side and the years slipped away all too easily. As his experiment with Henry Fitzroy had not met with the support he had hoped for, the only option would be to make another marriage, with a younger woman who had her fertility intact, and hope for a son from that source. It is quite possible that at this time Henry just did not know which road to go down. He was eager to forgo the marriage, which had promised so much and actually produced so little, but he must have been aware that it was not likely to be a popular move, or one simple to achieve.

However, Popes were known to be amenable to the necessity of kings to provide heirs, knowing the importance of secure succession. It was enough to mull over, even at a time when he had many more pressing concerns to occupy his time.

When Henry had agreed with the Emperor to share the costs of the French enterprise, he did not expect to hear that not a penny of his money had actually reached Bourbon. However, Charles V was destined to have far more success in the venture than Henry had had. One of the worst decisions King Francis would make was to go into Italy personally. There had, of course, been rumours that Charles V was not only in poor health, but chronically short of money, and that since Bourbon's defeat he was 'very desirous for peace and weary of war'.[5]

Brewer states that Francis was so determined to go to Italy that he did not even discuss it with his mother, for fear that she would manage to dissuade him from the idea. He was to face there a series of disastrous military reverses, which were to leave his army defeated and himself a prisoner of the troops of Charles V. Francis had gone directly to Milan. With the main force of Imperial troops only 20-odd miles away at Pavia it could hardly have been a worse decision. He attempted assault, then a siege and then had the winter to face. However, by January 1525 the enemy had reformed. Francis fought on stubbornly but was severely attacked and soundly defeated. Pavia was to be his downfall and he found himself in the humiliating position of actually being the prisoner of the Emperor. When Charles heard of the capture of the French King, he treated the matter not with joy and triumph, but with grave and considered solemnity. The outcome of the Battle of Pavia had placed that young man at the head of a real Empire.

If Charles considerately thought that the physical capture of a fellow monarch was somehow shameful, Henry VIII certainly did not. He was delighted at the news, which served to re-ignite all his own hopes of a successful invasion of France. If he could not manage to win in France against its king, surely he could succeed when that king was a prisoner? A less than chivalric intention, but it would crown the year for him if he could find some success there. The usual problem was, of course, lack of money. Henry had to have substantial sums to be able to make any attempt.

He decided to extract a 'loan' from the people, merely another form of taxation, which would be based on previous assessments of available assets. This time there was no time to waste in the process of collection. Henry was all on fire to get to France while it lay weakened. To expedite matters, he decided that 'donors' to this scheme would simply be informed what they would have to pay. Unfortunately for his idea, the 'Amicable Loan' was far less than amicably received. It was to lead to riots, threatening refusals and even to priests openly denouncing the demands from the pulpit. The backlash from it all fell on Wolsey. He was again blamed for the exactions demanded by the King. He was also blamed by the King for his inability to provide the funds needed for the French adventure quickly. His reputation sunk to an all-time low over the King's demands, particularly in view of the fact that he had already started to dissolve a few of the smaller religious houses, intending the funds thereby released to pay for his improvements at Cardinal's College, Oxford (now Christ Church).

This was a sensible move in itself, closing the smallest and least viable houses for amalgamation into larger and more thriving ones. Fortunately for his own peace of mind, he would not be there in the future to see what this precedent would lead to, when Henry would remember the lesson Wolsey had taught him, that religious houses were not necessarily sacrosanct. It was a lesson he would store away for future use, and one that he would one day use to devastating effect, when a need for money would be paramount.

The situation left Wolsey dangerously exposed. The common people were never quite as obedient or devoted as Henry liked to think they were. On the other side was Henry with his dreams of conquest tempting him onwards. Wolsey certainly did his best. He changed the name of the 'Loan' to the softer sounding title of a 'Benevolence'. This also failed to inspire the people to throw their money into

Henry's venture, and it became clear to Wolsey that he faced an uphill struggle to make them give anything at all. There was fierce opposition, from all sides.

The Dukes of Norfolk and Suffolk also did their best to carry out the task of collecting these 'Benevolences', but with no success. They began to fear downright insurrection. They also made it clear to the Cardinal that the common people were laying the blame for the whole sorry business squarely at his door. Warham had written to him from Kent, to warn him that the people were speaking openly and dangerously about him. Wolsey had attempted to retreat somewhat from the stance of 'requisition' into one almost of entreaty, declaring that the King would 'require no set sum, but would be happy to accept from his loving subjects whatever each of them might be inclined to give'. He ended with, 'I now ask for a Benevolence in His Majesty's name'.

This was another unfortunate allusion, as these so-called benevolences had been one of Edward IV's favourite methods of raising money by extracting funds from increasingly unwilling donors. One citizen was actually courageous enough to stand up before the Mayor and Corporation of London to remind Cardinal Wolsey to his face that, by a Statute of King Richard III, such benevolences were illegal. This led to a furious retort by the Cardinal on the lines of the usual Tudor propaganda regarding the posthumus reputation of the said Richard III, but the brave complainer stood his ground. He said that 'in his time were many good acts, made not by him only, but also by the consent of the body of the whole realm, which is the Parliament!'.[6] It was a sharp reminder of illegality which Wolsey – and Henry – could well have done without.

That was the root of the problem. The demands that Henry (through Wolsey) was making were without the backing and consent of the realm. Henry was to learn the hard lesson that it was not possible to do as he wished without the support of Parliament. Cardinal Wolsey had been obliged to retreat even further, and merely asked the London merchant to 'grant privily whatever he would'.

It was also Wolsey's first real failure to carry out Henry's wishes to order, and would be a salutary lesson to them both. Wolsey was aware of the antagonism towards him while going about Henry's business and Henry, in his turn, was beginning to realise that his Cardinal was not omnipotent.

But he still hadn't entirely given up his dream of French conquest, and he floundered for some time, vainly trying to raise the necessary funds. He tried asking the Pope for a loan, but was met with a polite refusal and the explanation that His Holiness had a 'duty to be a common father to all Christian Princes'.[7] Therefore he could not take sides in disputes between them.

After that rebuff, Henry faced the even greater humiliation of asking for assistance from Charles V himself. However, the advisors to the Emperor calmly informed Henry that Charles had no spare money to give towards the project. Henry was obliged, most reluctantly, to realise that this particular dream was destined to come to nothing.

In the meantime, the thing troubling him the most was still on his mind. That was his, to him, barren marriage. Katherine of Aragon still saw their daughter, Princess

Mary, as the heir to the Crown of England. She was satisfied, having known the upbringing of the most warlike and capable queen of her generation, her mother Isabella of Castile. She was ready to train the Princess Mary for the great position awaiting her.

Henry felt differently. While he was fond of his daughter, and saddened at the memory of all the wasted pregnancies that had come to nothing, he did not consider the matter irrevocably closed. The unprecedented elevation of his bastard son proved that he was considering other ways of dealing with the succession. He was still desperately fishing around for a satisfactory solution, and by the end of 1525 he believed that he had found it.

He had been toying with the attractive idea of a new marriage on and off for some time. He had discussed it with his chief minister and finally agreed with Wolsey that emissaries would be sent into France, to sound out the idea of a female relative of the French royal house becoming his bride. Wolsey was happy to comply, while putting the ball firmly back in Henry's court by leaving him the difficult task of informing Katherine of Aragon of the news that she was to be supplanted. Not an easy task for any man, and certainly not for Henry, who had made an art form out of dropping every unpleasant job into someone else's lap. The relationship between himself and the Queen was already strained and she would certainly suspect his motives when she realised the situation.

In the meantime, another complication was arising. When Thomas Boleyn's daughter Anne had been exiled from court over the ill-fated Percy romance, Henry had become interested in her. Perhaps, initially, merely wondering what it was about the young woman that would make Henry Percy risk everything to have her. She had been at court already, without stirring the King, but now he looked again. Not as wife material, of course, that was unthinkable, but as a diversion. She was most unusual in her looks and in her manner, and would certainly be different from her too-compliant sister. With his marital problems at home and his disappointment abroad, Henry no doubt thought that he was fully entitled to a little fling to take his mind off his problems. But there lay another problem. The girl had ideas of her own, and they certainly did not include following her sister into the King's bed. She had seen Mary Boleyn's involvement with Henry end with little more than a marriage to a courtier, children whose paternity would always be in doubt and a shameful lack of a decent reputation. She had also seen the way that Elizabeth Blount had been cast off. That lady may well have given the King his beloved son, but she was exiled from court and would remain so. Now even her son was taken from her.

There is no reason whatever to suspect Anne of less deep feeling than Percy had displayed. She had been almost broken by the loss of her hopes. Others had noticed her, but she had involved herself with none of them.

Thomas Wyatt was a neighbour of the Boleyns from Kent, and had already made his interest in Anne Boleyn clear in the fashionable manner, by writing poems about her beauty and his broken heart. There is no evidence to suppose that Anne considered Wyatt more than a close family friend. He was a married man, therefore dangerous, and Anne was not prepared to allow herself to fall into that trap, pleasant though it was to have such a man declare himself in verse.[8]

She had no intention of falling into that trap with the King either. She did her best to avoid his increasing attentions in the early stages of his interest in her. It is not to be expected that her father was pleased at seeing another daughter risking herself. Anne had profited most from her advanced education, and her father's guidance. He would not wish to see such investment wasted on a mere affair.

It is not correct to assume that the Boleyns were performing a dance with Henry, cynically drawing him closer, with Anne's attractions as the bait. The evidence available for this period of her life shows that Anne did not want to become the King's mistress, but that her genuine reluctance inflamed him further. That is hardly surprising when it is remembered that Henry was a man who had rarely been refused anything. Nothing in the King's previous behaviour had given anyone the right to expect that he was likely to be a faithful lover, or even generous after the event to those he became involved with.

The conventions of 'courtly love' in England were in their infancy compared with the situation usual in France, and greatly lacking the refinements Anne would have seen during her stay there. There a successful mistress of a king could rise very high indeed, gathering lands and titles, influence and security. Henry would expect the discarded lady to fade discreetly into the background, once her day in the sun was over. It was not what Thomas Boleyn wanted for his most promising daughter, and it was certainly not what Anne wanted for herself.

The Butler match had definitely gone off the boil, and whether the stain of the Percy scandal had spoiled it or whether the families simply could not agree terms (as was rumoured) was not clear. If Anne were to give in to Henry, and soon after become just another of his cast-offs, there would be no line of suitors waiting to marry her respectably. She would be obliged to take what she could get, as her own sister had done. Small wonder that her father appeared no more eager for her to warm the King's bed than she was herself. The whole situation was becoming embarrassing. However, Henry's attentions continued. By all previous criteria, he should have become quickly bored with the unsuccessful chase, unwilling to risk humiliation at the hands of a young woman. But in this case, his determination not to lose gradually fed the fire of his imagination, and what had started as merely a salacious interest became infatuation. Henry was caught in the net of his own desire, just as Anne was, but she must have realised that the situation was a dangerous one for her, and for her family. If the King became annoyed, he could cast the Boleyns down further than he had raised them up. She had to move carefully, without causing that reversal of feeling that could ruin everything for her relatives. This knowledge is likely to have engendered fear in her, every bit as strong as any feeling of triumph or pride at the idea of a king being involved.

He began to send her notes and small gifts, and eventually so committed himself as to begin to write love letters to her. In these he claimed that if Anne should give herself to him 'body and soul' to become his mistress as he wished, he would 'seek no other, casting aside all others but you' and that he would 'serve' her alone.[9]

Even this magnanimous gesture had no effect on her and his feelings towards her began to change. In his private thoughts there grew the idea that so different, so rare a woman as she must be might be worth the ultimate accolade. In any case, his heart was now involved, and why could he not actually marry the woman he wanted?

On Anne's side, we will never know when she realised that she was trapped.

That Henry's increasingly obvious attentions towards her were doing more than causing Thomas Wyatt to write her a beautiful farewell, but might also be blocking the path of any other man of nobility who might be prepared to offer her legal marriage. No man looking for a wife would be likely to step in while the King was making her conspicuous in such a way. As the faintly ridiculous situation became fixed, it was becoming apparent to Anne, and to her father, that all her education, and talent, all her expensively and painfully acquired accomplishments, might be wasted after all.

Cardinal Wolsey was aware of the King's growing infatuation for the girl he had spoken contemptuously of over the Harry Percy affair. But, like most other people, he considered her to be no real threat. True, he generally disliked the Boleyns, and did not wish to see them become any more prominent than could be helped, but he did not expect Anne to be any more of a fixture than her sister had been. She would either give in to the King, or he would grow bored and turn his attentions to some other lady. Either way, she would be no more than a passing annoyance. That everyone was deliciously aware of what was going on meant nothing – except to Anne. She was to show herself to be a woman who was possessed of a rare pride in herself, what might in more modern times be called an 'awareness' of herself, independently of others who affected her. Later, at the crisis of her life, a time of great grief and shame for her, she would supposedly write a poem, which showed that her greatest regret was the besmirching of her good name.[10] There is no reason to doubt the fact that she was indeed shamed and grieved to find herself infamous without just cause.

There is no reason to suppose that she was enjoying the pressure she was under. The wagging tongues, the sniggering whispers at court. Open talk of whether or not she had given herself to the King. If not, then why not? We know enough about her as a woman to know that it would have outraged her dignity, shamed her, to be the object of such common gossip, but there was no remedy. The King persisted, he could not be shaken off.

By the following year something fundamental had changed. We cannot know when the idea of matrimony between the two of them was first considered. But sooner or later it was mentioned, and it was to alter everything.

Anne was by then fully aware that her reputation would not survive the situation intact. There were enough wicked tongues and doubtful minds at court to ensure that she would be blamed for the act, even if she never performed it. Her reputation would be in tatters either way. She would never find a suitable husband of her own rank, for such a man would not be content to take the King's leavings.

When the King finally mentioned the magic word 'marriage' Anne had to look at the situation differently. If a legal relationship with Henry was second-best to the true love of her life, then it was a very good second-best. It would eventually raise her to the throne, above all the people who still disapproved of her family, and all those – including Wolsey – who had considered her to be not quite good enough to marry Henry Percy. She could become mistress over all, able to secure the future for all those people she loved, and she could hopefully produce the much-needed son and heir, ensuring that her own child would sit on the throne. All her training and skills could be used, her knowledge of languages, her culture, her philanthropic instincts, so carefully cultivated by her father. These would all enhance a queen.

But any understanding between her and Henry would have to remain a very private thing. However, she was to make a delicate and impressive gesture to signal to him that she was prepared to throw in her lot with his. She did not merely say 'yes' as any lesser woman might have done. What she did do was to commission a jewel, a pendant to be worn on a lace or chain, made of gold. It would have been enamelled and we know from the letter sent to her by Henry when he received it, that it also held a 'fair diamond'. It would have been an expensive item – did her father pay for it? It would certainly have been something she would discuss with him.

This jewel showed, as Henry mentioned in his letter of thanks to her, a 'ship, in which a solitary damsel is tossed about'.[11] Henry would have been able to understand the message implied in the design. He would see Anne as the damsel. It would have been designed to flatter his sense of strength and reliability.

But, was there a second and deeper meaning to the trinket? Anne wasn't the type to lean heavily on the man in her life, she was a strong woman, sure of herself. In this instance, she seems to have been less sure. It is quite possible that the real meaning of the 'tossed about' damsel is that she was still not convinced she was doing the right thing. She would know that she was sacrificing any real marriage (and surely even then ladies still hoped for a marriage that included affection, despite the pecuniary motives). Henry may have been delighted at what he saw as her surrender to him, but it meant more than that. She was also saying that she was still not entirely his, and that she was not prepared to become intimate with him until she was secure. Her determination was the only thing she had to ensure that she did not end up as the mother of another of his bastards. It would prove to be a situation just as fraught with strain and danger as its alternative.

For the time being it would not do for Katherine or Wolsey, and certainly not for the Pope to know, what they had privately agreed. It is certain that her family did know, at least its closest members, but others would work better if they worked in the dark.

What they would need to help them through the approaching minefield was the support of the Duke of Norfolk, Anne's maternal uncle. This man, by then 52 years old, had recently returned to prominence. He was the son of the hero of Flodden, but the family had lost everything by backing the wrong side at the Battle of Bosworth. The Howards, now rising again at this point in history, would remain influential for the remainder of the reign and Thomas Howard was again England's premier Duke (excepting Fitzroy) by 1525.[12]

However, Thomas Howard, though at this stage of her life a supporter of Anne's, was not her champion for her own sake. In all noble families the notion of the 'family' was as an entity in itself, rather than individual personalities within it. Thomas Howard was prepared to encourage and uphold his niece because of the good she could bring to the family, not because of any personal liking between them.

Unlike Anne's own father, Thomas Howard had no appreciation of the finer points of her education, or her grace or charm, except in that such accomplishments could be used. They were saleable commodities. Anne would never find a solid and true supporter in him and, once their paths began to diverge, and their relationship fractured, it would be irreparable.

The Duke of Norfolk provided all that was necessary for the women of his household because it was required of his rank that he do so. His stepsisters were married off well, and his stepmother, Agnes Tilney, the Dowager Duchess, had retired in comfort to her property at Horsham St Faith near to Norwich. There she kept a large household in accordance with her status.[13]

The Duke had a difficult relationship with his wife, Lady Elizabeth Stafford, daughter of the Duke of Buckingham. That lady was twenty-three years her husband's junior, but she was said to be a termagant, who lived apart from him when possible, at her dower house at Redbourne.[14] There are, of course, two sides to every story, and it was claimed on the Duchess's behalf that the Duke had treated her cruelly, instructing servants to hold her down and sit on her 'until she spat blood!'. Whatever the truth of their pitiful marriage, it seems certain that the Duke had better relationships with people of a lower social class than he did with his equals. Perhaps that was merely due to the fact that, in such encounters, he would have a measure of control, which he could not always exercise over his peers. His long-term mistress, Elizabeth Holland, was the sister of his steward.

He now based his authority on his willingness to do the King's bidding, and took enormous pride in the service he offered to his sovereign. So long as his niece Anne was working for the same ends, he would be content to be her partisan.

That was not the way in which Anne's relationship worked with her brother. She and George had met almost as strangers but with recognition that they were two halves of a pair. He was to show himself to be his sister's firm bedrock and support through all the difficult years ahead. His own marriage was not as happy as he had expected it to be. It is possible that the bride was to feel jealousy at her husband's close friendship with his sister. Whatever the truth of George's relationship with Jane, there were no children of the marriage, although there were persistent claims that he had fathered an illegitimate child, a son. Details of this claim are difficult to find and there is no record of whether this son was supposed to have been born before, or during, his marriage to Jane Parker.

George was certainly in favour at court. As one of Henry's 'minions' he had close access to the King, he was wealthy and as well educated and cultured as his sister. He was the most likely person in whom Anne would confide her secrets, particularly the dangerous but exciting news that the King was suggesting a marriage between them.

Katherine of Aragon may have appeared middle-aged and part of the 'old order' that was being pushed aside by the heedless new crowd, but she was still Queen of England. She was still a daughter of Spain, a lady of unassailable dignity and recognised virtue; she was still the maternal aunt of the Emperor Charles V, now ruler of most of Europe. This man, like the Pope himself, was to be a firm champion of his aunt's right to remain as Queen, and as Henry's wife. Henry had also realised that he would need allies, and his eyes had yet again turned towards France.

King Francis was released from his captivity in 1526, in exchange for granting certain considerations. These were harsh. First, his two young sons were to spend some time in Spain, under the 'protection' of Charles V. They would be respectfully and suitably treated as Princes of France, but were obviously hostages for their father's good behaviour. Francis also had to cede his hard-fought-for Italian possessions to Charles, along with lands in Flanders, Artois and Burgundy. It was a humiliating list of concessions, likely to provoke Franco-Spanish enmity for good.

Henry thought that Francis' experiences with Spain would be sufficiently painful that he would jump at the chance to see a Spanish-born Queen removed from the English throne. He was banking heavily on Francis' sympathy and support and also that the Pope would also show some sympathy for Henry's situation with regard to his 'barren' first marriage.

Francis appeared to be amenable, particularly if there might be a good chance of the second wife of the King of England being a Frenchwoman. It was, fortunately, hidden from him at that time that, before too long, he would also be obliged to accept a Spanish princess as a wife, if ever his poor tormented country was to have a proper and lasting peace with Spain.[15] His wife, Queen Claude, had died in 1524 and, by 1530, he would be married to Eleanora of Austria, sister to Charles V himself. Despite this, Henry would continue to look towards Francis for encouragement in what by then he was determined to do.

Henry was like a new broom in his eagerness to sweep away all the stuffy and confining ideas that had once been so comforting and suitable. He was grasping at more than a new wife. He also wanted the whole package. Anne represented youth and the future, along with the young people who were friends to her brother and herself. They were a fresh breeze, promising a new start and a new life. Together with a son, which he looked to Anne to provide. He was to follow that dream with a tenacity few would have believed him capable of, a dogged persistence eventually to trample underfoot anyone who stood in his way.

Thomas Wolsey cannot have been expected to approve the new interest. Holding grimly onto his power, working hard, being useful, he could not spare too many hours of his precious time on such a matter.

Queen Katherine may have felt differently, realising Anne was too clever to be so easy a conquest. She had her background and her religion to sustain her, along with the private certainty that kings did not throw aside a marriage of nearly twenty years in order to marry their sweethearts. If her heart was sore in the knowledge she had lost Henry's interest, she could feel secure with her honourable position and the power of her nephew.

Wolsey had only himself to rely on, for the difficult times when Henry seemed to have lost all sense of what was fitting. He must have realised that this lady was more ambitious and cleverer than the others, but one day she would cease to please and the matter would be ended.

Wolsey had already seen so much, and still waded through. He had been a witness to Henry's despair, when the sons were not born and the years were passing. When the King had even toyed with the idea of pushing his illegitimate son onto the throne. Wolsey held no brief for Katherine and if a new match would replace her with a French princess then she would have to live with it. She would not be the first queen to sacrifice her own wishes on the altar of her country's desperate need. She and the Princess Mary would be well provided for and the Queen could console herself with the rightness of the act and that the Pope would approve it.

Even while Wolsey's brain buzzed with such ideas, he would have had other concerns. No mention now of Henry's intention to bring in 'new' men to handle his diplomatic secrets. Other men could not be trusted. Only Wolsey could be trusted with difficult matters.

For one thing, the expenses of the King's household had again swelled to immense proportions. They seemed to inflate year upon year. Henry wanted this matter dealt with too, for who knew what further expenses he might be expected to meet in the near future?

There would certainly have to be retrenchments, and the King could not court possible unpopularity by appearing to insist on economies, he was above having to deal with such things.

Henry knew that there would be a need for meticulous detailing, firm handling and the sort of careful accounting that was the Cardinal's particular forte, and that Wolsey would faithfully leave no stone unturned in finding ways to regulate the chronic situation.

Henry had made no attempt to curb his own profligate tendencies, while Wolsey had come to believe that even the King should be accountable for his use of the public funds.[16] Wolsey would have to instigate internal reforms, from the attics to the kitchens, even taking an interest in the clothing for the scullions in those kitchens, under the aegis of the three master cooks. They would ensure that kitchen servants received 'honest and whole garments' which would be kept 'without such uncleanness as may be to the annoyance of those by whom they shall pass'.[17]

Naturally, it is easy for people to take offence when new orders are sent down and they are expected to comply. Not only humble people were irritated by Wolsey's high-handed manner. Even the Duke of Suffolk, still in debt to the King over the matter of his runaway marriage to the King's sister, Mary Tudor, came in for a sharp reminder that most of that debt remained unpaid. The Duke, no doubt seething, was forced to retire from court for a time, and establish his own household retrenchments. He was to lead a frugal existence until he was able to raise some money to service his debt to the King.

But re-organising kitchens and account books did not end Wolsey's attempts at reconstruction. He particularly wanted to deal with the things taking place within the King's Privy Chamber. This was on more delicate ground, among the King's closest gentlemen. These people had the King's ear, which gave them influence, but also opportunities to ask for things for themselves or their families and friends. This exacerbated the problem of the rising expenses, and made them almost impossible to control.

This all too easily led to abuses, particularly with the King's known open-handedness towards people he liked. This constant begging for favours and offices was an accepted part of court life. It formed one of the main reasons why people wanted access to the King and why competition for any such appointment was fierce.

Wolsey's vigorous reform of the Privy Chamber meant a severe cutting back of the numbers of gentlemen employed within it. This would mean a saving directly, on wages, but also obliquely, as there would be fewer men asking favours. Fewer attendants on the King, meant fewer attendants on the gentlemen. Each gentleman of the King's Chamber had gentlemen and servants of his own. Lodging at court was expected not only for the Privy Chamber gentleman, but also for his personal servants; sometimes his wife and her servants; his grooms, horses and even hounds.

However, even though Wolsey was perfectly correct in trying to stamp out the more obvious abuses and cut down the constantly escalating costs, he took the opportunity to pick and choose a little among the gentlemen; to decide who would, and who would not, remain in the King's intimate service.

William Carey stayed, as did Henry Norris, William Brereton and Francis Weston (who became the King's page), but George Boleyn lost his place. It seems almost too obvious that this man, Anne Boleyn's brother, should be dismissed, when others remained. There was no reason given for his dismissal, except that the Cardinal was reducing the numbers of people in close daily contact with the King.[18]

However, George Boleyn was still one of the King's favourites. If Wolsey had attempted a little spiteful manoeuvring regarding George's removal from the King's presence, it very quickly backfired.

George's name was on the list of 'those assigned to have lodging in the king's house, when they should repair to it'. George was to be paid £20 per year, in addition to his own £80, as a salary for his new post as cupbearer. The list states quite clearly that he was appointed as 'one of the King's cupbearers, when the King dineth out'.[19]

This meant that George was still in the King's presence. He still had free lodgings at court for himself, his wife, his servants and horses. Actually, 'when the King dineth out' meant that he would be in attendance on Henry at every occasion on which the King dined in state, anywhere other than in his Privy Chamber.

It meant that George was certainly still in a position of prominence. If Wolsey had given in to the hope of getting rid of him, he had failed.

The Register was as meticulously checked by the Cardinal as all of his other amendments, and the document in which there is the reference to 'Mr. Boleyn's' post is clearly ticked as approved in Wolsey's own hand.[20] The Cardinal had obviously had to bow to Henry's own wishes and authority on the matter of George Boleyn.

Chapter Seven

The Pope and the Italian princes had actually welcomed the presence of Francis I in Italy. Their main area of concern was the growing power of Charles V. After Pavia and the capture and imprisonment of Francis, and after the humiliating agreement of the Treaty of Madrid, Charles was in a greater position of power than ever. Once Francis was free he let it be known that he would be willing to join with the Pope in opposing the Emperor, and subsequently on 22 May 1526 the Holy League was formed. This included France, Florence, Venice and Francesco Maria Sforza II (the last Duke of Milan; he had ambitions regarding Milan and joined the League in opposition to Charles V, who had taken over Milan in 1521). Henry VIII was not actually a member, though he was made 'Protector' of the League. By including him in this manner the members hoped to encourage him to contribute to the defence of the Holy See. The hopes of the Pope had risen, temporarily, at the idea of some defence from outside Rome. Pope Clement had written to Wolsey and Henry to thank them personally for bringing France into the group, and told them, flatteringly, that but for their help the alliance could not have been made at all.

Despite the flattery, Henry did not wish to join any real activity. The League was too weak to mount more than a token resistance to Charles, and Francis, revelling in his freedom, spent his time with pleasures, rather than concerning himself with the problems of the Pope. Nor did he make any attempt to safeguard the possessions he had gained there. The League was useless in real terms against Charles, and could offer no military resistance. By this time he had large forces in Italy, but disliked the idea of paying the men under his command. This meant they lived by plundering the countryside. It was reported that there were 'great excesses of the Imperial army, wherever they lodge. The like whereof could scarcely have been done by the Turks ...'.[1] Not only for their greed, but also for their cruelty were the Spanish troops disliked. Their German Lutheran mercenaries behaved in such a way as to make them feared, though the Lutheran mercenaries in Rome could hardly be expected to show much respect for the Pope. Clement was obliged to confine himself to sending pleas for help to Henry VIII and to Wolsey. Wolsey's replies to the Pope were full of concern, advice and encouragement, but Henry declined to make any attempt to assist.[2]

Clement did not effectively use what powers he did have, lacking respect from Charles to his position. This was surprising in a man brought up as Clement had been. He was the illegitimate son of Giuliano de' Medici and his father had been murdered about a month before his birth. His mother, whose name is unrecorded, gave the child to his uncle Lorenzo (the Magnificent) to rear, and he was intended for a military career. He grew very close to Lorenzo's son (his cousin Giovanni, who became Pope Leo X) and was to abandon all plans for a soldier's life in favour of a career in the Church. He was forced into a military situation when the matter of the long-unpaid troops swarming over Italy came to a head.

Almost 35,000 of these troops mutinied and forced their leaders to march towards Rome. This meant that the Pope was under personal attack. His ongoing difficulties were made worse by the actions of his enemy, Cardinal Pompeo Colonna.[3] He and his supporters were in open opposition to Clement, and Colonna had gone so far as to ride at the head of troops towards the city a few months previously. Clement had made a point of pardoning Calonna, but it had achieved little other than to show his weakness, and Clement's physical safety could not be guaranteed while he remained at the Vatican.

By May of 1527 it was obvious that the position had grown desperate and the Pope was prevailed upon to leave for a place of greater safety, while Rome lay helpless under the heel of the invading troops.

On 6 May the Imperial army attacked the Vatican itself and the Swiss Guards were massacred on the steps of St Peter's Basilica. Renzo de Ceri led 5,000 militiamen in defending Rome, along with only 500 Swiss Guards, under the command of Kaspar Roist. There were only 189 Guards on duty when the Vatican was attacked and only 42 of them survived to attempt to form a rearguard around the person of the Pope. Their leader persuaded Clement to escape along the Passetto di Borgo, the high brick wall running from the Vatican to the Castel Sant'Angelo, containing a tunnel.[4] Kaspar Roist was killed defending the Pope during his flight, while he and his closest advisors were successful in scurrying down the narrow internal corridor to safety.[5]

The Pope was to remain there while Cardinal Colonna entered the city on 8 May with his peasant army behind him, and a thousand defenders of the city were executed by Imperial troops. By 6 June Clement had no choice but to surrender, agreeing to a ransom of 400,000 ducati in exchange for his life. Charles V made a show of being embarrassed at the flight and endangerment of the Pope, but his rampaging troops had shown Europe where the true power lay and Pope Clement heeded the warning. He would never again make the mistake of openly opposing Charles. This would have a very deleterious effect on Henry VIII when he needed the Pope's support against Spain. He was to realise that Clement had learned his lesson well, and would not find against the cause of Katherine of Aragon when she asked his aid against Henry. Weak he may have been, cautious to a fault he certainly was, but his course was fixed and Henry would ultimately be the loser.

If Henry had been able to show indifference to the plight of the endangered Pope, Wolsey was a man of more worldly experience. When news of the Sack of Rome finally reached England, Wolsey wrote, 'If the Pope be slain or taken, it will hinder the King's affairs not a little, which have hitherto been going so well.'[6]

The first secret approach to the Pope regarding Henry's proposed divorce had been made in the summer of 1526. On 13 September of that year, John Clerk, Bishop of Bath, wrote from Rome that he had spoken with the Pope and that he could handle all the matters that Wolsey had submitted to him, but that the 'cursed divorce' would not be easily granted.[7]

Not only did the matter need to be kept as secret as possible, but Henry's real aims were being kept secret from Wolsey. He had seemingly more important matters to deal with than the King's wish for a change of wife. Pro-French he may have been, but he was not blind to the difficulties the King was entering into when he wished to prove that his queen had been no more than his paramour for almost twenty years. They were exacerbated by Katherine's popularity with the ordinary people. But the real problem hinged more on the fact that what one Pope had pronounced good and valid, Henry now wished another Pope to revoke. Moreover, that Pope was the one man who could not afford to offend Spain. The intolerable burden of what Henry wanted from him must have settled like King John's cope of lead around Wolsey's shoulders.

Wolsey would later tell George Cavendish that he had 'fallen on his knees for the space of an hour or two' in his attempts to dissuade Henry from setting out on a course that was almost guaranteed to fail.[8] However, once Wolsey became convinced that Henry was adamant in his determination, the Cardinal was equally determined to serve his king to the best of his considerable ability.

It was Diego Hurtado de Mendoza, the Spanish Ambassador, who first sent word to Charles V of the King of England's intention to divorce his wife. He placed most of the blame onto Wolsey. Mendoza's intention had been to stop any closer alliance between England and France. He sent news that was guaranteed to surprise the Emperor, to the effect that the 'Cardinal, to crown his iniquities, was working to separate the King and Queen'.[9] This belief might have been understandable. Wolsey had, not long previously, arranged for the Duke of Suffolk, husband of Henry's sister Mary, to tidy up his unfortunate and confusing marital track record and the matter had been confirmed by Rome. Spain suspected Wolsey of intending to do the same with regard to Katherine of Aragon. To the end of the whole business, Katherine would neither accept nor admit that Henry had not been manipulated, or that he had personally been the driving force behind the divorce question.

Henry's first official move was to call a Tribunal on 17 May 1527 at Wolsey's residence at York Place, at Westminster. There the King admitted to 'a terrible doubt' with the original dispensation given for his marriage to his brother's widow, claiming that it had been in error. He said he believed that he and Katherine had been living in sin all their married life, and that this sin was responsible for the fact that all their boy children (the heirs in his eyes) had died. He claimed that it was illegal for him to have married his sister-in-law and that the Bible confirmed that fact. Probably none of the people present at York Place on that date were under any illusions about the required outcome. The King wanted the 'charge' against him, i.e. of living in sin with his late brother's wife, to be found proven. Katherine had not been informed that the meeting was taking place, so she was not present to make any defence.

Wolsey may even have said something at an earlier time, which gave Henry the idea of running towards Leviticus' 'if a man shall take his brother's wife it is an impurity, he has uncovered his brother's nakedness, they shall be childless'. Wolsey was to remark later that it was 'best to be well advised and assured what manner of matter ye put into his head, for ye shall never pull it out again!'.[10]

Henry had already appeared, on Shrove Tuesday of the previous year, at the jousts at Greenwich, wearing 'Declare I dare not' as his new motto, so few of those present could be in any doubt that he had another lady waiting in the background. Did they also turn a blind eye, expecting a short-lived love affair?

Whether Wolsey had planted the original idea of an invalid marriage into Henry's receptive mind; whether he sincerely wished he had kept quiet on the subject; he was to be the one expected to make it all happen. The King's relationship with Anne did not seem relevant. What the King wanted was to discard his long-standing marriage to the Emperor's aunt, and that was where the real problem would be. Few people could believe that there would be a quick or simple solution to expecting Pope Clement to disregard the interests of Spain after the fright he had had.

It would be discussed only in whispers for the time being. However, whispers have a habit of spreading and Katherine was not stupid. Mendoza had already observed that 'she sees that they do not tell her the truth ...'. He was then referring to diplomatic matters, from which the Queen had gradually been excluded, but she had her spies too, and on the following day Mendoza wrote to Charles V that the Queen already knew what was planned.

> The king is so bent on this divorce, that he has secretly assembled certain bishops and lawyers, that they may sign a declaration to the fact that his marriage to the queen is null and void on account of her having been his brother's wife. It is therefore feared that either the Pope will be induced by some false statement to side against the queen, or that the Cardinal by virtue of his Legative authority may take some step fatal to her marriage. I am perfectly aware, though the queen herself has not ventured, and does not venture, to speak to me on the subject, that all her hope rests, after God, with your Imperial Highness.[11]

Wolsey's scheme was making the assumption that Henry's marriage was invalid. The participants were also taking it for granted that Katherine would not fight, and would facilitate matters by discreet withdrawal, once the decision was made against her. It was not to be.

On 20 May the court met again and after a further adjournment a copy of the Bull of Julius II was produced, which had granted the original dispensation.

On 31 May, Richard Wolman (one of the King's chaplains) produced a set of objections to the royal marriage and the court was again adjourned. News of the recent Sack of Rome then reached England and the court was not to meet again in the original form. However, Wolsey had already been working at sounding out bishops and others for their opinions on the legitimacy of the King's marriage, behind Katherine's back.

It was not until 22 June that Henry gathered his courage to visit Katherine and tell her personally what was being done. The conversation did not go smoothly.

Katherine was horrified, and reacted not with reasoned argument, but with a flood of tears. Henry was forced to try to pacify her with assurances that the proceedings he had instituted were merely to confirm their daughter's legitimacy.[12]

Whatever the difficulties of the recent Sack of Rome, the Pope's situation gave Wolsey another idea. If the Pope were a captive – or if not actually captive, then under the influence and control of Charles V – could he, as Cardinal Legate, assume power to make a decision on the matter on behalf of the King? It seemed logical that the Pope should delegate power to some Cardinal not subject to Imperial restrictions.

Wolsey had been appointed Plenipotentiary for conducting a League of Peace between Henry, Francis and the Venetians, during the captivity of the Pope. A further commission empowered him to make arrangements for the prospective marriage of the Princess Mary with a French prince (possibly the Duke of Orléans), together with a general commission enabling him to form an offensive league against the Emperor. Before leaving for France, Wolsey received a message from the King via Dr Wolman. This suggested that Henry suspected him of wavering in his desire to promote the 'Secret Matter'. Wolsey hastened to reassure Henry that he was convinced of the invalidity of the marriage and that the Queen still seemed obstinate in the matter. He advised Henry further that 'til it were known what should succeed of the Pope, and to what point the French king might be brought, your Grace should handle her both gently and doulcely'.[13]

Wolsey left for France on 3 July accompanied by a train including Sir Thomas More. Modesty was never one of his virtues and, although a few ecclesiastics did make a show of humility, that had never been Wolsey's style. They were living in a period when display was a sign of status and Wolsey went to France much as he had done previously, with all the razzmatazz expected of him. He considered it a duty to his position.

All his yeoman wore their tawny coats embroidered with his cipher under a Cardinal's hat. His mule, and his spare mule, were similarly ornate being trapped with crimson velvet. Before him were carried the usual two great silver crosses and two large silver pillars, along with the Great Seal of England, his Cardinal's hat and even a gentleman who carried his heavily embroidered cloak bag, complete with cloak.[14]

Wolsey was received at Calais with ceremony and met King Francis at Amiens before travelling with him to Compiègne, where the full court waited, including the King's mother and his sister-in-law, the young Princess Renée. This was the lady who would be presented as the object of the King of England's marital intentions.[15]

However, the visit was not entirely without incident. George Cavendish, Wolsey's gentleman usher, showed a strong dislike for the French, calling them 'slaves'.[16] This was due to their penchant for spying and whispering against his master, but also for their petty thieving. A standing dish of silver gilt was taken by a youth, but after official complaints the boy was captured and pilloried. But more serious annoyances were to come.

Wolsey was not aware that, while on the road to France, Henry (instead of taking part in the usual summer progress) had gone to Beaulieu, which had been sold to him by Thomas Boleyn. With him was a party of friends and 'advisors' intending to hold private discussions regarding the marriage. Although Wolsey was on official business dealing with the divorce and remarriage of the King, these intimate discussions were excluding him from the real centre of power. The private Beaulieu talks began in July. The party briefly visited Castle Hedingham during early August for a couple of days relaxation in hunting, but on 7 August Dr William Knight (Henry VIII's new secretary, who replaced Richard Pace) was instructed to write to Wolsey asking for 'Dr. Stephens' to be sent to Henry. This was Stephen Gardiner, later Bishop of Winchester and Lord Chancellor, but at that stage in his career he was working as one of Wolsey's confidential secretaries. It was stated that Henry needed him to 'communicate and confer divers things to him' or to have private talks, which would effectively take control of the divorce proceedings out of Wolsey's hands. The Cardinal was immediately aware of the implications and refused to allow 'Dr. Stephens' to return to England, indulging in a flurry of makework to keep him busy and show Henry that the situation was progressing. Wolsey excused all delays, but pointed out that he had heard about the proposed divorce via the Archduchess Margaret in Flanders. It was clear that all of Europe was talking about it.

By the end of August the 'Beaulieu party' had dispersed, heading back to court, but Dr Knight then set out towards Rome, intending to visit Wolsey in France on the way. He was carrying with him Henry's personal requests for the Pope. But it is essential to realise that Knight was Henry's envoy, not Wolsey's.

On 5 September Wolsey received a letter from Knight informing him that he was on his way to Rome on the King's business. He made it clear that he was being sent to see Pope Clement with particular requests from the King. Wolsey was annoyed that Knight should be sent on such a mission without his knowledge or approval, but when Knight actually arrived in France with his instructions, which he showed to Wolsey, mere annoyance gave way to dismay.

Henry had instructed Knight to see the Pope and to ask for two dispensations. One of them was for Henry to have permission (once his marriage to Katherine was dissolved) to marry a woman whose sister had been his mistress. This blew the whole charade wide open. Not only had Wolsey no idea that Henry was writing to the Pope behind his back, but the proposed dispensation quite obviously did not refer to the Princess Renée. It did not take Wolsey long to realise to whom it did refer. He would have been more than horrified, he would have been furious. Yet he could not show it, even when he read the even more ridiculous second suggestion from Henry. That asked the Pope if, in the event of the marriage to Katherine not being dissolved in a reasonable time, Henry could be allowed to marry another lady anyway. In effect, could he have two wives, with the offspring of the new one to be also considered legitimate.[17] Wolsey must have been almost apoplectic at the stupidity of Henry's request. In view of the careful work already done, and the efforts made to convince the Pope that Henry's doubts were purely due to his fear of illegitimacy in his present marriage, it must have seemed that Henry had lost all common sense.

Wolsey was obliged to write to Henry, and it must have been one of his most considered and carefully worded communications. Not only was it obvious that Henry was not thinking sensibly for himself, but also that he was ferreting around behind Wolsey's back, rather than letting him get on with the work he was sent to do. He had entrusted secret and indeed dangerous papers to a third party, allowing a totally inexperienced man to step into the labyrinth of Roman politics on a very sensitive issue, which would make a veteran shudder. A minefield had just opened under Wolsey's feet and he realised that there were powerful people around the King who had managed to convince him that the matter could be managed without recourse to the Cardinal. Therefore, Wolsey had become surplus to requirements.

It cannot be over-emphasised what a shock it must have been. He prided himself on his ability to deal with difficult diplomatic manoeuvres, yet he found he had been treated as nothing. His mission had been usurped, and he had only found out about it by accident. It now appeared that his embassy to France was being used by Henry as a smokescreen, while papers of the utmost importance were carried direct to the Pope.

When he sent his carefully worded letter to the King he knew that he was writing for his life, his career, everything he had so carefully built up. His dignity, his Legatine position, all meant nothing if Dr Knight could simply bypass him, even while he was on diplomatic service. In any lesser man such sudden knowledge, such shock and anger, might have brought on a stroke. But this man was different. Somehow, despite the betrayal of the King's actions, despite the fact that the King's real intentions regarding Anne Boleyn were now well and truly out in the open, Wolsey managed to gather his thoughts and calm himself sufficiently to write. It was a masterpiece. In it he assured the King that he was doing all in his power to assist Dr Knight on his way to Rome. But he could not resist adding that he was worried that the King, without consulting him, was taking steps of his own to allow him to marry Anne Boleyn.[18]

Wolsey decided to return to England without delay. He set off on his journey laden with gifts from Francis, including a set of silk tapestries and a golden chalice, worth in total some 30,000 crowns.[19] He was probably so concerned about the problems awaiting him at home that he could take little pleasure in treasures. His mind must have been turning over the betrayal and loss of influence. He knew that the only chance he had of keeping anything like the favour he had always enjoyed with Henry was to obtain the divorce he was determined to have. Even though it now seemed that the new queen would not be some French princess, but Anne Boleyn, a daughter of the family he already distrusted and disliked.

According to Mendoza, the Cardinal and his train went immediately to Richmond, where the King was staying. He sent word to Henry, asking where it would be convenient for them to meet, as 'was the custom when a Legate needed to communicate with the king, for them to retire to a private closet'.

Unfortunately, Anne was with the King when the message arrived. Before Henry could reply to the messenger, she is reported to have said, 'Where else should the Cardinal come? Tell him to come here, where the king is!'[20]

The remark showed Wolsey that in his absence things had changed, and not for the better.

It seemed that the Pope had initially been amenable to Henry's dispensation suggestion, and hopes had risen. Once he had escaped to Orvieto it was clear that his opinions had changed. By the Easter of 1528 after several meetings with the Pope in his near derelict palace, Stephen Gardiner and Edward Fox (later Bishop of Hereford) were trying yet again to interest him in Henry's plans. They had arrived in Orvieto in March, and had their first audience with the Pope on the 23rd. French troops, led by Lautrec, had by that time reached Naples, and that is probably the only reason the Pope was prepared to make concessions. He must have been sick of Henry's constant demands.

What Henry wanted was a new dispensation to marry Anne Boleyn, but along with that he required a commission for Wolsey to assume full power to try the matter in England. This was the real sticking point. While Clement might, in principle, be prepared to allow Henry to marry Anne (once his marriage to Katherine was dissolved), he did not want to give Wolsey the full powers he asked for. It was obvious that the Spanish-born Queen's marriage would be dissolved immediately, without further investigation. Henry would be free to marry Anne within weeks. It was Wolsey's desperate last throw to regain power.

Finally, a compromise solution was suggested, whereby Clement would agree to allow a general commission, in which Wolsey would be one of two judges of the matter. The other judge would be the Pope's choice and would be sent from Rome. It was not exactly what either party had wanted, but was better than stalemate. It was decided that Cardinal Campeggio would be Wolsey's co-judge, and by 13 April all was signed and sealed and Foxe set off for England. Gardiner, by then suffering from illness, stayed behind.

Foxe made excellent time on his return journey and travelled straight to Greenwich. Wolsey was at that moment unavailable, so Henry ordered Foxe to report straight to Anne. He put the best possible face on the result of the negotiations but when Wolsey heard that he would be merely a co-judge along with the Pope's own representative he was not pleased. He needed that Decretal Commission and he needed full control. He immediately arranged for one John Barlow (a priest, who was devoted to the Boleyns and their cause) to travel to Orvieto with further instructions for Gardiner. But by 28 June there was at last some good news – Cardinal Campeggio was on his way to England, and was bringing a Decretal Commission with him.

Cardinal Lorenzo Campeggio was the best possible man for the job. He was a man of the world, and had English experience. Born in 1474, he had been married and widowed before taking Holy Orders. His wife, Francesca, with whom he had had three sons, had died in 1509. He had two further children, illegitimate daughters, so as well as diplomatic skill he could be expected to have a tolerant view of Henry's matrimonial entanglements. His first legation to England had been in 1518/1524 at which Henry had made him Bishop of Salisbury. While he was willing to take on the task assigned, and Henry and Anne were desperate for his arrival, he was unfortunately a sufferer from gout and his journey through Europe was to be extremely slow.

While Campeggio was taking his time travelling from Rome, there were plenty of other worries. The first of these, presenting another annoyance for Cardinal Wolsey, concerned what would otherwise have been a minor matter. Elizabeth Shelford, the Abbess of St Edith's at Wilton Abbey, in Wiltshire, had died on 24 April 1528. There would be candidates eager to replace her in a rich and influential house, in which many of the nuns were members of aristocratic families. Two main contenders disputed the place. One, backed by Wolsey, was Dame Isobel Jordan, while her main rival was Dame Eleanor Carey, sister to Anne Boleyn's brother-in-law William Carey. Naturally, Anne would have been approached by the extended family and asked to aid Dame Eleanor, and so became involved through familial duty.

There was contention between the factions and a lot of mud-slinging took place. Anne had promised that she would speak with Henry so that Dame Eleanor Carey should be successful. But the matter could not be easily settled.

On 16 June one of Anne's ladies-in-waiting fell sick of the sweating sickness. It was at the beginning of a progress, and everyone was busy packing for the journey.[21] They intended to soon leave Greenwich, stopping first at Waltham Abbey in Essex. As soon as the cause of the woman's illness was known, the plans for the progress were abandoned. The court scattered, Henry setting off for Waltham with a reduced train, while Anne was returned to her father at Hever. Anne seems to have been surprised at Henry's sudden abandonment of her and he had to write to her to take away her 'unreasonable thoughts' on the matter. He made it clear that he was concerned for her safety and health, but consoled himself with the thought that 'few, if any, women were affected', already forgetting the lady whose illness had started the panic. Henry did not stay long at Waltham, preferring to keep on the move. His fears at the time, and lack of an heir in the event of his death, must have concentrated his mind and made him all the more determined to end his marriage to Katherine. For the time being, even that plan seemed to go awry, for word soon reached him that Anne herself had been taken ill. Her father was stricken too.

Wolsey, workaholic as ever, had remained at his post, waiting for Campeggio's arrival, finding time to send Henry suggestions for medicines to keep his health. When he heard of Anne Boleyn's illness he must have felt elation at the idea that the whole sordid matter might soon be ended.

Henry was more practical and after his first disbelief and anguish he moved quickly. First, he wrote to Anne to console and reassure her. Second, to send to her one of the royal doctors. George Boleyn, in attendance on the King (then at Hunsdon), also fell sick but appeared to recover quickly. However, Henry only had thoughts for Anne, as his letter to her clearly shows:[22]

> There came to me in the night the most afflicting news possible, for I have reason to grieve on three accounts. First because I have heard of the sickness

of my mistress, whom I esteem more than all the world, whose health I desire as much as my own and would willingly bear the half of yours to cure you. Secondly because I fear to suffer yet longer that hated absence which has given me such pain already and as far as I can judge is like to give me more. I pray God to deliver me from so importune a rebel. Thirdly because the physician I most trust is absent from me at the moment when he could do me the greatest pleasure, for I should hope by his means to obtain one of my principal joys in this world, that is my mistress cured. Nevertheless, in default of him I send the second, and the only one left, praying God that as soon as he may make you well, then I shall love him more than ever.

Further bad news was to follow. A letter from Heneage to Wolsey said that on 23 June 'this night as the king went to bed' news reached Henry that Anne's brother-in-law William Carey was dead of the disease.

Thomas Boleyn took longer to recover from the dangerous illness than Anne, but Henry had little sympathy. He was immediately in correspondence with him about his daughter Mary Carey, recently widowed. Henry was concerned that Mary might look to him for support and financial help, and he was quick to point out to her father that he had a duty towards her. 'I have caused Walter Walsh [Henry's groom of the chamber] to write to my lord my mind therein ... it cannot so stand with his honour but that he must needs take her his natural daughter, now in her extreme neccessitie ...'.[23]

By the end of the month Anne was recovering and Henry had settled at Tittenhanger after 'finding further removals useless'. There had been several other deaths, including Henry's close companion Sir William Compton.

Although fretting about his separation from Anne, Henry wrote, 'as touching abode at Hever, do therein as best shall like you, for you know best what air doth best with you. But I would it were come thereto (if it please God) that neither of us need care for that, for I ensure you that I think it long ...'. Despite Henry's impatience to see her, Anne was prepared to stay at Hever.

Meanwhile, the matter of the Abbess of Wilton's replacement was waiting. The Carey family were eager for the advancement of Dame Eleanor. Most of the convent favoured the appointment of Dame Isobel Jordan, but Thomas Benet, in a letter to Wolsey, admitted that 'there will be great labour made for Dame Eleanor Carey'. Further investigation was to reveal that Dame Eleanor had a very poor reputation. Dr John Bell, Archdeacon of Gloucester, had examined the ladies in question and Dame Eleanor had admitted to him 'having had two children by two sundry priests, and since having been kept by a servant of Lord Broke'. Wolsey then appointed Dame Isobel to the satisfaction of the convent.

However, on 10 July Dr Bell wrote to him that the King was 'somewhat moved' at the arrangement. That 'though at the report of the dissolute living of Dame Eleanor he was content to desist, his mind and expectation was that in no wise the prioress [Dame Isobel] should have it, at which some will find themselves aggrieved'.[24]

Henry followed it up with a letter of rebuke to Wolsey for acting against his wishes and then 'cloaking your offence by ignorance'.

Henry suggested that a third lady be given the appointment, which would have been annoying and humiliating to Wolsey, who had confirmed his own preference in the post, also the preferred choice of the nuns themselves. Henry was unwilling to displease Anne but his interference was making the situation worse and causing resentment between Anne and Wolsey. Isobel Jordan was still Abbess of Wilton in November of that year, so she was most likely not removed from her newly appointed role.

There is no reason whatever to assume that Anne was aware of the bad reputation and behaviour of the Carey candidate. She is unlikely to have known the woman, being asked to do a favour to a member of the extended family, as would have been expected of her. It was Henry's heavy-handed treatment of the matter that made a mountain out of a molehill. What it also did was to show Wolsey that Henry was quite prepared to rebuke and criticise him on Anne's behalf, which would sour any future relationship between them.

On 21 July Heneage wrote to Wolsey that Anne was to return to court with her mother in that week (probably to Ampthill where the court must still have been). However, 'my Lord Rochford (Thomas Boleyn) was to have come, but because of the sweat he remains at home'. Anne's father was still suffering from the sickness.

The matter blew over and life returned to normal. Wolsey, however, had received another indication that Henry's patience was short. Cardinal Campeggio was still wending his slow way towards England, and Henry was relying on Wolsey to expedite matters as soon as he arrived. The pressure to perform and fulfil Henry's requirements without much delay must have been enormous. For Wolsey there would have been the knowledge that if he did manage to do what Henry wanted, the future did not look particularly welcoming with a Boleyn queen in power. Wolsey was now as trapped as Anne had originally been, with Henry pulling the strings of both his puppets.

There must have been a distance growing between Wolsey and Henry, an awkwardness that negated all the years of close friendship. It would make any normal gesture of affection or trust embarrassing. Henry had made it clear, very firmly, what he expected of Wolsey and intended to have his way. Homage was also now expected, which in the days of friendship was not enforced.

It was certain that the pleasant days of intimacy were over.

Katherine of Aragon, Henry VIII's first Queen, from a miniature by Lucas Horenbout.

Chapter Eight

By September 1528 Henry had begun to be alarmed at a rising tide of support for Katherine. Despite the matter not yet being officially public, and the other Cardinal from Rome still not arrived, the divorce was a 'secret' matter no longer. Everyone discussed it and gave opinions on it. Henry became very indignant at the idea that the lower orders were discussing what he still considered to be his private matter, although Anne Boleyn did not seem to mind that everyone was now aware of what was going on. Perhaps she saw it as a form of insurance. The more open the matter was, the more real it seemed. If the whole world knew of Henry's intentions it would be more difficult for him to back out in the face of difficulty.

For Wolsey the public awareness of such a private intention would have been painful. He could not welcome it. Katherine certainly blamed him, but that was her own form of denial, that she could not hold Henry responsible. It was far easier to blame Wolsey. The common people also blamed Wolsey. Far from being pleased and proud that one of their own had reached such eminence, they were resentful. The nobles had never liked him, always begrudging having to defer to him.

Anne and the other Boleyns had no more love for him than he had for them, despite the need to pretend amity. From Anne's point of view, he still bore the brunt of the responsibility for the loss she had suffered over Henry Percy. Perhaps that residual affection towards the man she could not have showed where her real feelings still lay. If that were truly the case, then she is to be as much pitied as anyone else involved in the whole business. She was on the treadmill that Henry's desires had created for them all. He was still the centre, the instigator who was turning all their worlds upside down.

Cardinal Campeggio had left Rome in June of 1528. Partly due to his infirmity of gout, which was sometimes so painful that he could not travel at all, and partly because of the problems in Europe, which included foul weather (and a month-long halt in Paris on the way), he did not reach Calais until 29 September. It was 1 October when he finally set foot in Canterbury. By then nothing else mattered more than that Henry and Wolsey should receive him with every honour, along with hope that he could help them to finalise the matter.

Did Wolsey, even then, have some suspicion about the Cardinal's visit with the French King? Did he fear that Campeggio's motives were more aimed at mending the marriage with Katherine, than ending it? If so, then the outlook was bleak for them all, for freedom from Katherine was the only outcome Henry would accept. Wolsey knew who would take the blame if the marriage did not end quickly.

The earliest sessions with Campeggio would have done little to reassure him. His opposite number seemed to do nothing towards granting Henry his dearest wish. Campeggio had had a miserable journey, made more so by the reaction of the people.

They had misjudged the reason for his journey and had shouted their support for Queen Katherine at every opportunity. Even taking to his bed in pain shortly after his arrival did not prevent Wolsey from visiting him, disturbing his recovery with arguments for the King. Campeggio did his best to establish the Pope's point of view, and try to discuss alternatives, but had to write to Rome regarding his abortive talks with Wolsey. 'I have had no more success in persuading the Cardinal, than if I had spoken to a rock!'[1]

Henry was impatient to speak personally with Campeggio and demanded that they meet on the 22nd of the month. 'Although I could neither ride, nor walk, nor sit without discomfort, yet I was compelled on the 22nd to go for my first audience', he reported. He may as well have not bothered. Henry used the same arguments Wolsey had already given to support his case, and refused to listen to any mediation. Only one thing brightened Henry's stubborn expression, which was when Campeggio suggested that Katherine might enter a religious house, which would absolve her of her marriage vows. Henry immediately granted leave for Wolsey and Campeggio to visit Katherine to put the proposal officially. They then spent a fruitless couple of hours with the Queen, using all their powers of persuasion. Katherine could be as stubborn as her husband. She declared that there was nothing wrong with her marriage, and there was no reason for her to retire from court. She would not hear of it. Campeggio, tired by his illness, pleaded with her to reconsider, to take the easy way out, for everyone's sake. He was seconded and supported by Wolsey, pleading volubly that she would be giving up nothing that mattered, that other queens had stepped aside in similar cases, that she would be rewarded not only by the Pope's approval, but also by Henry's gratitude. He would deny her nothing if only she would make the way easy. They might as well have saved themselves the journey.

Wolsey was finding himself in second place behind Campeggio, particularly when Katherine requested that the Roman Cardinal should hear her confession. It took some considerable time, but then Katherine gave Campeggio her permission to reveal the content of it. She insisted that 'although she had slept in the same bed with Arthur for seven nights, she was still a virgin'. She made it clear that she did not see any reason why she should lose her place, and that she intended to die in the state and position to which God had called her – as Henry's wife and Queen of England.[2]

Both Cardinals sent a message to the Pope, asking for a more explicit commission, which would allow them to proceed at once to trial. They did not receive a reply, and despite Campeggio's journey from Rome, it was beginning to look as if things might drag on indefinitely.

On 8 November 1528 Henry called a gathering of the courtiers and other men of standing, at which he claimed that he was being forced into his present position by his qualms of conscience. He declared that he was concerned for the status of his marriage to the Queen, as it affected the legal position of the Princess Mary. Wolsey's warning about giving Henry ideas was to prove prophetic. Yet if Henry had imagined that he would gain sympathetic supporters by his semi-public declaration of concern, when everyone knew that Anne was back at Hever, while he put on a show of friendliness with Katherine, he was deluding himself.

Anne had her supporters, certainly. Mainly driven by personal or family ambitions or by the lure of something new. Katherine had hers too, mainly traditionalists and those who preferred the old form of religion (like Wolsey himself). The Boleyns threatened the old ways and were feared, as new things often are. Probably nobody believed a word Henry was saying and he was the only person present convinced that he had altruistic motives. Katherine might have been gratified by the show of friendship from Henry, as it demonstrated that she had enough support among both the courtiers and the common people to cause Henry some disquiet.

Anne, back in Kent, was probably seething at Henry's perfidy. She had been back and forth between Hever and the court often. Being a totally straightforward person, she could envisage only a straightforward answer to the problem. A couple of years later, a little nearer the throne and a little less concerned about public opinion, she briefly adopted a motto that had been adapted from that of the Archduchess of Austria. Anne's said '*Ainsi sera, groigne qui groigne*', or 'Thus it will be, grudge who grudges!'[3]

It showed clearly the mounting pressure she was living under, which she was transmitting to Henry. That was the real problem with the situation, intensified by Katherine's absolute refusal to remove herself in a dignified way, along with the apparent inability of anyone to make her do anything against her will. Henry could fret and fume and Anne could rage, but the years were still slipping away.

That must certainly have been the thing frightening Anne the most. The idea that the Queen, now barren and growing old, would not allow her younger husband to take a younger wife and try again for the heir he needed. For Anne the years were to be feared. She was probably already in her late twenties, and although that age seems nothing, in the sixteenth century it was more than old enough. Girls were married and mothers in their teens. Anne's cancelled engagement to Butler and her ill-fated attachment to Percy were all time-wasting, and now she was trapped in time-wasting again. She was afraid of the years sliding away. She began to panic, allowing her fears to shorten her temper with those around her.

Naturally, Henry's sympathies were with Anne. It was only right that a young woman should want legal marriage and the blessing of children before it was too late. If Henry had taken steps to safeguard the position of the Princess Mary, the stalemate might have been broken. As his sister, Margaret of Scotland was to find, if a couple had married 'in good faith', later finding that there was some impediment to the legality of the marriage, the Pope could instruct that any children of that marriage would be considered innocent parties. Therefore they could retain legitimacy. This happened after the divorce of Margaret of Scotland from the father of her daughter Lady Margaret Douglas. Lady Margaret Douglas was considered legitimate and treated by Henry as his blood relative. This concession would have been a small matter for the two Cardinals to arrange with the Pope, in the event of Katherine stepping aside.

The truth is, Henry did not want that. He wanted his marriage to Katherine to have never taken place. What he required was not a divorce, but an annulment. He wanted his marriage to Anne to be his first legal marriage and any children of it to be his sole heirs. Naturally, Katherine could not be expected to accept that.

Henry and Anne had looked forward eagerly to Campeggio's arrival, confident that it would mean a prompt decision, allowing their own marriage to take place within a few weeks. The time had already spread out due to his tediously slow journey, then it seemed that he was incapable of speeding things up. Henry was convinced that Wolsey could do something to push Campeggio into making a quick decision, but the endless talks achieved nothing.

Henry was disgusted at Campeggio's dilatoriness, and surprised that Wolsey seemed to suffer a loss of confidence, rather than leading. Did Wolsey suffer from weakening of resolve? He knew the importance of speed, and also that his own career depended on his ability to set Henry free, but instead of forcing the pace, he seemed to hesitate. He allowed Campeggio to waste time on repeated efforts to negotiate with Katherine, who was not prepared to budge an inch.

Wolsey did suffer from a temporary loss of confidence and it was directly attributable to Campeggio. Wolsey, who had not had personal dealings in Rome, nonetheless revered its power, the sight of the other man, secure and confident in his position, must have made him realise how precarious his own position was. Campeggio was the perfect Cardinal. Experienced, worldly, diplomatic and unaffected by the pressing matter. Not for him the anxieties regarding present success and future position. He could take all the time he needed to discuss alternatives with Katherine and Henry. He could prepare for a Legatine Court at his leisure, and face its decision with equanimity, unaffected by its outcome. Then he could return to Rome, secure in the knowledge that he had done what was required of him.

Wolsey once was similar. Exuding confidence. Knowing that the King would listen to him with attention. All that had gone. Wolsey could only face the lengthy talks with fear of failure. No wonder he suddenly felt weak, unsuited to the task, afraid of the ordeal ahead and how long it all would take.

There might also have been that suspicion in his mind that Campeggio was not being altogether straight with him. Campeggio was almost too calm and confident, considering the matter in hand involved a king, a queen and the succession to a throne. Was Campeggio's sanguinity ominous? Was there a secret agenda from Rome from which Wolsey was excluded? Pope Clement was wily with a weak man's deceitful cunning, were he and Campeggio already aware of the outcome? The suspicion that something was not quite right must have added to Wolsey's unease. The constant pressure Anne was putting on Henry and Henry was pressing onto Wolsey must have made his days fraught and his nights sleepless.

Anne was back at court again by December of 1528. This time there was no pretence about her position. She was lodged in semi-royal state at either Durham House or Bridewell Palace. Not only did she prefer a place of her own, where she could live comfortably and entertain Henry more informally, but it was no longer fitting for her to lodge as an attendant on the Queen. Certainly, by the time the court moved to Greenwich for Christmas, Anne had her own separate suite.[4]

It is recorded that Katherine did not join in with the festivities that year. The King marked the occasion with jousts and both Wolsey and Campeggio were welcomed with respect. On Twelfth Night Henry made one of Campeggio's sons (who had travelled to England with his father) a knight, and gave him a golden collar in recognition of the event. 'But the Queen showed them no matter of countenance, and made no joy of nothing, her mind was so troubled.'[5]

Although many people admired Katherine's behaviour at that time, she had her Spanish royal lineage to fall back upon as a support, along with a sense of right.[6] Anne, whose behaviour occasionally shattered into temper, had only Henry's affection to uphold her. Even knowing that he appeared eager to go ahead, she must have felt the ambiguity and insecurity of her position.

Quite apart from calm dignity, the Queen did have one surprise up her sleeve. She presented to Campeggio a copy of a second dispensation, issued by the late Julius II. This was sent to her from Spain and was supposed to have originally been obtained by her father at the time of her betrothal to Henry. This purported to fill in any gaps or flaws in the original one. Unfortunately, Henry was basing his claim for divorce on the original one, which he insisted did not allow him to marry a woman who had been his brother's wife. Katherine's denial that she had ever been Arthur's wife in truth, i.e. that they had not consummated their marriage, was made unnecessary by the newly produced dispensation. This allowed permission for her to marry Henry 'even if' she had lost her virginity to Arthur. It effectively blew Henry's claim out of the water. But was it genuine? Either way it was a dangerous document. Henry gave Wolsey the task of obtaining the original of it.[7]

Wolsey wanted Katherine to ask the Emperor to send the original document to England, and told her that the lack of it 'might be the extreme ruin of your affairs and no little danger to the inheritance of your child'.[8] Unfortunately, Katherine fell for Wolsey's wiles and sent a letter by her chaplain Thomas Abell. The chaplain was a better friend to her than she realised, for he was to tell the Emperor that she had written the letter requesting the dispensation under extreme pressure, and that it should be ignored. The Emperor's response was to reply that he would send the document direct to the Pope instead. Before he did so, the English agents in Spain were allowed to examine it in situ, and they declared their opinion the document was not genuine.

By January of 1529 Mendoza had begun to spread the word that he had heard Henry was seriously considering ridding himself of Wolsey, as a direct result of the Cardinal having failed to fulfil the King's expectations.[9] Such speculation seems a little premature. Certainly there had been delays, but they had not been of Wolsey's making and once Campeggio was safely in England things could be expected to make some progress. Despite Campeggio having tried to persuade Henry to accept his recommendations regarding Katherine and the false trail of the new dispensation, by following these leads Wolsey could be said to be safeguarding Henry. Such thoroughness would prevent any later accusation that Henry was trying to rush the thing through without due process.

Campeggio, in the spring of 1529, complained to Henry about 'heretical books' that were being widely read and circulated at court. One of those was Simon Fish's *A supplication for beggars*, which attacked the pomp and rapacity of the clergy. More worrying still, even while preparations for the forthcoming Legatine Court were being made, the King's agents had begun to compile a dossier on Wolsey. They began collecting a long list of all the offences and irregularities, however apparently trivial, which the Cardinal was supposed to have committed over the previous fifteen years.[10]

Even more portentous was news that the Pope was dead. Unfortunately for the carriers of the news, and for Henry who must have received it with a sudden leap of hope, it was false. Clement had certainly been very ill but when the couriers had been sent out with the news that he had been given up for dead he began to recover. It took a long time for him to regain full strength. Henry, disappointed to hear that the Pope who was blocking his divorce had not been removed by death, tried to make what he could of the situation by sending new instructions to his envoys in Rome. These were that they should make every effort to ensure that Wolsey would be elected as Clement's successor in the event of a relapse. Failing that, if Wolsey should prove too unpopular, then Campeggio should be pushed forward for election by any and all means possible.

Mendoza had earlier remarked that 'at present there is nothing that annoys the king so much as the idea of not accomplishing his purpose'.[11] By early May of 1529 the English envoys made another attempt to force Clement to declare the brief from Spain to be a forgery. Dr Stephen Gardiner, their leader, is said to have 'used the Pope roughly' in his language towards him.[12] But, although Clement had responded to the verbal attack with tears, he still would not budge. Gardiner reported back to England that there was talk in Rome of the commission of the Legates being recalled, so they backed down from their aggressive stance, pinning all their faith on the Legatine Court, which was soon to take place at Blackfriars.

By the end of May the licence was issued to Campeggio and Wolsey to begin proceedings and the court was almost ready, although Mendoza was busy spreading bad news. He told the Emperor that Anne was working against Wolsey and that her speeches to the King were beginning to have effect.

The lady who is the cause of all this disorder, finding her marriage delayed … greatly suspects that the Cardinal puts impediments in her way … in this suspicion she is joined by her father and the Dukes of Suffolk and Norfolk, who have combined to overthrow him. In this they have made no impression on the king, except that he does not show the Cardinal so fair a countenance as he did, and it is said that he has had some bitter words with him.[13]

It is possible to feel sympathy with Wolsey at this point. Working hard in a matter he disliked, he was beset on all sides, even by Henry for whom he was straining every nerve. Yet all his efforts went unappreciated and talk designed to ruin him was coming in from all sides. No wonder he envied Campeggio his easy security.

The court was finally opened in the Great Hall at the Dominican House of the Blackfriars on 31 May 1529. This building was a place often used for conferences and meetings requiring a neutral venue. It was also, oddly, the place where the sets and costumes for the court revels were made and stored.[14]

Everything had been done to emphasise the importance and solemnity of the proceedings. The court had been prepared carefully with two chairs covered with cloth of gold for the Legates to use, with a table before them covered with tapestry. To the side of the court was a chair for the King, cushioned for his comfort and with a Cloth of Estate. Opposite a similar one was prepared for the Queen. The officers of the court sat in front of the judges and the Archbishop of Canterbury and all the bishops of the realm were seated in a semicircle in front of the Legates. Stephen Gardiner was the chief scribe with Dr Sampson (later Bishop of Chichester) and Dr Bell (later Bishop of Worcester) heading the team of counsels representing the King. For the Queen, Dr Fisher (Bishop of Rochester) was her chief prop and stay, supported by Dr Standish (Bishop of St Asaph).

Once the court was settled the judges commanded the crier to call for silence. The commission from the Pope was read, then the crier called out, 'Henry, King of England, come into the Court', to which the King replied, 'Here, my Lords'. Turning, the crier then called 'Katherine, Queen of England, come into the Court', expecting a similar reply.

Instead, Katherine rose to her feet and headed towards the King. Due to the positioning of the judges she was obliged to walk around them to approach Henry, and when she reached him she kneeled down in front of him.

To his obvious embarrassment, she then began to remind him how she had always done as he wished, even to details such as welcoming friends of his who were not hers. More importantly, she reminded him that they had produced 'divers children' together, 'although it hath pleased God to call them out of this world, which hath been no default in me'. Then she went to the crux of the matter, as she saw it. 'And when ye had me at the first, I take God to be my judge that I was a true maid, without the touch of man, and whether it be true or no I put it to your conscience!'

It was a direct challenge to Henry, demanding his reply, but what could he say? He made no reply. Katherine, after a long and awkward pause, went on to say that she had no impartial counsel in the Court, since the men appointed to represent her were Henry's subjects. She said:

> Therefore I most humbly require you, in the way of charity and for the love of God, who is the just judge, to spare me the enormity of this new Court until I may be advised what way and order my friends in Spain will advise me to take. And if you will not extend to me such impartial favour, your pleasure then be fulfilled, and to God I commit my cause.[15]

Bishop Fisher, the staunch defender of the rights of Katherine of Aragon.

She rose to her feet, made a low curtsey towards the King and headed for the door, taking the arm of her receiver, Master Griffith, as she did so. The King signalled to the crier to call her back again into the court, using the same words as before, and Master Griffith was heard to say to her, 'Madam, ye are called again.' 'On!' she replied, 'It makes no matter. For it is no impartial Court to me, therefore I will not tarry. Go on your way.'

She left the court on the arm of her gentleman, with whispers and speculation circling the room. After a few moments the King called out, 'I will in her absence declare, to all the Lords here present, that she hath been to me as true, obedient and conformable a wife as I could in my fancy have wished for or desired. She is a noblewoman born for if nothing were in her but her qualities they would well declare the same.'

Cardinal Wolsey, rattled by the awkward incident and fearful of taking more blame, said to Henry, 'Sir, I most humbly beseech your highness to declare before this audience whether I have been the chief mover or inventor of this matter to your Majesty, for I am greatly suspected by all men herein.'

The King replied, 'I can well excuse you herein. Marry indeed you have been rather against me in setting forth.' He then went on to repeat that only his conscience and fears for the legitimacy of the Princess Mary prompted his actions. He further claimed that all of his bishops had signed a declaration regarding the fears over the marriage, but to this Katherine's ally Bishop Fisher of Rochester interjected with the words, 'No Sir, not I! You have not my consent thereto!' Henry lifted the document, dangling with seals, so that everyone could see it, asking, 'Is this not your hand and seal?' 'No, Sir,' the Bishop said firmly, 'It is not my hand, nor my seal!'

The Archbishop of Canterbury, attempting to pour oil on troubled waters, stepped in and claimed that Bishop Fisher had asked him to sign it for him, to which John Fisher turned angrily on him, shouting back, 'There is nothing more untrue!'

Henry hastily adjourned the court to avoid any further argument over the falsified signature. It was a very inauspicious beginning to what Henry had expected to be a formal matter. Queen Katherine's refusal to attend any more of the sessions, or to acknowledge the Court's jurisdiction at all, together with Bishop Fisher's public refutation of the declaration he was supposed to have signed, were all performed under the eye of Cardinal Campeggio. They made the worst possible impression.

Subsequent days were no improvement. In Katherine's absence the counsels argued back and forth on purely legal points, before hearing witnesses, who claimed that they saw the young Prince Arthur in bed with the Princess Katherine at the start of their marriage. There was so-called evidence from elderly men boasting about their sexual prowess at the same age as the late prince, on the premise that if they could manage to perform, then so could he.

After many tedious days Henry sent for Wolsey to attend him at Bridewell Palace and the Cardinal was with him from 11 o'clock until after 12 noon. When the Cardinal emerged from the meeting with Henry he was visibly upset. Waiting for him in his barge at Blackfriars Stairs to go with him to his house at Westminster was the Bishop of Carlisle. On seeing Wolsey's condition and that he was obliged to wipe the sweat from his face, the Bishop politely attributed it to the weather. He remarked, 'Sir, it is a very hot day.' Wolsey ignoring pretence, replied sharply, 'Yes. And if ye had been as well chafed as I have been this past hour, ye would say it were very hot!'[16]

As soon as Wolsey reached his house he retired to lay on his bed, having removed his clothing for comfort. But he was not allowed the rest he needed, nor time to think. Within the hour Thomas Boleyn, Anne's father, now Earl of Wiltshire, disturbed him, saying that he had been instructed by the King to tell Wolsey to go immediately to Katherine and convince her to surrender her case into Henry's hands.[17]

Seeing Thomas Boleyn before him, demanding further efforts from him in the name of the King when he was already exhausted, was the last straw. Wolsey, doing his best to please everyone, was pleasing nobody. He was still stinging from the rebukes Henry had thrown at him at Bridewell and here again were further instructions, demanding that Katherine be made to do what she plainly would not agree to. Wolsey did what any man might have done. He lost his temper.

He said a good deal of what was on his mind, blaming Boleyn 'and others' for putting 'fancies' into the King's head 'whereby ye are the causes of great trouble to all this realm and at length will get yourself small thanks, either of God, or of the world!'.

George Cavendish tells us that these sharp words caused Thomas Boleyn to kneel by the Cardinal's bedside in tears. Eventually, he and Wolsey took a barge, together with Campeggo, back to Bridewell where they wasted further time begging the Queen to be amenable to the King's wishes.

Katherine was adamant. 'Those I intend to put my trust in be not here!' but she eventually took pity on the obvious distress of Wolsey and took him and also Campeggio into her private chamber.

The Cardinals reported back to Henry the results of their latest meeting with Katherine. It was a dispiriting business and the Court was still sitting while the statements of 'witnesses' dragged on. At length, even these ran out of steam and the time came for judgement.

On Friday, 23 July the King appeared in person and sat in a gallery near to the door. From there he could see the judges clearly. All the proceedings were read again, in Latin, and then the King's counsel called for the judgement.

Before any of the officials could speak, and to Wolsey's obvious astonishment, Campeggio rose to his feet and declared:

> I will give no judgement herein, until I have made relation to the Pope of all our proceedings, whose counsel and commandment in this matter I will observe. This case is too high and notably known throughout the world for us to give hasty judgement, considering the highness of the persons concerned and the doubtful allegations, considering also whose commissioners we be and under whose authority we sit here.

He went on to say that he did not intend to put his soul into jeopardy of God's displeasure for the favour of any prince in the world, which was a remark most calculated to make Wolsey cringe. Campeggio repeated that he was concerned for Katherine, who was without impartial counsel, 'considering the king's own high dignity and the authority he has over his subjects in his own realm'.

For these reasons, he repeated, 'I will not damn my soul for any prince or potentate alive' and declared that he intended to speak with the Pope and such of his counsels who had 'more experience and better learning in such laws' than he had. Then came the crux of the matter, 'I will adjourn the Court for this time, according to the order of the Court of Rome, from whence this Court and its jurisdiction is derived.' He sat down, leaving it obvious that the whole proceeding had never intended a final judgement to be given.

Wolsey must have been in utter shock, realising that Campeggio had known all along there would be no final judgement. The court was to be adjourned to Rome, from where it would never return, and a decision would never be made. He must have been groping for something to say, but for a short while there was silence. Henry, equally shocked at the duplicity of the Roman Cardinal, said nothing at all.

Suddenly, the Duke of Suffolk stepped forward in a fury, shouting towards the table of the Cardinals. 'It was never merry in England' he declared 'whilst we had Cardinals among us!'

Campeggio, secure in knowing that he had done exactly what he had been ordered to do, could sit serenely. Wolsey could not and he was stung to reply angrily to Suffolk's attack.

'Of all men in this realm you have the least reason to be offended by Cardinals! If I had not been, you would at this moment have had no head on your shoulders nor tongue to make in such report as to despite us!' swiftly reminding Suffolk that he had saved him from disaster after his irregular marriage with the King's sister.[18] Wolsey berated the Duke for his ingratitude, while Henry left the court without a word.

At that moment, Wolsey could have refused to accept Campeggio's decision to revoke the case to Rome. He was equal with Campeggio in status and also held the Pope's commission to conduct the business at Blackfriars as Papal Legate. He could have decided for the King there and then, which would have instantly restored him to Henry's favour. The temptation to declare that it was an English court, deciding an English matter, and the decision was required there and then must have been almost overwhelming. To give the required decision and have the thing ended. But he was also aware that the result of such an action, temporarily pleasing to the King, would actually place him in exactly the same position with regard to any second marriage, as he was with the first. Authorities abroad would never accept it without the Pope's sanction and it would be considered invalid. Any offspring of it would be illegitimate in the opinion of anyone who still mattered. Henry, after the first euphoria had evaporated, would have been no better off.

Wolsey, choosing to remember from whom he drew his real power, took the second course.

He did as Henry had once suspected he might. He accepted Campeggio's decision to revoke the case, thereby throwing in his lot with Rome. It would mean annihilation of Henry's regard but, if the case could be resolved legally, it might give Henry a deferred, but valid, divorce, which was what he needed, not merely what he wanted.

It would also, for Wolsey, give him what Campeggio had claimed – his soul back. Perhaps it had been towards Wolsey that those words had been aimed 'not to damn my soul for any prince or potentate alive!' Had they been said as a rallying cry to remind Wolsey, as another Cardinal, where his real loyalties lay? If so, they did the trick. Wolsey at the final moment chose Rome. Suddenly, doing the right thing, rather than merely the approved thing, meant more. Having 'a good name in Christendom' became more important to him than riches.[19]

The decision would make him real enemies, not only the Boleyns but also Henry. But at the final count it would reinstate his position in the eyes of those abroad who had for many years watched him descend the slippery slope in doing Henry's will. He had finally defined his limits and would stick to them. He would confine his actions to what could be done with the Pope's agreement and in doing so would rise above all the years of avarice which had marked him out. As he contemplated the loss of his great career, it would be as a more honest man, and a far better churchman.

It was the action of a man unable to struggle any further, but it was also the action of a man shaking off the chains preventing him from being free. He would suffer for the decision he had made. But he would realise that he had made the right, indeed the only, decision.

In the eyes of the King he had thrown everything away. If he could explain to Henry that it had been for his ultimate good, perhaps something could be saved. But on that day, with everyone against him, what he probably desired most was rest, and for the world to leave him in peace.

Chapter Nine

The lack of progress at the Legatine Court had disgusted Henry. It left him out on a limb with both Katherine and Anne. Any decision to be made by Rome was likely to favour Katherine anyway, as had been made clear by Campeggio's concern at her position and lack of impartial counsel during the Legatine Court itself. He would naturally make his recommendations to the Pope to that effect, and as Clement was likely to go along with Campeggio's suggestions, Henry could expect little assistance from that direction.

Anne had returned to Hever immediately after the debacle at Blackfriars, declaring that she would not return to court unless she was forced to do so. She may very well have been testing Henry's resolve, expecting him to prove his affection by following her and imploring her to return, as he had done many times before. But it may also have been rather more than merely a display of feminine temper. She had put considerable faith in the trial at Blackfriars, assuming that, as it was actually being held in the presence of the Pope's own representative, it must mean something. She had hoped for a final decision from it. Its failure to reach any conclusion at all, to be revoked to Rome, had seriously damaged her confidence in any English court's authority or ability to proceed in the matter. She had been buoyed up with anticipation, strained by all the waiting, but still hopeful, only to find that all had been for nothing. This realisation seemed to plunge her into depression.

At length Henry went to Hever to escort her back, but only after having spent some time trying to reconcile her to the new situation they faced.[1] They would have to confront it together, and angry as the King was, he was also aware that the present disaster could not be blamed entirely on Wolsey. The Cardinal had worked hard on his behalf. Once the court was adjourned and the need for the show of friendship towards Wolsey no longer necessary, the full whispering campaign against him started in earnest.

Henry had already gone so far in his suspicions as to institute investigation into his activities, both public and private. No man in public life is ever free from the possibility of censure, and Henry was confident that evidence would be found against Wolsey. On the Cardinal's own part, he was aware that the smear campaign was in full swing and that he would be lucky if he could make Henry listen to anything he had to say.

Anne's need of a quick decision, allowing her to marry without delay, was now crushed and she would ensure that Henry heard only unfavourable reports of Wolsey. From this point the gloves were off, and both sides knew it. Due to Wolsey's failure to refuse Campeggio's decision to revoke the case, Anne found herself in a more ambiguous position than ever. Her difficulties with lack of respectability, and the opposition of those who supported her rival, were to make her enmity towards Wolsey venomous.

With the assistance of her brother George, still close to Henry, Anne had the best possible opportunity to fuel Henry's anger and resentment at the futile waste of time and to eat away at any lingering affection he still had for his minister. The failure of the Blackfriars court, humiliating as it had been for everyone but Katherine, could only be washed away by ultimate success. They were determined to tackle the problem head-on by using the brilliant idea on which Cranmer had already started work; he had found a way that would suit their purposes.

During this period, Wolsey was definitely out of favour. The King was not disposed to see him and would not allow him to explain. To the courtiers, who had seen his great rise, and perhaps suffered under his grandeur, it must have seemed as though he had recently fallen down a pit. Even the courts where he still attended regularly, priding himself on his ability to deal with many matters at once, had suddenly emptied. It was as though his presence began to carry with it a taint, which affected all that he worked with. There could have been no greater indication of Henry's anger towards him than to find himself cast out, as if his closeness to the fount of power had never been. The court went on in his absence, pretending that it could get on well enough without him.

Any raising of spirits did not last long, as further blows were to fall. It soon became apparent to Henry that all the foreign policies with which Wolsey had taken such pains, had been brought to nothing. This was due to the signing of a peace treaty between the Emperor and the Pope at Barcelona, and a further one between Charles V and Francis I signed at Cambrai. These were specifically designed to leave Henry out in the cold, and gave little hope that the Pope would ever be in a position to make any independent decision in the matter of the divorce.[2] It was yet another wall being built between Henry and what he wanted, which would force him to consider other methods rather than continuing to wait helplessly for Rome.

Cranmer's earlier idea of canvassing the universities would prove to be a good one, a purely secular one. By its very nature it took attention away from papal authority and directed it towards the intellectual community. In its scope and daring it was thoroughly Boleyn in character, and the Boleyns would take it up gladly. It emphasised that they were the proponents of the new radical school, not prepared to run to the Pope for the answer to every question. In fact, the neat, clear, common sense of the idea was diametrically opposed to the regular delaying tactics of the Papacy's working method, in which discussion and procrastination were endemic, often intended to blur the original question, confuse or even obliterate argument.

The Boleyns now appeared to represent a fresher approach, which had rather more likelihood of being effective. Henry was by then almost pathetically eager to grasp at the new concept even though it would inevitably mean a break with the Cardinal. It would also finally mean a break with the Papacy itself, although Henry never intended to turn Lutheran. The authority was what he desired. It was to be a particularly English decision. Anne was to represent the future, the casting off of the old order, while Wolsey, Katherine, and the traditionalists were the old order. Henry, desperately trying to hold on to his rapidly eroding youth and virility, saw Anne as a lifeline, and as such, irresistible.

Anne would eventually be blamed for the changes coming about, once the break was made. She disliked, and also probably feared, Wolsey. He was clever, so a worthy adversary. It would be a triumph to defeat such a colossus.

Anne was to break down many of the barriers confining women, but was still ultimately subject to Henry's will and as dependent on his favour, or otherwise, as Wolsey. Once Wolsey's fall from favour was certain the Boleyns could move forward from their ambivalent position and become far more vociferous in their condemnation of him, with less fear of censure. The previous dissembling, little notes and requests, were very much against Anne's nature and had been forced upon her by the situation and often by Henry's spoken wish. Wolsey had behaved the same way towards her, despite his dislike and distrust, because Henry demanded it. He, too, was obliged to cover his known antagonism under a show of civility, and hide his dismay at the way she had infiltrated Henry's affections.

Once it became obvious that the way to the divorce did not lead through Rome, the Boleyns could move into prime position, to bring forward their own candidates to take over the matter. This shift in loyalty was by no means confined to the Boleyns. Other rats deserted the sinking ship Wolsey had become. Chief among these was Thomas Cromwell. He had been Wolsey's secretary, yet he had absorbed none of Wolsey's gracious urbanity. Of a similarly humble background to Wolsey, he was to rise fast and high, propelled by burning ambition and greed for wealth and status, though Cromwell never became, nor was accepted as, a gentleman.

The position of friend to the King, vacated by Wolsey's fall, would be taken by Thomas More. He was possessed of different attributes, lacking the flexibility that had characterised Wolsey. Despite Henry's many coarse and selfish acts, he did have a core of refinement that Cromwell could not share, but Thomas More could.

Born in 1478, More was thirteen years older than Henry. He was Oxford educated and a scholar, a man of many talents. Henry imagined that he would be useful in replacing Wolsey. He could not, at that point, realise that he would never succeed in filling that huge gap. More had become a member of the Privy Council in 1518 and was knighted in 1521. By 1525 he was Chancellor of the Duchy of Lancaster and apparently a good friend and advisor to the royal family.[3] He took an interest in Henry's intellectual pursuits and discussed with Queen Katherine the correct upbringing for daughters. Wolsey was not then ousted, but Henry may have already thought that he had a replacement ready, when required. Because of this, the lack of Wolsey's help and advice did not at first appear to be the tragic loss it would eventually prove.

More would show that he had fixed limits within which he was prepared to work. He was not blinded by the King's charisma. He believed that a man of honesty and solid worth would always find his level.

Cromwell admitted to no limits, no boundaries he would accept. His greatest ability lay in his desire to make anything the King wanted become reality. By doing so, he would rise to prominence, initially on the coat-tails of the Boleyns, but eventually on his own account, because Henry found him useful. Whereas Cromwell could engineer ways to make the future happen, Anne would be blamed for what he did during her lifetime. Wolsey was also about to become a casualty of Henry's determination. Unfortunately, each of the people closest to Henry would in turn be shown that they were merely puppets, and would realise too late that he was pulling all the strings.

Latterly, of course, Henry had done plenty of dissembling on his own account. Particularly in his dealings with Katherine, even going so far as to claim publicly that the lady was everything he desired in a wife and queen. The falsity of that claim had been shown for what it was, when Clement had called his bluff by offering to make good whatever might be wrong with the original dispensation. Henry had, of course, considered himself above such a patching-up job.

Ironically, he had ascended his soapbox on the matter of divorce back in 1527, when his sister, Margaret of Scotland, was petitioning for a divorce from her second husband, Archibald Douglas, 6th Earl of Angus. This was to be on the grounds of his precontract with another lady making their marriage invalid.[4] The Pope had decided in Margaret's favour and also agreed that as she had married and borne a child 'in good faith', that the child, the Lady Margaret Douglas, could keep her legitimacy. She was therefore considered to be the King of England's legitimate niece with no stain upon her birth. However, Henry had thundered his displeasure at Margaret's divorce, oblivious to the fact that he was already considering a similar action. Such was his capacity for self-delusion. He did not wish to go down the same road with regard to the legitimacy of his daughter by Queen Katherine. Henry's unfortunate attempt to make his first wife nothing more than a strumpet and his royal daughter a bastard was to have repercussions long after he was dead and gone.

The two peace treaties signed by Charles V, Francis I and Clement VII forced Henry into a show of bravado, attempting to show indifference to the men who had marginalised him. With this intent, he indulged in a hunting trip to Northamptonshire, taking Anne with him. It was then time for Cardinal Campeggio to return to Rome, to make his formal report to the Pope, but Henry did not feel inclined to make the departure easy.

Campeggio, along with Wolsey, who was obliged to accompany him for his formal leave-taking with the King, would be forced to travel to where Henry then was to make their goodbyes. Those at court who enjoyed witnessing the discomfiture of others would have been looking forward to the next move, wondering how the Cardinals would be received.

The two Cardinals met the King at the Manor of Grafton in Northamptonshire. The manor was to prove to be a favourite of the King's for hunting parties, but it already had its place in England's history, being the birthplace of Elizabeth Woodville, in around 1437. She would later become the Queen of Edward IV and eventually mother-in-law to Henry VII. Henry VIII had purchased the 'fayre manor of Grafton and the goodly parkes and lands thereabouts' from Thomas Grey, Marquess of Dorset. It had been 'in great ruyne and decaye' but Henry had spent money on it, and brought it up to date.[5] It became a regular stopping place between Ampthill in Bedfordshire and Woodstock in Oxfordshire.

On 19 September 1529 the two Cardinals arrived, travelling from The More in Hertfordshire where they had been staying. Campeggio was greeted with all respect, but to Wolsey's great dismay it was obvious that no lodgings had been prepared for his reception. This was a deliberate insult as Henry was aware that Wolsey would be accompanying Campeggio. There was a period of embarrassment, when it did not seem clear that anyone had orders to put the matter right, then Sir Henry Norris stepped forward and offered his own lodging for Wolsey's use, to rest and change his clothes, while his servants could find him alternative rooms nearby. This compromise was gratefully accepted and shortly afterwards Wolsey's servants were able to report that they had found him lodgings at Euston, about 3 miles away.

Eventually the Cardinals were called into Henry's presence. Wolsey must have been expecting further humiliation, after his unfortunate reception. However, Henry's mood had changed again. He greeted Wolsey cordially. After the usual formalities, he even led Wolsey 'by the hand to a great window, where they talked until dinner'.[6] However, despite the friendly greeting and the withdrawal away from straining ears, there was still resentment. Cavendish, who was present, was later to write:

> The King was in long and earnest communication with my Lord, insomuch as I heard the King say 'How can that be? Is this not your own hand?' and he plucked out of his bosom a letter, or writing, and showed him the same. I believe it was so answered by my Lord that the King had no more to say in that matter, but he then said to him 'My Lord, go to your dinner, and all my lords here will keep you company. After dinner I will resort to you again and will commune further with you in this matter.' And so they retired.

The King retired to his privy chamber, to dine with Anne, who had already had word of the favourable reception of the disgraced Cardinal and was fuming. She dared to argue with Henry on the subject, claiming that:

> There is never a nobleman in this realm that if he had done but half as much as the Cardinal hath done, he were well worthy to lose his head. If my Lord of Norfolk, my Lord of Suffolk, or my Lord my Father, or any other noble person within this realm had done much less than he, they should have lost their heads before now.

The King replied, 'Why then, I perceive that you are not the Cardinal's friend?' To which Anne replied, 'Forsooth sir, I have no cause to be. Nor hath any man who loves your Grace. No more has your Grace, if ye consider well his doings!'[7]

The last thing she could afford at that point was for Henry to take him back into favour. On the seesaw of political balance, Wolsey's success could only mean her failure. Supported by her friends, she must have worked on Henry over the evening, because when Wolsey came back from his lodgings on the following morning, eager for another in-depth discussion with the King, he found Henry and Anne already prepared to leave on another hunting trip. The King had already taken his formal leave of Campeggio and Wolsey was curtly informed that he was to ride with him back to London.

Cavendish, fond of his master, shows disgust at the outcome in his biography of Cardinal Wolsey. He reported that 'the King's sudden departing in the morning, was by the special labour of Mistress Anne, who rode with him only to lead him about, because he should not return until the Cardinals had gone'.

It was 20 September 1529 and Wolsey would never see Henry again. In just over two years the Boleyns had succeeded in driving out of office the most powerful man in England.

Henry might have been less cordial towards Campeggio before he left England, if he had known that the Cardinal was taking with him to Rome seventeen of Henry's love letters to Anne, which had been stolen from Anne's chambers and were secreted in Campeggio's baggage. These would make unedifying reading for the Pope, and made certain that Henry's claims of a tender conscience were a complete fallacy and could safely be disregarded.[8]

Henry had expressed concern about the lax security within Anne's chambers, and that their private matters were not being kept private enough.[9] The loss of his letters to her must have created a scene of epic proportions once it was discovered, but we have no record of what was said. Not only would Henry's love letters make salacious reading for the Cardinals in Rome, they would effectively bolster Katherine's case. They showed that Henry was more prompted by the stirrings of lust for a younger woman than he was by stirrings of conscience.

However, Henry's attitude towards Anne did not outwardly change. Perhaps he realised that it was practically impossible to keep secrets safely in the situation in which they were living and any servant or retainer could be bribed to steal. The Ambassador Cardinal du Bellay, at the end of 1529, made clear the King's continued obsession. 'Mademoiselle Boleyn has come to court at London and the King has set her up in a fine lodging, which he has furnished for her very near his own. Greater court is paid to her every day, than has for a long time been paid to the Queen.'

Wolsey's usefulness to Henry was over and he was aware of it. For a little while longer he managed to cling onto dignity, but even then there was always work going on against him in the background, including a Writ of Praemunire, an old-fashioned weapon that would absurdly charge him with procuring Papal Bulls into the country.

Eventually, of course, the situation had to be brought to an end. The Dukes of Norfolk and Suffolk visited him to extract from him the Great Seal, his badge of office as Chancellor. Characteristically, he refused to surrender it to them without the King's authority in writing. They went away, but not for long. They were soon back with the necessary papers in their hands. When Wolsey saw Henry's familiar signature on the order, he is reported to have wept.

All of his property was then inventoried and he was informed that he must remove himself from London to his country house at Esher.[10] For a man such as

Wolsey death would be infinitely preferable to exile and disgrace. When a small token, or 'bauble', was taken to him by Sir Henry Norris, with a kind word from the King, he was again reduced to tears. He was only 54 years old, but his world had completely crashed. For a time he would suffer abject despair.

He was not alone in his fears of a bleak future. Cavendish would later write that he had spoken at this time with Thomas Cromwell, Wolsey's man of business, who had appeared very greatly distressed. Thinking that his show of emotion was on Wolsey's behalf, the loyal gentleman asked, 'Why Master Cromwell – is my Lord in any danger, that you lament thus?'

'Nay', replied Cromwell. 'It is for my own unhappy case. That I am like to lose all that I have worked for all the days of my life.' He then recovered himself a little, and went on, 'But I intend, God willing, to ride to London and so to court, where I will make, or mar, ere I come again.' Therefore, Henry was to gain one of his replacements for the great Cardinal from Wolsey's very household.[11]

Henry would soon begin to gather his forces in the light of the Cardinal's fall. Cromwell, Gardiner, Cranmer and Sir Thomas More would all be used in the future in attempts to fill the gap left after Wolsey's exile.

As one man left court, another arrived. He was Eustace Chapuys, the new Imperial Ambassador. He was to prove to be Anne's immediate enemy and Katherine's supporter. He came from a family of notaries from Annecy, a relatively modest start in life, but he was a competent and determined man, who had clawed his way up the ladder of service, until he reached the position that noblemen often filled. He was a generally well balanced man, by then 40 years old, and a realist, though even he must have been slightly startled to hear that the King had gone on a hunting expedition in the company of both Queen Katherine his wife and the Lady Anne his sweetheart. Although the idea of divorce was unpopular, most of the courtiers would be wary of showing their real feelings to him. The whole atmosphere at court must have been apprehensive and uneasy in the extreme, not only had unusual things already taken place, but still worse was expected.

When Henry met Chapuys he introduced him to the faction which surrounded the Boleyns and the Ambassador quickly realised the extent to which the Queen, despite still being at court and often in Henry's company, had already been marginalised. Though Katherine and her household still maintained an aura of indifference to what was happening, the strain showed. Chapuys could admire her courage, even though he was aware that any real defence of her marriage in such an atmosphere of suspicion would be difficult, as it became increasingly obvious that Henry would not tolerate any idea of defeat.

Katherine didn't help by being in denial about Henry's motives. When Wolsey had confirmed the Legatine Court's authority by agreeing to the matter being revoked to Rome, her worst fear – that of being ousted by an English court – had been removed. She had been afraid that her marriage was about to be declared null and void there and then, and when that did not happen she found a new strength and optimism. She fully expected her nephew Charles V to stiffen the Pope's resolve and force him to declare on her behalf, though just what kind of relationship she envisaged with Henry cannot be imagined. Perhaps she still believed that he would docilely return home to her, if she kept patience long enough.

In that strange time, when the Legatine Court was shown to be a waste, and Wolsey had been exiled, it might not have seemed to be such a ridiculous idea, partly because Henry honestly did not know what to do next.

The polling of the universities was continuing and Henry and Anne were pleased to see the further inventories of the great Cardinal's personal goods. These had been left behind when he retired to Esher, and were surprisingly extensive. However, such things were on the surface. At Greenwich, things were still unsatisfactory, with Henry, Katherine and Anne all living under one roof, albeit in separate apartments. Katherine would have been aware that her husband still fussed over his lady, but he still occasionally dined with her, possibly glad to relax as in the old days. If it had been possible to continue that way, seeing them both, Henry might have been perfectly comfortable and happy to leave things much as they were. But of course, that situation could not provide an heir.

Anne must have been keen to see Katherine leave, as the Cardinal had done, but Henry was not yet ready to take the step of banishing her from court, although he did not allow the Princess Mary to visit her mother. On one occasion, when Katherine remarked wistfully that she would like to see Mary, Henry said roughly that she was perfectly welcome to join Mary as soon as she liked. The implication being that she should not return.

The living arrangements could not continue indefinitely, and four months after Blackfriars, Katherine and Henry quarrelled openly, a dispute started by Katherine's complaint that he did not spend enough time with her. He retorted angrily that it was because he was not her husband, and that she had no claim on him. Katherine then lost her temper, telling him that she, too, could find supporters, 'Let me but collect opinions as you have done, and for every doctor or lawyer of yours, I dare say I could find a thousand to hold that our marriage is good and indissoluable!'[12]

Henry was always stunned to have open opposition and he fled Katherine's presence, intending to receive sympathy from Anne, but he found none. She told him firmly that he should have more sense than to quarrel with Katherine, as she would always win. Then her own strains snapped her temper. One day, she raged, she knew he would go back to Katherine, as being the easiest way out, then what would happen to her? She had wasted all those years, passing up any chance of honourable marriage and the hope of children, 'which were the greatest consolation in the world'. 'But alas,' she declared, 'to my time and youth spent to no purpose at all!'[13]

The listening servants must have had a field day at the sight of the harassed King, stamping furiously along the corridors from the rooms of his wife to those of his lady, and receiving nothing but arguments. However, his affections still rested with Anne, being the younger of the two, and the most likely to provide him with that all-important heir. It was for that child's sake that he was putting himself through the present situation.

Katherine must have realised she was fighting a battle that could not be won. If Henry had safeguarded the inheritance of his daughter Princess Mary, as the legitimacy of his niece had been safeguarded, would Katherine have given in? Saddened and tired, she might have done so.

Cardinal Wolsey was still a problem to be dealt with. He had gone so far as to write to Anne Boleyn to ask for her help in regaining Henry's favour. Cromwell, by then a member of the Privy Council, pleaded his old master's case and word came that Wolsey was far too ill even to leave Esher, where he was staying. Henry panicked, and replied by sending Dr Butts together with a message for Wolsey, bidding him be of good cheer.

However, he became even more concerned when Dr Butts returned to report that the outlook for the Cardinal was poor. 'I warrant your Grace that he will be dead within these four days, if he receives no comfort from you shortly!' Butts declared. Henry replied 'Marry, God forbid that he should die! I pray you Master Butts, go again to him and do your cure upon him, for I would not lose him for £20,000!' He then gave Dr Butts a ruby ring as a gift for the Cardinal, along with a message, 'Tell him that I am not offended with him in my heart, and that he shall believe, and God send him life very shortly. Bid him be of good cheer and pluck up his heart and take no despair. I charge you, come not from him until you have brought him out of all danger of death.'

He turned to Anne, who was standing by, and asked her to 'send the good Cardinal a token, with comfortable words, and in so doing ye shall do us a loving pleasure'. Anne removed a gold tablet from her girdle, and gave it to Dr Butts to give to Wolsey, along with 'very gentle and comfortable words in commendation to the Cardinal'.[14] What else could she do? She had received a direct request, in public, from the King.

Wolsey's illness must have been far more of the mind than of the body, for such reassurances from Henry made an immediate improvement in his health. Rumours quickly spread that Henry would soon forgive the Cardinal and that he would be reinstated, particularly as Henry had not yet signed an Act of Attainder against him.

As soon as Wolsey's recovery appeared complete he was able to move from Esher to The More. This was a favourite house of his, and du Bellay had once reported that it was even more splendid and attractive than Hampton Court. Wolsey had spent a good deal of money on it, making it into a sumptuous moated palace. Originally built in the fifteenth century, of brick, it would have been a very pleasant place for the Cardinal to retire to, but it was shortly afterwards to suffer neglect, like the Queen herself who would be living there in exile in the winter of 1531/2.

Anne and Henry then moved to Waltham, where in the neighbourhood Foxe and Gardiner would meet with Thomas Cranmer. They would talk of the divorce and Cranmer would reiterate his view that the royal marriage was invalid. He also repeated that the matter should be easily settled by asking the opinion of the two universities. When his words were eagerly reported back to Henry, he declared, 'He has the right sow by the ear!', subsequently summoning him to Greenwich for further discussions and telling him that he was to 'study the problem with an indifferent eye'.[15]

Henry's spirits had risen at the thought and he celebrated by giving Anne precedence over all other ladies of the court, including even the Duchess of Suffolk. This could not be expected to go down well, particularly with Mary Tudor who had always had plenty of spirit of her own, and was not on friendly terms with Anne Boleyn. She provoked her husband, Charles Brandon, to protest to Henry about the altering of court etiquette, which irritated Henry and a quarrel ensued during which Suffolk lost his temper and claimed that Anne had once been the mistress of Thomas Wyatt. This was untrue, but Thomas Wyatt's fondness for Anne was well known, so it was a safe accusation to throw. However, Henry vehemently denied it and the Suffolks were obliged to leave court. While the Duchess then remained in the country, being unwilling to share the centre stage, which had always been her prerogative, with Anne Boleyn, her husband shortly after saw common sense and returned to court and to Henry's side after making suitable apologies. He obviously did not consider the matter worth losing his favoured position for.[16] It was obvious that any open enemy of Anne's would not long survive at court.

However, Henry could find no further comforting advice from the men with whom he had replaced Wolsey. Norfolk, Gardiner and Sir William Fitzwilliam could offer no more, while Sir Thomas More refused to become involved. Henry was frustrated at the continuing lack of progress, finally forcing the pace by moving away, taking the court elsewhere. Chapuys raged at his actions but Henry ignored his tirades.

In March of 1530 the Earl of Wiltshire had received a rebuff from the Emperor at their meeting at Bologna and Henry actually began to fear that Charles V might finally go to war over Katherine's rights as Queen. Chapuys smilingly told him that he had more to fear from his own subjects, as it looked as if rebellion might be the price of his separation from Katherine. Henry could not afford to lose the support of his Parliament or of his people, so he decided to proceed with caution. In the spring of 1530 he composed a petition for the Pope, asking him to acknowledge the invalidity of the marriage with Katherine, quoting the learned opinions he had collected. It was politely and courteously phrased and signed by over seventy nobles and other notables, such as abbots and bishops. Although it was polite, it made clear that the continuing delays were intolerable, but after strong protests from those unfortunates expected to sign, he toned down his indignation. Henry later confined himself to a letter to Clement, protesting he felt he had been treated unjustly.

After some further delay, Clement countered with the astonishing suggestion that he thought that Henry might do well to marry Anne immediately, after which he might be able to do something about the invalidity. He might also be able to speak to Charles V on Henry's behalf. It was a lot of 'mights' and was exactly the same outrageous idea Henry had suggested at an earlier date. He now coldly refused it, declaring that he had no wish to be accused of committing bigamy. Perhaps the real reason for refusing it was that he no longer trusted Clement. If he were to take such advice he would be in a terrible position if the Pope went back on his word. The possibility that he was being tricked did nothing to improve his temper. Chapuys had remarked that it was becoming shorter, with his rages occurring more frequently.

The duplicity of the suggestion infuriated Henry and he declared that he would remind the Pope of that offer when he declared him a heretic.[17] He also firmly refused any idea of being called to Rome personally on the grounds that no Englishman could legally be summoned to appear before a foreign court. He replied that the case must be submitted to the Archbishop of Canterbury.

A little while after this, Chapuys and the Duke of Norfolk were interrupted in a discussion about the divorce by the Earl of Wiltshire. His subsequent verbal abuse of Pope Clement reached such a level that Chapuys was obliged to leave the room. He was to later write to the Emperor, 'If she and Lord Wiltshire remain in power they will entirely alienate this Kingdom from the Pope.'[18]

Wolsey, meanwhile, had recovered a little from the shock of his loss of status and had begun to write abroad – to France, to the Emperor and finally to the Pope. He, too, had decided that the only way to get England back on an even keel was to find some way to separate Henry from Anne. He had begun to correspond with people who backed Queen Katherine, hoping to get their support.

Wolsey's physician, Agostini, was noted to be very busy with errands for his master, and although Wolsey's return to activity caused some comment, Chapuys wisely kept his distance. He judged that Henry's spy system was as effective as that of the Cardinal, and that to become involved in whatever Wolsey was plotting would be extremely foolish.

However, Wolsey's intention to return provoked great strain in the Boleyn camp. Anne had a real fear of what the Cardinal could do if he did return to power. Her father was aware that he had written to Pope Clement offering his support against the King's divorce, and even going so far as to put forward some plan for Anne's dismissal. The idea of such a thing was terrifying. She was aware of her own unpopularity and just what her own future was likely to be if Henry was to cave in to such pressure. At that point Wolsey was actually in London, staying with the Duke of Norfolk, Anne's own uncle. The implications were appalling. She was surrounded by people whose allegiance was extremely unreliable and who waited to see which way the cat jumped. Anne was by then desperate. All she could actually do was threaten to leave Henry, throwing down the ultimatum she had used successfully so many times before. It was a move of sheer panic, but it was effective.

Henry gave in to her at once, with copious tears, begging her to abandon any idea of leaving him. 'He could not appease her,' Chapuys reported, 'nothing but Wolsey's arrest would satisfy her.' This may seem harsh, but was hardly surprising, considering what Anne's own future would hold if she were to be dismissed as her opponents intended. The knowledge that Wolsey was sufficiently recovered to be working against her, and with members of her own family, was enough to bring the dislike and distrust between them into open warfare. She had to defend herself, and bearing in mind the forces ranged against her, she would have to fight dirty, using the only weapon she had, her hold over the King. However, Henry would not agree to the arrest of Wolsey, promising only that he would be sent to his diocese, which he had never yet visited.[19] Anne had to be satisfied with that.

The newly arrived Venetian Ambassador, Savagnano, reported that he disapproved of the King's proposed repudiation of Katherine, and that the King's relationship with 'a young woman of noble birth' was unpopular. He admitted that the King still showed some care towards his Queen and his daughter the Princess Mary, who was living at Hampton Court. He did not meet Anne, nor could he understand why the Cardinal was in disgrace. Anne could have told him.

She was then standing on a knife-edge with only Henry to support her. All pretences were at an end, it was either Wolsey or herself. There was no room for them both. Henry had shown an ability to hanker after old friendships, which Anne knew could easily lead to her own failure.

Wolsey's sudden frightening closeness with Norfolk had kicked away any support she may have expected from that quarter, and she was terrified. If she were ever to win through, she would have to win at once, and defeat the Cardinal.

In September of 1530 Cardinal Wolsey left for York. He was not accompanied by the ceremony of the old days, but his entourage was not meagre. He had with him over 600 people. Agostini went with him, but what Wolsey did not know about his trusted messenger was that the physician had already betrayed him to the Council. According to Agostini, Wolsey had declared openly that all his hopes now rested on the Queen, and that he had actually advised Pope Clement to take a stronger line in her defence. He had gone so far as to suggest the use of the 'secular arm', i.e. the forces of Charles V. It was no less than a suggestion of armed insurrection. There had been a hint that Clement should excommunicate Henry, and order him to dismiss Anne.

This news was being mulled over by Henry as Wolsey made his journey north. He was to settle at Cawood, the country house outside of York that was his as Archbishop of York, until his formal progress into the city for his installation at the Minster.

He cannot have realised that he had been betrayed by the man to whom he had entrusted his messages, though since his illness his plotting had been obvious. Even Chapuys had seen disaster looming. Wolsey seems to have lost all sense of discretion. He and Anne were only aware that each was the nemesis of the other.

Each had weapons the other lacked. For Wolsey, the years of diplomatic experience, political infighting with a proven success record. His age was against him, and also his treachery against the man who had discarded him. Anne had her youth and her firm grip on Henry, which had not yet begun to slip. Wolsey's personal prestige in Europe could be countered by Anne's hold over Henry's affections, which, while it lasted, was a formidable weapon. Wolsey's status as Papal Legate was countered by Anne's promise to Henry that she could give him sons, for which he was desperate.

If these two fierce protagonists could only have found some way to work together, how different things could have been. Wolsey's sound advice and European experience would have benefited England enormously, while Anne's presence as wife and mother would have soothed Henry. England's final break with Rome need never have happened, thus saving the country from the appalling upheavals ahead. Anne herself, if accepted and secure, could have sailed into more placid waters with motherhood, without the constant plots and stresses which would prevent her from fulfilling her potential in that area. Between them, those two would have been able to work out some way of providing a nursery full of children without damaging and destroying the happiness of the one child he already had. Katherine could have been left in peace with the religion she revered, and the religious feelings of the majority of the population need not have been changed by force.

Change is necessary and natural, but change imposed is very different from change occurring in the normal course of events. It could have been a gradual process and England need not have suffered catastrophic disorder. Unfortunately, the two people most influential in Henry's adult life could only fight over him, each aware of the opposition and hatred of the other. It was a battle with a tragic conclusion. So damaging that both parties would be weakened to the point that even the apparent victor would then be easy game for the next contenders for power.

In this fight to the death between the people Henry had trusted the most, there could be no ultimate winner. Wolsey was destined to fall first, but Anne's own defeat would not be too far in the future and she would crash and burn with far more of a spectacle, far more collateral damage, than attended Wolsey's demise.

Wolsey had also turned over a new leaf with regard to religion. He had spent time each day at the Charterhouse at Richmond 'in godly contemplation', as his man Cavendish was to report. Ironically, it was the Duke of Norfolk, veering in his allegiance again, who said to Cromwell, 'Me thinketh that the Cardinal your master makes no haste northward. ... if he does not go away shortly, tell him I will, rather than that he should tarry still, tear him with my teeth!'. Norfolk had already conveniently forgotten those private talks with Wolsey, which had so frightened Anne. Or possibly he had been reminded? Perhaps the aggressive speech was his form of demonstrating that he had finally remembered where his best interests lay.

Wolsey left for York at last and ahead of him went a letter from the King asking for 'loving and favourable assistance of the noblemen and others' for the man who had been his closest advisor.[20]

A friend of Norfolk's, Sir John Gage, wrote to Cromwell to complain about the 'sumptuous fashion' in which Wolsey travelled. He reached Peterborough on Palm Sunday and attended Masses in the abbey. Passing the property of the Earl of Shrewsbury, some gentlemen of the Earl's household came out to welcome him and invite him to hunt on the Earl's preserves. He replied kindly that he had not come into the North Country for pleasures, and though he thanked them kindly more than once, he rode onwards. He was by then wearing a hair shirt under his fine robes. He stayed for some time at a house at Scrooby in Nottinghamshire which was owned by the diocese of York, before moving on to Cawood Castle, near Selby, in Yorkshire.[21]

On this, his first journey into Yorkshire, the people were impressed by the man whose fame had been so great. Now he appeared to be very different. Gone was the proud Cardinal, glorying in his magnificence. In his place was a priest, eager only to help the people. At Ferrybridge he confirmed 200 children who had waited to see him pass, before mounting on his mule again to complete his journey to Cawood. His old desire to build seemed to remain strong, as he gave orders for the repair of Cawood, employing 'above the number of three hundred persons daily'.

Whatever he did now would seem to his detractors to be subversive, even the settling of quarrels between local gentlemen, as he did at Cawood, between Sir Richard Tempest and Mr Brian Hastings. It would be impossible for him to cast off the past completely, and it is recorded that he was concerned for the fate of the colleges he had founded. To his grief, he was to lose those too. William Capon, Dean of the College of Ipswich, wrote to express his sorrow at the Founder's 'heaviness' and to say that all the company of the college prayed daily that he be restored to the Prince's favour. Others, however, were to take advantage of Wolsey's absence and disgrace simply to poach his tenants' livestock. When one man named Vesey was apprehended he declared that 'My Lord Cardinal was not worthy to wipe his horse's feet' along with other similarly unsuitable abuse.[22]

Wolsey was to beg personally from Henry that his College at Oxford be saved, writing 'humbly on my knees, with weeping eyes, to recommend unto your excellent charity and goodness the poor College at Oxford'. The plea went through Cromwell, who was quickly growing in importance and even more quickly forgetting duty towards his old master. He replied sharply that he thought that Wolsey was conducting a whispering campaign against him. Wolsey, by then cut off from honest reports, and aware of his disadvantage, replied quite humbly that he heard that Cromwell 'had not done him so good offices as he might have, concerning his colleges'. However, he did add that he did not believe the reports he had heard of Cromwell's indifference.

Despite all the new humility he showed, many people at court still watched his every move, afraid that he might manage a comeback. Even in October, Chapuys reported that Henry, complaining that his Council did not act according to his liking, had raged that the Cardinal was a better man than any of them at arranging matters. He repeated the angry statement twice, before storming out of the room. Such incidents were to keep Wolsey's memory fresh, but were not destined to make him any more popular. Chapuys went on to say that, since then, the Lady Anne and her father Thomas Boleyn 'had not ceased to plot against the Cardinal. Especially the Lady, who does not cease to weep and regret her lost time and honour, threatening the King that she will leave him, in such sort that the King had much trouble to appease her.'[23] Anne was worried about Henry's lingering affections for the Cardinal and afraid that he might bring him back to court.

It is hardly surprising that Anne feared Wolsey's return. He was beginning to gain some popularity among the common people, and Henry was openly bemoaning his loss. She was no further forward despite her opponent's fall and must have feared that Henry would tire of her tempers and threats, even though she seemed unable to control them.

The Cardinal had arranged that 7 November 1530 would be the date of his formal installation as Archbishop of York. He was, in fact, waiting for the rents to be collected from his tenants, so that he could put on a feast appropriate to the occasion and his position's dignity.[24] Such a mundane matter would have caused him no concern at all in the old days, but in the new life he had to be careful of money.

There must have been fears in London what he might do next, as he seemed to have become suspiciously quiet. It was remembered that he had asked for the divorce to be recalled to Rome. Was it possible that he was still plotting against Henry in Katherine's favour? Or could it be made to seem as if he was?

The news of the Convocation called by Wolsey to attend his Installation reached London at the same time as a Papal Bull issued against Henry. The two were not connected, and the timing was unfortunate, but it might be made to seem as if the incidents were linked. As if Wolsey had arranged for one, while plotting for the other.

At the end of October 1530 the Cardinal was at dinner with his household. There was a slight accident at that time, when his physician knocked over a large silver cross, which struck Wolsey's personal chaplain, Dr Bonner. When Wolsey asked Cavendish 'Has it drawn any blood?' Cavendish was obliged to reply, 'Yes my Lord, as it seemeth to me.'

Wolsey looked very grave, then muttered 'Malum omen'. Disturbed by the incident, he retired to his chamber to pray.[25]

On Friday, 4 November, only three days before his planned Installation at York Minster, the Earl of Northumberland arrived at Cawood unannounced. He had attendants with him. Wolsey greeted him warmly, welcoming the attendants by name in many cases. Only Wolsey's volubility betrayed his nervousness, but he took Northumberland into his private chamber where they could speak in private. Wolsey's gentleman usher, following to stand by the door, was the only witness to their words.

The Earl seemed to be as nervous as the Cardinal, but eventually he laid his hand on Wolsey's arm and said 'in a faint and soft voice', 'My Lord I arrest you for High Treason.' Wolsey, probably very shocked at the sudden reversal, said nothing.

Cavendish, standing at the door, then heard someone shout, 'Go in then traitor, or I shall make thee!' and Dr Agostini was pushed through the door, followed by Walter Walsh.

On being asked to show his commission to the Cardinal, the Earl refused, and Wolsey demanded to know under whose authority he acted. He then turned to Walsh, who also refused to show his commission, saying that it contained other, private, instructions in addition. Wolsey, however, was prepared to yield to Walsh as he was a member of the Privy Council. He said, 'for the worst person there is a sufficient warrant to arrest the greatest peer in the Realm, therefore I am ready to be ordered and disposed at your will'.

Cavendish then tells us that the Cardinal and his unexpected guests attempted to dine together, but it must have been a miserable meal, as Cavendish reported,

'Notwithstanding, my Lord did eat very little meat, but would many times burst out suddenly into tears, with the most sorrowfullest words that have been heard from any woeful creature.' Also reporting, 'and thus he passed his dinner, in great lamentation and heaviness'.

On the following Sunday, Wolsey was to leave Cawood with five servants, Cavendish, his chaplain, his barber and two grooms of his chamber. The rest of his household had been shut away to avoid any disturbance when the Cardinal left, but he had insisted on saying goodbye to them. When he mounted his mule he realised that there was a noisy crowd gathering outside the gates, which were later estimated at 'not less than 3,000 persons!'. Cavendish was afterwards to state that these people ran after the party through the town, calling out blessings on him and encouraging him, as well as calling down curses on his enemies.

When they had gone some distance towards Pontefract, Wolsey, who had been deep in thought, asked permission for his man to go back to Cawood, to retrieve something that he said he had forgotten. 'Then,' said he, 'let the messenger go to my Lord of Northumberland (who had stayed behind to close up the house), and desire him to send to me the red buckram bag, lying in my almonry in my chamber, and sealed with my seal.'

The messenger did so, while Wolsey continued on his journey towards Pomfret. Later, when the man returned with the required bag, it was taken immediately to Wolsey after he was in the chamber prepared for him at their temporary lodgings 'which was delivered ... very secretly'.[26] A later inspection showed it to contain merely hair shirts.

In London, awaiting the Cardinal's arrival, there were rumours that he was to be put into the Tower of London. It was believed that he had corrupted the people of the north in his favour and Dr Agostini's testimony gave Wolsey's enemies all the fuel they had been looking for to fire their hatred. Chapuys reported that Agostini 'is singing the tune, as they wished him'.[27]

For two further weeks, at Shrewsbury's house, Wolsey rested, and became more and more depressed. At dinner one day, Cavendish noticed that his master's colour had changed several times while he was eating. When he enquired whether his master was ill, the reply was that he had 'been taken suddenly about the stomach with a thing that lieth overthwart my breast, as cold as a whetstone'. A little later Wolsey, rallying, said it had been merely wind. He then asked for some remedy 'to break wind upward'. This proved not to be a simple request, because Master Walsh had refused the Cardinal the use of any drug 'which might enable him to escape this life'. Cavendish was obliged to speak to the Earl of Shrewsbury to ask for 'a powder' which was finally granted. The Cardinal took the drug and immediately 'voided exceeding much wind upward'. He then rose to go to his prayers, but shortly afterwards a seizure of the bowels came upon him and he was 'forced to go incontinent to his stool'. While he was there, news came that Sir William Kingston, Constable of the Tower, had arrived at the house, along with twenty-four yeomen of the guard. It was the final humiliation, the sum of all his fears, that he would be paraded through the streets of London, tried as a traitor and probably expect to suffer a traitor's death.

Cavendish, in anguish, to protect his master, tried to pretend that Kingston's men were merely a form of honour guard, sent to escort him to London in style. Wolsey was not fooled and he answered, 'I perceive more than ye can imagine, or do know. Experience of old hath taught me.' He then retired to his room again, complaining of his bowels.

The following day Shrewsbury enquired after his health, also pretending that Kingston was merely an escort for him. Kingston even attempted to confirm this himself, saying that 'the King beareth you as much good will and favour as he ever did and willeth you to be of good cheer'. However, he did go on to add that, though the King did not believe the reports of Wolsey's crimes, to prove his impartiality he would still ask him to stand trial. Wolsey was not stupid, and he knew it was the end. He replied, 'all these comfortable words which ye have spoken be but for the purpose to bring me to a fool's paradise. I know what is provided for me.'[28] He agreed to be ready the following morning.

At this point the party stopped briefly at Hardwick upon Line, in Nottinghamshire. Cavendish reported, 'When night came, my Lord waxed very sick through his new disease, which caused him continually, from time to time, to go to the close stool all that night, insomuch as from the time it took him, to the next day, he had above fifty stools, and the matter that he voided was wondrous black …'.

During that night he was ill again, the sickness that had so suddenly come upon him ensuring that he spent another night on his close stool. He was by then very weak.

When he went out the following morning to continue his journey, he looked so ill that it brought tears and expressions of affection from the old retainers Kingston had with him. The party lodged overnight in Nottinghamshire, but they were in Leicester by the Saturday and approaching the Abbey of St Mary of the Meadows. This was a house of the Greyfriars, and Wolsey's weakness had increased so much that Cavendish said, 'it looked at divers times as if he was likely to have fallen off his mule'.

It was night-time when the party was received by the abbot with great reverence. Wolsey said sadly to him, 'Father Abbot, I am come to leave my bones among you.' He was immediately taken to a chamber and put to bed.

By the Monday morning, Cavendish reported that 'I beheld him, as me seemed, drawing fast unto his end.' It was about 8 a.m. but still dark, at the end of November. The candles were burning in the chamber, and Wolsey seemed to have become confused and asked for the time. On being told it, he appeared surprised, even stunned, repeating, 'Eight of the clock? That cannot be, for by eight of the clock ye shall lose your master. My time draweth near that I must depart this world.'

By dinnertime Kingston was fussing over some money that Wolsey should have had with him, questioning Cavendish about it. Cavendish advised Kingston to ask the Cardinal, 'but I would not advise you to delay the time with him, for he is very sick and I fear me that he will not live past tomorrow morning'. So Kingston went into Wolsey's chamber to question him about the missing money with the words 'My Lord of Northumberland has found a book at Cawood, with reports that ye had, of late, £1,500 in ready money, yet not one penny of it can be found.' He went on to demand, in the King's name, that Wolsey answer for it. Wolsey, weak as he undoubtedly was, still had enough spirit left to retort sharply, 'I have nothing, nor never had, that I esteemed or had delight or pleasure in, but that I took it as being the King's goods, having myself the bare use in my lifetime and bound after death to leave all to the King, wherein he hath but forstalled my intent and purpose.'

He went on to say that the money had not been his, but borrowed, and if Henry were to take it from him he would have to ask that the lenders should be satisfied 'for the discharge of my conscience'. He then gave a full list of the people from whom he had borrowed the money, but Kingston still pressed him as to its whereabouts. 'It is safe enough,' Wolsey said, 'And in an honest man's keeping, and he will not keep one penny from the King.' Kingston then left him, probably remembering all the treasures that the King had already had from the Cardinal, the palatial houses and their fabulous contents, tapestries, plate, horses, lands and now even life itself.

Later Wolsey asked Cavendish to bring him some food, and he was given a little broth in a bowl. He did not manage to drink more than a few spoonfuls, then asked Cavendish what it was made of. Cavendish replied that it 'was of a chicken' and Wolsey put down his spoon. He said it was a fasting day, therefore he could eat no more of it.

Cardinal Thomas Wolsey, who died after his failure to secure Henry VIII's divorce.

Kingston continued throughout this time to pester Wolsey with visits, and they had some desultory discussion from time to time on subjects ranging from the Lutheran threat to the uprisings of the common people, but Wolsey was obviously far weaker and losing interest. He was fading fast. Eventually he said, 'Master Kingston, farewell. I can no more, my time draweth on fast. I may not tarry with you. Forget not I pray you what I have said … when I am dead you may peradventure remember my words much better.'[29]

Kingston, then trying to calm Wolsey in his extremity, said, 'ye be in such grief and pensiveness, fearing which indeed ye need not fear'. Wolsey replied, 'I see clearly the matter against me, and how it is framed, but if I had served God as diligently as I have done the King, he would not have given me over in my grey hairs'.

The abbot then went to attend to him, and Cardinal Wolsey died as the clock struck 8. Exactly 24 hours after he had said he expected his death. It was 29 November 1530 and he was 55 years old. It was certainly no great age, even for those times, but he had packed a very great deal into those years, and was worn out.

It is not surprising, given his years of greatness, that he had no intention of allowing Henry, for whom he still had a genuine fondness, to make a humiliating spectacle of him on his arrival in London. Henry's discarding of him had been the final straw, the end of all hopes, and it is plausible that Wolsey had taken some 'powder' or other to end his life and escape from the horrors awaiting him in the capital. It would not only be in character for him, but it was his right to decide.

There is no evidence at all that Wolsey had been ill before his arrest at Cawood. On the contrary, he was busily engaged with the arrangements for his Installation in York. That had been due to take place only forty-eight hours after the arrival of the Earl of Northumberland. The 'illness' that was earlier reported by Dr Butts to Henry, after which Henry sent Wolsey tokens and kind words, can easily be discounted. Despite the prognosis of that doctor, the malady swiftly evaporated as soon as Henry's cheerful words and gifts were received. It was not until he was actually arrested that Wolsey became aware of what his future held and his final illness certainly stems from then.

Although shock and fear certainly loosen the bowels, the ailment does not last so long as Wolsey's did, nor does it kill. His fatal illness was extremely sudden in onset and coincided with leaving Cawood to head south for trial. There is also the mystery of the bag, apparently so important to Wolsey that a rider had to be sent back to retrieve it, yet when it was later examined it was found to contain nothing except worthless old hair shirts. It was perfectly possible for it to have held something far more important, which was removed by Wolsey when the bag was taken to him 'secretly' leaving its more innocuous contents to be seen later, when the bag was checked by others.

If there was some preparation in the bag, for Wolsey's use a little later, it may have been stored for some time by him, ready for just such an eventuality. If that were the case, it may explain why Wolsey's death was more long drawn out and exacted more suffering from him than he had expected. Such preparations, incorrectly stored, can very often degrade in quality and efficacy, thereby working at a different rate to the one expected.

Wolsey's questioning by William Kingston over a missing sum of money adds a bizarre twist at the end, confirming Henry's purely mercenary motives and lack of any real concern for the man's welfare. It was an interrogation Wolsey would have been spared if his chosen means of suicide had worked correctly. His sudden 'flux of the bowels' and subsequent severe weakness is entirely consistent with him having taken a poison.

Of course, lacking positive proof (which cannot be forthcoming unless his body is recovered), this can only be conjecture. However, his final illness appears very suspicious and quite in the context of Wolsey refusing to face the public shaming that Henry had doubtless planned for him.

Even Shrewsbury's remarks about him not being 'allowed powders' show that just such an action was expected from him.[30] Sebastiano Giustiniani said as much in a letter to the Doge and Signory of Venice, and Chapuys made a similar suggestion when reporting Wolsey's death to Charles V. Most modern historians have tended to ignore – or even discount – the idea, but it is difficult to see why, when all the available evidence so clearly points that way.[31]

Any contention that such poisons would not be available to Wolsey, or that for some reason he would not choose to use them if they were, is far too simplistic. Wolsey had far too much character to allow Henry to lead him into imprisonment, and even the scaffold, like a lamb to the slaughter. Regarding the contention that poisons would not be available, this is simply ridiculous. Even in the second century the Greek physician Nicander of Colophon wrote widely about white lead, red lead oxide, aconite, henbane, hemlock and opium, in all their applications. He is known to have experimented on criminals to refine his knowledge of the effects of such poisons. Nearer to Wolsey's own time, arsenic was certainly widely used in the sixteenth century (indeed well into the early twentieth too), and its effects were quite indistinguishable from food poisoning or dysentery, as is the use of antimony, which creates similar symptoms in the sufferer.

Until the late 1700s there was no way of testing for arsenic, and even when a test was developed, the results were extremely unreliable.[32] Wolsey's stools having been reported as being 'wondrous black' indicates bleeding, which is in itself a pointer.

Frankly, it is a relief that he managed to finally outwit them all, and cheat them out of their triumph over him. He left behind a life that had become insupportable for him, and he left it on his own terms, with the affection of the common people and the abbey community surrounding and supporting him. It was no more than his due.

His poverty and humility towards the end of his life provides a very telling contrast to his previous way of living and is entirely in keeping with his return to his religious roots. The foundation of that had been laid when he made his fatal decision to opt for Rome at the end of the Legatine Court at Blackfriars. It finally allowed him to transcend the malice of his enemies and make a fitting and private end in the mediaeval tradition of a great Churchman, for such he certainly was.

Chapter Ten

George Rochford had moved into place as his sister's chief supporter. Although he did not possess the social or ecclesiastical prestige of Norfolk or Cranmer, or indeed the political clout of a man such as the quickly emerging Cromwell, George was the person Anne trusted. He was the one she felt closest to and the man who shared her religious opinions. He had become her dearest friend. He had benefited from Wolsey's fall. During the distribution of Wolsey's wealth George had received a £200 annuity from the Diocese of Worcester and another annuity of 200 marks from the revenues of the rich Abbey of St Albans. This particular award had to have been dated after 8 December 1529, as the document refers to him as Viscount Rochford.

George was in France at that time, entrusted with the mission of trying to persuade the court and the universities to back Henry and agree to his contention that Julius II had not the authority to issue Katherine's original dispensation. It was not quite such a wild assertion as it may sound. Wolsey had earlier come to the same conclusion – that the Pope did not have the power to dispense in such a case – and this is shown by his letter to Sir Gregory Casale, dated 5 December 1527, in which he says '*quad Papa non potest dispensare in primo gradu affinitatis* ('no power to give a dispensation in the first grade of affinity)'.

George was young for such a task, but he had with him John Stokesley (later Bishop of London). This man was intended to deal with the universities, while George met with the King. It was assumed, as with all novice diplomats, that George would defer to the greater experience of the veteran.

Nonetheless, it was a very good training ground for the man who would shortly be the King's brother-in-law. Letters went ahead of the party asking that the Viscount be given all consideration. This also shows Anne's affection for, and trust in, her brother, and her desire to bring him forward.

Despite Katherine having begun a campaign of her own, aimed at preventing the universities from deciding against her, Lord Rochford was able to persuade King Francis. He reminded him that, even if he did not fully agree with Henry's stance on the matter, he would not wish to lose the King's friendship, or his money. Francis was convinced enough to press, through an intermediary, that the universities in France should favour Henry's case over Katherine's. It seemed to be a substantial success for George, though he had been receiving experienced support. He had managed to keep the business moving when it had appeared to be running out of steam.

He managed a meeting with his father, who was also travelling across Europe. In the Earl of Wiltshire's case he was to represent Henry at the meeting between Clement VII and Charles V. George was then free to return home, where he quickly resumed his normal duties as an esquire to the King.

Sir Thomas More, Chancellor since Wolsey's disgrace, still refused to soil his hands on the matter of the divorce, and the rise of Thomas Cromwell as Henry's 'fixer' could only mean bad news for the traditionalists. Furthermore, the rise of the Boleyns and their friends was now taken for granted. Chapuys, in writing to the Emperor, reported on the attitude of Anne Boleyn:

> She is braver than a lion, and has said to one of the Queen's ladies in waiting that she wished all Spaniards in the world were in the sea. When the other replied that for the Queen's honour she should not say so, she said that she cared nothing for the Queen, and would rather see her hanged than acknowledge her as her mistress.[1]

Chapuys was incensed at the triumph of the Boleyns once the Cardinal was out of the way. Anne was in the ascendant and at times her arrogance showed. Whatever Anne's faults, hypocrisy was not one of them. She played the part Henry demanded of her, of initial civility towards the Cardinal and the Queen. Her own feelings were close to the surface and her temper easy to arouse. In Anne's eyes, Katherine could easily have finalised the matter by stepping aside, but her stubborn insistence on her rights dragged out the inevitable ending. For Anne, it was a deliberate wasting of time, when she could have been breeding children.

Henry had his own problems. These centred upon a stand against the Pope and Church complicated by knowing that personal letters to Anne were in the Vatican. Clement had issued another Brief as a result of Henry's refusal to visit Rome for a hearing. He had forbidden him to marry until the cause was decided. Henry knew that if he and Anne married any children they produced would be bastards. After all the years of waiting, they were little further ahead.

As well as requiring a certain standard of behaviour from Anne to Katherine, Henry practised it himself. On 8 January he dined with Katherine and then spoke genially with the Ambassador. There is no mention of 'the Lady' having been present at Greenwich with the royal party, and possibly Anne was still at York Place for the festival. She had not been forgotten, she received from Henry £100 as a New Year's gift. It was a considerable sum, useful for a lady who needed to make 'la bella figura'. Despite the slow pace of the holiday season, things were beginning to move under the surface.

Parliament met on 16 January and Henry had instructed the Attorney General to begin proceedings against the bishops for recognising the Legatine power of the Cardinals the previous year. He ignored the fact that he previously had high hopes of it. He now considered that it had constituted Praemunire, which would mean the loss of all goods and chattels to the Crown – as in Wolsey's case.

The members of the Convocation of Canterbury were immediately alarmed, and offered the King a 'free gift' of no less than £100,000 if the proceedings against them were dropped. It was what Henry was waiting for. He said he would gladly accept the gift, and give them free pardon – *if* they would acknowledge him as Supreme Head of the Church in England.

Cromwell, recently made a member of the Privy Council, was the messenger. It was a task he undertook several times during the next few years. His bullying tactics were to become infamous, but this time ineffective.

The Convocation took fright at the suggestion and backed off, withdrawing the offer of money. However, Praemunire was a very serious weapon and, threatened with the penalties for treason, the Convocation had to think again, and acquiesce. They did acknowledge Henry as Supreme Head of the Church in England, but they added the qualification of 'insofar as the law of Christ allows'.

The next stage was to enforce the same confirmation from Parliament, and Henry met with opposition. He was ready for them, granting a pardon in advance to the laity, without extracting further requirement from them. For the time being, Henry was prepared to accept that the people should not be pushed too far.

The speed with which such a damaging matter had been forced through alarmed Katherine, and by 21 February Chapuys reported that the Queen was surprised that so little had been done on her behalf in Rome. But Chapuys' furious letters were to be countered quite neatly by Cromwell. He called the Members of Parliament together in order to inform them again 'that there were some who said that the King pursued this divorce out of love for the Lady, and not out of the scruple of his conscience, but that was not the truth'. He went on to reiterate that the King 'was only moved thereto in discharge of his conscience, which through what he had read and discovered from doctors and universities, was in bad condition due to his living with the Queen!'.[2]

The Princess Mary had been ill and asked permission to visit her mother at Greenwich. The request was brusquely refused. Chapuys immediately blamed this on the influence of 'the Lady' claiming that if the King praised the Princess in any way, Anne would become angry. He also claimed that Henry had spoken to the Duke of Norfolk, and had complained that Anne was not like the Queen, 'who had never in her life used ill words towards him'.

The Princess Mary was more of an obstacle for Anne than the Queen. Henry was determined to rid himself of Katherine, but Mary was still his daughter and his heir. In the event that Anne did not produce a son – or was not given the opportunity to do so – Mary would retain that position.

Anne had to endure a vigorous campaign of calumny directed towards her by the supporters of the Queen and Princess. While they enjoyed their stance on the moral high ground, they were still willing to speak out and make trouble, particularly in the spreading of ill-natured gossip. One of the things that Anne was to be accused of was persuading one Richard Rice, a cook in the household of Dr Fisher, Bishop of Rochester, to put poison in the broth he had made. That something caused illness and death in the household is well recorded, and the cook was executed after admitting to the crime, though the Bishop survived his indisposition. But there is, however, no evidence to connect Anne with the crime. If Anne had been tempted to kill, she would have done better to poison the Queen. She had nothing to be gain by making an attempt on the life of the Bishop.

The unpleasant matter comes to us from Sanders, an author violently anti-Boleyn in his opinions. This line was followed and copied by such people as Henry Clifford. Burnet in his *History of the Reformation* took pains to investigate the accusation against Anne and found no evidence against her whatever. The idea of blaming her for the incident seems to stem from Chapuys, who remarked on it in a letter to Charles V on 1 March. He was the only person who laid the blame on 'the Lady and her father' for what had happened.[3]

Legends of Anne's 'evil' nature abounded, with claims of her unchastity. These vituperations were not unexpected but must have hurt her deeply. Her lifestyle with Henry, platonic as it most probably was (for fear of an illegitimate pregnancy), was something that an outsider was unlikely to understand. Her precise relationship with the King was bound to be the subject of speculation and Katherine's position would lead to blame for Anne. The situation in which they lived was of Henry's making, and was pushed on even when Anne showed signs of being tired of it.

The Pope was still making threats regarding Henry's proceedings in Rome, and by the end of May 1531 Henry was very tired of that too.

He made a further attempt to influence Katherine, sending a deputation of nobles, including Norfolk, Suffolk, Northumberland and Wiltshire, along with the Bishops of London and Lincoln and Drs Lee, Sampson and Gardiner. It must have been a strange procession to arrive at Katherine's door at 9 o'clock at night, but she was not intimidated by it. Chapuys, always eager to boast on Katherine's behalf after the event, reported that 'they worked hard and counselled long, and devised fine plans, but were confounded by a single woman!'.

The deputation was forced to return to Henry defeated, telling him that Katherine had said that she was prepared to be guided by him in all things, except two. When asked 'What?' the reply was 'God and her conscience, which she would not destroy for anyone.' Despite Henry's determination and Katherine's defence of what she believed to be true, patience was wearing thin. The matter had dragged on too long and hostility to the idea was widespread. Henry took refuge in hunting with his favourites, including Anne, to take his mind off his many problems.[4]

Chapuys, as usual, had a good deal to say about it, although his sources are often suspect and in many cases sheer gossip. On 17 July, while the hunting party was still away from court, Chapuys recorded, 'the Lady is preparing for royal state by degrees, she has just taken an almoner and other officers. She goes with the King to the chase, and the Queen, who always used to follow, has been commanded to remain at Windsor.'

Only a week after this came rupture between Henry and Katherine. In the twenty-third year of their marriage, Henry had left Windsor to take his hunting further afield. Katherine sent him a message expressing regret that she had not seen him leave, but an angry reply came back from the King. He told her that he wanted no goodbyes, or enquiries after his health and he reviled her for all the trouble she'd caused. Katherine's reply was immediate and Henry took three days to respond to it. He was furious. He told her that she defended the non-consummation of the marriage to his brother, and preached it to the world. She had no witnesses to it, and from then on she had better not write to him again.

On 19 August, Chapuys reported that the King had sent word that he wished to return to Windsor, but did not wish to see the Queen. She was to retire to The More, and the Princess Mary was to go temporarily to Richmond. Katherine protested, but without result, and she had to remove herself and her household. The break was final.

It may have seemed a move forward, even a triumph, but was not to be. Anne was to suffer increased attacks on her character at home and abroad. A letter to the Doge and Signory of Venice claimed that the 'King was living with a young woman of noble birth, though of bad character, whose will is law to him'.[5]

Twice in December of 1531, Dr Ortiz, an Imperial agent, wrote to Charles V claiming that 'the King's wench' had miscarried.[6] This continued what was being said of Anne by others, including Simon Grynee to his reformer friend Martin Bucer. Grynee had come to England at the instigation of Erasmus and been introduced by him to Lord Mountjoy. As well as research, Grynee had developed a line in common gossip, including:

whether she has children or not by the King I do not know, they may be brought up in private, (which if I am not mistaken I have heard more than once). Though there are those who say that the King has not had intercourse with her ... she is young, good looking, of a rather dark complexion, and likely enough to have children.

Christmas Eve of 1531 was marked by a feast given by Anne with the new French Ambassador, Giles de la Pommeraye, in attendance. He had come with special instructions from Francis, who intended to assist Henry in his matter of the divorce – for a consideration. Francis had remarked that Henry seemed to have lost nothing from the death of Wolsey, as the Lady had more credit than the late Cardinal had. It should not be necessary to pay her the 25,000 crowns as the French had to Wolsey. In Anne's case, flattery and promises would be enough.

Now a new treaty between England and France was being proposed. This guaranteed that they would aid each other in the case of any attack from the Emperor. Henry was hedging his bets in case the casting off of Katherine should bring any military repercussions. The Treaty of Alliance was signed by April, but Francis had already by then begun defending Henry's case in Rome.

The correspondence details this fraught period, when Henry stood out against the Papacy and Spain. There is a letter from Clement VII to Henry, asking him for his help in fighting the Turks, in case they invaded Italy. Henry had already written to Ghinucci and Casale, his Roman agents, telling them to use every possible means of getting Clement to adjourn the case longer. Henry's other agent, Benet, had written to Katherine, asking her pardon for seemingly working against her. He told her that her affairs were in a good position in Rome, and that he was her faithful servant. These people had no difficulty in managing to compartmentalise their lives, and saw no problem playing one side off against the other.

Chapuys, playing the role of doom-monger, reported that the Queen had been treated 'unkindly' at the New Year. She sent Henry a gold cup as a gift, but he sent it back, and refused to allow others to receive gifts from the Queen. 'He has not been so discourteous to the Lady', Chapuys reported miserably. 'She presented him with certain darts of Biscayan fashion, richly augmented. In return he gave her a whole room, hung with cloth of gold and silver and crimson satin, with rich embroideries.' Anne's family did well for gifts from the King. Silver plate went to Anne's mother Lady Wiltshire, Lady Rochford (George's wife) and Lady Mary Rochford (Mary Carey). Lady Shelton (one of Thomas Boleyn's sisters) was appointed to the court. Anne was by then attended by almost as many ladies as Katherine had been, but, despite all the privileges and the luxuries, the divorce still seemed to be stuck.

Henry suggested to Pope Clement that the matter should be tried by three English prelates, but the Imperial ambassador was pressing the Pope. His immediate desire was for Clement to issue a Brief, commanding Henry to cast off 'his concubine Anne, within fifteen days, and return to the Queen'. He was to be disappointed.[7]

When Clement did make a move, it was only to admonish Henry mildly, about the scandal being created. He ended with the hope that Henry would take back Queen Katherine and put away Anne. It was easy to ignore.

The Duke of Norfolk was to make the next step. He called together some of the peers and members of the Commons and put it to them that matrimonial cases should be judged by lay tribunals, not ecclesiastical ones. Chapuys claimed that Anne's father had said that no Pope had any power to exercise such jurisdiction or make any law in the matter. But it was to go no further. Henry became angry at the failure of what he considered a good idea. He was almost tempted to take the French line of marrying Anne, taking the invalidity of the first marriage as read. But on reflection, he realised that this was what Wolsey had saved him from. Even Lord Wiltshire opposed such a move, though Anne quarrelled with her father and her uncle of Norfolk over it. She had begun to believe that they were opposing her personally.

She even began to fear that her uncle Norfolk was plotting for the hand of the Princess Mary for his son Henry Howard, the Earl of Surrey. To counter this, she pressed forward with the original plans for Surrey to marry Frances Vere, the daughter of the Earl of Oxford. It did not help the relationship between Anne and the Howards, and Norfolk began to behave in a friendly manner towards the Imperial ambassador, guaranteed to make Anne feel more insecure.

Chapuys reported, quite gleefully, to Charles V that had it not been for the Duke of Norfolk and the Earl of Wiltshire, the marriage between Henry and Anne 'would have taken place a year ago!'.[8] Although it is difficult to see how preventing the union between Anne and the King would have benefited either family. What Henry hated the most was the 'bruiting abroad' of personal business to the common people. In March of 1532 he ordered the arrest of a priest for the crime of preaching against the divorce. He gave instructions that all future preachers should support him. The Friars Minors, or Observant Friars, at Greenwich, had always been firm favourites of Queen Katherine, and they took up her cause. On Easter Sunday 1532 one William Peto (the Provincial of the Order) preached very boldly before Henry in person, even going so far as to cry out 'where the dogs licked the blood of Naboth, even there shall the dogs lick thy blood, O King!'. Henry remonstrated with him, but made no move against him, except to send one of his own chaplains, Dr Richard Curwen, to preach on the following Sunday and to contradict all that Peto had said. Peto would be arrested, but the Observant Friars were seething with discontent against the King. When Peto was finally released he went to live in Antwerp, but the Greenwich convent was suppressed by Henry in 1534, one of the first to suffer for their opposition.

The Pope continued to send Henry documents until his temper snapped and he expressed astonishment that the Pontiff should believe that he would ever take Katherine back. He sent her further afield, to Easthampstead, where she was to lodge in very uncomfortable circumstances with the Bishop of Lincoln, who was unfriendly towards her.

Henry sent for the Speaker and twelve members of the Commons on 11 May 1532 and told them that he had discovered that the clergy were not his loyal subjects. He claimed that this was because they took two oaths, one to himself but also one to the Pope. He intended to provoke a quarrel between the Parliament and the clergy but he also 'by menacies' forced the clergy to make submission to him, by promising that no new canons or constitutions would be made without his consent, and also promising to revise the existing ones. This was agreed on 16 May, which was also the day upon which Sir Thomas More finally resigned his Chancellorship.

Why had More accepted the position in the first place, knowing what was happening and his own strong feelings about it? If he could not agree to Henry's intentions, had he hoped by his presence to alter or modify them? Surely his years of friendship with the King made him aware that Henry would never back down once his intention was made clear? Or was More merely the martyr born, provoking Henry, by his moral superiority, offering himself as a sacrifice on the altar of the Church's supremacy? He would have been wiser not to accept the office of Chancellor if he had intended to oppose the King. He could hardly have expected that Henry would continue to ignore his attitude.

When, in 1530, the Lords had sent a letter to Pope Clement asking him to annul Queen Katherine's marriage, More had refused to sign it. For a man in private life to do that was bad enough. For a man who was a friend of the King, and his chief minister, to do it, knowing that the eyes of Europe were on him, was not only unforgivable, but also ridiculously suicidal.

Henry had appeared to forgive, or lay the matter aside. In 1531 More had agreed to the Oath of Supremacy, but 'only so far as the law of Christ allows'. A direct reference to Praemunire again. Henry was angry and More offered to resign, but Henry refused, knowing what Europe would make of it. Was that why More had continued? Using his disapproving presence as a form of moral blackmail? He knew that in any such contest Henry would lose. Thankfully, the old belief that Thomas More was a saintly character has been eroded in the light of his hypocrisy and religious bigotry. He was not above using his reputation as a stick to beat Henry with. But he finally overplayed his hand by the way he held himself disdainfully aloof from the problems surrounding the throne. When, in 1532, he again offered his resignation, Henry accepted. More should have been warned.

He was to retire into private life, but even as a private citizen his opinions meant something, and he had already made his feelings plain. For the time being, Henry would leave him alone, but such blatant resistance to the King could not be allowed to go unpunished.

More had been replaced by Thomas Audley, a friend of Cromwell's who had previously been the Speaker. He was knighted and made Keeper of the Great Seal, then Chancellor. Cromwell became Master of the Jewels and seemed to have acquired great influence over Henry, but always under the aegis of Anne.

The marriage between the Earl and Countess of Northumberland was causing trouble. The Countess had claimed that her husband had told her that their marriage was invalid due to his prior contract with Anne Boleyn. Whatever Anne's remaining feelings might have been for Harry Percy, his foolish words were the last thing she needed. Scandal had already made free with her good name despite all efforts to show herself to be innocent of wrongdoing and Harry Percy was, by thoughtless talk, making things worse. Henry, too, was to be displeased.

The Countess of Northumberland had written to her father, the Earl of Shrewsbury, and he had shown the letter to the Duke of Norfolk. Whatever his personal disagreements with Anne, Thomas Howard was aware that if her chance of becoming Queen was destroyed by sordid revelations it would adversely impact upon the whole family. They had all invested a great deal in the prospect of a Queen of Howard blood becoming the mother of the heir to the throne.

Norfolk took the offending letter to Anne, who in turn showed it to Henry. He was angry but more concerned about the future legal position. If not immediately refuted the matter could become a serious impediment to their marriage. Whether or not Harry Percy had ever made such a claim, during an argument with the wife he detested, he now would have to swear that he did not, and he would have to do so both legally and quickly.

He went to the Archbishop of Canterbury and then to the Council, and in both cases swore that he had not said any such thing. He also had to swear that no contract of any kind had ever existed between him and Anne Boleyn.[9]

Later, when marriage with Anne had soured, Henry would refer to it again. But had Anne and Henry Percy ever sworn vows to one another? Would it have meant anything if they had? Percy was already contracted to Mary Talbot then, so he was not free to make vows to anyone else, even though he was in love with Anne. Anne had been technically free, as her proposed marriage to James Butler had never reached the point of a legal contract. However, such vows would always be a problem, and even the suspicion of them could make difficulties due to the very awkward nature of those sixteenth-century contractual agreements between two consenting adults.[10] The very possibility of them having made vows, particularly if such vows were followed by physical intimacy, could present any marriage with extremely difficult legal questions. A formal marriage was not necessarily required to form a bond, and that could easily pose awkward questions and make a mess of any subsequent matrimonial connection.

Did the Countess of Northumberland, trapped in an abhorrent marriage, decide to make use of what seemed to be the only legal way out? She had plenty of reason to feel aggrieved towards Anne Boleyn, considering her husband's lack of interest in making their marriage work. It seems to have been the only romantic attachment Henry Percy ever had, but it marked him. Whether or not he was actually still in love with Anne, he had become a bitter and melancholic man, who found it extremely difficult to maintain decent relations with his spouse or his family. It is possible that he would have developed into such a character anyway, but it is reasonable to assume that his wife thought he was hankering after a lost love. It was easy for her to blame the subject of that early infatuation for spoiling their chances of married happiness.

It was a very dangerous thing for her to attempt. The King had made it clear that Anne Boleyn was the woman he wanted to marry. Whether or not the Countess's accusation had any basis in fact, it was likely to spur the King's jealousy and make him angry. The Countess could leave her husband and return to live with her father, if she and the Earl preferred it, but any suggestion that Anne was involved in their separation must be very quickly and efficiently doused.

The Earl of Northumberland's rapid acquiescence showed just how dangerous the matter was. It is likely that he would have been delighted to have been rid of his Countess but Henry's flare-ups at any new difficulty were not to be provoked lightly. Whatever the truth, it was not worth the probable consequences. Once Northumberland had sworn before all the necessary authorities, he must have exited the court with great relief.

Wolsey's shade may have been laughing. Years before he had issued a warning that any idea put into Henry's head could be impossible to drag out again. So it would prove. The time was not yet, but the filing system that constituted Henry's memory had just received another item, placed in reserve.

His unwanted Queen was exiled and stubbornly refusing either to agree with, or acknowledge, the ending of their marriage, and his heir, the Princess Mary, was living away from court. She was beginning to develop into what in the twenty-first century would be a teenager with problems. Her love for, and support of, her mother was well known, and perfectly understandable in the circumstances.[11] She was upset and bewildered by her father's obsession with a woman she considered an interloper, and her own chances of a fruitful marriage were slipping away with the years. This was not only due to Anne's presence, although she and her mother liked to think it was, but due to the blight of suggested illegitimacy, which her father's negation of his marriage to her mother had thrust on her. She was to fall back for support on the few constants in her life: her mother's royal blood and her own, the Holy Church which approved of and supported their cause, and their relationship with the Emperor Charles V upon whose assistance they still relied.

Many traditionalists were in agreement with them and with the Emperor. Unfortunately, the Emperor, lavish with words, was less so with actions. He still showed no sign of doing anything to reinforce their position. Indeed, he could not. Fortunately for their safety in England, King Henry was to remain on tenterhooks of uncertainty that he eventually might.

For the Princess Mary the situation was a disaster. It drove her inward and intensified her reliance on religion. It would ruin her judgment and eventually her ability to rule when her turn came. It would alter her from being a pleasant and accomplished young woman, into a person so out of touch with the changes of the world, that she never had any real chance of becoming an effective Queen.

Henry, still besotted with Anne, must have felt resentment that his daughter, in whom he had once delighted, had retreated from him, and taken her place among people who would remain inimical, even hostile, towards him. That relationship he had once enjoyed with his daughter would be irredeemable.

Henry was by that time working on the premise that all who were not wholeheartedly with him, were most certainly against him, and probably traitors into the bargain. There could be no nuances of opinion. Friends could become enemies without warning and, along with Anne, he was by then desperate for some chink of light in the darkness, to break up the everlasting deadlock.

His temper had become unreliable since the summer progress. Henry had been keen to have Anne with him but wherever they went they seemed to meet with groups of women, pockets of resistance. These people were ready to remind the members of the royal party that they did not approve of the plan to divorce their Queen, and that they wanted Katherine back! An intolerable situation for Henry, who had convinced himself that he was working in the best interests of the country. For Anne, the demonstrations in Katherine's favour were unsettling at best and frightening at worst. Small wonder that she occasionally gave way to tantrums when Henry had difficulty in soothing her.[12]

Finally, in 1532, the ever-present clouds began to disperse a little. Enough to provide a glimmer of hope again.

It started on 21 July, when an invitation was received from King Francis. He asked Henry to meet him in France later that year. Henry was delighted to agree. It was a show of solidarity, and he was not only eager to go, but keen for Anne to accompany him. But how? She was neither mistress nor wife. How would she be received abroad, what train should she take, how would Henry arrange it in the face of his exiled Queen, or even his Archbishop of Canterbury? Warham had, like More, attempted to hold himself aloof from the business of the King's affections. Although he had mistresses of his own, it had taught him nothing about human frailty. Henry, not only aware of the Archbishop's status but also his advanced age, had tried to exercise some restraint in his handling of him.

Warham had declared his belief that the famous St Thomas of Canterbury (another man who had unfortunately opposed his rightful king, with tragic consequences) 'was rewarded by God with the great honour of martyrdom. Which is the best death there can be; which is the example and comfort of others, to speak and do, for the defence of the liberties of God's church!'[13]

Such declarations must have made the King impatient, but however tempted he may have been to give such intransigence the martyrdom it seemed to desire, it was a road he could not go down. On 23 August 1532, Archbishop William Warham of Canterbury solved the problem by dying. It must have been very pleasant news for Henry to receive while making preparations for his visit to France. One obstacle in his path had been removed. The first steps towards the destruction of papal authority in England had already been taken. Although there would continue to be considerable resistance to it, the process, though gradual, would prove unstoppable. Warham could, and would, be replaced with a man less likely to be intractable.

Henry intended to replace him with Cranmer.

Cranmer had been in Italy on Henry's business since early 1532 and was not recalled until 1 October. He would be travelling as winter approached, therefore slowly, and would not reach England until January of 1533. He would then realise what the King wanted from him.

Cranmer was 43 years old, with a wife in Germany. He was quite a timid man, but a reformer at heart. The prospective position of Archbishop of Canterbury may have been a difficult but inspiring one. He would prove to be another very useful tool to Henry's hand.

Again, no Wolsey, but far more malleable than Warham had been. William Warham had veered with the wind, until More's surrender of the Chancellorship had stiffened his resolve to help him to speak out more firmly in favour of Katherine. Cranmer might sway with the breeze, but it would always be in the direction of Henry.

There was, of course, a problem. To avoid schism Cranmer's appointment would have to be ratified by the Pope; only then would he be Archbishop. Only then would his pronouncements hold any weight, even if he intended to perjure himself – which he did.

Anne, though relieved that Warham could no longer prove to be an obstacle, would need to be occupied with feminine matters. The trip to France was definite, and she would accompany Henry. Who would receive her? Not the Queen of France, or indeed any lady of rank who considered her position, for Anne's own position was still ambivalent.[14] Francis had made the suggestion of the Duchess de Vendôme, but she was hastily rejected as her own reputation was such that it would hardly enhance Anne's.

Anne was cheered by Henry's insistence that she go to France attired as a queen, even if that position had not yet been achieved. He showered her with jewels, all part of the intention to bolster her apparent rank, and his insistence on making her his official wife as soon as Cranmer could validate it.[15]

Despite there having been an informal agreement between the two kings that the expenditure for the visit should be kept to a minimum, Henry did not consider that such an arrangement could refer to either himself or to Anne. No doubt many of the courtiers who were to attend were glad of it, and relieved that they would not have to bankrupt their estates, as many had done for the Field of the Cloth of Gold.

Anne's clothes, as magnificent as Henry's own, were designed to be the perfect foil for the jewels. He had demanded the return of many of them from Queen Katherine, who had at first refused the order. She retorted that she would not surrender them to adorn 'the scandal of Christendom'.[16] However, her initial refusal was ignored and she was forced to return them to him. Katherine was not of a mercenary nature, but the value of the jewels was not the issue, it was what they represented.

There was another thing Henry could do for Anne. Her title of Lady Anne Rochford was held by her in right of her father's position as Earl of Wiltshire. Normally, she would have no other title until she married, then she would hold her new one in right of her husband. Henry could give her one of her own. It was unusual, but not unheard of, for a lady to have her own title, and Henry was determined to raise her to the peerage in her own right before they went to France. It would make his intentions towards her crystal clear. She would accompany him as his acknowledged future wife.

There had, of course, been speculations regarding the trip, despite Anne's preparations and the costs involved for extravagant jewels and clothing. It was suggested that Henry was going to France to arrange a marriage for himself with the eldest daughter of King Francis.[17] Another of the rumours going around, contradictory to the first, was not so far off the mark. It said that Henry intended to marry Anne secretly while they were in France. Even the King's idea of raising her to the peerage before they left was the subject of gossip, the suggestion being that he was about to put her aside and the title she would soon receive was a reward for the years they had spent together.

It is far more likely that Henry, now waiting eagerly for Cranmer's return, was taking steps to elevate Anne to the peerage, so the next step – only achievable after Cranmer was home – would not seem to be as much to take. If she were already a peeress in her own right, she would not seem to be lowly born at their marriage.

On the 1 September, at Windsor Castle, the usual Sunday routine was disturbed by an impressive ceremony. Anne was to be formally invested. She wore ermine, the royal fur, trimmed with crimson velvet, and her long hair was loose.[18] She was attended by Garter King at Arms, and her cousin Mary Howard, with the Countesses of Rutland and Derby. Her uncle Norfolk's letters show that the original intention was for her train to be carried by his wife the Duchess, but Elizabeth Howard had refused to accept the honour. She was Katherine of Aragon's good friend and supporter. To avoid any impasse, her daughter Mary Howard, Anne's first cousin, took her mother's place.

Henry waited for Anne flanked by the Dukes of Norfolk and Suffolk and surrounded by all the court. The French Ambassador was guest of honour.

Anne knelt while Stephen Gardiner read aloud the patent conferring on her the new title 'in her own right and upon her future offspring' of the Marquisate of Pembroke. That title had its own royal associations for the Tudors, as it had previously been held by Jasper Tudor, Henry's great-uncle. Rather than being made a marchioness, Anne would be referred to as 'Lady Marquis' to emphasise that she did not hold the title through the right of a husband. Henry placed on her shoulders a mantle and put her new coronet on her hair. Into her hand he placed the Patent of Nobility along with another, which granted her lands worth £1,000 per year. The ceremony was followed by a High Mass at St Gregory's Chapel which was sung by Gardiner. Henry and the French Ambassador, on behalf of King Francis, took advantage of the holy atmosphere to swear to abide by the terms of a new treaty between England and France. The Mass finished with a *Te Deum*, and the day was rounded off with a great banquet within the castle. It had been the greatest day of Anne's life, so far.[19]

All the rumours and speculation ended on Friday, 11 October when Anne took ship with Henry at Dover. They crossed to France on the *Swallow* and by 10 a.m. Anne was in Calais after an absence of almost twenty years. This time she received a very different greeting for now she was with the King, listening to a royal salute and acknowledged as the King's intended wife. She had with her personal attendants numbering 30 ladies, but these were totally swamped by the 2,000 nobles and other men attending the King.

Anne was to spend ten days at Calais with Henry, being treated as if she were already Queen of England. A delegation from Francis arrived on the 15th to offer an official welcome and on the 21st Henry left to meet Francis at Boulogne. He stayed there for four days, after which Henry returned to Calais with Francis on Friday, 25 October.

Anne kept discreetly out of sight while Francis was received at his lodgings at Staple Hall, though his reception was far from quiet, with the firing of 3,000 guns in welcome. Despite Anne's non-appearance, her presence was felt, and Francis sent her a gift of a fine diamond, worth £3,500. A banquet was planned by Henry for the Sunday afternoon, 27 October, and all preparations were aimed towards that event, while Henry kept the French King occupied.

For the banquet itself every display was ordered. Seven shelves full of gold plate, hangings of cloth of gold and silver tissue, and gold wreaths with pearls and precious stones inset were all on show. All the ostentatious wealth was illuminated by twenty candelabra of silver and silver-gilt, each one holding a hundred wax candles. But it was not until the dinner was over that Anne appeared, leading a masque of six ladies 'gorgeously apparelled'.[20]

Mary Carey was there in attendance upon her sister; so was George's wife, Lady Jane Rochford. Their aunt, Dorothy, Countess of Derby, another aunt, Elizabeth, Lady Fitzwalter, and Lady Wallop, who was the wife of the Ambassador to France, along with Lady Lisle completed the party.[21] Lady Lisle was Honor Grenville, and was married to Arthur Plantagenet, then Lord Deputy of Calais. This man was one of the many bastard children of King Edward IV, and half-brother to Elizabeth of York, which made him the uncle of Henry VIII.

The ladies wore matching gold cloth overdresses, with sashes of crimson satin. Each was masked and attended by four maids of honour, richly dressed in crimson satin. Each lady chose a partner to dance with, but King Francis was, of course, partnered by Anne. After a short while, Henry removed the masks the ladies were wearing and, while general dancing continued, he and Anne, with King Francis, spent the rest of the evening in private conversation.

The following day was one of amusements, ranging from attending a Chapter of the Order of the Garter, to enjoying watching a troupe of Cornish wrestlers. It was not until Tuesday, 29 October that Henry escorted Francis back to the border between Calais and France itself.

There was then a general scramble among the crowds of attendants to get back to England before the weather changed for the worst. Henry and Anne did not join the rush. They were to take their time, and those who had embarked for home too hastily regretted their rashness. They had to face a fierce north-westerly gale which scattered the ships, sending some vessels back to Calais while some unfortunates found themselves driven as far away as Flanders.[22]

While waiting to avoid the worst of the gales (which did not abate until 4 November), the royal party would not have become bored. The Exchequer building, where they lodged, had everything to please and entertain visitors, from separate gardens for the King and Queen, to indoor conveniences such as tennis courts and a large gallery, in which the ladies were able to take walking exercise when the weather was bad. Anne occupied the Queen's lodging there, which consisted of seven main rooms, including one great chamber overlooking the Queen's garden. Furthermore, those rooms backed on to Henry's, and had interconnecting doors.[23]

Did Henry and Anne take advantage of that particular convenience at that time to finally consummate their relationship? It would have provided them with a little more privacy than they could expect from their apartments in England, where every ear listened and every eye watched every move. At least in Calais they had only their immediate attendants around them, chosen for discretion.

Of course, they could well have crossed that particular hurdle at a previous date, but the lodgings at Calais seemed perfectly situated to provide the opportunity for them to spend some private time together. Also, the start of their physical relationship at around that time fits with the ensuing pregnancy of Anne.

It seems likely that, with things beginning finally to go their way, with Francis friendly and supportive and Cranmer on his way home, Anne might surrender her virginity. She would certainly not have done so lightly, she was no fool and could hear rumours as easily as anyone. She may have gambled that, now that she was a peeress in her own right, the time was ripe and if she finally lost the gamble, she would still have come out of it better than Henry's other ladies. She would not be cast off with nothing to show for her years of waiting. But why should she now expect to lose? It is far more likely that she was convinced of his sincerity towards her, and that their formal marriage could not be much longer delayed. It was time for them both to relax a little, to enjoy each other's company once the banqueting was over. They had a little time for themselves, while they waited for the weather to improve.

Their party finally left Calais on 12 November at midnight, when the wind changed. However, they did not land at Dover until early on the Thursday morning, 14 November, after an unpleasant crossing lasting 29 hours. The weather had been so poor that a *Te Deum* was ordered, to give thanks for their safe return but Henry seemed in no hurry to return to London and did not reach Eltham until 24 November.

This appears to have been their true honeymoon period, a lazy journey home after a successful meeting with Francis. A final surrender from Anne for which Henry had waited too long, and for her, a relaxation of tension, perhaps a feeling that she had reached a safe plateau.

By the end of December 1532, Anne was already convinced that she was pregnant.[24]

Chapter Eleven

Rumours of what might have been planned for Calais spread around during the summer of 1532, ranging from fairly sensible to ridiculous assumptions. What was obvious was that Henry appeared to have relaxed. Anne too. Their leisurely return to London appeared to have become something of a holiday. Henry was very genial and generous, so much so that his good mood was remarked upon.

Anne had certainly decided to make the final concession, but she had not waited all those years in order to do so thoughtlessly. A rather tenuous exchange of vows, followed by carnal copulation, might technically be all that the Church required to validate a relationship, but that would not be enough for either her or Henry.

Anne had no intention of being cast aside if Henry's feelings should undergo a change. Likewise, Henry still saw the possibility of a legitimate son as a beacon for the future of England, and he had no intention of risking that child being another bastard.

The chronicler Hall and many eminent historians have concluded that some form of ceremony must have been performed, probably on 14 November, St Erconwald's Day, which the general consensus of opinion has marked out as being special.[1] The suite in attendance upon Henry and Anne would not be in ignorance that something was going on, therefore the date has not been plucked out of the air, but seems to be representative of the opinions of the people who were in the know.

However, whatever pleasure and hope for the future Henry may have been basking in, the stark fact remained that, to the Catholic leaders of Europe, Henry was still married to Katherine. But he had his plan ready for that, which involved Cranmer's ability, once he was officially Archbishop of Canterbury, to decide on the matter and declare Anne to be Henry's only lawful wife.

While still awaiting Cranmer's return, Henry took Anne with him to inspect the rebuilding at the Tower of London, which had begun the previous June. Building and renovation work cannot be hidden, and rumour was busy. The Venetian Ambassador reported that Henry was fortifying the place. Chapuys had also remarked on the 'considerable repairs' being undertaken, but completely missed the mark when he wrote that 'It is the King's intention to send the Queen hither.'[2] It is quite ingenuous of him to imagine that Henry would want to have Katherine, who was out of sight and as much out of mind as possible, to be lodged in London.

By December the work was progressing well and Henry, still in generous mood, had allowed Anne to choose from the Jewel House such items of plate as she would soon require for her household. The list is recorded under the heading 'parcels of plate given by the King's Highness to my Lady Marquess of Pembroke in the month of December'. It was a very extensive list, comprising cups, bowls, pots, chandeliers and spoons, with a total weight of 5,000 ounces of precious metal and an impressive total value of £1,200.[3]

All the plans for the future centred by then on Anne's belief in a pregnancy. It must have been a huge relief to her to have conceived quickly and Henry was no doubt delighted that all the difficulties of the past years could be wiped out at a stroke.

On 15 November the Pope had written to Henry lamenting that he had 'during the past two years altered his conduct without any reasonable excuse'.[4] He went on to say that he hoped that Henry would return to his former attachment, and reminded him that he had previously committed his case to the Legatine Court in England. While the matter was still under consideration he ought not to have taken any new steps and yet he was publicly cohabiting 'with a certain Anne'. Henry was exhorted, on pain of excommunication, to return to Katherine.

On hearing about the letter even Chapuys was dismayed at its weak tone, and despaired of there ever being any proper decision. He deplored the fact that the Pope made no attempt to give a final decision or pass any sentence, but preferred sending useless letters, easily ignored.

The Pope and the Emperor were due to meet at Bologna, but the Emperor clearly had more important things to consider than his Aunt Katherine's marriage. The Turks were a concern, as was the growing Lutheranism in Germany, and these both hinged on the authority of the Church, which Henry was flouting. Moreover, the matter of the Pope's niece, Catherine de' Medici, being due to be married to the second son of the King of France, was more worrying than anything Henry might be getting up to. It presaged a new closeness between Francis and the Pope that Charles could only deplore.

It was intended, once the Emperor had returned home, that the Pope and Francis should come to some arrangement whereby they could direct Henry towards 'some good end'. However, the cynical Francis was already well aware of the level Henry's relationship with Anne had reached, and that any further talks on the matter were futile. Henry was busily preparing the Tower of London for Anne's Coronation, planned for the following summer, and although he heard of the plans the Pope was formulating, they were just a waste of time.

Henry had heard it all before. The proposed meetings and discussions, the trial in some 'neutral' court, the need for everlasting patience while nothing definite happened. Although he thanked the Pope for his concern, he was clearly unimpressed as well as determined to wait no longer. He had taken the matter into his own hands and was quite happy with the results. All he required of the Pope was that Cranmer should be confirmed Archbishop as quickly as possible, so that the whole could be legalised.

It was a very cold winter, but Cranmer must be hurried home. Cromwell sent his friend Stephen Vaughan to meet him. Vaughan was to report on the appalling travelling weather, saying that he 'expected not to come back without a broken leg' due to the roads being so icy. However, by Christmas he fully anticipated being in England, with Cranmer in tow.

Cranmer had been travelling even more slowly than the conditions warranted, and the fact that 'Mr. Cranmer is disposed to make only very small journeys' was also reported back.[5]

It was not until the middle of January 1533 that Cranmer arrived at Greenwich. Henry informed him that it was his intention to make him Archbishop of Canterbury, although Cranmer was aware of that already, hence his reluctance to return.

Cranmer had left a wife in Germany. That may not only have given him some insight into Henry's feelings, but also made him less willing to be the King's tool in the matter, even though the Archbishopric was a powerful lure. He at first refused the honour, having given as his reason that he had scruples about taking an oath to the Papacy (necessary in order to obtain the Bulls of Appointment), then being required to swear to uphold only Henry and his interests, which would conflict. Legal experts were consulted and he was persuaded to put forward a compromise. This was to assert that he did not acknowledge the Pope's authority. He would reserve the right to speak against the Papacy in the future whenever he (or Henry) considered it necessary. His Proctor would be obliged to swear his Oath to the Papacy, in order to secure the all-important Bulls, but Cranmer would personally make a different Oath at his Consecration.

It begs the question that if Cranmer's 'genuine concern' about vowing himself to loyalty to the Papacy, when he immediately intended to act against it, was so strong, then how could such a concern be so easily salved? If the man had the most fleeting of genuine scruples on the issue, then that perjured, double-oath should have made them worse. The man was a toady, happy to do whatever was necessary to obtain the authority to impose his idea of the new learning on England. His only fear was for his own skin, and he was completely without the courage of his convictions. He preferred that the responsibility for his double-dealing be taken by others, leaving the impression that he had been forced. That was the true reason for his pretended reluctance to assume the position.

Such a compromise would never have satisfied a Fisher or a More, and Wolsey had recognised and acknowledged his true allegiance at the last. For the more elastic conscience of Cranmer it would do the trick well enough. It was clearly the solution of an essentially weak man, overborne by and hiding behind Henry's stronger personality. That was to be the case for the remainder of his time with the King. He would oblige his master with whatever shifts and contrivances were demanded of him. Cromwell and Cranmer were to be the tools Henry had looked for, but they would prove to be a slippery duo, even while they helped him to trample justice underfoot. Cranmer's willingness to begin even his Archbishopric with a perjury was to define his future relationship with Henry and damage his standing in perpetuity.

Henry and Anne were to undergo a marriage ceremony at the end of January of 1533, which Cranmer would always deny having performed. Whether it was their first, or their second, such exchange of vows can never now be proved, though it has been suggested that the 1533 nuptials were designed to cover any deficiencies in the one that had been celebrated during the previous November. However, it was a moot point, as Henry's marriage to Katherine had still not been officially declared void. But in his own eyes he was a bachelor and free to make a marriage with anyone he chose. His supporters concurred.

Once the New Year of 1533 had opened, there was an air of optimism, along with a need for speed. Anne was certainly pregnant and Henry required William Benet to press the ambassadors to make every effort to ensure that the divorce be committed to a decision in England, where Cranmer could deal with it immediately. On 6 February Henry authorised that Cranmer should receive the sum of £1,000 to cover his necessary expenses.[6]

On 11 February Henry signed a further warrant authorising Cromwell to pay another £1,000 to the Italian merchant Antonio Bonuisi, which was for transfer to Benet in Rome and was intended to cover the question of the annates payable on issue of the Bulls.[7]

At the same time, the Emperor was with the Pope at Bologna and Chapuys wrote to him urging him to intervene to prevent the issue of the Bulls, in an attempt to stop Cranmer having the authority to dissolve Katherine's marriage. He demanded that nothing should be done until sentence in the matter had been pronounced in Rome, or at least a clause should be inserted that would forbid Cranmer interfering in the matter.

It is possible to feel sympathy with Chapuys at this time. His obvious despair at the flaccid support of the Pope and the complete indifference to what was a sensible suggestion must have been immensely frustrating. No notice was taken of his letter, and on 21 February 1533 the Pope issued the necessary Bulls to Cranmer's agents in Rome. There was not even the insertion of any clause restricting his ability to interfere in a matter still under the Pope's jurisdiction. It seems quite incomprehensible that the Pope would not have taken that most obvious step to prevent Cranmer from taking the matter into his own hands and assuming papal authority. Hawkins reported to Henry that the whole thing was virtually settled, and for a very modest outlay, though he did remind Henry that another 1,000 ducats would be needed at the next consistory, in order to obtain Cranmer's Pallium, which was the outward sign of his authority. It was done, and done almost with the connivance of the Pope, who could at least have made some effort to restrict Cranmer's power.

Despite Henry's impatience, the Bulls did not arrive in England until 26 March, but Cranmer was ready and was Consecrated Archbishop only four days later, on 30 March 1533. On the day of his Consecration, by Henry's order, the Archbishop elect went to St Stephen's Chapel with four witnesses, and declared on oath that the oath of obedience, which he was about to make to the Papacy, was 'for form's sake only'. He swore openly that he did not intend to bind himself to that oath, or to anything contrary to the law of God, or anything in any way prejudicial to the rights of King Henry. He then went straight to his Consecration, to make oaths to the Papacy he had already forsworn.[8]

On 14 March Parliament introduced a Bill into the Commons which proposed a statute that the Pope should have no authority in England. This met with enough opposition for it to be delayed for two weeks, but the complaints were less to do with the religious question and more to do with fears that trade with the conventionally Catholic countries might be affected badly.[9]

Katherine's supporters suggested that if Henry would agree to submit the decision on his marriage to a general council, he would receive from them a grant of £200,000. Tempting though this undoubtedly was (around twice the amount of his annual revenues), it was already far too late for any such bribe to have any appeal for him, in view of Anne's pregnancy.

The Act in Restraint of Appeals of 1533 was to become the most decisive and important single statute of the sixteenth century. It was to emphasise that the delayed justice, expenses of appeals and encroachments upon personal liberty made by the 'See of Rome' were in themselves contrary to the estate and dignity of the King of England. It went on to declare that only sentences pronounced by the King's courts should take effect, and that any attempt to procure an interdict, or appeal, from Rome should be treated as a matter of Praemunire. Henry was to rest his claim to independence from Rome on the Statute of Praemunire of Richard II dated 1393. In effect, all matters could in future be decided within the realm only. The Pope's jurisdiction over England was totally abolished, leaving only the Parliament – and Henry who controlled it – to decide on all matters, both spiritual and temporal.

While Parliament debated the Act, a Convocation defined the theology of marriage, in preparation for the moves that Cranmer was to undertake.[10] Henry was impatient for the matter to be ended and continually urged them to bring in their decision. Only Bishop Fisher dared to deplore the haste, along with the suspicion of intimidation being used. However, his voice was only one among many and most of the others involved were falling over themselves to please Henry, so, as Chapuys reported sadly, 'the Queen (and he) now consider her cause to be desperate!'. The new Archbishop appeared in Convocation on 5 April to receive the votes and, unsurprisingly, each question under consideration was carried by a large majority.

Henry kept an eye on public opinion. He was on friendly terms with Francis of France, as yet there had been no open breach with the Emperor Charles and the strain between England and the Papacy was kept quiet for fear of provoking unrest. Henry arranged for the Pope's representative to attend the House of Lords for the Opening of Parliament in February. The matter then under discussion was of no importance. The actual presence of the Nuncio was the point of the exercise. Again, a little later, the Nuncio was invited to attend the Commons, and the aim was to give the impression that relations with the Papacy were normal.

During this time there were rumours that Henry had already married Anne, or, if not married, they were betrothed. The new Archbishop was usually cast as the man who had performed the ceremony, though he continued to deny having any involvement with it.

Preparations had been made for the Pope's meeting with Francis, to which Henry had not been invited to send any representative. Francis had made a suggestion that the Earl of Wiltshire should attend, as any matter under discussion regarding

Henry's affairs touched him more closely than most. However, in the middle of March, Henry decided to send Anne's brother George, Lord Rochford instead. He had instructions that he should tell the French King that Henry's great desire for a son was the reason for the new marriage, and that he hoped for Francis' support if the Pope should show signs of intending to excommunicate him. However, these discreet and sensible sentiments were spoiled by Henry's private message to Francis about Anne's pregnancy in which he remarked 'which, to all appearance, is in a state of advancement already'.[11]

One of the things Henry attempted to urge upon Francis was the cancellation of the proposed marriage between his son Henri and the niece of the Pope. He claimed that Catherine de' Medici was not the equal of the French King's son to whom she was betrothed. Due to the 'base place, blood and house from which the Pope's niece springs …'. Such sentiments were an insult to the Pope's family and another example of Henry not knowing when to keep his mouth shut.

Henry did not realise that he was expecting too much of Francis. By putting a strain on their friendship at a time when Francis was arranging the marriage for the benefit of his country, Henry expected him to insult the Pope on his behalf. He assumed that Francis was in agreement with him.

Henry admitted, 'we have effectively proceeded to the accomplishment and consummation of our marriage' and went on to say that he expected Francis to hasten to obtain the necessary ratification of it from the Holy See. He even went so far as to send Francis a draft letter to copy out.[12] One wonders why Henry thought it so important, since he had already taken steps to abolish the Pope's authority over England.

As soon as the Cranmer matter had been concluded and all ecclesiastical appeals to Rome had been abolished Henry sent a deputation to Katherine (on 9 April 1533), led by the Dukes of Norfolk and Suffolk, to tell her that her case was virtually settled. She need make no attempt to return to him, or see him, because he had already remarried. Katherine was also informed that she must no longer attempt to use the title of Queen, reverting instead to the one used after her widowhood, that of Princess Dowager of Wales. Henry had already taken the precaution of having John Fisher, Bishop of Rochester, arrested to prevent him from making the expected fuss while these plans were put into action.

Once this was done, and due to the open secret of Anne's pregnancy, on Good Friday, 11 April, Cranmer wrote to Henry. He asked permission to proceed to the 'execution, determination and judgement of the cause of matrimony touching Your Highness'.[13] Henry took exception to the letter he received from Cranmer, considering the manner in which it was written to be insufficiently humble. He insisted that Cranmer rewrite the letter, with minor but important alterations in tone. The second version was submitted to the King immediately. The real reason the letter had to be redone was not due to any fault in the wording, but because Henry had no intention of handing over to Cranmer any of the authority of the position. By emphasising that he was the master, Henry made it clear that Cranmer's authority as Premier Archbishop stemmed from him, and although Cranmer was empowered to 'summon' him to the new court, it was only because he had been ordered to do so.

After that, Henry graciously approved the request and gave permission for the court to be convened in order to finally 'judge' the matter.

Anne openly assumed the rights and title of Queen, attending Mass on Easter Eve with a suite of sixty ladies. The King ignored the Spanish Ambassador's critical looks. He was more concerned with the problem of how Anne would be received by the people. To oil the wheels, he urged the Lords to pay their respects to her, telling them that she was to be solemnly crowned shortly after Easter. In confirmation of this, Anne's household was reorganised on more formal lines.

Her uncle, James Boleyn, became her Chancellor; Lord Burgh was appointed her Chamberlain, with Sir Edward Boynton as Vice-Chamberlain. George Taylor became Receiver General of the new Queen's household, with John Uvedale as Secretary. Sir William Coffin became Master of Horse to Queen Anne. The Ladies-in-Waiting included Anne Savage (who had been a witness to Anne's marriage); Anne Savile, Anne Gainsford (later Lady Zouche), Elizabeth Holland (the Duke of Norfolk's mistress) and a relatively unknown Jane Seymour. They all took Oaths of Allegiance to Anne as Queen.

Before she could be crowned the ending of the first marriage had to be completed. It was to follow the line of the Blackfriars Court. Queen Katherine refused to attend or acknowledge that it had authority, so the court would again convene in her absence, but this time be speedily concluded. However, perhaps the haste with which it had been convened had compromised its efficiency. The key witness to Katherine's response had not shown up, and neither had two ancient ladies who were to have testified that Katherine's marriage to Prince Arthur had been fully consummated. Even the King's own statement was apparently not available, neither were the 'determinations' of the Universities, or even Cranmer's instrument of opinion.

Despite all the administrative blunders, and the inefficiency regarding its essential paperwork, Katherine's absence told against her and the court proceeded with its business.

Also, perhaps intentionally, the court's rural situation meant 'few or almost none were present at the place of judgement ...'.[14] The proceedings were heard almost in private, and the deficiencies of the preparation mattered less. Cranmer, always conscious of the King's requirements, ensured that the court received as little publicity as possible. His only fear was that Katherine might change her mind and turn up, but she did not.

By 17 May Cranmer was able to tell Henry that the final sentence would be given 'on Friday next now ensuing', which would be 23 May. On that day he reported, 'I have given sentence in your Grace's great and weighty cause.'

Chapuys had complained about the proceedings of the Dunstable Court on behalf of Katherine, but was resentful about a humiliating warning he had received on 8 May. On that date he had been summoned (at the King's order), by the Earl of Wiltshire, to appear before the Privy Council. While there he was accused of 'deceitful dealing' and was cautioned officially that he was not to go too far in his condemnations, and not to interfere in English affairs. From that date he kept largely away from court, unless an appearance could not be avoided. However, he still spoke – and wrote to the Emperor – as if he knew everything, claiming to know far more than he did.

It was finally over. Not in Katherine's eyes, nor in the opinion of the Pope, the Emperor or any of the faithful Catholics watching the situation with dismay. But in Henry's eyes it was done. Cranmer had performed the task he had been summoned for, raised to high position for, and in Henry's opinion he was vindicated. His first marriage to Katherine of Aragon had never been valid, Crammer would see to it that his union with Anne was the only official one, and the child Anne was carrying would be sole heir.

Now Anne could be crowned to become worthy of bearing Henry's prince. The dissatisfaction of those who did not agree could not only be ignored but could eventually be eradicated. Henry and Anne were triumphant, and were busily engaged in preparing for the greatest show on earth.

* * *

The fuss surrounding the Coronation of Henry's new Queen was unprecedented. In a fairly short time, scores of people were mobilised, either as attendants or participants in the Holy Rite itself, or as artisans responsible for the constructions, decorations, feasts, clothing or bejewelling of those who were fortunate enough to be invited. Also the provision of horses, trappings, boats and barges, street decorations, triumphal arches and otherwise helping to make the great day not only happen, but be a success.

Anne was to be the last of Henry's tally of Queens Consort to have a Coronation and it needs to be remembered why he needed to make it so spectacular. Not only was he affirming his right to remarry, but emphasising his personal choice, which Anne's pregnancy, now in its fifth month, helped to confirm and justify. By her pregnancy, she had become something different, no longer the sweetheart. She was now the chalice, the holder of the Blood Royal, and with her safety and well-being went all the hopes for the future royal line.

That was the reason for his insistence on every royal privilege for Anne. To ensure that all who saw her were made aware that she was not only his Queen, but that the child she carried was a royal and legitimate one, and his heir.

Whit Sunday, 1 June 1533, was the date chosen. Despite Henry's concern for the child, he had planned a long and arduous trial for Anne. She would be required to be the centre of all eyes for days on end, without any sign of tiring. It was a substantial expectation for a pregnant woman who knew that not all the spectators were sympathetic towards her.

Henry had arranged a journey by water from Greenwich to the Tower of London 'to see the city ordered and garnished with pageants, in places accustomed, for the honour of Her Grace, when she should be conveyed from the Tower to Westminster'.

There were different levels of functionaries, nobles and lords appointed to serve; those taking part in processions and those who were to be knighted in honour of the occasion. They were led by Lord William Howard, who acted as Earl Marshal in place of his brother the Duke of Norfolk, who was away on embassy in France with George Boleyn. Charles Brandon, Duke of Suffolk, was appointed Constable for the Coronation. His wife, Princess Mary, the King's sister, was not present. Brandon had escorted her home to Westhorpe where she was to die on 25 June. For Suffolk it was more important to be present at the Coronation of the new Queen, to show support for Henry.

Lady Cobham was appointed as one of the attendant horsewomen to follow the Queen, but she had to provide white palfreys for herself and her own attendants. Although her robes for the occasion were to be supplied, she had to equip the ladies with her at her own expense, 'as unto honour and that solemnity appertaineth'.[15]

The full celebrations lasted four days. First, the Queen would be escorted by river to the Tower of London. Then the second day would be devoted to court rituals.

The third day was for a procession on horseback from the Tower, through the city, to Westminster itself.[16] The fourth and final day was for the actual Coronation ceremony, to be followed by feasting in Westminster Hall. It was the intention that the show be on an outstanding scale, with everything proclaiming joy and excitement. Various 'pageants', at specified points of the route, were paid for by foreign merchants, to show their appreciation.

The Spanish residents of the city could not be expected to make any demonstrations in favour of the new Queen, but there were plenty who would. Despite Chapuys' grumpy reporting of the events, there were hundreds of people who enjoyed the pleasure of turning out for a royal show, regardless of the participants. Although there would have been pockets of disaffection, most of the Londoners and visitors to the capital had a good time. They enjoyed the sight of the boats and barges, the pageants cleverly designed and made, the beautifully dressed court ladies and gentlemen and had a share of free wine. They cheered the Queen, smiling graciously from her barge or her litter and surrounded by pretty young ladies gaily dressed.

The water pageants were considered particularly good, and had been organised by the Lord Mayor of London, Christopher Ascue. He did Anne proud with the scale and originality of the delights on offer.

At about 1 o'clock on Thursday, 29 May, fifty barges of the London Livery Companies set off from a rendezvous at Billingsgate. They were followed by many smaller boats and were dressed overall with flags, bunting, gold foil which twinkled in the sunshine, and with numerous little bells, tinkling and chiming in the breeze. The boats were filled not only with notables, out in their best robes and chains, but also with musicians who were plucking at, or whistling through, every instrument that was small enough to be carried. There were also cannon on board, ready to give the loyal salutes. It is fair to assume that many of the vessels were grossly overcrowded and dangerous enough, without the addition of cannon, but nobody seemed to care. The Livery Companies' fleet was led by a wherry, upon which was a mechanical dragon. This was not only able to move its limbs, and presumably also its wings, but also to belch out flames.

There were several other models of monsters, along with men dressed as 'wildmen' who cheerfully threw blazing fireworks. It is just as well that all this inflammatory fun was on the water, in case anyone became over enthusiastic, as a few no doubt did.

Behind them came the Lord Mayor's own barge, with Christopher Ascue and his Aldermen and Councillors in their best scarlet robes. Following them came the 'bachelors' barge', hung with cloth of gold and silk, with two great banners showing Henry's arms and Anne's, with thirty-six shields along the side, painted with their two coats-of-arms impaled.

A further barge held a huge model of Anne's well-known badge of the white falcon, perching on a tree root (representing the Plantagenet line). This sprouted red and white roses (representing the new Tudor dynasty) and the huge bird stood proudly holding a sceptre and with its crown on its head, to show that Anne was now Queen. The whole edifice was surrounded by 'virgins singing and playing very sweetly'.

It took the procession 2 hours to reach Greenwich and in the afternoon Anne made her appearance, stepping into a 'sumptuously decorated' barge with her ladies. A second barge contained more court ladies, then came the King's barge, which was full of guards and musicians all 'in best array'. Further barges followed, all glittering and jangling in the sunlight.

Reports detailed 'banners and pennants of arms of their crafts, beaten of fine gold, reflecting against the sun, standards, streamers waving in the wind, trumpets blowing, shawms and minstrels playing ... a right sumptuous and triumphant sight to see, and hear, as they passed upon the water, to hear the marvellous sweet harmony of the instruments ...'.

Approaching the city, the salvoes were so many and so loud that the observers were unable to count them. It must have been deafening. As they came in sight of the Tower, the gunners 'loosed their ordinance, four at a time' and there was another burst of gunfire as Anne's barge pulled in to the steps of the landing stage.[17] There she was greeted by an official party before entering the Tower, where Henry was waiting.

Chapuys was to report that a sulky Anne had received a muted welcome, but the evidence shows otherwise. London was *en fête*, Henry was delighted and 'with many goodly words' thanked the citizens. Anne must have been stunned and bewildered by all the glitter and noise, but pleased, proud and grateful too. For a pregnant lady it was a tiring day, but there was more to come and Anne rose to the occasion, delighting in this great triumph for which she had waited so long.

He had even more reason than Anne to feel pleased with the way the first day had gone. Henry had just pulled off a clever move. It was not only a piece of theatre, but a manipulation of the Londoners, the playing off of one side against the other. The

146 Tudor Victims

Lords, the nobles, the Lord Mayor and Aldermen, the Livery Companies, were all out that day. They had spent large sums on honouring the new Queen. Therefore, naturally the common people would assume that all those important people, bending the knee, bowing and smiling, fully approved of all that the King had done. From the other side, the common people, dizzy with noise and excitement, delighting in a free show accompanied by food and wine, cheering and waving, were having a good time. It looked to the notables that the commons approved of the marriage, and the lovely, smiling, pregnant Queen. Each side took the apparent enthusiasm of the other as proof that the marriage to Anne, and her Coronation, was not only accepted but also in principle acceptable.

The few discontents could easily be discounted. Katherine still had her partisans, but a Coronation, like a royal wedding, draws people together, transcends boundaries, erases differences. It was a masterly act on Henry's part and it worked well. Only he could know what concerns there must have been, but the blinding, glittering, noisy, brilliant show did the trick. The new Queen was carried down river on a wave of enthusiasm and hope, and that potentially difficult first day was a great success.

Anne must have been glad to rest. Henry could not be expected to understand the swollen ankles, the headaches caused by noise, the nervous excitement and the sheer exhausion of a pregnant woman after a long day. But Anne, revelling in the triumph, had smiled, bowed and waved and he was proud of her. She had looked elegant and beautiful and she had carried his heir unflaggingly. But there must have been a rush to bring cushions, take off shoes and anxiously raise feet, when the ladies were finally alone.

These were the new rooms, upon which Cromwell had been working. Anne had a great chamber, and a room in which to eat privately. There was a new wooden walkway leading to a private garden for her pleasure and relaxation. She would spend 48 hours there with Henry, resting before the procession on the Saturday, which would complete her journey to Westminster Abbey.

While Anne rested, other things were taking place, unseen by the crowds of people milling outside. Eighteen Knights of the Bath were created in honour of the new Queen. The ceremonies attendant upon their elevation lasted from dinnertime on Friday to the Saturday morning and included an overnight vigil in the White Tower. This was a particular honour for Anne, as the creation of new knights was usually only in conjunction with the crowning of the sovereign, not a consort.

These knights included Sir Francis Weston, William Windsor, Henry Parker (brother-in-law to George Boleyn), the Earl of Derby (husband of Anne's aunt), Thomas Arundel (who was married to Anne's cousin), Henry Savile and Thomas Lord Darcy, among others. There were also Knights Bachelor and Wynkyn de Worde gives forty-six names of the gentlemen so honoured.[18] Cromwell was one of these, along with Henry Norris, William Brereton and the Earl of Derby. It was an impressive line-up of mainly Boleyn sympathisers.

Cromwell moved into position alongside the Boleyns at this stage. His agent, Stephen Vaughan, had been approached by Anne in the previous year as a link between those people interested in the new learning. Anne had already shown herself to be a champion of the free-thinkers and had already assisted Thomas Alway and Richard Lyst when they had fallen foul of the Observant Friars at Greenwich. She had also worked to obtain the release of one Thomas Patmore from Hadham in Hertfordshire. He had been imprisoned in the Lollard's Tower for two years, and once his plight was brought to her attention she spoke on his behalf to the King. Cromwell, of course, could see the immense benefits to be gained from aligning himself with the new seat of power, at least while the Queen had the King's ear.

Saturday, 31 May 1533 was a perfect day. The houses along Cheapside were hung with cloth of gold, velvet or tissue, shining in the sun and at Cornhill and Gracechurch Street there were hangings of red and gold, arras and tapestries. The procession was rather late in starting out, but it was designed to impress. The new French Ambassador, Jean de Dinteville, had decked out all his servants in yellow and blue, with white plumes in their hats. King Francis would later pay him the equivalent of £100 to reimburse his expenses for Anne's procession.

The gentlemen of the royal household followed in a procession over ½ mile long, and they in their turn were followed by the Judges, the Knights of the Bath, the council, the higher clergy and then the peers. Ambassadors from France and Venice, the Lord Mayor, Earl Marshal and Lord Constable of England (Charles Brandon, the King's brother-in-law) also took part. The Duchess of Norfolk had stayed away (understandably in view of the state of her marriage to Anne's uncle and the fact that her rival was now one of Anne's ladies), but she was an expected absentee and not missed.

Thomas More had been sent the sum of £20 with which to purchase himself a robe so that he could attend, but he refused. It was a foolish move, and one that was to lead him to the Tower within the year.[19] His intransigence would do nobody any good but would bring great harm to himself and to his family. However, a man who is a martyr born is not likely to consider the feelings of anyone else while he makes his journey to doom.

Finally, behind all the long, winding, colourful, glittering lines of courtiers, officials and nobles, came Anne herself. She was riding in a litter of white satin, decked out with 'white cloth of gold' both inside and out. The two white palfreys supporting it were also covered with white, this time in damask. Anne also wore white, with a gold coronet on her dark hair, which hung loose, flowing to her waist. The Barons of the Cinque Ports carried a cloth of gold canopy. Her riding palfrey followed, with twelve ladies dressed in crimson velvet also on palfreys.

Two carriages held older ladies of the household, then more riders, more carriages and thirty gentlewomen in black velvet, all on horseback. The King's guards followed them, wearing new coats of goldsmith's work and the servants came last, all finely decked out in the liveries of their families.

The *Cronico del Rey Enrico* was dismissive in the extreme, although its content was generally vehemently anti-English and consisted of rumours and falsifications rather than facts.[20] The Venetian Ambassador, who was the most sensible and most reliable of the foreign witnesses, remarked not only upon the magnificence of the show, but also on the 'Utmost order and tranquility' of the day as a whole.[21]

Holbein had designed the arch and pageant for the Hanse Steelyard, from which Anne's praises were sung. Reformers such as Nicholas Udall and John Leland were also effusive in their verses, written for the occasion.

Again, Chapuys reported lacklustre celebrations, played out before largely resentful and silent crowds, but that is simply untrue. Probably to his disgust, London greeted everything with pleasure. What Chapuys disliked most, and could never admit, was that many Londoners were tired of the restrictive religious policy of men like Thomas More, with its arrests and executions of people who merely wanted to enquire about new ways.

Ideas were changing, and a large number of people were eager to explore, and embrace them, particularly after seeing the prosperity of the merchants of the Low Countries, and hearing something of their beliefs. Old ways still held firm in the north, and indeed in most isolated corners of the country, but London had always prided itself on being up to date, on its forwardness and modernity, and a large number of people now realised that the old way was not the only way.

Queen Anne Boleyn, second wife of Henry VIII from 1533–6.

The really big day was, of course, still to come. Sunday, 1 June 1533, Whit Sunday, would be the most stressful and tiring day of all for Anne. The procession began to assemble at 7 a.m. and Anne joined them just before 9 a.m.[22] She was to walk along a railed route, which had been fully carpeted in blue cloth, all the way from the Hall to the Abbey at Westminster. Everyone of any importance was there, wearing best robes, gold chains, even borrowed jewels. Nobles, Lords, Archbishops, Bishops, the Lord Mayor and Aldermen, the Judges and the monks and staff of the Chapel Royal.

Anne wore robes of purple velvet, furred with ermine; the gold coronet on her head and the gold canopy borne over her. Her hair was loose, and her very long and very heavy velvet train was carried by the Dowager Duchess of Norfolk, who was followed by the ladies and gentlewomen, all dressed in scarlet.

The King was to watch the entire ceremony from a specially erected stand behind a screen, to make sure that Anne's great day was hers alone. He was attended by the Ambassadors of France and Venice. Cranmer officiated and Anne performed the ritual and listened to the High Mass with dignity. She was anointed and then crowned with St Edward's Crown, which was later exchanged for a lighter one when she took the sacrament and made her offerings.[23] That was another singular honour for her, for a consort usually only wears the lighter crown. After a short break for a rest, the procession wound slowly back to Westminster Hall, past five cisterns spouting free wine for anyone to help themselves.

After a further rest, there was the final ordeal of the great banquet to get through. Anne must have already been exhausted, but one can imagine her rallying her strength for the climax of it all. She would be the centre of all eyes, almost alone on the dais, which was twelve steps higher than the tables of the throng who dined with her. Anne sat alone under the Cloth of Estate, with Cranmer sitting to her right, but at a distance and not under the Cloth. The new Earl of Oxford stood almost behind her with the widowed Countess of Oxford on her right and the Countess of Worcester on her left.

Two ladies of her household crouched on the steps at her feet, ready to do her service in case of need.

Looking down onto the hall, she would have seen the four tables, each 24ft long. On the one to her left sat the Lord Mayor, city officials, Aldermen and several merchants. The next table, almost in the centre, held her ladies, including Jane Rochford, her sister-in-law, with her mother, Lady Morley. Anne's mother, Lady Wiltshire, and her sister, Mary Carey, were with the others. Slightly to her right the long table held Lord Morley, with his son, Anne's father, Lord Wiltshire, the Knights of the Bath and other notable lords and friends of Henry. The table to Anne's extreme right seated the Judges, leading churchmen including Archbishop Lee, Bishop Gardiner and other eminent clerics and lawyers.

On that day 800 people were fed at Westminster Hall, and the number of courses makes one blanch. Despite all the grandeur of the crowds around her, Anne may have missed having George present to exchange a smile with. However, Henry had certainly done his best to please and honour her. Even the marble chair in which she sat, which was in the highest place in the Hall, had been made more comfortable by the addition of a padded inner chair, to ease her back. Henry again watched everything from a specially built box, along with the French and Venetian Ambassadors.

The Duke of Suffolk performed the duty of High Steward, wearing a doublet and jacket dripping with pearls and riding a horse trapped in crimson velvet. Also on horseback, and in crimson, was Lord William Howard. His horse's purple velvet was embroidered with the Howard white lion. These horsemen escorted a first course of twenty-eight dishes carried in by the Knights of the Bath. Thomas Wyatt performed the service of Chief Ewerer for Anne, pouring the water for her to wash her hands.

The second course of the meal consisted of twenty-four dishes and the third of thirty. Each came in accompanied by the horsemen, trumpets and minstrels. The Lord Mayor's table had two courses of thirty-two dishes each course. As well as the actual food to be eaten, there were many 'subleties' and devices, including great ships made of wax which were particularly admired. By the end of the meal Anne must have been grateful for the ladies 'sitting at her feet' and also for the presence of the Countess of Worcester and the Dowager Countess of Oxford. Those ladies held a cloth, raised up to cover her face whenever she needed a moment of privacy. She was on show for over 9 hours that day, quite an ordeal for any lady in the middle of a pregnancy. If she felt ill, if the heat and the smells of food and burning candles made her feel sick or the noise of chattering and shouting voices, the clattering of horses and dishes and the sounding of the trumpets gave her a throbbing headache, she did not show it. Everyone knelt to Anne as she finally rose to leave the hall, and she smiled and said, 'I thank you all for the great honour ye have done me this day.' She gave Christopher Ascue, the Lord Mayor, a gold cup, as a commemorative gift.

Although the banquet officially ended the ceremonies, Henry was loathe to finish. After all, he too had waited years for this, and did not want the celebrations to end. On Monday, 2 June the day was devoted to jousting, dancing and another 'goodly banquet', this time in the Queen's chamber.

The 'great jousts' must have been the first ones to be held in the new tiltyard, which was opposite the entrance to the Palace of Whitehall. The public was admitted to enjoy the day but the new tilt, or central barrier, did not seem to be a success, as many of the horses veered away from it, rather than keeping in line, and did not seem to be controllable. Nicholas Carewe was blamed for this, as he was a known enemy of Anne's, but it is hardly likely that he would do anything guaranteed to provoke the King's anger on such a day.

Anne issued her own medal to commemorate her Coronation. It shows her wearing the gabled English-style headdress and wide sleeves, with the inscription referring to her as 'the Moost Happy'. She had good reason to feel happy, for she had achieved what no other woman would have even dared to attempt. There were plenty of women at court, some of them more physically attractive than Anne herself, yet in her presence they tended to fade. She cannot have been merely 'that foolish girl about the court', as Cardinal Wolsey had once dismissively referred to her. Even he had eventually been obliged to alter his opinions.

The celebrations gradually began to wind down and Anne's Chamberlain wrote to her brother, still in France, to report that 'pastime in the Queen's chamber is never more. If any of you that be now departed have any ladies they thought favoured you, and would mourn at the passing of their servants, I can no whit perceive the same, by the dancing and pastime they do use here.'[24]

Even the death of the King's sister, Princess Mary, Duchess of Suffolk, did nothing to put a damper on the general feeling of euphoria. On 28 June Anne received a wedding gift from King Francis, a magnificent litter with three mules to carry it. It had been sent to Anne at Greenwich via her brother, George. Delighted with the gift, Anne immediately went out and travelled 3 miles in it.[25]

It was good that she so thoroughly enjoyed the period of pleasure around her Coronation. She had the coming months to get through, when she would become more unwieldy and less able to make merry. She had come through so many difficulties, she was married to the King, crowned Queen and carrying the heir. All she needed to do for the rest of her time was relax, both in body and mind, let nature take its course. She had achieved everything and the coming period of time was for waiting, and for making those essential preparations for the birth of the child whose appearance would both crown and confirm it all.

She knew that Henry was expecting a son. He had already listened to, and believed, those people who claimed to be able to tell the sex of unborn children. All were in agreement that it would be a boy.[26] Did Anne have any doubts? Did she fear the outcome? Or, carried along on a wave of optimism, did she, too, simply trust that all would be well?

She could not then know that, in the glorious and triumphant summer of 1533, she had already reached, and passed, the pinnacle of her personal achievements.

Chapter Twelve

The Coronation was the greatest triumph of Anne's life. Nothing would ever compare with that special occasion which had paid for all the agony of waiting. After it was over she could hope to concentrate on the approaching birth. The King was naturally concerned that she should rest, that nothing would be allowed to disturb her peace, cause her any anxiety or provoke the famous temper. Such upheavals were widely believed to be detrimental to the expected child.

But the outside world was impossible to shut out entirely. Not everyone was sympathetic towards the new Queen's need for rest during her gestation, or prepared to let the matter rest.

The Duke of Norfolk was at Lyons on 11 July when he heard that the Pope had finally made a move after so many ineffectual letters. He had excommunicated Henry, and not the King alone, but Cranmer, the new Archbishop of Canterbury, along with him. It was said that he had 'cursed the four Bishops of England, the which have been the cause of the King's Grace's marriage'. The other three referred to were Gardiner, Lee (of York) and Longland (of Lincoln).[1]

Any person whose ideas tended towards the 'new thinking', as Anne's did, might be expected to receive such news with equanimity, but that did not apply to Norfolk. He was still a devout Catholic and to him, and others like him, such news from the Vatican was devastating. It is reported that when he heard it he fainted. As soon as he was able, he sent George Boleyn back to England to break the terrible news to the King. Perhaps also to bear the first brunt of Henry's wrath, but Henry immediately ordered Norfolk's return.

The Pope had sent 'terms' along with the news of excommunication. These terms stated that Henry had until September of that year, during which to cast off Anne and reinstate Katherine. With Anne finally wed, crowned and pregnant, it was an impossible demand. Whatever Henry may have felt about the blow from Rome, he had to brazen it out. He could hardly have expected the Pope's reaction to be less, but after so long and so many placating letters, it must still have come as a shock.

Far worse than loss of the Pope's favour was the implication that Henry's loyal Catholic subjects, still in the majority, would be shaken by the news. It would have the effect of dividing their loyalties. Henry could not afford to show concern. He must behave as if the matter was nothing and that such a break from the Papacy was his intention all along, he already taken the first steps towards just such an eventuality. His defence towards the news was to reassure those around him, particularly Anne, that there was no cause for concern.

Also in that July, Lord Mountjoy sent to Cromwell a reminder list of all that would be required for Queen Anne's lying-in. Henry, to reinforce his authority in defiance of that blast from Rome, sent instructions to Katherine that he wanted the christening robe that had been worn by the Princess Mary. As he might have expected, Katherine not only refused outright, but also insisted that her household would continue to address her as Queen, irrespective of whatever title her husband chose for her.[2]

Preparations for the birth of the new heir went ahead. These were made according to the rules laid out by Lady Margaret Beaufort for the household of Queen Elizabeth of York, Henry's mother. However, at the end of August Anne was still at Westminster with Henry, and did not travel to Greenwich to begin her confinement until the 26th of that month. It was usual for a queen to 'take her chamber' a full month before the expected birth. She would not be expected to re-emerge until approximately six weeks after the birth, when she would be 'churched' or underwent the blessing ceremony that was intended to remove the 'stain' of childbirth.

This was the origin of the term 'confinement' when alluding to giving birth, which is still sometimes used, although the modern woman does not live in seclusion. The actual period of time varied, royal women changed the rules to suit themselves. Even Katherine of Aragon's mother, Queen Isabella of Castile, was loath to waste her time on such seclusion. When Katherine was born her mother was engaged with war against the Moors, and her time could not be squandered. In any case, being imprisoned in a set of stuffy rooms, at the tail end of a hot summer, was hardly Anne's idea of pleasure. Even in her eagerness to show herself worthy of her new position, there were limits beyond which an active person would not wish to go.

The rooms had been prepared to receive her in the accepted manner, and however pleasant Greenwich might normally be, with the river air and the sunshine at its windows, Anne would be about to forgo it. The rooms were tapestried, with all windows but one covered over to keep out evil odours, as well as fresh air. The large bed was a hot and uncomfortable tent of heavy drapery and other couches had been added for the ladies in attendance and the midwife herself, which would successfully exclude the slightest privacy. The delivery would take place on a separate couch, often at the foot of the 'official' bed, or sometimes on an actual birthing chair, and there would be an altar in the room for the necessary prayers.

The Queen would be escorted to the door of her chamber, where prayers for her safe delivery were said and blessings given. She would then be handed over to the women of the household and all the men, including her husband, would retire from her life until it was over. The prayers were not ceremony for its own sake. For women childbirth was just as dangerous as battle was for their husbands. Many men had several wives over their lives, as the dangers of parturition took their toll. Henry had ordered special prayers for Anne's safety and fruitful delivery, which would be repeated in all churches. However, he was too impatient to stand about waiting for the result. He went off hunting.

True to form, Chapuys took the opportunity to claim that Henry had already allowed his eye to wander towards other women. He stated that when Anne had protested at this, she had been roughly told to 'shut her eyes, as her betters had before her!'. This ludicrous story has been picked up and regurgitated too many times. It is known that Chapuys could not be relied upon for veracity at his best, and Anne's success put him at his worst, prompting him to spout venom with no attempt to verify his accusations. Only the previous year he had claimed that Henry had already abandoned Anne, which was nonsense.[3] Any idea that Henry would be foolish enough to cause her anxiety, when she appeared about to justify everything, is too ridiculous to be seriously considered.

Henry was extremely concerned about Anne's welfare, and made every effort to show her honour as the mother of the expected child. Chapuys, living on the periphery of court life, after his warning, was obliged to send in his reports and was frequently driven to compile accounts combining half-truths and sheer fantasy. He was so rarely at court that he must have been desperate to find enough scandal to justify sending in reports at all.

Henry's escape from the stifling atmosphere was far from unusual. So long as all the preparations were well in hand, there was little he, or any other man, could do but wait with as much patience as he could manage.

He did not have to wait for long. On Sunday, 7 September 'between three and foure of the clock at afternoon, the Quene was delivered of a fair Laidie, for whose good deliverance Te Deum was sung incontinently and great preparation was made for the Christening'.[4]

All had gone smoothly enough and Anne was sufficiently recovered to write personally to Lord Cobham, on that day, to record her thanks for the 'good speed in the deliverance and bringing forth' of the child.

There must have been disappointment at the child's sex. It would be futile to pretend otherwise. Both Henry and Anne had allowed themselves to become keyed up at the idea of the child being a boy. It would have been so fitting, would have rounded everything off perfectly. But life is rarely perfect and things rarely go entirely as hoped. Although mother and child were doing well, and Anne and Henry put a cheerful face on the matter, it must have been a huge disappointment for them. Henry would appear to be no better off than before, and Anne's opponents would be pleased.

However, it was not all gloom. Anne had conceived quickly, had carried her child without problems and borne it without danger. The baby girl was enough to warm any father's heart and Henry was susceptible to small children. The child would have her mother's pointed face and dark eyes, topped by a cap of true Tudor-coloured hair. More importantly, she was healthy and that was something to be thankful for. The lusty child was a promise for the future and Henry would accept her as such.

The jousts and tournaments were cancelled. But they had been when Princess Mary was born back in 1516, so too much must not be read into this. Henry saw the girl child as a forerunner for a brother. There would be enough people delighted that the child was the 'wrong' sex, without the father giving them more fuel for speculation.

The King did what he could. He visited Anne to reassure her of his devotion and pleasure and admired the baby. He may have been satisfied by the vivid colour of her hair, so obviously his child. He ignored the people who were inclined to gloat, and he arranged a very splendid christening for his new daughter, referring to her as his heir. In the meantime, nobody would be allowed to believe that he regretted the choices he had made.

A Herald immediately proclaimed the child the first of the King's 'legitimate' children and the *Te Deum* was sung by the Chapel Royal of St Paul's. Letters announcing the birth of the Princess were sent out in the usual way and the date of the Christening was set for Wednesday, 10 September, after which there would be bonfires of celebration, accompanied by free wine with which to toast the child's health.

Edward Hall was to describe the ceremony in the most lavish terms; starting with a procession from the Great Hall at Greenwich, to the Church of the Observant Friars, along a carpet of green rushes, between arras hangings and with an escort of over 500 lighted torches. The French Ambassador was the guest of honour, and he noted that 'the whole occasion was so perfect that nothing was lacking'.[5]

The Marquess of Exeter carried a taper of virgin wax, while the Duke of Suffolk escorted the baby and John, Lord Hussey, helped to carry the canopy. The Marchioness of Exeter was one of the godmothers. If those supporters of Katherine felt less than joyful taking part, feelings would have been exacerbated by the necessity of offering a costly gift. There were plenty of Boleyn and Howard relatives present too.

Among twenty-one participants Hall mentioned as being present, there were eight Howard connections along with Anne's father, the Earl of Wiltshire, and her brother, Lord Rochford. Cranmer was the child's godfather, and a friend of William Brereton was present, along with John Dudley, who was a friend of Cromwell's. Thomas Cromwell was there in person, and was quite likely to have been one of the organisers.

For Anne it would have been pleasant. Her child was being christened with the ceremony of a Princess of England. Anne did not attend. It was customary for the mother to wait in her bedchamber, where the child would be brought when the ceremony was finished. After that, gifts would be offered.

All the deference shown to her and her child would be gratifying, but Anne was not stupid. However grand the ceremonies were, however well Henry was taking it, she knew that the birth of a daughter was not enough. It was not what he had married and honoured her for. However loved this child would prove to be, she was keeping the cradle warm for her brother. Until then, Katherine's many supporters could claim that she had achieved nothing special. Anne knew that she would have to recover her strength quickly, and make sure that she conceived again as soon as possible.

She also knew that any apparent failure in that direction would be laid squarely at her door. A man like Henry, with his image of himself, could never admit that any lack of a male child could be his own fault. It did not take much to realise that Henry's record as a breeder could have been better. He was not in the league of Francis I. Of the women known, or suspected, of having been his mistresses (and there were several) there are very few leads towards putative offspring from these liaisons. Henry of Richmond is, of course, the one firm example, but where are the others?

We know that the King frequently used his friends as panders and that they arranged assignations for him with the wives of other court gentlemen. It is also obvious that offspring resulting from those transient relationships would generally be accepted as the offspring of the woman's husband. It was one good reason for a man to associate only with married ladies. Everyone knew how to behave. But, except for the children of Mary Carey (both of which have been suggested as the offspring of the King), there were few others who could lay claim to a strain of royal blood.

At this distance in time, such evidence can only be circumstantial, and there will be those ready to spring to the King's defence. Katherine came from a line rich in daughters and poor in living sons, but conceiving was not a problem.[6] She conceived regularly during her fertile years. She conceived enough times to have filled the royal nursery twice over, if all her pregnancies had resulted in a healthy child.

Anne would have reason to regret those wasted waiting years, which had tipped her over into her early thirties before her first child was born. Although Anne had produced Elizabeth with apparent ease, there was always the problem of infection, introduced during parturition, having a deleterious effect on any future pregnancy. It was known to be a dangerous business, and not every woman who attempted to bear a child in her thirties survived, even if she had successfully produced children.[7]

Despite Anne's successful first attempt, she would now need to produce another child which must be a boy. It might be interesting to inform those men who have made the life of some woman miserable for failing to produce a son, that they were responsible for the sex of the child. For Anne, and thousands of other women who would suffer, such knowledge would come too late.

Henry's record as a sire was not good enough to ensure that his wife could conceive easily. Did he ever think that the fault might lie with him? Perhaps, deep down, he may have been aware that there was a problem, which would not be unusual reaching middle age, but which he could never admit. Increasing age, and increasing girth, would add to the problem Anne faced over the next couple of years.

Before Anne had taken to her chamber, a report had been made to Cromwell by one Brother Lawrence, who was a lay friar at Greenwich and one of Cromwell's part-time spies. Lawrence had reported that he had been watching two of the Observant Friars who were supposed to be in England on behalf of one Friar Peto to collect books for him. Friar Peto was unable to collect them himself because he had recently fled to Flanders after writing some inflammatory nonsense regarding the King's divorce.

These two Friars had visited Katherine at Buckden. Their arrest and questioning was ordered, when they were back in London. But this was not the only report Friar Lawrence was to pass on, and his second revelation was far more damaging.

His main concern was with regard to Elizabeth Barton, who was a nun and known as the 'Holy Maid of Kent'. She had already made a name for herself by claiming visions during fits and hallucinations, and many people had been impressed by her apparent sanctity. Unfortunately, her opinions were at odds with those of the King, and she was hostile to his divorce from Katherine and his marriage to Anne. She had gone so far as to make foolish prophecies regarding the deaths of Henry and Anne. Cranmer had already been in touch with her and 'with his consummate talent for dissembling' had managed to convince her of his belief in her.[8]

Cromwell had sent Cranmer a list of questions to put to her, regarding her predictions, and she walked into the trap set for her. She was arrested and sent to London, where several other persons, clergy and gentlefolk, were to find themselves dangerously embroiled. These people had their papers seized, and had to face the examinations of Cromwell's agents. The list of those involved soon became long and impressive. It was to include the names of Sir Thomas More, Bishop Fisher of Rochester, the Marchioness of Exeter, the Countesses of Derby and Salisbury, and Lord and Lady Hussey, among others. Many of these people were in close contact with the court and yet showed strong sympathies towards Katherine.

Katherine was to deny that she had ever had any contact with Elizabeth Barton and Cromwell had to admit that there was no evidence to implicate her.

It seemed at first to have been little more than the ravings of a demented woman, a few disaffected people had been foolish to believe in. Barton was made to stand at Paul's Cross and read out a confession. She had to listen to a sermon detailing her faults, then returned to her prison. Cranmer was in favour of sterner measures being taken, and Cromwell created an opportunity to frighten the people whose names appeared on his list, letting them believe they stood in danger.

The Bishop of Winchester was in France, where he hoped to meet the Pope, not arriving until 11 October. Clement was to refuse Henry's request that the sentence of excommunication made against him should be revoked, on the grounds that the acts of the cause were still in Rome. Gardiner informed Henry that he was likely to be disappointed in his hopes of a cancellation of the sentence. Shortly after, on 20 October, a disputation was held at the lodging of Cardinal Duprat, Chancellor of France. The Cardinal complained that although Anne's marriage had been annulled, and her newly born child declared illegitimate by the Pope, she had not actually been made to answer to the charges against her. He said that she should be given the opportunity to defend herself. There was then a long discussion over whether Anne should be cited or not.

Henry had caused to be drawn up a deed by which he agreed to the case being reheard at Avignon, in front of special Legates, and the Pope seemed to go along with that. On condition, of course, that Henry should submit himself entirely to the Pope's authority and accept as final any judgement that Clement might make. Gardiner declared that he could not bind his King to such conditions and did not have full powers to do so, which made Francis angrily claim that the King of England had duped them.

Shortly afterwards, the marriage between the Pope's niece, Catherine de' Medici, and the King of France's second son, Henri, which had been the purpose of Clement's visit, was celebrated (on 27 October). There was no further reference made to the King of England, who had originally hoped to prevent it, fearing closer alliance between the Papacy and France.

By 25 October Henry was in receipt of Gardiner's letter of the 17th, which reported Clement's refusal of Henry's suggestions.[9] Henry was furious and made no effort to hide his feelings, declaring that he had been betrayed and that the King of France was not the friend he had thought. He continued to rail against the Pope and was for some time unable to calm himself. There were many witnesses to his anger who were pleased at the rupture between Francis and Henry. Cromwell was particularly glad that there was no arrangement with France, and no subservience to Rome.

Anne had become very concerned at what Henry was trying to do. The idea of the divorce from Katherine being reopened, with all its implications affecting the validity of her marriage and legitimacy of her child, was anathema. It is easy to understand her alarm when the King, after the ceremonial of crowning and the birth of her child, should ludicrously appear to be prepared to discuss the matter with the Pope. It was obvious that any such attempt to get the Pope's approval for any of his actions would involve Henry in accepting the supremacy of the Papacy.

Henry's actions at this time appear very confused. Why was he attempting to re-negotiate with the Pope at all? He appeared to be preparing to backpedal over what he had done, seeking approval from the authority he wished to usurp. Was it that he was beginning to fear a Catholic backlash in England? That would be natural enough, but it was not like Henry to show his insecurity so blatantly. Did he suddenly have doubts about his own invicibility, due to the birth of a daughter instead of the son he had confidently expected?

We can never know the feelings of any individual, but Anne, who may until then have thought she knew him, must have felt a chilling sense of betrayal at the time when she needed his support. Cranmer too must have been dismayed at Henry's move. He had been brought to England for the establishment of Henry's rival church, giving up his own life, and his marriage, only to find that its founder appeared to be changing his mind.

As it was to turn out, Henry had gone too far for any regrets. There was no longer any common ground between his policies and the Papacy. If he had felt doubts created by the precarious position into which he had put himself, he would have to live with them, without the safety net of the Church he had spurned. Agreeing to acknowledge the authority of the Pope was too much for him to accept. After a period of angry blustering he reverted to his original stance and the spectre of Katherine's re-emergence faded into the background.

Cromwell and Anne, each for their own reasons panicked by his changeability, combined to prevent him from considering the matter further, and by the time the courier arrived on 1 November 1533 Henry was again in defiant mood. His instruction to his ambassadors was that they refuse the Pope's suggested concessions, and make appeal against the proposed council.[10] Once his reply was received by his agents in France, they were loath to submit the dispatch, despite its urgency. They knew that it would be easily construed as an insult to both King Francis and to Pope Clement. Francis declared:

> Your King thinks himself a wise man, but he is simply a fool! He is working for the interests of the Queen, for by this appeal he admits that he knows of the sentence of 11th July, yet he disregards it. Let him know that if, in consequence of his behaviour, he is excommunicated, I declare that I shall not assist him against the Pope.[11]

Eventually, on the 7th, Dr Bonner went to see the Pope in person, taking with him Girolamo Penizzoni as a witness. When Clement read the letters he spoke bitterly of Henry's disrespect and ingratitude.[12] He also spoke angrily of King Francis, stating that he should forsake any alliance with the King of England, and unite instead with the Holy See. Despite Francis' obvious annoyance with Henry, he was reluctant to have an open breach with him, and the Pope finally offered him Calais as a bribe to turn him against Henry. Francis was to engage in a quarrel with the English ambassadors, declaring, 'as fast as I study to win the Pope, you study to lose him …'. The Pope was so incensed by Henry's attitude that he did not attempt to extend his stay in France, choosing to leave on 12 November. The matter of Clement's proposal to Francis, regarding Calais, was to go no further, as Francis, on reflection, saw no point in abandoning Henry. The Spanish considered that Calais was probably better off in the hands of the English, than it would be if controlled by the French.

The French Ambassador in England, de Dinteville, was about to be replaced by de Castillon and he took the opportunity offered by his imminent withdrawal to speak plainly. The King was ready for him and hardly gave him an opportunity to speak, breaking into recriminations rather than listening to what he had to say. Henry accused France of double-dealing and spoke with such impudence that de Dinteville was amazed. The Duke of Norfolk was shocked by Henry's behaviour towards an ambassador and spoke later to de Dinteville, when he admitted that what Henry said did not always tend to be the truth.[13]

While the upheavals in France were infuriating Henry and causing concern for Anne and Cromwell, matters in England could not described as placid. To counteract any future difficulties, it was appropriate to enforce Henry's spiritual supremacy. This took the form of the Declaration, which claimed that Convocation had declared Henry and Anne's marriage to be lawful, and the Princess Elizabeth to be the King's only legitimate heir. The nobles and higher clergy were to sign it, and recusants were threatened with the King's extreme anger and put in fear of their lives. There was some attempt made to persuade Princess Mary to renounce her rights, but this she had stoutly refused.[14]

The Princess Elizabeth had been moved to Hatfield by the end of 1533. This establishment of a separate household was normal practice for royal children. The new household was to be governed by Lady Shelton, Anne's aunt, who was the sister of Thomas Boleyn.

Hatfield Palace was the nursery of choice and the King's elder daughter was informed that she would join Princess Elizabeth's household there. This reduced Mary in stature, as a sign to those who considered her the true heir. Lady Shelton was charged with the care of Elizabeth, but also with reducing the obstinacy of Princess Mary, as Henry was determined to make her defer to his authority.

This was all the more important as Queen Anne had conceived again. The King and Queen, greatly relieved at the swift second pregnancy, were praying for a son. Anne's condition had reassured Henry and given him a new burst of confidence. He knew that Mary looked to the Emperor for support and at Christmas 1533 he had used threatening language towards the Marquess of Exeter on the matter. He had said that she would submit to him, for he feared neither the Emperor nor anybody else. He went on to say loudly that all those people who played him false would pay for it with the loss of their heads.

After hearing complaints from Anne regarding reports of Mary's behaviour at Hatfield, Henry gave orders that she should be more closely guarded and both the Duke of Norfolk and George, Lord Rochford upbraided Lady Shelton for being too lenient towards Mary. Lady Shelton was ordered to treat her more severely to remind her of her bastard status.

Mary's stubbornness and refusal to co-operate had progressed to refusing to dine with the household. She had begun taking her meals in her room, costing Henry an extra 10*s*. each week. This was a considerable sum, which was resented.[15] Mary's attitude was upheld by letters from her mother, who assured her all would be well if she obeyed her father in everything, except assaults on her conscience.

It is understandable that a teenage girl who had seen her secure family life overturned by her father's infatuation for a younger woman should feel resentful. Henry should have expected resistance, but totally lacking any understanding, he took it as an opportunity to show everyone that he intended to be firm. It is to Mary's credit that she did not then blame Elizabeth for the situation, and was able to form a bond with the child.

Elizabeth Barton, the Holy Maid of Kent, had been defended against censure by a book written by a friar named Dering, who had been imprisoned. Cromwell began to make new arrests, and a Bill of Attainder was framed against Barton, accusing her and her main supporters of High Treason or Misprision of Treason. This, at its simplest, referred to anyone hiding, or not reporting, any relevant information about a possible act of treason being accused of being traitors.

This charge could affect anyone who had had any contact with Barton. This caused a anxiety at court, as people often consulted 'holy' persons for advice. In this way Henry was able to push through his Bills of Succession. He bridled opposition by creating an atmosphere of fear in those likely to have listened to the Holy Maid's pronouncements.[16]

The Act of Attainder against Elizabeth Barton was to condemn a total of seven people to death. Elizabeth Barton, her spiritual advisor, Dr Edward Bocking, John Dering, who had written on her behalf, two Observant Franciscans (Hugh Priest and Richard Risby) and two secular priests (Henry Gold and Richard Master).

Their executions took place on 20 April 1534. A letter from John Hussey the Younger to Lord Lisle, written on that day, gives the details: 'This day the Nun of Kent, with two Friars Observant, two monks, and a secular priest were drawn from the Tower to Tyburn and were there hanged and headed.'

Another chronicle, by Londoner Richard Hill, says: 'The Holy Maid of Kent, called Elizabeth Barton, was drawn on a hurdle along to Tyburn, and there hanged and headed ... all the heads were set on London Bridge and on the Gates of London'.

These executions were carefully timed to 'encourage acquiescence' in the Oath to the Succession, the Oath being administered to the citizens of London on the day of the Holy Maid's public execution.[17]

Also in April 1534 Bishop John Fisher and Sir Thomas More were arrested and sent to the Tower. Like other Catholics of standing, they had communicated with Barton, but the reason for their arrest was their refusal to sign the Oath. This time there was to be no escape and Henry was prepared to make an example of men whose fame was widespread. He showed England, and the world, that he expected loyalty from his subjects, irrespective of their standing. Nobody would be exempt from obeying him.

By early in 1534 Anne's pregnancy was obvious and appeared to be progressing well. Henry showed his pleasure by ordering a very elaborate silver cradle for the coming child, from his goldsmith Cornelius Hayes. It was ornamented with Tudor roses and precious stones and was accompanied by gold-embroidered bedlinen and a set of cloth-of-gold clothing for the infant.[18]

The happy expectations continued throughout spring and into summer. All was to end tragically in July, when Anne miscarried.[19] Chapuys did not report it until 23 September but he had been out of touch with the court and the miscarriage had been kept quiet following the loss of the child. It must have been a shattering blow for Anne after so promising a start, and a huge disappointment for Henry, so certain that all was well.

There had been no obvious reason for it. Anne was not suffering the level of stress that she would experience later. She had had a triumphant start to her queenship and had produced a healthy child and conceived again within three months. All families suffered such losses, but in Anne's position, with Katherine's record of maternity as a guide how not to do it, she would have been worried.

In the light of later events, it would seem Henry was even more worried. The birth of another girl child might be considered no more than a delay in the production of the boy he had been reassured of by the quick second pregnancy. Now it wasn't well, and he was aware of the list of miscarriages he had lived through with Katherine.

There had been some incidents of nastiness directed against Anne. One of these was calculated to upset and distress a pregnant woman. This had concerned her favourite lapdog, Purkoy, which had been a successful gift from Lady Lisle and had been delivered into Anne's hands by Sir Francis Bryan.

That favourite pet had been killed after 'falling from a window' which seems to be unlikely to happen to a small dog in the normal course of events, with the small window openings at the time. Anne was so fond of the animal that nobody dared tell her of his fatal 'accident'. Henry took that duty himself, dealing with the resulting shock, disbelief and grief.

Chapuys was, a short time later, to make a malicious joke about certain surprised courtiers 'looking as shocked as dogs falling out of a window' which suggests that the poor animal's demise was not an accident, and that he and others were fully aware of it. It was a deliberate act of cruelty on the part of someone wishing to hurt the Queen, and distress her enough to have a miscarriage. It was unfortunately successful.[20]

There is reason to believe that from this miscarriage, in the summer of 1534, there was a slight change in Henry's feelings towards Anne. He would not, at that point, have allowed anyone to suspect that he had regrets, or had made a mistake. He would never want Katherine back, so what was he to do? He could not put himself in the wrong by another divorce so soon, but there was, from that point, the earliest appearance of dissatisfaction.

There were also signs of a flirtation. This was reported by Chapuys. Jane Rochford had been forbidden the court, for taking sides in the quarrel. The attractive Margaret (Madge) Shelton, Anne's cousin, had recently entered court service. Had Henry been guilty of a little too much admiration towards the newcomer? It would never have happened in the old days, when his thoughts had been entirely centred on Anne.

In the old days Anne had been the sweetheart. Now she was the wife. With many men the promotion of sweetheart to wife means a vacancy for another sweetheart. Henry was romantically inclined and many young women would be flattered by attention from him. Anne was younger and more attractive than the previous Queen, but she was the official consort, and it was natural, to him, to look around for some pretty young thing to pay compliments to.

All would depend how Anne handled the matter. The relationship between her and Henry had been one of sexual attraction, unusual in royal marriages, so she had some advantage.

Their partnership had been kept fresh by the 'sunshine and shadow' of her changeable temperament. But now stresses were greater. Not only was there a wife in the background, stubbornly insisting upon her rights, but there were many people who did not consider Anne to be the rightful Queen. Any one of them might take a chance to push forward a pretty daughter and profit by Anne's example. Whether or not people actually liked Anne personally – and those who served her intimately grew very fond of her – it was what she represented that counted.

There were still many people also who did not appreciate that Henry meant what he said. It was too easy for what Anne represented to become stained with the blood

Henry shed in his quest for dominance over every aspect of English life. This would rob Anne of the opportunity to be given the benefit of the doubt, or any credit for her genuine attempts to become a charitable Queen, separate from what became Henry's bloodthirsty rampage. Her short tenure of the throne would be defined by whether she bore a male child.

Anne did try, and as she was neither a fool nor a wanton she was able to succeed on a personal level. She intended her household to be 'merry' with music and dancing, without becoming loose. She wanted to establish a respectable, even learned, court. She proved to be quite a strict mistress, keeping her ladies on a tight rein with regard to their behaviour. These ladies were expected to be able to discuss politics and religion as easily as the latest fashions or music. They did the usual beautiful embroidery (some of Anne's survives), and we know that she bought books from Antwerp to display in her chambers, so anyone could read them, even if they could not afford to buy them.[21] She also presented her ladies with miniature psalters, or prayer books, for their personal use.[22] These were not the actions or interests of a foolish airhead.

A number of people were closely involved with the Queen's search for books, including William Lok, the mercer, who ran errands for her in the Low Countries, bringing back books and other things. His daughter, in her old age, remembered how 'Queen Anne Boleyn, that was mother to Queen Elizabeth, caused him to get her gospels and epistles written in parchment in French, together with the psalms.'[23] William Latimer would be on a book-buying trip for the Queen when he heard that she had been arrested in 1536.[24]

Despite all Anne's endeavours there would be many upheavals in that disappointing year of 1534.

Anne's desire to show that she was capable of running a learned and well-behaved group of ladies was scuppered by her sister Mary, the widow of William Carey. Anne and Mary do not appear to have been particularly close, so it may have not come to her attention that there was gossip about her sister until it was impossible to ignore. Mary's name was again besmirched by scandal, as it appeared that she was pregnant. It did not help Anne retain a high moral tone when her sister was the subject of malicious talk.

This time Mary was able to redeem herself. She claimed that despite having started a new relationship she was not wanton, but secretly married. The man who was her new husband was one William Stafford, who was the younger son of Humphrey Stafford of Blatherwick in Northamptonshire. The family was not wealthy, although it did have some good connections. It was better than nothing, but was not a suitable match for the sister of the Queen.

Anne may have felt some resentment at the pregnancy of her sister, as she had lost her own child, whose loss was more important than any pregnancy her sister may have started.

Mary Boleyn was one of those people who, while stumbling through life, still manage to get along all right. She seemed less ambitious than the rest of her family, content to take life as she found it, and make the best of things. She was to find that she had, despite appearances, chosen wisely in Stafford, who was to prove to be a good husband.

But the early days were not easy. Anne withdrew from her sister for a time, and Henry was angry, perhaps allowing resentment against Anne to show as criticism of her sister.

Feeling herself abandoned by those closest to her, Mary was driven to write to Cromwell, asking for his help in regaining the favour of the King and Queen. The letter was sent from Cottered in Hertfordshire, where the couple were living with Sir Humphrey Stafford. In it Mary begs for understanding.

> Master Secretary ... I am sure that it is not unknown to you the high displeasure both he and I have, both of the King's Highness and the Queen's Grace, by reason of our marriage without their knowledge. Wherein we both do yield ourselves faulty and acknowledge that we did not well to be so hasty, or so bold. But one thing Good Master Secretary consider, that he was young and love overcame reason. For my part I saw so much honesty in him that I loved him as much as he did me, and was in bondage, and glad I was to be at liberty ... I saw all the world did set so little store by me, and he so much, that I thought I could take no better way but to take him, and to forsake all other ways, and live a poor honest life with him. If we might once be so happy as to recover the King's gracious favour and the Queen's. For well I might have had a greater man of birth, or a higher, but I assure you I could never have had one that loved me so well, nor a more honest man.[25]

It was a heartbreaking plea from the woman often considered the black sheep of a successful family, who had again done something foolish. However, as events were to turn out, Mary Boleyn was to be the only survivor of her immediate family, the grandmother of some of the people who did so well at the court of Queen Elizabeth. She was the carrier of the family bloodline and a woman finally at peace with herself. She would live a relatively simple life in a domestic setting, rearing her children and grieving for her clever siblings, whose comet-like brilliance would explode and ignite fire in a family once so united.

Mary would escape most of that fallout. Already an exile, she was not blamed for the tragedy that extinguished Boleyn hopes, but in her more modest life she was safe and content.

Chapuys, glorying in anything bringing discredit upon the Queen's family, wrote with grim pleasure of the matter to Charles V. 'The Lady's sister was banished from the court three months ago, it being necessary to do so, for besides that she has been found guilty of misconduct, it would not have been becoming to see her at court enceinte.'[26] The only thing taking the gloss from Chapuys' gloating was that he reported the matter as 'being three months ago'. This emphasised that he was not at the centre of events. It took him so long to hear 'latest' gossip that it was old news.

Queen Anne, after the loss of the second pregnancy, began to face the reality that whatever she did, she would never be fully accepted. Added to the slight, but definite, change in Henry's feelings towards her, she became anxiously aware that without a son she could never be safe.

Much is made of the changeable nature of Henry's affections, particularly towards his wives, as if they should not have trusted him. For the first two of his wives there was no warning, no dangerous precedent set. They were the precedent.

Katherine is to be sympathised with because she simply could not believe that her husband would cast off a marriage of two decades' standing to marry his sweetheart. It was unheard of. Kings often had mistresses and in some courts it was customary for these women to attain power and influence. But they did not become queens. Katherine's stubborn denial of what had happened to her and to her daughter is perfectly understandable. Henry's behaviour had been totally aberrant, quite beyond the norm.

Anne, also, deserves sympathy. For her sake this man had overstepped all boundaries, done the impossible thing. He had put her in the place of his Queen with all honour and ceremony. Surely, then, it must mean that he loved her above all women? He had appeared to, and declared that he did. Surely she could expect that their unusual relationship would last? But after little more than a year of marriage Anne could sense changes in him.

He had appeared to believe that they were pre-ordained as a couple, that Anne had been put into his life for good reason. That the changes to England's way of life and religious beliefs, which they would make when they were able to marry, would be for the benefit of all. Once he had done for her what he could, raised her higher than any woman had ever been raised, she was expected to fulfil her part of that bargain and promptly present him with a prince.

But she had failed. That first year, when the son should have been born, there was another girl. He had rallied, regaining his confidence in her and the rightness of his actions. Then another failure, with the miscarriage a reminder of the losses he had suffered with his first wife. Was that all to begin again? It was not what he had discarded Katherine, enraged Europe or broken with Rome for.

The time was not ripe for him to have to make changes. He was still proving to the world, and his bewildered and reluctant subjects in England, that he had made no errors of judgement.

But Anne, in the closest possible proximity to him, could surely see the difference. For one thing the deference was gone. She was no longer his inspiration or delight, his reason for struggling against overwhelming odds. She was now just another woman, another unsuccessful wife. As such she was not only suddenly fallible, but also extremely vulnerable.

The time would come when she would envy her sister her modest obscurity.

Chapter Thirteen

The situation at court during 1534 might have seemed the ideal opportunity for the supporters of Katherine of Aragon and the Princess Mary to push on with plans to oust the Boleyn faction. While this may have looked like a lost cause, they still entertained hopes of achieving it. At the very least, there was a possibility of spiriting away Princess Mary, putting her under the protection of Charles V abroad. Katherine's appeal to Rome had been made five years earlier, but despite all that had happened since, there were those who felt strongly that the matter was not resolved.

What Katherine could no longer do on her own behalf, she might be persuaded, or pressured, into doing for her daughter. Mary was still, in Katherine's eyes and in the eyes of many others, the heir to the throne. Her safety was paramount. There were many people who feared that a frustrated Henry, quick to destroy opposition, might turn against Mary, since she persisted in demanding rights as his legitimate daughter.

When Pope Clement passed that long-awaited judgement in Katherine's favour, he made it clear that he feared the situation for her and her daughter might worsen because of it. He expressed his very real concerns at the time. 'I am afraid that I have committed a great sin, for the Queen may suffer death by it!' he declared. Even before Katherine actually heard that the sentence was finally passed in her favour, there were fears for her safety in Europe.

Cromwell, already pressing on with Henry's changes, selected many new members of Parliament himself, to ensure that he would have the support needed for the more radical of those changes. These were to include the Act of Succession, which confirmed that the Princess Mary was officially a bastard and the marriage of Anne was 'true, sincere and perfect …'.

The Act contained a dig at Rome, stating the Pope could not encroach upon the 'great and inviolable God-given rights of the King of England' in decisions within his own country.[1] To do so would suggest interference from outside which would not be tolerated. The dreaded Praemunire had been used before and would be used again, preventing any Catholic from obtaining assistance or advice from the Papacy, throwing them back without resource while the familiar way of living was dismantled.

The danger lay in the fact that the country would be expected to swear to observe and abide by the Act, which placed Katherine's supporters in line for horrendous punishments. It was intended to spread terror, and it succeeded.

Cromwell wasted no time in making it clear that he intended to enforce it, with the greatest possible severity. Elizabeth Barton had already suffered, but the Act would force insidious tendrils into the lives of ordinary people. The most obvious and helpless suspects standing in the line of fire, increasingly viewed as subversive, were the religious orders. Particularly Katherine's much-loved Friars Observant. They were men with little to lose, except their lives. They had no great wealth like the large monasteries, which would become such a temptation to Henry and Cromwell. They had only their religious convictions, which to Henry were uncomfortable. By June 1534 they had been carried into the Tower of London, literally, by the cartload.

Katherine was in anguish at what might happen to the Friars, and others who risked themselves to support her. But many other people had backed off out of a sense of self-preservation. They avoided confrontation and attempted to sit out the dangerous times.

Despite the Pope's belated support of Katherine's cause, it seemed already too late. Henry had wrested the reigns of power out of the hands of the Church. It was becoming too dangerous to stand out openly in favour of Queen or Princess. Many still did, resolute souls who did not fear to speak against injustice, but in almost every case their actions were followed by retribution, too awful to contemplate.

There were spies everywhere even at the lowest levels. In one sad case (representing the general oppression) a woman in childbirth, recently delivered and still confined to her bed, had declared her pleasure in her midwife. She claimed that the woman's skills were such that she was good enough to serve a queen. 'Though not Queen Anne', she rashly added, 'for she is a wanton'. Her words were reported and the following day she was arrested and questioned. She was subsequently hanged.

Most people did not consider the brief pleasure of speaking one's mind worth dying for. They tried to remain neutral. It meant burying one's head in the sand, the consequences of offending Henry were not worth the risk.

Even the Emperor, in no way afraid of Henry, did not consider the matter worth a war. He could not afford one. When the sentence was passed, which should have guaranteed Katherine's future, Charles' ambassador in Rome, Cyfuentes, openly rejoiced that the Pope's declaration did not carry with it any demand that it be enforced by Spain. In England Chapuys was in despair. He remained convinced that if Charles would show his fangs, Henry would back down. He knew that without Charles' armies behind it, the sentence from Rome meant nothing, and was unenforceable.

By May of 1534, once the news reached Katherine, her letters to Charles V changed in tone. No longer begging assistance, they became enigmatic. They made the point that Charles 'knew' what needed to be done. However, her position was to change. She didn't really want a war, any more than her nephew did. Even Chapuys recognised this when he wrote to Charles V in July of 1534. He stated Katherine's case clearly: 'But she is so scrupulous and has such great respect for the King, that she would consider herself damned without remission if she took any way tending to war!'[2]

Whether Katherine believed that Charles would support her to the extent of sending troops to England, she considered herself bound, by the rights and duties of a queen, to increase the pressure on her daughter Mary. Living apart from her mother, she might have done better to receive more letters of support and affection, rather than regular demands for defiance, but Katherine had a streak of iron will. Mary must be seen to be unbroken in spirit, upholding her rights at all times. This instruction was to make life more uncomfortable for Mary than it need have been.

When Elizabeth's household was moving from one house to another, Mary refused to move. She would not be considered a member of her half-sister's entourage. Her defiance resulted in her being forcibly bundled into a litter, and taken against her will. Such indignities were a part of the new way of life imposed upon her. Although she wished to support her mother against her father's new wife, such problems were too much for a teenaged girl. They made her existence stressful and unhappy.

Katherine, with her demands, her increasing pressure, was pushing her vulnerable daughter over the limit of what she could bear, and the process was beginning to alter the Princess's once sunny disposition into one of suspicion and wariness. This came to a head when Richard Featherstone, Princess Mary's Latin teacher, obtained an interview with her during which she confided her problems. Shocked at the strain she was under, he informed Chapuys, who contacted Katherine. He told her plainly that she was pushing Mary too far. That it was one thing for Mary to be strong, but another for her to put herself in danger by confrontations with her father. She should be able to obey, without seeming to renounce her rights. It was reasonable to do so with reservations, and it would be understood abroad that she was under duress, so long as that had been made clear.

It was a compromise solution but one acceptable to Emperor and Pope, given the Princess's confinement. It would not benefit anyone for her to break down under the strain. It was a way for her to live more easily, so long as she did not swear the Act of Succession.

This seemed to do the trick, leading to a softening in Mary's attitude and Henry's too. By September of 1534 the courtiers had begun to visit the Princess. Chapuys reported to Katherine that tensions had eased and her general health had consequently revived.

These improvements in the circumstances surrounding Princess Mary could have only a detrimental effect on Queen Anne's peace of mind. She was already uncomfortably aware that Henry had tried to make a 'deal' with the Pope even after their marriage. This, together with the knowledge that he was disappointed in his expectations, greatly increased her insecurity. It must have been difficult for her to continue with everyday routines when the man upon whom everything depended was becoming less reliable. There was one bright spot, Henry had begun to consider offering their daughter Elizabeth as a bride for a son of the King of France. That showed that he still considered the child a viable pawn for royal marriage, which should have eased Anne's mind.

Such a betrothal of the Princess to the French King's younger son, the Duke of Angoulême, would confirm Elizabeth's position, whatever Anne's detractors chose to say. The Princess was being considered for marriage suitable to her rank, but Anne's sense of unease was still not fully soothed. The negotiations proceeded slowly, and were never finalised. The preliminary talks ran into difficulties by February 1535 because the French negotiators asked Henry to renounce the large annual pension he was taking from them. Henry's goodwill did not extend to losing the money and he replied to their suggestion 'it was a strange recompense when he was offering the heiress of the Kingdom to a younger son!'. He declared, 'they ought rather to have given something, than to ask!'.[3]

By May of 1534 Katherine had moved to a new residence at Kimbolton, in Huntingdonshire. Her health was beginning to fail and the moves from one cold and half-furnished house to another did nothing to allieviate her discomfort. She did make her own situation there worse than it need have been, due to her refusing to be served by anyone who addressed her by her 'new' title of Princess Dowager of Wales, rather than her own marital title of Queen. This resolve meant that she spent the majority of her time in her chamber, attended only by her closest retainers, while the life of the household went on without her. She had withdrawn and marginalised herself. Henry had been spending £4,000 per annum on expenses for Katherine's household and intended that she should live in honourable retirement. Suitable accommodation, proper service and vetted companionship had been an intended part of the arrangement. That this was more for the sake of appearances than any personal concern was irrelevant. Henry was aware than any arduous way of life imposed on Katherine would reflect badly on himself, and do his reputation in Europe more harm than good. He would have been satisfied if she accepted the arrangements, and lived quietly but comfortably in the country, as his brother Arthur's widow. He was expecting too much.

Katherine's own insistence on withdrawal from any who did not acknowledge her proper rank, impinged on her health, mentally and physically. It robbed her of basic comforts and of necessary contact with the outside world. She inured herself to the lack of the queenly household, using her strong religious faith to counteract her change of circumstances, but the lack of contact with others was to isolate her more than Henry had intended.

She had begun to live in a bubble, into which she retreated on a point of honour. Those restrictions, self-imposed though they were, would begin to threaten her health.

Chapuys, to his credit, remained as attentive as possible, though he was to find it difficult to maintain contact with the Queen. He would send messages to her and to Princess Mary, as often as possible, and the delays were not his fault. He did his utmost to play the part of watchdog over them both, still believing that his master the Emperor could, and should, have done more. Although he accepted, reluctantly, that there would be no troops asked for or sent, he felt that it would be safer to get Princess Mary out of the country. In Europe, rather than under her father's control, she could be better protected, and also have the Emperor's support for future claims.

Chapuys' fervour in serving Katherine's interests sometimes led to him being reprimanded by Charles V, who reminded him from time to time which person he was supposed to be working for. Chapuys was to find it difficult to deal with Henry in person, actually finding Cromwell easier to get on with on a business level. He recognised that there was a man whose 'cold, calculating, unemotional logic he could at least understand', even though he was never foolish enough to trust him.[4] He wrote on one occasion to the Emperor that 'Cromwell's words are good, but his deeds are bad, and his will and content are incomparably worse!'. It was a fair assessment and one that people would realise to their cost in the years ahead.

By the autumn of 1534 Henry's hopes were raised. Pope Clement's sentence had done little good, except push him on, in irritation, to enforce his will even more. But by September of that year the Pope's life was to come to an end.

He was only 56 years old and was to go down in history as a vacillating, weak man, but such a simplistic dismissal is not entirely fair. Being elected to the Papacy did not ensure either a safe or easy tenure. Popes had been deposed, even killed, in the bloodsoaked years of the Papacy's history, but usually, underneath the conflict, was a sense of respect for the office, if not for the man who held it.

Clement VII (Giulio de' Medici) had been respected while he was a Cardinal, when he was advisor to his cousin, Pope Leo X. He had served as advisor to Pope Adrian VI. He was a patron of literature, the arts and an admirer of Michelangelo, as might have been expected from his background. In 1519 he had been sufficiently trusted to oversee the administration of Florence, after the death of his uncle, Lorenzo de' Medici. He was hard working, known to be efficient and genuinely pious. Nor did he stain his Papacy with scandals.

On becoming Pope in November of 1523 he had begun to face challenges he could not have imagined, which few Popes could have dealt with. Europe was changing, not only due to religious and political pressures, but at that time it was being led by a clutch of most assertive rulers, unwilling to be either led or controlled.[5] Any Pope must become a strong intermediary between the constantly warring factions.

Charles V still saw the Papacy and Spain as a spiritual partnership. He also saw himself way out in front of his royal brethren in the struggle to be acknowledged as the closest and most trusted son of the Church. But there were other contenders. France, where King Francis wanted to make a name for himself, and also England, where Henry VIII demanded to be taken seriously and be ranked as an equal. Henry's requests would seem to be like the jealousies of a schoolboy, but he was a dangerous person to deal with if he considered he was not treated with respect.

Charles V had been embarrassed by the Sack of Rome, initiated by the troops ostensibly under his command. Clement's subsequent period of seclusion in Castel Sant'Angelo marked a breach in the papal/Spanish relationship which would take some mending. Charles had been very disappointed with what he saw as Clement's weak and wavering loyalties as well as his patience with Henry VIII, when a show of firmness might have been appropriate. But Clement had believed that Henry could be reasoned with, shown the error in his thinking. He relied on the idea that Henry would eventually become weary of the difficulties and retire from the field, and the problems he'd created would disperse.

Charles had referred to Clement as 'a shepherd who left his flock, and returned as a wolf!'. But Clement deserves sympathy for the situation in which he found himself. Respect for both the office, and the man who held it, had reached an all-time low. The kings he was supposed to guide and advise considered the person of the Pope a prize, to be 'captured' by one side or another and used as a trophy.

The Sack of Rome had seriously damaged the old relationship with Spain, but it also damaged Rome's feeling for its Pope. The people would never forgive what they saw as abandonment of them, as though he had been to blame for what had happened.

Henry VIII could never understand Clement's position. The loss of England to the Catholic fold was not Clement's fault, it was entirely Henry's, but Clement had bent backwards to accommodate the King, show patience and to give him time to see sense. Henry appreciated none of it. He made his demand and was refused. He wanted the Pope's unqualified agreement, which could not be given, and so in frustration had flung himself and his people away.

Even in the excommunication, Clement had been reluctant to take the final step. He neither supported Katherine nor chastised Henry sufficiently. His forbearance towards an increasingly belligerent Henry lost him respect, and Henry broke free anyway.

Clement was to enjoy just two triumphs. One was the marriage, in 1533, of his niece Catherine de' Medici, into the royal family of France. This girl was to go on to become a major player in the struggles of the country of her adoption. The other was the marriage of his nephew to a daughter of Charles V. It might be inferred that he was still sitting on the fence, but a kinder interpretation would be that he was still trying to keep a balance between the two countries.

It would be said of him that he was 'a great Medici, if not a great Pope' and that where Medici interests were at stake he could prove himself to be a great statesman. It was also said 'Clement's inability to inspire loyalty was nothing compared to his main defect, which was the inability to make up his mind.' That epitaph might also be considered as simplistic. Clement may have been unwilling to give opinions either way, but the result of such caution was the posthumous reputation as a weakling. He was faced with a period of upheaval equal to any faced by earlier Popes, many of whom did not survive the experience.

Clement died on 25 September 1534 and was buried in Santa Maria Sopra Minerva in Rome. He left behind one son, Alessandro de' Medici, Duke of Florence.[6]

He is remembered for his role in that most easily recognised period of European history, and his difficult relationships with Charles V, Francis I and Henry VIII were to complicate and define his reign as Pope. He was succeeded in October 1534 by Alessandro Farnese, who reigned as Pope Paul III.

Paul III was a far more effective and decisive character than his predecessor. More willing to show Rome's iron fist under its velvet glove of fatherly concern. Paul was a cultured man, but was not prepared to allow the ridiculous situation caused by England's King to continue. After taking advice from his Cardinals, he would made it clear that the dilatoriness that marked Clement's rule was not his way. He would prove himself to be the enemy of the enemies of Rome.[7]

Paul III had been born in 1468 and was the last of the Cardinals created by Pope Alexander VI (Rodrigo Borgia). He was brother of that Pope's mistress, Giulia Farnese, and owed his elevation to her influence. For a time he was known in Rome as 'Cardinal Petticoat'.[8]

He was no better morally than the others, and had fathered four illegitimate children before becoming Cardinal. Two of these had been declared legitimate by Julius II. Paul in his turn raised two of his grandsons to Cardinal, one aged 15, and the other while only 14 years old. He expected to become Pope on the death of Leo X, and again when Adrian VI died. Incensed at the election of Clement VII, he declared that he blamed Clement for robbing him of ten years of his Papacy.

His accession was a turning point for the Church. Under Paul III it would not sit helplessly by while the new religion swept across Europe. Paul was to be the founder of the Counter-Reformation and there would be a great resurgence of religious orders and a strong backlash against those who fought the Church. He would show firm support for those who suffered under the oppressive rule of men like Henry. One of those sufferers, a man of unusual piety and probity, was John Fisher, Bishop of Rochester.

Bishop Fisher, a Yorkshireman born in Beverley in 1469, had been recommended for the diocese of Rochester by Henry's grandmother, Margaret Beaufort. He became Bishop in 1504. Not for him the extravagance of a Wolsey, he had no desire for any display. Fisher was an aesthetic, frugal and remote, his eyes set firmly on Heaven and on his spiritual life. Seemingly cold, he was respected for his clear good sense, which was never sullied by self-interest. Where Wolsey had striven for his place at the political centre of events Fisher was a pure churchman first and last. His piety isolated him from the shallow and selfish world he inhabited. He had notably written of the court of Henry VIII at that time: 'Here there are many chalices of gold, but almost no golden priests!' This was a damning indictment of the way in which the giddy new world had, in Fisher's opinion, contaminated even the priesthood.[9]

But even a man like Fisher could not escape the mainstream. He had become involved in the matter of the Holy Maid of Kent. Fisher had been cleared of any complicity in that dangerous matter (on payment of a fine of £300), but the swearing of the Act of Succession was a very different matter entirely. It was to trip up many a person of innocent intentions, even Fisher.

On 26 April 1534 he had been arrested over his refusal to take the Oath of Succession. As a supporter of Henry's first marriage there was little else he could do. However, a man of such renown could not be allowed to make himself a figurehead for dissenters. He was sent to the Tower, where he was to languish for over a year, in conditions that were so bad that even he, who had lived without luxuries, wrote to Cromwell to lament the severity of his captivity. However, his grim circumstances did nothing to persuade him to submit to Henry's demands. Other churchmen, including Tunstall and Gardiner, could slide with equanimity into the schism engulfing England, Fisher remained obdurate.

Another who fell foul of the Holy Maid of Kent episode and the Oath of Succession was Sir Thomas More. He had also escaped censure over the Holy Maid of Kent, but incurred Henry's anger over his refusal to attend the King's Coronation to Anne.[10] Sympathisers offered him money for a suitable robe for the celebrations, due to his straitened financial circumstances, but he was unwilling. He had been a trusted and respected advisor of the King. A companion if not an intimate friend. Henry took his refusal as a snub.

More's reasoning was different to Fisher's. He had made it perfectly clear that in his opinion the King was within his rights to marry any lady he wanted. As an anointed king he also had the right to decide the succession, leaving the Crown to any person of his choosing. He had no intention of involving himself in secular concerns he did not consider himself qualified to oppose. But he could not, and would not, agree to the King's Supremacy. He could never accept that Henry had a right to usurp the Pope's role as Head of the English Church. On 13 April he was questioned and had refused to take the Oath. Four days later he was arrested and sent to the Tower, so that before Bishop Fisher went into the fortress, Thomas More was already there.

Both were to have plenty of time to reconsider their decisions, but neither would waver. It must have been a grief to Fisher to learn that from 2 June 1534 his See of Rochester was declared vacant. Less painful would have been the knowledge that in November he was to be attainted for Misprision of Treason and all his goods forfeit, backdated to the previous March.

Henry would not have gained much from an inventory of the goods of the Bishop. There would be no lists of treasures to gloat over, as when the possessions of Cardinal Wolsey had been forfeited. Fisher had little to lose materially. His reputation was the important thing. He would not allow that to be disgraced by capitulation to Henry, even if his life was to be sacrificed. For him there could be no accommodations. He had never been tempted by life's pleasures, had no need of flattery or position to uphold him. Many men relied on outward show as evidence of their place, but that meant nothing. He had his sense of right, and his genuine piety. He was to remain unbending, whatever blandishments were offered or threats made. He was 66 years old and seemed older. He belonged to an earlier age, and was ageless. He was prepared to be a martyr.

The great danger towards the clergy continued while Fisher and More were in the Tower. The Royal Supremacy was a barrier over which many could not climb. The Prior of the London Charterhouse was executed, followed by the Carthusian Priors of Beauvale and Axholme. Later the Vicar and Procurator of the London Charterhouse would suffer the same fate. It would be a long, cold winter for those awaiting their fate in prison, and they could have no hope of reprieve.

Paul III looked on Fisher's arrest as a personal affront and he began to consider re-issuing Henry's excommunication. This rumour added to the difficulties of

Anne's position, as it would turn Catholics even more against her. Even worse, Henry was rumoured to be showing interest in other ladies. Anne was helpless. With a son in the nursery she could rise above such tawdry escapades, but without that security she was adrift.

Whether Henry was taking flirtations to their natural conclusion Anne did not know. But they became for her a source of great anxiety in that winter of 1534 to 1535. The King might have been looking for an escape from Anne's swiftly changing moods.

What is exciting in a mistress is less so in a wife, especially when a man has problems. Probably worse if most of them are of his own making.

He was not ready to give up on his marriage to Anne, but Anne's state of anxiety helped to drive him further away. One young lady was enthusiastically 'taken up' by Chapuys, who described her as 'both intelligent and beautiful' as well as a friend to Princess Mary. Jane Rochford became involved in intrigues against this person and was sent from court in the second week in October, which made Anne look a fool and lowered her prestige further.

A little later Anne visited Richmond, where Elizabeth's household was in residence. During this visit she was disconcerted to realise that both the Dukes of Suffolk and Norfolk, with several of their retainers, had left her to pay respect to Princess Mary. The visitors remained with Mary until time for Anne to leave.[11] Her complaints to Henry about their disrespectful behaviour were ignored.

It was not entirely gloomy towards the end of 1534. The consent of Parliament to the Treason Act strengthened Anne's position considerably, making it a capital offence to impugn the marriage, speak disrespectfully of the King or call him a heretic. By December of 1534 Chapuys was forced to admit that whatever attraction the new young lady had for Henry, it had done nothing to damage his marriage. He said the King and Anne (referred to as 'The Lady') seemed on good terms.[12]

Chapuys' versions of English court life were criticised by Sir William Paget. He was one of Henry's secretaries and was known to be a decent, unbiased man. He had come to know Chapuys well, but his opinion of the Ambassador's probity was not flattering.

'I never took him', Paget said, 'for a wise man, but for one that used to speak without any respect for honesty or for truth, so as it might serve his turn. He is a great practiser [plotter], tale-telling, lying and flattering.'[13]

It seems a fair assessment of the man who has left behind a rich legacy of letters and reports showing his great devotion to Spain and to the Spanish-born Queen. But which also show that he had a talent for fantasy. His desire to appear to be at the centre of events frequently led him into serious errors of judgement. Many of his reports were based on sheer malice and he regularly painted very blackly any person he disliked. It was a pity such a man, holding a position of trust and responsibility, left behind so much material of extremely doubtful veracity. He could easily have been a beacon, giving later generations a unique insight into the lives of people he met at a time of great changes. Chapuys' loyalties to Spain increased his spite against Anne and her followers, and his reports became so virulent and unreliable that they are effectively worthless. Francis I's championship of Henry's marriage to Anne aroused his ire, and was the cause of violently prejudiced reports.

It is understood that an Ambassador was in a peculiarly difficult position. One that entailed more than being his country's representative and his master's mouthpiece. He was expected to act as a spy, and spread false information. Sir Henry Wooton once said, 'An Ambassador is an honest man who is sent abroad to lie for the good of his country.' However, Chapuys' lack of knowledge of the English language did him great disservice, preventing him from understanding the nuances of what he learned, or being able to keep up with events as they evolved. He was reliant on paid informers so was unable to differentiate fact from fiction, and his own strong feelings led him into errors when he allowed vindictiveness to get the better of common sense.

Francis I's new envoy, Admiral Chabot, was invited to a court entertainment on 1 December 1534. He was to sit on the dais with Henry and Anne as an honoured guest, to watch the dancing. Henry remarked to Anne that she had not yet had the opportunity of receiving Monsieur Palamede Gontier, who was the Treasurer to the French Embassy. Rather than sending a page to summon this dignitary, Henry went in search of him personally. Anne, watching the King's progress through the throng, suddenly burst into hysterical laughter, which she found hard to control. Chabot, wondering if he had done anything to provoke such amusement, asked her, 'What Madame? Do you laugh at me?' Anne said to him, 'The King told me that he was going to find your Treasurer, but on the way he has met a lady and stopped to speak with her, completely forgetting his errand!' Chabot made no comment, and Anne regained her composure, but Chapuys was to report it in the New Year.[14]

He had also been feeding stories to the Emperor regarding supposed ill-treatment and the subsequent failure in health of Katherine of Aragon. The Emperor, believing the tales, complained to Henry who refuted the allegations. Mary had also been spreading tales that she was being treated like a second-class citizen and was forced to act almost as a servant to Elizabeth. This in spite of the fact that her journey to Richmond during the previous summer had been made in a velvet-covered litter, exactly the same as Elizabeth's own.[15]

In October 1534 Princess Elizabeth had been weaned at the age of 13 months. This was an important moment and the decision was taken at the highest level. Sir William Paulet, the Comptroller of her Household, put the matter before the King on the advice of the women in attendance. The King had been pleased to agree the decision that she be removed from her wet-nurse and weaned. She had also recently been proudly shown, 'Quite naked', to a visiting French delegation, one of the opening moves in negotiations for her prospective marriage to the French prince.

By that Christmas, Anne had begun to feel anxious that the negotiations were no further forward. She was not only devoted to Elizabeth as her daughter, but also very protective of her rights as a princess. But she was also afraid for the child's safety.

There was a strong Catholic lobby, and while ever Anne had no son, or any other child at all, Elizabeth stood in danger. Although not everyone was prepared to suffer a terrible death by speaking out against Henry, it did not mean that they would always let him do as he liked. Anne knew that she and her daughter stood on very shaky ground when her own uncle, the Duke of Norfolk, could openly refer to his Boleyn relatives as 'heretics'.

Despite problems, the King and Queen were reported to have kept 'a great house' that Christmas and the King appeared to be 'in his most hearty manner'. The undercurrents would, unfortunately, ensure tension beneath the facade. All eyes were on the royal pair, and there would have been wary glances in Henry's direction, despite the smiles. He made people nervous and Anne's popularity had not improved. Everyone was waiting to see a male heir, who should have already been born, but with Henry's waning interest and waning virility, it was proving difficult.

The Pope had sent polite messages but it was obvious that he would not be the pushover Clement had been, or Henry had come to expect. The imprisonment of Fisher and More caused friction, not only with Rome. Intellectual Europe grieved for More's predicament even as the Church grieved for Fisher's. This matter would drag on into the coming year but could have no good ending. Henry's rapid cruelty towards the Friars had pushed him towards the edge of the precipice, and it did not need Chapuys with his ready facility for mendacity to suggest that the 'merriment' was uneasy that Christmas.

Chapter Fourteen

Since his sister's rise in status, George Boleyn had done very well. The position of brother-in-law to the King brought with it many advantages, as Charles Brandon had discovered.

George, Lord Rochford, had the honour of being sent on several embassies abroad, even missing his sister's Coronation as he was in France. By October of 1533 he had been granted the right to establish himself at Beaulieu in Essex, which caused Chapuys concern as Princess Mary had the property assigned to her. She had been obliged to move out of the main house into another nearby, to accommodate the Queen's brother. Her resentment added to Chapuys' indignation, as he considered the latter property inferior and unsuitable. After this event Chapuys' complaints rose to such a degree that the King decided that it would be easier, as well as economical, for Princess Mary to share the household of Princess Elizabeth.

Lord Rochford had been present on 20 March 1534 when the Act of Succession was presented to the House of Lords, which had passed the Act on the 23rd.

George was in France in April of 1534, when he accompanied Sir William Fitzwilliam. Their efforts had achieved some conciliation with France, on the surface at least, and Henry VIII had been pleased at their success.[1] Chapuys reported to Charles V on the English King's praises, which were lavished on the envoys.[2] The King and Queen also expressed their pleasure by dancing together in public, after dining.

The French Ambassador had arrived at the end of May 1534, and suggested a meeting between Francis and Henry the following August. Francis did not intend to change his relationship with the Holy See at the behest of the King and Henry's unfortunate outburst about the unsuitability of the late Pope's niece, Catherine de' Medici, to become the daughter-in-law of Francis would be remembered. But Henry was willing to show pleasure at what he considered Francis' attempt at friendship. He rewarded George Boleyn for his latest mission by making him Constable of Dover Castle and Warden of the Cinque Ports, which took effect from 16 June 1534.[3]

But by the summer of 1534, when Anne had been pregnant, then lost the child, the visit was called off.[4] George's instructions referred to Anne as being 'not mete to be conveyed over the tombling sea' so George was sent to France instead. He was entrusted with messages to the Queen of Navarre (Marguerite d'Alençon) who begged that the visit be put off until the spring.

George had established very good relations with the Queen of Navarre in France in June of 1533. On this occasion he was back in England by the end of July.[5] It is likely that, on hearing news of Anne's miscarriage, George made a hasty return trip. Henry's growing irritation with Anne was to spill over onto George. He began to feel a withdrawal of Henry's favour as Anne had. George was no fool. He was as aware of the danger of new female favourites as Anne was.

There was also the problem of friends turning away, when preference was withdrawn. George had some disagreement with Sir Francis Bryan, which became blown out of proportion when others took Bryan's side. It became more serious when Henry himself turned his face from George, and also took the side of Francis Bryan.

As Chapuys reported, 'the said King recently showed disfavour to Lord Rochford in some question he had had with Master Bryan'.[6] Chapuys' report is dated 19 December of that year, and it is known that this disturbing incident happened sooner, but Chapuys' reports were sometimes many weeks behind events.

George went to Dover to greet the Admiral of France, Chabot, who arrived on 11 November. The Admiral's journey had been very slow, and on 11 November George had written to the Duke of Norfolk to explain that, although the visitor had arrived 'at the tenne of the clock', he was in no hurry.[7] He insisted he should rest the first night, before making his leisurely way towards Canterbury. Once there, he asked that he might 'also tarry Friday all day' so that his train could meet up. Many of his retinue had been scattered, some arriving at Dover, some at Sandwich 'and somme in other places!'. Chabot finally arrived in London on 20 November and was immediately received. He caused surprise by his declaration that the object of his mission was to ask for the hand of Princess Mary as the prospective bride of the Dauphin Francis.[8] Francis I had decided to ask for the King of England's elder daughter, due to something he had heard from the Emperor Charles V.

The Emperor had been indignant at what he considered 'disgraces' inflicted upon his relatives Katherine and Mary. He declared that he 'wanted to do some good for them' and if, in the process, he could ruin England's new Queen, so much the better. He intended to try to make other sovereigns take interest in his kinswomen, and hopefully put some pressure on Henry. It was not a war, but it might become a war of attrition, and might seriously disturb and inconvenience England. Charles had even proposed Mary as a bride for the King of Scotland (James V), a direct challenge and insult to Henry, as if Charles, not her father, had the right to dispose of her in marriage.

Scotland was a very weak ally for Spain and Charles thought better of it, deciding that he would be more effective if he could include Francis against Henry. He pressed for the marriage with France, which, as Mary was officially a bastard, showed Henry that other nations considered the Princess differently.

Francis, more wily than Charles gave him credit for, pretended he did not like the idea. But in truth, it appealed. Although Charles suggested the Duke d'Angoulême, Francis' third son (six years younger than the Princess), Francis preferred to offer for Mary on behalf of his heir.[9] This would not only be a suitable match (assuming Mary could be considered legitimate), but would give France a very valuable claim to the English Crown. Francis had sent Chabot to deliver the thunderbolt and make what negotiations he could. Francis asked for the daughter of Charles V for the Dauphin, just in case the English idea failed. It was a move worthy of Henry.[10]

Learning of the real mission of Admiral Chabot that Christmas, Anne's nerves were stretched to breaking point. If her husband decided to grant Mary to the French, it would mean her reinstatement in the line of succession. Could it also mean reconciliation with Katherine of Aragon? If so, what of Anne's position, and her daughter's?

Fortunately for Anne, there were other requests that Chabot was instructed to make to Henry. There was the question of the French pension. He was highly unlikely to give that up. Nor would he be amenable to the idea of the second item, that he was to take steps to reconcile with the Holy See. Henry professed himself shocked, particularly at the second demand. He would never admit that what he had done regarding Anglo-papal relations had been wrong. There could never be any rapprochement unless the Pope was made to agree. Following the death of Clement VII and the recent election of Paul III such an idea was ludicrous. Henry had no intention of giving in, nor would he give up his title of Supreme Head of the Church in England, which had been bestowed upon him only two days before Chabot's arrival.

At this worrying juncture, Anne was actually relying on Cromwell's support. This did not mean that he was any more friendly towards her, knowing that her hold was beginning to slip. But Cromwell, who had been 'Master Secretary' since October of 1533, could do without any alliance if it meant the slightest concession to Rome. He was responsible for all religious policies in England and encouraged Henry's reluctance, advising him to refuse all demands from others that he reconcile with the Pope. This newly strengthened attitude reassured Anne, and helped to establish the 'merry' Christmas that was reported.

But, Henry liked the idea of a French alliance, and the proposal made for Elizabeth. If that were accepted, it solved problems regarding Mary's equivocal status. Although the French King's son was 12 years old, and Princess Elizabeth barely 18 months, it was not considered a difficulty. The Prince would wait for his bride, if she were the heiress of England. The age difference would be on the right side, a bridegroom ten years older than his bride was acceptable. Henry's counter proposal was passed on and Anne could breathe more easily.[11]

If the marriage of the Princess Elizabeth to the French Prince went ahead, would it further anger the Pope? Francis wavered, tempted, but irresolute. Only further dissent between him and Charles V caused him finally to come down in favour of the daughter of Henry rather than Charles. But he was determined Henry would not have things all his way. Henry hated the idea of giving up the French pension, but there were other demands that Francis could make, and he made them.

First, he demanded Elizabeth be declared officially 'Henry's only sole and true daughter, and heir'. She already had been by the previous year's Act of Succession, but Francis made it clear, considering Charles' manoeuvring on behalf of Mary. He wanted confirmation if Henry and Anne had no son that Elizabeth would receive the Crown of England 'without any impediment or contradiction'.

Secondly, he estimated Elizabeth's dowry at an annual revenue of 50,000 crowns. Instead of paying this amount, Francis wished Henry to lower the amount of the

French pension, paid in accordance with the latest treaties, until the sums levelled out.[12] The remainder, of approximately 60,000 crowns, Francis demanded he be cleared of.

Henry had already rejected all proposals regarding the pensions. Francis hoped he might reconsider. He said, for the meeting in April of 1535, he would bring his sister, Queen Marguerite of Navarre, and his two daughters, the Princesses Madeleine and Marguerite.[13] There had been a time when such a proposal with the recognition that it implied would have been accepted with alacrity. But it had come too late. Henry was already less than satisfied with his marriage, and appeared unmoved. He declared that Francis could not keep a foot in both camps, and that until he was absolutely sure of Francis' loyalty towards himself he would have 'marvellous great suspicions' and would guard against 'speaking or engaging himself' too much with Francis.[14]

Gontier did his best to reassure Henry that his master was less friendly with Spain than he believed, and while Henry appeared satisfied it was not to the extent that payments made to England would be discounted.

Elizabeth's rights he could agree to, her dowry and its payments he accepted, but he could not accept that the pensions from France could ever form a part of any agreement between England and France, even at the price of Elizabeth's future marriage.

Gontier had no authorisation to make changes to the instructions he had received, and the negotiations seemed stuck. It was only the fact that Henry's interest in the 'maiden' with whom he had flirted for the past months had waned that allowed Anne's position to improve. Henry had begun a new interest with a new woman. This was the Boleyn cousin, Margaret Shelton, who was the daughter of Lady Shelton, governess to Princess Elizabeth.

That Henry felt the need for a mistress, in the aftermath of the greatest love affair of his life, was sad. But at least the lady concerned was a relative who would not do any harm to Anne, upon whose continued success they depended. Madge Shelton was likely to strengthen the position if she influenced Henry at all. This seemed to happen, and Henry appeared more conciliatory. He no longer refused to cancel the pensions, but requested that claims from both sides should be examined. Mistress Shelton had worked well and Elizabeth's proposed French marriage still seemed viable.

Henry wanted Gontier to take back to France a declaration he wanted Francis to sign. This was that Henry's marriage with Anne was valid, and Princess Elizabeth was the only legitimate heir to the French. It was a triumph for the Boleyns if they had Francis' approval and apparent support.

However, Henry no longer wished to take part in the visit the following spring. The possibility of Anne meeting the French royal ladies on equal terms had not tempted him. He suggested sending emissaries instead.

George Boleyn expected to be chosen, but Henry appointed Secretary Cromwell and the Duke of Norfolk, with Sir William Fitzwilliam.[15]

Cromwell became ill and unable to go, so George was appointed in his place. He was qualified and experienced enough to be entrusted with the post, but Madge Shelton may have had something to do with Henry's change of heart towards his brother-in-law. John Hussey wrote to Lord Lisle on 4 May 1535 that 'The King's deputies for the Conference in Calais are to leave on the 11th of this month, where Lord Rochford, the Lady's brother, will go in Master Cromwell's place.' It is interesting to note the use of the word 'Lady' rather than 'Queen'. It is possible that Cromwell's illness and subsequent withdrawal from the embassy was diplomatic. There are reports that he was genuinely ill, with breathing difficulties, and was unable to work for some weeks. Whatever the truth, George was going to France on sufferance, and not as a first-choice candidate. It was a change, after the rapid rise and goodwill he had enjoyed.

For other members of Anne's family it was a similar picture. Mary Boleyn's cry for help after her marriage to Stafford did her little good. Cromwell's reply to her letter has not survived, if there was one. He had already begun to dissociate himself from the Boleyns and never had the slightest interest in people who could bring him no advantage, Mary Boleyn's affairs could draw attention in the worst way.

Anne and Mary do not appear to have been particularly close companions, but as time progressed Anne may have felt the need for family around her. There is no actual record that Mary Boleyn returned to court after her marriage with Stafford.[16]

We know she spent the rest of her life in obscurity though that may have been no bad thing. The court had always been a seething centre of intrigue, and anyone not fully capable of keeping up with it, pushing with the rest, was far better outside of it than in.

Mary's son, Henry Carey (by then 10 years old), was living apart from his mother. After the death of his father, William Carey, Anne had been given wardship of her nephew. By 1535 he was at Syon Abbey, a Brigettine nunnery in Middlesex. It was a large and wealthy abbey, which had long enjoyed Royal patronage, and was famous for its fine library. It was the ideal place for a well-born boy to receive a good education. Anne had taken her duties as his guardian seriously and done her best for him. In 1535 she found him a well-respected tutor, named Nicholas Bourbon, who had been obliged to leave France due to his lack of belief in the worship of saints.[17] He found refuge in England, and patronage in Anne, who had been recommended to him by Dr William Butts, the King's physician, with whom he lodged. We know Bourbon was employed to teach not only Carey, but Henry, heir to Sir Henry Norris, prominent at court as Groom of the Stool, and a member of the Privy Chamber. Also being taught was Thomas Hervey, the son of Sir Nicholas Hervey, a courtier close to the Queen, who shared her reforming principles.

It must be emphasised that despite Anne's posthumus reputation as a great reformer, her reforms tended to be aimed at necessary changes, within the Established Church rather than making any attempt to overthrow that Church. This is a difficult position to uphold as changes, once begun, tend to escalate and run out of control. Rather like 'jumping out of a window, and wishing to change one's mind halfway down', as one of Anne's biographers noted.[18]

Anne lived, and died, as a Catholic, albeit one of the Henrican persuasion. This belief occupied a shadowy ground of opinion trying to find its way.

Mary Boleyn's second husband, Stafford, was to go further, becoming so much a Protestant that he could not live in England during the reign of Queen Mary, exiling himself to Germany, where he became a friend of John Calvin. Mary Boleyn's daughter, Katherine would also marry a man known to be a Protestant, although by the next generation it would be far more acceptable to have such opinions. Mary Boleyn would not live to see such vast changes, but her daughter would live with and serve her cousin Queen Elizabeth, when such beliefs were the norm, based on the foundations Anne had helped to lay. That was for the future. After their exile from court, Mary and her husband were not sure what their prospects were. It appears that William was employed by Lord Lisle, possibly at Calais, as we know that he was there in 1537 and 1539. In 1539 William Stafford would be one of a group of people given the task of welcoming Princess Anne of Cleves on her journey through the town, on her own way to an ill-fated marriage to Henry VIII.

There is evidence that Mary Boleyn, despite disfavour and disgrace at court, continued to receive an annuity. This was the sum of 100 marks, and was referred to by Robert Blakeney, new Prior of Tynemouth, in a letter to Cromwell in April of 1537. 'My Lady Mary Carey, now Stafford, had an annuity of 100 marks under Convent Seal of my House, for no cause except that it should be for preferring my predecessor in his position …'. The Prior had been attempting to stop payment, but was commanded by the Lord Chancellor that it be reinstated.[19] That this pension should be continued despite the horrors of the previous year, has been taken by many as proof that Henry VIII was not paying for Mary herself. He could no longer have had the slightest interest in her, as an ex-mistress or the sister of his disgraced second wife. However, the payment could have been for the upkeep of her children, one or both of whom may have been sired by him.

It might be interesting to digress, to consider this question. Was Katherine Carey, born in 1524, Henry's child? It is possible. Katherine Carey would marry Sir Francis Knollys. She would bear her husband nine children, two of whom died young. Her eldest surviving daughter, Laetitia (Lettice Knollys), would become the rival of her cousin Queen Elizabeth for the affections of Robert Dudley, Earl of Leicester, and Lettice succeeded in marrying him in 1578.

Despite the mutual dislike between Elizabeth and Lettice, there was an acknowledged resemblance. Letttice possessed the long face and dark eyes of the Boleyns, together with the royal-Tudor red hair, as Elizabeth did. Her looks and colouring suggest not only the same female line but perhaps also a trace of the same male line.

If Elizabeth's father, Henry VIII, was also the grandfather of Lettice Knollys, it would explain their obvious resemblance to each other, as well as the pension that continued to be paid to Mary Carey. There can be no confirmation of this most interesting speculation, but questions may be raised regarding the true paternity of Katherine Carey.

Mary was only mentioned again, indirectly, when Anne Boleyn was divorced by Henry VIII before execution. A 'secret' reason was given to substantiate the divorce from Anne, and it is logical that Henry would use this old affair with her sister as an impediment. By the standards of the time, association with Mary Boleyn formed nearly the same impediment to Henry's second marriage as the marriage of Katherine of Aragon to Prince Arthur had his first. In either case, he chose to ignore the impediment, and it has been said of his elastic conscience that he 'forgot it when it suited him to forget, and remembered it when it suited him to remember!'.[20]

Anne seems to have attracted a particularly violent level of derogatory remarks aimed at her morals.[21] In one instance, the Abbot of Whitby, a man of presumably peaceful and decent habits who had never met Anne, still felt qualified to express his thoughts regarding her in the strongest terms. He declared, as if it were a fact, that 'The King's Grace is ruled by one common stewed whore, Anne Bullen, who makes all the spirituality to be beggared, and the temporality also.'[22] That this man had no personal knowledge of her at all did not prevent him from referring to her as if she were a common prostitute. Henry's actions had unleashed a tide of spite and malice which, while it was difficult and dangerous to direct at the King himself, was apparently in order to direct against his Queen. This was not only painful and distressing for her, but extremely perilous. Henry would play on the bad reputation she had innocently acquired, and when the time came would use it for his own ends against her.

A side effect of this was something Henry had not wanted. That was for every common person in England to feel free to discuss the King's business, and freely to give their opinions on it. Henry had complained about this earlier, when he had first attempted to break with Katherine and had objected to his affairs being talked about 'in every alehouse'. Unfortunately, the problem had not gone away, in fact it had become more widespread.

One example, from the previous year, had concerned two men at the White Horse in Cambridge. During a conversation, one man had asked the other if he knew that there was no longer a Pope. The other expressed his belief that there was still a Pope, and that anyone who thought otherwise was a 'strong heretic'. The first man claimed that King had 'played his part' in the current situation and the second man lost his temper. He declared that both the King and the other man were heretics, and also that 'this business would never have been if the king had not married Anne Boleyn!'. The dispute then descended into a fistfight in the stableyard.[23]

Such displays of public dissent could have been repeated anywhere in the country, between people who had never seen the King, or Anne Boleyn or Queen Katherine either, and never would. We know of such clashes because of the work of Thomas Cromwell, who was tireless in creating a spy system which could monitor every instance of friction, where the King's name was being besmirched.

Anne was widely believed to encourage the King in his excesses and in the establishment of the oppressive regime. Henry had his own fears, particularly with regard to Katherine of Aragon. He did say of her that 'the Lady Katherine is a proud and stubborn woman of very high courage. If she took it into her head to take her daughter's part, she could easily take the field, muster a great array, and wage against me a war as fierce as any her mother Isabella waged in Spain.'[24]

That Katherine still felt herself unable to take such a step was something Henry could never feel entirely sure of, and it was another source of tension to add to those that he and Anne were struggling to live with.

One of the Duke of Norfolk's reasons for his dislike of his Boleyn relatives was his feeling that Cromwell, whom he saw as their creature, had moved into a place that he was, by birth at least, totally unfitted for. That move had ousted Norfolk. The Duke considered that he should be at the centre of affairs rather than Cromwell. He had felt a strong dislike and jealousy when Wolsey occupied the central position, but now that feeling was aimed at a man who had been nothing but one of Wolsey's minions. Even the marriage of his daughter, Mary Howard, to the King's illegitimate son, the Duke of Richmond, did not seem to be enough to satisfy his need to occupy the central position. It was not, to him, sufficient recompense for being sidelined. Cromwell had moved out from his original place, standing modestly behind the Boleyns, into a very powerful position of his own. This made him obnoxious to the Duke, who had his own fixed ideas regarding the status of individuals and the disposal of power.[25]

Wolsey had certainly seen the need for reform, and had instituted reforms, but within the Church. He had loved the glorious ceremonial, designed to take men's minds higher than the mundane, and had no wish to see it destroyed. He had been, in that at least, closer to Anne than either of those two old enemies would have cared to admit. They both wanted changes, but still both died as professed Catholics.

Cromwell, on the other hand, was truly agnostic. Whichever way the religious cat was to jump meant nothing at all to him, and all the arguments for and against left him unmoved. He would deal with Catholics or Protestants alike equally, because he believed them all to be equally deluded. Apart from his advancement and fortune, his only aim and wish was to be accepted as the gentleman that he was not. For that cause, he would support, or discard, any partners or colleagues, shift with any breeze, change sides as necessary, provided he could gain from it. That was precisely why he was so dangerous. He could not be swayed by altruism and was never subject to guilt. He was entirely pragmatic.

To a man like Thomas Howard, who, despite many faults, could still accept the curb of religion, Cromwell could only be regarded with growing horror, as a man totally without compunction or restraint, saving only the King's word, which had in itself become erratic and unreliable.

There were, very worryingly, rumours that Spanish ships were being made ready. Henry knew he had no fleet to repulse them, if the Emperor were to move against England at last.[26] He then decided upon a rather panicky attempt at conciliation. Not only would Fisher and More (both still in the Tower) receive concessions in their treatment, he claimed, but he would ensure that Katherine of Aragon would be treated extremely well. This, of course, all provided that Charles V made no move against England.

Annoyed with the Emperor, Francis then turned again towards the English alliance, but without going so far as to finalise it. Anne had expected quicker, and better, news. Francis was still playing for time by trying to insert ever more unenforceable conditions.

Anne saw Gontier in those first unsettling weeks of 1535, and he gave her a letter from Chabot. She retorted angrily, saying that 'she found herself in greater difficulties than before her marriage' and that Chabot needed to put matters right. He should have been looking after her affairs better for her. She then entreated Gontier to pray for the Admiral to help her, but declared that she could not tell all of her concerns then and there 'due to the prying eyes of the king and of the courtiers'.[27]

She also told him that she dared not remain in conversation with him, and Gontier was impressed with the level of her anxiety. He was to write to Chabot, 'I assure you, my Lord, by what I can make out, she is not at her ease.'[28]

The conditions in the newly prepared treaty were again not such as Henry could accept. Francis now demanded Henry's official renunciation of all claims to the title of France. Although Henry had no possibility of ever making good on those ancient claims, they were still dear to his heart and his sense of history and chivalry. He would be loath to reject them completely. Francis also demanded the total extinction of all pensions, arrears and all other payments that were supposed to be made by France to England and which totalled a very healthy 120,000 crowns a year. Henry was incensed. He would never agree to such terms – but perhaps that was exactly the reaction hoped for, and was why such extreme demands had been made.

By 1 February 1535 Gontier had decided that he would have to pay a visit to Cromwell. Up to that time, he had not been considered of very much value in the negotiations, but that was only because the French had not fully realised how high he had risen.

Gontier was to suggest that Cromwell might 'profit' from persuading Henry to agree to the French demands. However, Cromwell was too clever, or too fond of his own skin, to side openly with France in the matter, or expose himself to danger by an attempt to make Henry accede to the terms.

Gontier then went to Westminster, where he met with the Dukes of Norfolk and Suffolk, polar opposites to his last attempt, but where he received a rather more friendly welcome.

The King also spoke briefly with Gontier after dinner and showed his anger to him at the claims of the French King, and also that he believed that Francis was still negotiating with Charles V. He did, however, tell Gontier to pass on to Francis his pleasure at the suggestion that the Queen of Navarre and the Princesses of France would attend any meeting they would have.

Francis, in return for the honour had asked a favour of his own. This was that when the next vacant Garter was awarded, it should be given to a gentleman of his choosing. The two candidates awaiting the honour of the Garter were Lord George Rochford and Sir Nicholas Carewe. Though the King's brother-in-law might have seemed the obvious choice, it was to be Carewe who received the Garter, which was, for the Boleyns, yet more evidence of the changeable and fickle nature of the French King.[29]

The Council was then to draw up the official answer to the French proposals, and was to prove itself to be even more obdurate than Henry. Any suggestion of rescinding the pensions and payments was absolutely refused, and a demand made for proper Commissioners to be sent to England to debate the marriage conditions. Neither Anne's father, Lord Wiltshire, nor her brother, Lord Rochford, would be connected with the negotiations for the marriage of Elizabeth.

In February of 1535 the Princess Mary became seriously ill. Henry allowed Dr Butts to attend her, along with Katherine of Aragon's own physician.[30] Dr Butts appears to have been in favour of the removal of the Princess from the country, to secure her safety, and he made his opinions clear. Chapuys reported these to Charles V, along with his own remark that 'it was well for the King that he did not know with how little trouble he [Charles V] might make himself master of England'.[31]

By April Mary had been removed to Eltham and Chapuys was entertaining hopes that the Princess might be able to be taken from there to Gravesend, where they could take to the river and flee the country. Getting her actually out of the house would be the most difficult part of any escape plan, as she was guarded by royal servants under the command of Sir John Shelton. The government, already well aware of the proposed plans, kept the conspirators under close surveillance and they were refused permission to leave the court, where Cromwell's spy system could track their movements.[32]

Cromwell's show of support for Anne had been useful. But early in March of 1535 Fortune's wheel had again turned. When Cromwell had withdrawn from the embassy to France, to be replaced by Lord Rochford, the friends of Katherine and Mary had taken strength from the idea that he was seriously ill, and not conducting any business, and might be unable to thwart them.[33] They did their best to use their influence on Henry at that time, and he appeared to be willing to listen to their entreaties, but to their disappointment Cromwell recovered and took over control once again, with all his old energy. He had gone so far, according to Chapuys, to 'threaten' those who had tried to work on Katherine and Mary's behalf.[34]

In fact, their slight advance in influence was to be checked even more severely by the new form of Oath to which the clergy was then compelled to subscribe. A further proclamation, aimed at any of those people who still looked to the Pope, or used his name in the service of the Church, ensured that they would be punished severely.

This did not cause many problems for the secular clergy, already well attuned to obedience to Henry and who were likely to offer little opposition to him. But the monks were another matter entirely. They would certainly not give in to the King so easily, but they would be punished accordingly. At the end of spring, three priors and a monk suffered the full appalling penalty of the law, by being hanged, drawn and quartered in the presence of many witnesses from the court itself.

Henry was looking forward with confidence to the proposed meeting with the French Commissioners, but Cromwell was uncomfortably aware that the execution of the monks and priors was being viewed with extreme distaste outside of England.

These men were not merely Henry's subjects. They were also members of religious orders with Houses throughout Europe. Orders that commanded great respect and even reverence. Henry's cruelties towards these men, dying horribly for a matter of conscience, were already being denounced on the Continent, and in France itself feeling was already turning to a bitter opposition and unpopularity towards the English alliance.

On 19 and 20 May the English Commissioners (by then including Rochford since Cromwell's withdrawal) had arrived in Calais, but Cromwell's fears were to prove only too real. The French refused absolutely to accept the proposed conditions, as brokered by Gontier, and demanded further additions of their own. These included a clause stating that, if after the treaty was concluded, Henry should break off the proposed match, he would then forfeit all the money due to him from France. It was also made perfectly clear that not only would France not join with England in any actions against the Holy See, but that on the contrary, every effort should be made to make the English submit and bring the schism to an end.

Henry had had some idea of the young Duke of Angoulême being sent to England, where he would be not only a prospective bridegroom but also a very useful hostage to ensure the support of Francis and his good intentions. But his idea met with resistance.

The French believed Henry was the one who should be making any necessary sacrifices, not demands, and their resentment at the execution of the Carthusians just before the beginning of the conference made it impossible to be able to agree terms.

Therefore the conference, into which had gone so much work, and upon which so many hopes had hinged, was after such a long time of negotiation and counter proposal finally to break up without anything at all having been achieved. The marriage was off.

Given the disparity in the demands from either side, it was impossible to imagine that talks would ever be resumed. All the protracted bargaining had done was to exacerbate Henry's determination to have his own way. He was even more intent on being obeyed without question, at least within the bounds of his own shores.

It would bode ill for all those who opposed him, and bring to a head the fates of those unfortunate people who were entirely in his power.

Chapter Fifteen

The spring and summer of 1535 were to be one of the wettest known. One of the Queen's ladies became ill with measles, which raised concerns about the continuing health of the Queen herself, as she was reputed to be pregnant again.

As Anne was later to accompany the King on progress as usual, it may be that she had a miscarriage that summer. There has always been disagreement between historians regarding the number of times Anne was actually pregnant during her marriage to Henry, and the summer of 1535 is usually the time that features largely. Was she, or was she not, pregnant that summer? She has even been accused of pretending that she was, when in fact she was not, in order to keep Henry's interest on the boil. There is, of course, another possibility, a halfway house between actually being pregnant or downright pretence. There is the possibility that she at this time suffered from a false pregnancy, or pseudocyesis. This is known to present problems with women who are desperate to conceive, and is not purely imaginary, as all the usual symptoms of a real pregnancy can be present, including lactation. Anne's state of stress and her deep longing to produce the son could have caused her to display the symptoms of the false pregnancy, so very easy to confuse with a real one.

In Anne's day the problem would not have been recognised at all. If she did suffer from pseudocyesis, her mental anguish would probably have been exacerbated by the failure of what she had hoped was another chance of a child. There would also be the humiliation of having to admit her error, when she had genuinely believed herself to be with child. She would probably have had to face the criticism and even barely concealed pleasure of enemies, who preferred to believe that she had fabricated the whole episode. It would have added to the wall of mistrust and resentment, which was gradually but inexorably being built up between her and Henry.

The political problems were also adding strain. The Pope, Paul III, was preparing to show Christendom that he was far more decisive than his vacillating predecessor had been.

The fact that Sir Thomas More and Bishop Fisher were still imprisoned was a matter of great concern, touching more than merely their closest associates. These men, far more than most, represented not only the traditional viewpoint, but an open frankness of opinion that was certainly becoming rarer, due to the atmosphere of oppression.

That is not to say that Thomas More had not in the past indulged his own prejudices freely. He had on several occasions written extremely disparagingly of Protestants in general, ignoring any claim to genuine religious convictions they may have had, and doing so with a foul, bigoted hatred with which he disgraced himself more than them. He considered them to be cowards and traitors and recommended that the fullest penalty of the law be used to punish them.

Now that the wheel of fortune had come full circle, he faced his own imprisonment and mortal danger with an outward show of courage. He was willing to be sacrificed for what he believed in, even as he had sacrificed others.

Fisher, though outwardly more circumspect in his behaviour, also had a fixity of mind that could not admit of any opinion other than his own. He was, in essence, just as rigid as More.

However, to the ordinary citizen, who had been appalled and bewildered by the many sudden changes of the last few years, they still represented the safe, familiar orthodox view. That this was swiftly being eradicated made it more precious. In consequence they were seen as martyrs.

The Pope also revered them. He could see in them, and in their terrible plight, an excellent opportunity to chastise Henry and to use them as a lever with which to dislodge Henry's dangerous pretensions. He intended to make it clear, through his championship of Fisher and More, that no ruler had the freedom to do as the King of England was doing. No man could be allowed to endanger such other men, whose reputations were well known throughout Europe.

Diplomacy frequently hides an ulterior motive, and the decision to elevate Bishop Fisher to the Cardinalate was a prime example of this. Fisher would be unable to take advantage of the rise in status the Pope proposed for him, but that did not matter. By elevating him at all Paul III was making it clear to all of Europe that if Henry were to harm the man, it would not merely be another Englishman who suffered, but an acknowledged Prince of the Church, a man who should be beyond his authority to harm.

After executing the recalcitrant monks, Henry had turned eagerly to the punishment of devout evangelicals, distributing his displeasure even-handedly to both sides. He would not tolerate any who professed their respect and obedience to the Pope, but he intended to prove that he had not, by any means, turned into a Protestant. He was equally keen to punish those people who foolishly believed that the radical new ideas gave them the right and freedom to interpret the gospels for themselves. Twenty-three refugees from the Lowlands, including three women, were burned alive at the stake to show the people yet again that only Henry's own version of Christianity was considered to be acceptable.[1]

In an attempt to counter such atrocities as these, Pope Paul decided to create a batch of new Cardinals. Men who were mentally strong and willing to help force through a counter-reformation. He intended to resist the dangerous new ideas and the new Cardinals were to be at the forefront of this. The existing Cardinals were in many cases afraid of the implications of such an aggressive stance, but Paul was not to be intimidated and he wanted men to support him who were equally courageous. He would not allow the new ideas to tear Christendom apart. To this end, he was to choose seven new men, all well known for their zeal, to help him to resolve and vigorously oppose the advances, which were threatening the peace and stability of the Established Church.

The French envoy, Jean du Bellay, became one of them; later Reginald Pole would be another, but in 1535 the most influential of the new appointees had to be Bishop Fisher, who was consequently elevated to the title of Cardinal of St Vitalis.

Henry's envoy in Rome, Casale, was fully aware of the likely repercussions of the move, which was obviously intended as a direct challenge to Henry. He remarked sadly to the Pope, 'Your Holiness has never committed a more serious mistake than this!'

The Pope's move had been intended not only as a direct rebuff to Henry, but also as a way of showing England's faithful Catholics that they were not abandoned, despite the upheavals they were forced to suffer. His stubborn withdrawal from the fold had not excluded them, their problems were understood and they were still considered by Rome to be an integral part of the Church. Fisher's elevation was meant to be recognition of this and a means of support.

It inflamed Henry further, proving the fears that Casale had expressed. Fisher's life was to be the forfeit for the Pope's well-intentioned move to bring England back into the Catholic fold. When Henry heard that Fisher's Cardinalate was a fact, he became furious and declared that the Pope need not bother to send the Cardinal's hat to England, he would send the head to Rome to receive the hat.

His outburst was childish, a man who felt himself cornered. Was he capable of remembering the show and ceremonies that had accompanied the arrival of the last English Cardinal's hat, that of Wolsey in November of 1515? In retrospect those celebrations seemed a brighter time. The conferring of Wolsey's hat had generally been seen as an honourable thing. The intervening twenty years had brought great and irreversible changes.

Paul III was horrified at the danger to Fisher. He contacted Charles de Denonville, the Bishop of Mâcon, begging him to write immediately to Francis I to ask him to intercede with Henry VIII on Fisher's behalf. While the Ambassador was willing to write to Francis, he admitted that he held out little hope of any such intercession being able to succeed. The Imperialists were using the situation to sow discord between Henry and Francis and had intimated that Francis had been responsible for recommending Fisher to the Pope. If Francis was to plead for Fisher's life, it would appear that he had interfered in the matter and would provide Henry with yet another source of resentment.[2]

The Pope asserted that he had not been asked by any Prince to confer the Cardinal's hat on the Bishop of Rochester, in an effort to defuse the situation. The Bishop of Mâcon went on to suggest that, if Fisher's life were to be spared, he could promise that he would swear to the statutes imposed upon him by Henry. Then it might be in order for him to be allowed to go to Rome to receive his hat from the Pope's own hands. This in the hope that Henry would be glad to be rid of him, and would allow him to leave the country.

But Henry had no such plans. Henry was out for blood, and now that he was a Cardinal, even without the accolade of the hat, Fisher's death would make him all the more valuable as a sacrifice. The well-meant attempts to get Fisher to safety had not taken into account that Fisher was unlikely to take part in such a subterfuge, and would not foreswear himself.

Gregory Casale had written to Cromwell after the deaths of the Carthusians, reporting that the French had been disgusted by Henry's cruelty. This confirmed Henry's entrenched belief that Francis had betrayed his trust, and that some form of league was at work. He could not lash out at fellow kings or the Pope but he could make sure that his helpless prisoners suffered for what he saw as another example of treachery and double-dealing.

A special commission for the trial of the Bishop was issued and Fisher was arraigned in Westminster Hall before a court of seventeen judges. These included Cromwell, Lord Wiltshire and ten justices. The charge was treason. As Henry had officially deprived Fisher of his title of Bishop of Rochester, by Act of Attainder, he was to be tried as a common person, by jury, on 17 June 1535. The only testimony

Sir Richard Rich, later Lord Rich, the giver of false evidence in the trials of Bishop John Fisher and Sir Thomas More.

against him was that of Sir Richard Rich. He would prove himself a master of the art of reporting what he claimed to be 'admissions'. These were supposedly made as part of innocent conversation with the accused.[3]

The result was a foregone conclusion and Fisher was condemned to be hanged, drawn and quartered at Tyburn. That awful death was commuted to beheading, and Fisher was to be executed without any further delay, at the Tower of London, on 22 June 1535.

Once that was done, and the echoes of the shock reverberated throughout Europe, Henry struck again. Compelled onwards by disappointments, frustrations and belief that every other ruler was against him, he had an even greater card to play.

Thomas More was, in the King's opinion, another ingrate, another man who was openly disrespectful of his King's wishes, and was to become the next victim. More was too well thought of, therefore too influential, to be allowed to continue to resist the King's will. He had been in the Tower for fifteen months, where he had not been actively ill-treated, but the confinement had ruined his health. By the summer of 1535 he was suffering from regular chest pains and cramps in his legs.

He had also been subjected to family pressures, particularly from his wife, who had repeatedly begged him to give in to the King to save himself, but that good lady had no real idea of the calibre of man she had married. His favourite daughter, Margaret Roper, had more wisdom and more understanding of her father, though she too had tried to get him to take the Oath. She had begged him to do so both for his own sake, and for the sake of his fearful and grieving family. However, even with the qualification of 'so far as the law of God allows' it would not now do for More. He would by then probably have refused any such escape clause.[4]

During his incarceration More had not been idle. He had written several 'books', some in Latin and some in English, along with many letters of encouragement and strength to friends. In these he showed himself to be obsessed by suffering, both his own, and that of others.

On 3 June, he had again been examined by Cranmer, Cromwell, Audley and the Duke of Suffolk. Lord Wiltshire was also present. Yet again More refused to be drawn about whether he considered Henry the Supreme Head of the Church, or whether he did not. It was an unanswerable question. As Lord Chancellor, More had used that very trap to convict heretics, knowing that one answer would violate the conscience and the other would be considered treasonable. Now that same argument would be used against him.

The authorities had become aware that he had been in communication with Fisher, letters having been carried between the two of them by More's servant. As a result of this discovery, by 12 June More had been deprived of his writing materials and his books. This would have been a greater loss to him than any amount of luxuries or even freedom.[5]

Immediately after Fisher's trial on the 17th, three more Carthusians had been executed by the full, horrific, method of being hanged, drawn and quartered. This took place at Tyburn on 19 June. By the time Fisher met his own end, by beheading, on 22 June, Thomas More was faced with the realisation that his own time was to be very short.

Henry was indulging in an orgy of killing, lashing out at anyone around him who did not obey him. Only Fisher's status had protected him, saving him from the long-drawn-out suffering of the full traitor's death. That shameful death faced More, and he would have been aware that his own show trial and execution would not be long delayed. He would be determined to use that trial to try to put forward his own point of view.

What is obvious is that if More had felt able to take the Oath, even in some modified form, he need not have suffered the traitor's death. Henry would have been delighted to show him off as a convert to his policies. More shunned Henry's 'mercy' with the same calm with which he faced his approaching death. Perhaps he welcomed the opportunity to face death for his beliefs, in a final open defiance of his King.

He was tried at Westminster Hall on 1 July before a team of special commissioners and a jury. The judges, again including Cromwell, Norfolk, Suffolk, Wiltshire and Lord Rochford, could hardly have been less impartial. More was to claim that, unlike Fisher, he had never claimed that Henry was not the Head of the Church in England. He had merely refused to answer that vital question. This hair-splitting was unacceptable to the court, and Sir Richard Rich appeared, being summoned conveniently to remember a conversation he claimed to have had with More on 12 June. That was the occasion when he had been sent to collect the prisoner's books and writing materials. Whether it was at all likely that More, after so long a silence on a delicate subject, would foolishly confide such dangerous opinions to a man like Richard Rich, was barely necessary as an argument to convince the judges of More's guilt. Despite his firm denial that any such unguarded statement was ever made, and also despite a spirited speech in his defence, More was found guilty of treason. He was sentenced to the full punishment required by the law.[6]

He returned to the Tower, and was informed that he was to die before 9 a.m. on 6 July following. There is a tradition that he managed to write a final letter during those days, to his daughter Margaret Roper.

On the morning of 6 July 1535 he was beheaded on Tower Hill, after giving the very short speech that Henry had instructed him to make. As a final farewell it was masterly in its brevity. He told the watching people to pray for the King, then said that he died the King's faithful servant – 'but God's first!'.[7]

It was hardly the end that Henry had envisaged. It showed none of the humility he preferred. Due to More's luminous reputation throughout Europe he seemed to have achieved an ascendency of Henry, due to his calm acceptance of his fate and his absolute refusal to submit. It was not a triumph for Henry, and he was aware of it, despite his claims of having to clear the country of traitors.

Queen Anne was blamed by many for More's death. She was accused of having demanded More's head, and for a time Henry's frustrations caused him to lash out verbally at her. Even Chapuys did not seem to blame her openly for what had been caused largely by More's own intransigence, and any quarrel between her and the King over the matter was soon at an end. Henry declared that 'there never was a servant to his sovereign so villainous, nor subject to his prince so treacherous' as More.[8] It showed that Henry's attitude towards erstwhile friends could, and would, suffer a total reversal and that he would deny any former intimacy of confidence.

Despite the miserable weather of that summer, Henry and Anne set out on progress together showing every sign of being comfortable in each other's company. Chapuys had reported that when Henry's fool, Will Somers, had made some disrespectful joke at the expense of the Princess Elizabeth he was sent away from court in disgrace.[9]

Sir Thomas More, the flawed saint who sacrificed himself perhaps unnecessarily, to prove a point.

Whether this was due to any love for Anne, or merely a cynical protection of his investment on Henry's part is open to debate. His affection for Anne had suffered and he was open to romance. During that year's progress, one of the stops was at Wolf Hall, home of the Seymours. Sir John Seymour was Sheriff of Wiltshire, Dorset and Somerset, but the family had never figured largely at court. They had been tainted by a terrible scandal in the recent past. Sir John had been guilty of having an affair with his daughter-in-law, Katherine, the wife of his eldest son, Edward Seymour. He was considered to be the likely father of her two sons.[10] There had been a separation, but the two children, born in 1528 and 1529 were declared illegitimate. The scandal was still very fresh and it is highly unlikely that Henry would have taken Anne into such a notorious house when he was more careful to safeguard her reputation. Even if the progress was there only a short time, there must have been a very awkward atmosphere between Sir John and Edward, making the visit uncomfortable. Edward Seymour had already remarried, taking the forceful Anne Stanhope as his second wife. Henry knew Edward rather better than he did his lecherous father, for he had been a protégé of Wolsey's, one of his Esquires of the Body, and present in Calais in 1532.

While still at Wolf Hall, Henry received a message that the Emperor Charles V had defeated Barbarossa and his forces at Tunis. It was a great victory that thousands of prisoners had been captured along with a good part of the enemy's fleet.

Despite any pleasure at such a success for the forces of Christendom, Henry may have been dismayed by the news. Such a resounding victory would leave Charles free of immediate military responsibilities, and cause him to turn his attention to the English question. Henry was aware that Katherine and Mary were part of the conspiracy against him, and in recognition of that knowledge were closely guarded and watched. It would be possible for others to stir up trouble on their behalf, even if the two women were helpless and in Henry's hands.

Henry was to send Gardiner to France, in an attempt to form an alliance against Charles as a form of insurance against any such attack from Spain, but it was very much in his interests, as it was Anne's too, to appear to be quite unconcerned publicly. They left Wolf Hall after a few days, and were in Winchester by 2 October.[11]

Sir Richard Greville reported, 'the King and Queen is merry and hawks daily and likes Winchester and that quarter and praises it very much'. Sir Anthony Windsor also said, 'the King and Queen were very merry in Hampshire'.

They stayed at The Vine between 15 and 19 October and had returned to Windsor by the 26th of the month. It must have by then been easier to assume an appearance of cheerfulness and unconcern, because during that autumn's progress Anne had good news for her husband. She had good reason to believe that she was pregnant again.[12]

The King and Queen may have done their best to appear to be 'merry' and Anne certainly had reason to be hopeful but outside of England feelings were running very high regarding the deaths of Fisher and More. It was said that the Pope and the Cardinals were so shocked and disgusted at the killing that they wished to deprive Henry of his Crown, for the crimes of heresy and 'lesere majestatis'. Their justification for that was the English Crown was a part of the Holy See. The intention was that the Crown would devolve upon the Princess Mary, to rule in her father's place. Such a plan could hardly remain a secret, and once it became common knowledge Mary's life might be forfeit. It was apparent that Henry was not responding in the normal way, so the fear was that any move against him, however sensible or considered to be for the ultimate good of English Catholics, would rebound upon the innocent party. It would put Mary's life at risk.[13]

There was also the problem of finding a secular Prince to act on the Pope's behalf, to deprive Henry of his throne. As he could not be expected to give in to the papal order without strong opposition, and no other Prince seemed willing to carry war into England, the matter lapsed. The idea had been unworkable, but showed the strength of feeling against Henry.

There was also a good deal of hostility from the foreign Protestants. Rather than approving his actions, they were disgusted at his lack of control. It was considered that his excesses discredited their cause, so they had begun to distrust him almost as much as the Catholics. The executions had widened a breach between them and Henry, due to the death of Thomas More, for whose common sense they had the utmost respect. That Fisher and More had been killed filled both sides with astonishment and horror.

Realising that public opinion abroad had turned against him, Henry attempted to justify his actions by issuing 'memorials' in his defence. He claimed that the executions had been in response to the treason of the men killed. He went so far as to claim that Fisher's death had been an 'easy' one. He made similarly bizarre claims in the case of More and defended his own 'beneficence, equity, piety and mildness', declaring his virtues were 'so well known to the world that his reputation for such qualities could not be undermined by any calumny'.[14]

Henry had lost any sense of how he appeared to others. The undermining of his reputation was severe abroad, where the distance between him and other people provided them some security for the expression of their opinions.

His claims to be a model of kindness and generosity, despite all his public actions, caused others to consider him not only dangerous but actually deranged. He began to be looked on askance, as if his common sense could no longer be relied on. Few ruling princes would dare go so far as Henry had, let alone claim virtue and kindness.

The Northern Alliance was collapsing, Denmark was in ferment and Henry had been asked for an alliance to prop up the Danish claimant Duke Christian. It would have been an ideal opportunity to form new friendships abroad, with men like Gustavus Vasa of Sweden, Christian of Schleswick-Holstein and the Dukes of Prussia and Pomerania. These men were looking for a figurehead, perfect for Henry, giving him authority and a more solid standing in the face of hostility from France, Spain and the Pope.

Henry showed that he was not only ill-informed but not wise enough to take advantage of such a solution, placed almost in his hands.

Schwaben had travelled to Hampton Court in February of 1535 on behalf of Duke Christian to try to make a start on the negotiations. Cromwell had received him cordially. Henry was not so diplomatic. When he met the envoy he began by demanding why Duke Christian thought he had any right to rule Denmark. He declared that it was an elective throne, and the decision rested solely with the people. He went further, lapsing into aggression and arrogance, saying, 'Why should I not accept the Kingdom of Denmark, which has been offered to me?' The envoys were astonished.

After an unpromising start, the Ambassador had been kept waiting for some weeks, and was finally sent away with no reply for his master, and with a lack of courtesy.

Pope Paul III had been more sensible. Henry became very uneasy when he heard that negotiations were possible between the Papacy, the King of France and the German Reformers. If those groups should become reconciled with the Pope, the Northern States might well do so. England would then be alone and surrounded by enemies on all sides. Such was the dangerous pass that the security of England had been reduced to.

By the summer of 1535 Henry had decided to send Robert Barnes to Saxony in an attempt to counteract Francis' moves of friendship. Henry should, in view of Francis' continuing hostility towards him, have acted with extreme care, but he did not. He had been asked to provide men and money for aid, in exchange for the castle and town of Warburg, with a possibility that he could also take over the castles and towns of Malmö, Landskron, Copenhagen and Elsinore. Such was the desire to have his backing.

The idea at first appealed to him. So much so that it blinded him to the difficulties involved. He became eager to send men and money into Denmark, but before they could embark news arrived that the Swedish fleets had captured Admiral Skram's fleet. Suddenly the idea of him becoming the 'Leader of the North' seemed more hazardous, resulting in a change of feeling on his part. The ships and men intended for Denmark were ordered to return to the Thames.

Henry had involved himself in a great deal of trouble and expense in his attempts to establish a small empire, without proper consideration. The idea of sending Englishmen to fight abroad had proved unworkable. Henry had lost the opportunity of becoming an advisor to the Northern States, which would have suited him.

By the end of July 1535 Pope Paul, still on the offensive, had issued several briefs detailing the evil acts committed by Henry. These required all Christian Princes to have no further contact with him, or indeed with England. Francis received one of these and decided that he should inform Henry of the extremity of its terms. He chose de Dinteville, the former ambassador to England, to deliver the bad news. De Dinteville arrived in England by the beginning of September.[15]

It would be a mistake to imagine that King Francis' early warning to Henry about the terms of the Pope's action against him was entirely altruistic. De Dinteville had further instructions from Francis that, if he were to stand by Henry, he could then expect hostilities in his turn from the Emperor. To prepare for that event, he expected to request subsidies from Henry. Francis' position had changed, and his attitude had changed with it. De Dinteville was instructed to make clear that if Francis was to go to war with the Emperor on his behalf, Henry must consider himself bound to pay back one-third of all the costs incurred by the French.[16]

De Dinteville had also been briefed to try to get a 'feel' for the general state of England and the reactions of the English people. The report he gave to Francis on his return painted a dismal picture.

Henry's policies had had a deleterious effect on foreign trade; there was rupture with Spain and difficulties with the Pope, as well as the frosty atmosphere with France. Negotiations with Denmark which, handled better, might have given England a new and useful alliance, had ignominiously failed and Henry's reputation in Europe reached an all-time low. If there were any possibility of a war with Spain over the situation of the Princess Mary and Queen Katherine, it would affect trade with the Low Countries even further. That was the greatest fear of the London merchants. Their trade with the Low Countries, under Charles V's control, was what England depended upon. In France, though Francis was on fair terms with Henry, merchants were finding they were subjected to robberies and almost daily attacks, and they could expect no justice in recompense. Shipowners had become afraid to send their vessels into French ports, with safe-conducts being taken out for all those hardy souls who intended to cross to France to continue with their business interests.

Henry's mishandling of the Danish business had caused resentment there too, resulting in Gustavus Vasa claiming that he was only just beginning 'the game' against Henry, leaving an impression that further trouble was to be expected.[17]

The harvest had been very poor due to the unreliable weather, the corn yield being less than half what was expected. Chapuys reported that the people were blaming the execution of the Carthusians and believed that their present wretched state was a direct result of divine vengeance being visited on England.

Previously, when bad harvests affected the country, as from time to time they did in the normal course of events, the Hanseatic merchants could be depended upon to supply the deficiencies. However, England was then relying only on France and the Low Countries. This was a very insecure position to be in, at a time when Chapuys and the French Ambassadors were advising that the export of corn to England should be forbidden, as a simple and effective way to bring pressure to bear on Henry.[18]

De Dinteville made careful note of all these problems, but he passed on Francis' financial demands to Henry. By then Henry was quite unable to afford to pay the amounts Francis asked. It was estimated that Henry would be liable to find over £33,000 a month. Since the entire royal income, even in a good year, did not exceed £140,000 a year, it was impossible and sharp words on the subject were exchanged. It was a humiliating position for Henry, who a quarter of a century previously had found his father's coffers filled with more gold than any country normally saw.

Before leaving England, de Dinteville asked for permission to visit the princesses. His aim was to meet Princess Mary, to check whether she was still inclined towards marriage with the Dauphin. The French contingent visited Eltham, where Mary and Elizabeth were living. One of the gentlemen of the King's Chamber accompanied them and the ambassadors reported that this gentleman had told them, in confidence, that he had had instructions from Queen Anne to watch their movements and report whatever they said. This also gave a very bad impression, and they later confirmed to Francis that King Henry was not even able to trust his own servants.[19]

The visit to Eltham had been wasted. They were not to see Princess Mary as Lady Shelton had received instructions prior to their arrival that Mary was to keep to her room. Although the Princess was indignant, she acquiesced on Chapuys' advice, when he recommended that she make no open protest. He was concerned for her safety, in view of Henry's notoriously short temper.

Anne, meanwhile, had plenty to occupy her. De Dinteville had mentioned – and also allowed the rumour to be spread – that when Mary left Greenwich to travel to Eltham, her journey had been enlivened by 'a great many women' who had flocked to see her in passing. They had called out to her that, despite the new laws, she was still 'their princess'. A few of the higher ranking ones had actually been arrested, and Anne found that two of those ladies were her sister-in-law Jane Rochford and her cousin Lady William Howard. Lady Rochford had been removed from court previously for involving herself, though if she had in the past acted on Anne's behalf, her feelings had undergone a change. By the latter part of 1535 she was known to be on poor terms with her husband. She had formed a friendship with Lady William Howard, her cousin by marriage. Whether her estrangement from George Boleyn was due to her attachment to a lady known for opposition to Anne, her extremely foolish behaviour, in view of her position as sister-in-law to the Queen, was bound to cause the maximum amount of talk. It would mortify Anne, giving the impression she was not properly controlling her household, allowing freedom to persons who publicly humiliated her.[20]

Due to all the unrest, difficulties in government and a malevolent atmosphere at court, the French ambassadors reported that the proposed marriage between the Princess Mary and the Dauphin might still be possible. The new regime did not appear to be as secure as had been thought. But that they considered themselves in a position to speak openly of such a marriage infuriated Henry. He knew that any such arrangement would seriously affect his hold on his subjects and he deeply resented interference from abroad. He was stoutly determined to keep Mary under his own control, despite her being of marriageable age. Ideally, had Mary been married, she may have given him a grandson, ensuring the succession. That would, of course, have meant bringing in the authority of whichever husband was chosen, which would have lessened Henry's own authority. Likewise, in the situation in which he found himself with his second marriage, there would be opposition to any attempt to provide Mary with a husband of rank as her own status was disputed.

Cromwell was angry with the French over this. At that time he was favourable towards the Princess Mary, as a result of his relationship with the Boleyns having deteriorated. But he certainly had no wish to see England fall into the hands of the French, through any marriage of their Prince with Henry's elder daughter.

One effective way for the English ministers to snub the French was to give the impression that they were on rather better terms with Spain than they were. A new ambassador, one Richard Pate, had recently been appointed to the court of Charles V and Cromwell made a great fuss of the honours that Pate had been receiving at the Imperial court.[21] Chapuys suddenly found himself more popular at the English court than he had been for a long time and Henry openly praised the virtues of Charles V.

Chapuys may have been gratified at the seeming popularity, and willing to make the French believe in the sudden new friendship, but he still did not want the outside world to think that either he, or his master, approved Henry's recent actions. Nor did he cease from pushing for Princess Mary's situation to be improved. In any event, the English attempts to regain the Emperor's friendship were unacceptable and doomed to failure, as Henry refused point-blank to do anything for either Katherine of Aragon or the Princess Mary.

Henry had made it clear, through his actions of that dismal summer, how he intended to pursue his policies, though even his ministers were dismayed at his inflexibility. Even their harmless subterfuge he refused to go along with. However, Henry might have felt real consternation had he known of the friendliness between France and Spain, and of the courtesies that passed between Chapuys and de Dinteville, before the latter left England.[22]

By September of 1535 more trouble was brewing, as in Rome Paul III was preparing his Bull of Excommunication and Deprivation. This move was not opposed by any of the French Cardinals and ambassadors, who merely requested that it should not in any way involve reflections on the conduct of King Francis. Neither should it put him in bad odour with the Emperor. Paul III's only problem was finding some prince willing to execute the sentence on Henry. Francis and Charles had perfected the art of looking the other way on that subject, though Francis had suggested that he might help, if Charles did. The Pope's son, Luigi Farnese, went to Sicily (where the Emperor then was) to attempt to forge some such understanding between them. Unfortunately, Charles' mistrust of Francis had not lessened, and he feared being put into the wrong if he agreed to any alliance, without first receiving solid written assurances.

The French party in England had been so discredited in England that Anne had had further bitter arguments with her uncle the Duke. He had intended to send his second son to France, but first asked Cromwell whether any show of friendship with the French was truly at an end. Cromwell's reply was so negative that it helped him to decide to keep his son at home.

However, Cromwell had his own problems to occupy him. The coffers were empty and Henry had instructed him to levy taxes to raise money. Even though the move had been approved by Parliament, Cromwell knew very well that if he forced the people to pay new taxes at such a time it would cause a very dangerous situation. Due to the terrible harvest and the bad trade abroad, the people were already finding it impossible to pay their rents. Salaries to officials also remained unpaid, and the smaller religious houses were already being despoiled in a desperate attempt to raise the money needed. Unfortunately, Cromwell's efforts to do as Henry wished did not endear him to the people, to Anne or even to Henry himself, as he became aware of the seething unpopularity of the move.

It was probably at this time that Henry first began to consider that many of the difficulties and disaffection he presently faced could have been eased had he not been married to Anne. He believed that, deep down, his people loved him, and the unpopular marriage was largely responsible for his troubles. It would always be convenient for him to offload blame onto someone else, and this situation proved no different. Anne was the convenient target. There were two main problems in the way of any attempt to discard her. The first was that he had already been informed that if he wished to divorce the new Queen, it could only be to take back the old one. Henry did not want Katherine back at any price, but the second problem stood firmly in the way, Anne was pregnant. She might still be able to save the succession by producing the son the ageing Katherine certainly could not give him.

During the progress just completed Henry's eye had rested on Jane Seymour, at whose family home the progress party had briefly stayed. Shortly after the return to court, the French ambassadors had reported that they thought that the King had a new love. If he had decided that someone like Jane would be a fitting consort, it could only have been that the lady's temperament was the opposite of Anne's. The family she came from were tainted with appalling scandal, and the lady herself was certainly no beauty. What she did have was the Seymour family's drive and ambition behind her, with her two elder brothers ready and willing to take advantage of the slightest encouragement. The Seymour brothers must have deeply regretted that their other sister, Elizabeth, widely acknowledged to be the beauty of the family, was already married. However, they certainly intended to do the best they could with what they had available, and were to play heavily on Jane's apparently demure and quiet character, pushing her forward on the premise that her greatest attraction was that she was not Anne.

Henry could do nothing but wait, frustrating though it was. He had for a considerable time expected Katherine of Aragon's death, but that lady had repeatedly disappointed him by clinging stubbornly on to life, despite him several times speaking openly as though her demise was imminent. Her continued existence seemed designed to spite him. Even if Katherine were to die before long, Anne's pregnancy still had to be waited for. If he were lucky the boy child might still result. If, on the other hand, Anne was to miscarry or produce another girl child, Henry could plan changes. Katherine could not live forever, nor could Anne's pregnancy last forever. Katherine's death would certainly relieve him of the calumny of having three wives living, which would be his if he tried to divorce Anne during her predecessor's lifetime.

Cromwell was also waiting for Katherine's death, but for different reasons. Once Katherine was safely out of the way, he hoped that it would be far easier for England to begin a new friendship with the Emperor. But the obstacle the poor lady had become still clung to life despite the rigours of her existence at Kimbolton. Katherine was as obdurate as ever, and seemed to be indestructible. Despite her holding on, the waiting game could not endure and those who still cared for Katherine's welfare were anxiously aware that Henry's patience had strict limits and his temper was short. They continued to fear that the King would take it into his head to anticipate the end, despite all his previous assurances that he had no intention of harming the lady. It was only her birthright as a daughter of Spain, and her close relationship to the Emperor Charles V, that prevented Henry from breaking his promises. He would certainly not be afraid to move against anyone, if they were unfortunate enough to be one of his subjects.

Cromwell had shown that his abandonment of Anne's cause was complete. When this was remarked upon, he showed neither concern nor remorse, merely saying, 'The Queen cannot do me any harm!' His confidence in his ability to withstand any opposition from Anne showed he believed that her situation depended entirely on her ability to produce the son.

As the autumn of 1535 slid down into another winter, the human pieces on the royal chessboard of England had begun to move into their final positions.

Chapter Sixteen

During October Katherine of Aragon had written to the Pope repeating that all the things that had happened during the year were 'an offence against God'. She reminded him that 'if some remedy is not applied shortly, there will be no end to ruined souls and martyred saints'. She finished with 'we await a remedy from God and Your Holiness. It must come speedily or the time will be past.'[1]

She must have felt the passing of time keenly. Not only was she aware of her increasing age, but also during the year her health had begun to fail. There had previously been problems, and Henry had been carefully watching, knowing that if she should die, the impasse would reach an end. She had suffered in November from the pains and nausea that had plagued her for some time, but they had worsened with the full approach of winter.

In early December Katherine had written to Chapuys, in her own hand, asking him for money, so that she could give gifts to her devoted household at Christmastime.[2] She also authorised him finally to make application to the Pope, in her name, for the Executory Brief against Henry to be issued. The lack of Katherine's application for that, being the injured party, had stayed the Pope's hand and prevented any real intervention on her behalf. By then she appeared to have taken a firmer stand, and with her formal application the matter could be expected to proceed. Neither Pope nor Emperor could move against Henry without Katherine's direct appeal. If the Brief were issued, then Charles V would not be able to ignore it, and Chapuys knew that it would finally force his master's hand.

Chapuys was relieved and cheered by what he saw as a return to health and vigour for Katherine. If her attitude had changed, then progress might be anticipated. The letter had also mentioned that Katherine hoped that Henry would allow her to move to another house in the spring, which suggested a raising of her spirits, a looking forward to the future. She intimated that she would prefer a place drier and healthier than Kimbolton, which was an understandable request in the circumstances, but one far less likely to be agreed to. If the cold and damp of Kimbolton were affecting Katherine's health, then there she would stay. Henry could do nothing obvious to hasten her end, but neither would he do anything to aid her recovery.

By the end of the month, it was clear that her condition was deteriorating. Chapuys received an urgent note from her doctor, De la Sa, on 29 December, which told him that her health was worse, and that if Chapuys wished to see her, then he must travel at once to Kimbolton.

Henry had another reason for a rise in spirits at that time. Francesco II Sforza had died in Milan and this had reopened the Milan question, the succession of which had been the cause of disagreement between France and Spain. If Charles and Francis were to become embroiled in the old argument, that new crisis would undoubtedly take the pressure off the question of the Executory Brief, and its enforcement. It would be a much-needed reprieve from excommunication and deposition.

Katherine's change of heart was too late. It looked as if there would be war between France and Spain, in which case Charles V would very likely need England to be an ally. It was highly improbable that the Emperor, in such circumstances, would allow concern for Katherine to stand in the way of a required alliance.

Henry fended off Chapuys' requests regarding Katherine, directing him to apply to Cromwell for any money needed. With regard to the Princess Mary, still a concern, and eager to visit her mother in her extremity, he said he would have to speak to the Council. Henry suddenly found that due to the death of Francesco II Sforza he had room to manoeuvre again. This gave him a substantial boost, which improved his temper, and with casual affability he allowed Chapuys to visit Katherine, with the words, 'She won't live long. Go to her when you like.'

Leaving the King's presence, Chapuys met with the Duke of Suffolk in the corridor, who confirmed Henry's indifference with the words, 'When she is dead, there will be no barrier between my King and the Emperor your master.'

Chapuys reached Kimbolton on 2 January 1536, making good speed on his journey despite bad weather. Katherine made an effort to welcome him formally, as befitted the Emperor's Ambassador, by ordering the pathetically diminished household to assemble to receive him. She then thanked him for his visit, adding poignantly, 'Now I can die in your arms, not abandoned like a beast.'

Chapuys pretended optimism, telling her that everyone was anxious to hear of her recovery, and that all were sorry to hear of her illness. He made various promises, impossible to keep, implying improved living conditions when she was well, and told her that the unity of Christendom depended upon her return to active life. The interview was short and formal, but quickly followed by another more personal one, during which Katherine told him of her problems with money, and her debts, which even included such small sums as laundry and repairs to her clothes. He tried to reassure her, telling her that the Emperor would soon have time to deal with the English problem, and that the English people still remained loyal to her.

While he was staying at Kimbolton, another visitor arrived. Katherine's dear friend the Dowager Countess of Willoughby was outside the walls, demanding admittance with the assurance of any noble traveller caught in bad weather.[3] Once admitted, however, the Countess disappeared into Katherine's rooms and did not reappear. Katherine was delighted at her friend's arrival and for a time appeared stronger, giving Chapuys the opportunity to leave Kimbolton the following morning, at Epiphany.

The apparent improvement did not last, and on the following morning the pain and nausea returned. She was obviously dying. It was at that point that she wrote her famous letter to Henry, in which she begged him to remember the health of his soul, telling him it was 'which you ought to prefer before all considerations of the world or flesh'. She reminded him, 'for which yet you have cast me into many calamities and yourself into many troubles'. But still she could not be harsh with him, 'But I forgive you all, and beg God to do likewise.' She commended their daughter Mary to him, 'beseeching you to be a good father unto her', and begged him to provide for her maids, giving them a marriage portion, 'which is not much, there being but three'. But the ending of the letter is what gave it its heartbreaking poignancy, given the miseries she had endured over the last years. 'Lastly, I want only one true thing, to make this vow. That, in this life, mine eyes desire you above all things.'[4] Despite everything, she loved and trusted him still. Henry had thrown away the love and devotion few people are ever fortunate enough to experience.

On that morning she received extreme unction and prayed aloud for 2 hours for the souls of all the people of England, for her beloved daughter Princess Mary and particularly for her husband Henry. At 2 o'clock that afternoon, on 7 January 1536, she died. She would be buried on the 29th in the choir aisle of Peterborough Abbey, but with only the honours of a Princess Dowager.[5] The terms of her will, along with her claims to be Queen, were ignored.

Chapuys was greatly saddened, but also indignant at all the unhappiness she had been made to suffer. He was particularly angry at the reaction of King Henry, who was reported to have dressed in yellow 'for mourning' worn with cheerful white feathers in his cap. He danced openly with Anne's ladies, and declared, 'Thank God, that we are now free from all threat of war!'

But popular reaction was different. Not only was Chapuys saddened, but many others felt the loss of the woman who had been England's Queen. However, to his surprise and dismay, there was no violent rebellion against Henry, which he hoped for. There were, of course, the usual rumours that she had been poisoned.

Chapuys reported to Charles V that there had been no proper autopsy of Katherine's body. Merely the opening of her remains by the chandler in an effort to embalm her. He had reported that all her organs looked normal, except for her heart, which appeared to have a black 'growth' clinging to it. This naturally fuelled the rumours of some foul play, but it is more likely that she died of cancer. She was just 51 years old.

Fortunately for Katherine's peace of mind, she had never seen that she could have acted otherwise. As a decent and honest woman she had felt herself to be in the right, and to be fair, many people agreed with her. But it is also fair to say that it was Katherine's stubbornness, in the face of her inability to bear that living son, and refusing to step down as others had done, that brought tragedy upon the people she loved, and the country that loved her.

Anne was sensible enough to have realised that with Katherine gone her own security was even more precarious. Katherine had offered her shelter by her very existence. Now that shelter was gone, and Henry might decide to free himself from Anne too. It might be his chance to make that completely fresh start. It was gloriously ironic that the woman who had so opposed Katherine, and wished her out of the way, should be the one to feel some regret at her passing and realise that she was now more exposed. Only the child she carried then stood between her and possible disaster. Anne must have clung to the idea of the coming baby like a drowning man to a lifeboat, hoping against hope that all might yet be well.

Anne's fears may have been eased by the fuss Henry made of Princess Elizabeth. When news of Katherine's death arrived, Henry had not only put on his 'mourning' of bright yellow, but had taken Elizabeth to Mass with him, 'with trumpets and other great triumphs'. Elizabeth was at that time just 28 months old. It is an age when a child is fascinated by bright lights, colours and cheerful noise. She would have known nothing but smiling faces, signs of approval, bows and curtsies. Did she later remember anything of that time, when her huge and bellowing father had carried her about, delightedly showing off his little red-haired daughter?

Chapuys reported that Henry had 'done the like on other days since, and has had some jousts at Greenwich'.[6] Did Elizabeth ever connect those memories of her father's delight, of the music and dancing and joy, with the death of a lady who deserved better than the farewell he gave her when she was old enough to reflect how her father eventually treated her own mother?

For the time being, Henry seemed prepared to wait, with one eye on Anne's growing belly and the other on a more promising future, but Anne had immediately to work to secure her position. She sent a message to Mary, through Lady Shelton, telling her to 'lay aside her obstinacy towards her father' and that if she did so she would find in Anne the best friend in the world. Anne promised that she would be like a second mother to the Princess, that she would have her at court, taking her proper place, and that she could have anything she wanted. She would even be exempt from carrying Anne's train. These were great concessions from Anne. Lady Shelton urged them upon the Princess, but the young woman refused to consider any offer from Anne. The word of her continued obstinacy went back to the Queen. Anne must have been very angry at Mary's attitude, but was determined to show that she had made the effort and that only Mary's recalcitrance had prevented her from achieving her aim. She then sent Lady Shelton another letter, in which she appeared to have retreated from any further efforts on her stepdaughter's behalf. She assured Lady Shelton that she might desist in her efforts to bring the 'Lady Mary' to heel, and made it clear that it no longer mattered to her whether Mary was on good terms with her father or not. Anne declared, 'if I have a son, as I hope shortly, I know what will happen to her. Therefore, considering the word of God, to do good to one's enemies, I wished to warn her beforehand …'. Anne said that the King would not esteem the girl's repentance 'when she had no choice'. Anne finished the letter with, 'Mistress Shelton, I beg of you, do not think to do me any pleasure by turning her from any of her willful courses …'.[7]

The letter, by accident or design, was left where Mary would see it. Mary made a copy and sent that to Chapuys, who then forwarded it to the Emperor on 17 February 1536. By that time, the instructions contained in it were obsolete.

One of the tournaments Henry had ordered to 'honour' Katherine's death had taken place on the day of St Paul's Eve, 24 January. On that day the King had a fall from his horse so severe that Chapuys reported that 'it was a miracle that he was not killed'. He was also to claim, in a later letter, that the Duke of Norfolk had broken the news of Henry's fall to Anne in such a way that she subsequently blamed him for causing a miscarriage, through her fright. She suffered that miscarriage a few days later, on 29 January 1536, which was, coincidentally the day of Katherine of Aragon's funeral.

Another version of the 'blame for miscarriage' story was given in Clifford's *Life of Jane Dormer*. This claimed that 'the King, seeming to effect Jane Seymour, and having her on his knee, as the Queen espied, who was then thought to be with child. She for anger and distain then miscarried ...'. This second version would seem to be more fitted to Anne's previous loss of a child in 1535, due to the phrase 'then thought to be with child' which apparently relates to Anne's possible false pregnancy. By January of 1536 there was no doubt at all that Anne actually was with child, and she had seemed to be well with the pregnancy proceeding normally.

It is perfectly feasible that Henry having taken such a heavy fall that it caused concern for his life. He was then 45 years old and already far too corpulent.

When ordering a suit of armour during the previous year, his waist measurement was recorded at 54in. When in his twenties he was around 15 stone with a waist measurement of 32in. Slim enough for a frame slightly over 6ft tall. But before he reached his fifties his waist had expanded so much that it already measured 20in more than before, and his body weight had very nearly doubled.

He was balding, irascible in temper and often in pain. He was ageing badly and already looked far older than his actual years. The charming, handsome king whom Katherine had married had long since gone, and although he still strove to give the impression of being bluff, cheerful and athletic, the reality must often have been a struggle to overcome.

The Venetian Ambassador Giustiniani's report had stated that on St Paul's Eve, 'at a great jousting tourney, the King had fallen very heavily, with his horse rolling on him, and then lay unconscious for almost two hours'.[8] In the circumstances, Henry's severe fall and his resulting concussion were to have long-lasting effects. Not only was it taken for granted that from that time Henry would no longer take a fully active part in such tournaments, but also that he was suddenly acknowledged to have joined the ranks of the 'older' men. This would have done nothing to ease his increasing attacks of irritation, or his growing unwieldiness. Once strenuous exercise was curtailed, he was to reach vast proportions, with an accompanying growth of further resentment that he could no longer show himself as he wished to be. He did still continue to hunt, though with several changes of horses which tired out quickly under his weight, but even that must have been a great strain on him when pretending that all was well.

However, the worst of the long-lasting effects of his mishap was on Anne herself.

She must have felt a very real and sickening fear at the news of Henry's injury, knowing that if he should die she would be unlikely to survive him long. The extreme shock resulted – as Anne's enemies hoped it would – in a miscarriage. That final pregnancy was far enough advanced for the lost child to be seen to have been a boy.

There have been many speculations about the child Anne lost. The most extreme of these theories claimed that the child was deformed, and that was the reason Henry then wanted rid of Anne and accused her of having many lovers. That he could not be blamed for the 'mere heap of flesh' that she had produced, as it would probably not have been his child. There is, however, no evidence whatsoever for this idea.[9]

Chapuys, Anne's mortal enemy, and ready to report anything he heard to her detriment, would have been delighted to have jumped on the bandwagon, if there had been the slightest possibility of truth in it. There were no reports at all, or even rumours, that there had been any disability or deformity in the stillborn son. On the contrary, Lancelot de Carles sadly described the child as *'un beau fils'*, a beautiful boy.[10] The official report stated that Anne had 'miscarried of a child who had the appearance of a male, at about three months and a half old, at which miscarriage the King has certainly shown great disappointment and sorrow'.[11] It was considered a fact that Queen Anne had 'miscarried of her saviour!'.[12] She must have been devastated.

When Henry was sufficiently recovered to consider the matter, he must have realised that the closure of that particular door might have opened another. There are several, slightly differing, reports of his subsequent meeting with Anne. The gist of them is generally that he let his anger out, shouting that 'she would get no more boys' by him. He then ended with 'when you are recovered, I will speak to you further' and stormed out of the room.[13]

Chapuys had a slightly different version. He claimed that Henry said, 'I see that God will not give me male children' which is not quite the same thing, as it seems to imply some personal responsibility for the mishap. Perhaps the King's anger included both phrases, 'I see that God will not give me male children, you will get no more sons from me!'[14] As all these remarks were reported by Anne's inverterate enemies, such as Chapuys, Nicholas Sander and Jane Dormer, who thoroughly detested Anne and all she represented, perhaps they are apocryphal. It was in their interests to give the impression that Henry had been tired of her for some time, and was only awaiting the opportunity to seize upon the latest misfortune to make a change.

Their recent closeness does not entirely bear this out, so the exact nature of Anne's relationship with Henry in the early months of 1536 is hidden. By then there must have been times when he wished he had not bothered, but they shared many things, and hope was one of them.

He certainly had his eye on Mistress Seymour, but she was hardly a suitable substitute for Katherine of Aragon or Anne Boleyn, and flirting with a willing girl is a long way away from disposing of a Queen. To do so would have made him look an absolute fool in the eyes of Europe, as a man who could not make up his mind, very damaging to his dignity. There was also an element of 'I told you so' which was humiliating. Finally, there was absolutely nothing that he could latch onto to excuse his sudden change of mind and heart. Anne had had some unfortunate childbed experiences, but these were not unusual. She had been settling into her role as Queen very well, becoming noted for her love of learning, her charities and her firm control of her household, after the model of the late Queen Claude of France. To suddenly dispose of her without due cause and replace her with his sweetheart (who may well do no better) was a very big step for Henry to take. Certainly it was far too big a step to take precipitately.

When Henry left Anne at Greenwich, it was not so much in a show of temper, as to open the new session of Parliament. Anne would have been keeping to her chamber, to recover her strength after her ordeal, and there are reports that she was quite ill at that time. It was stated that, 'she had been brought to bed afore her time, with much peril of her life'.[15] Therefore the contradictions of this period of Anne's life are easily misunderstood and will probably always remain clouded.

There is no doubt at all that if Anne had carried the child full term and produced it as a healthy male heir Henry would have been absolutely delighted and would have felt absolute justification for everything. Mistress Seymour would have remained nothing more than a passing fancy. Henry would never allow anyone to endanger the mother of his heir and the future of England would have been changed.

The loss of the child left Anne wide open to plots. Her entire faction was disliked, not just Anne personally, and had gathered many powerful enemies. But speed would be essential. If Anne's position, obviously unsteady at that moment, was to be undermined permanently, it was necessary to do so while Henry might be open to persuasion. But it was perfectly likely that Anne would recover and begin to cast her charm over the King again, as she had done before. There had been several disputes between them, but she had always won him back. She was also still young enough to bear further children, and clever enough to regain her position.

Mistress Seymour, quiet, plain and apparently unassuming, could never hope to compete with Anne once she was in full possession of health and vigour. That was the whole point. If Anne's detractors wanted to make a move against her, it was far easier to do so while she was out of action. This was the reason for the plot against the Boleyns being begun at that time.

Cromwell, in allying himself to the Seymours by the marriage of his son Geoffrey to Elizabeth, the widowed sister of Jane, could hope to achieve a great deal if the family to which he had bound himself could be eased closer to the throne. That the woman they would be obliged to use for this move was one unlikely to be able to charm the King for long was a pity, but if she could become pregnant everything would be changed. Henry liked, and was accustomed to, intelligent and cultured ladies, but that did not matter immediately. A great deal could be done by pushing Jane towards Henry, by starting a whispering campaign, which the Seymours could assure him was common knowledge at court. Particularly if they could show that another, more amenable, woman could also bear a child for him, they might be able to present the Boleyns with a fait accompli.

Cromwell's need for such an outcome was greater than most, as he had already made his defection clear. Others also disliked the Boleyns, but it is debatable whether Cromwell actually liked, or even disliked, any of the people with whom he came into contact in the course of his career. His attitude towards his old master is an example of the coldness that the man showed, even to those who had been good and useful to him in the past.

At his fall, Wolsey had been deeply concerned for the welfare of the colleges he had founded. He feared that the revenues, necessary for their upkeep, would be diverted, as indeed they were. He wrote to Cromwell, in deep sorrow, fully aware by then that his erstwhile colleague was being far less than honest with him. Wolsey had declared that he was so grieved that he was 'put from my sleep and meat in consequence of the news of the dissolution of my colleges'. He went on to say that he 'could not write any more for weeping and sorrow'.[16]

Cromwell cared nothing at all for Wolsey's grief, and considered his concerns worthless. Neither did he feel any need for pretence. In the last surviving letter he wrote to Wolsey, dated 18 October 1530, he actually threatened the Cardinal, warning him not to try to make any accusation against him with regard to maladministration of the funds. It ended with a warning tone, 'Truly Your Grace in some things overshoots yourself. There is regard to be given to what things you utter, and to whom ...'.[17]

Therefore, to Cromwell, turning against a woman who had failed the King, and might prove dangerous to himself, would provoke no qualms of conscience. Anne's continued presence at Henry's side might prevent Cromwell from moving forward, particularly with the Dissolution of the Monasteries. Anne had had no difficulty with their dissolution per se, but her opinions of the uses to which the vast sums released could be usefully put greatly differed from Henry's, and from Cromwell's. He knew Henry needed money very badly, and money would therefore have to be found. It was also certain that in the quest for such cash, to be given as bribes, to pay debts, to bolster Henry's throne or simply to fritter away as had already been done with Henry VII's vast hoard, a substantial and very useful amount could stick to Cromwell's own fingers. If advancement for himself and his family meant the crushing of a woman, that would be a small and insignificant price to pay.

Cromwell also knew that once he had moved against the Boleyns in an attempt to drag them down, he had better succeed. Henry was still notoriously fickle. There must be no possibility of him turning back to Anne and the Boleyn faction, leaving their opponents exposed. Cromwell knew that any plot to bring down the Queen would have to be, by its very nature, sufficient to draw the King to his side, and enlist his help in the work. He would have to convince the King that he had his interests at heart, and that the Boleyns' actions had driven them so far beyond the pale that there could be no forgiveness. Whatever move he made would have to strengthen his own position and that of the Seymours, to whom he was then allied.

It was doubtful that Mistress Seymour would be able to fight for her position as Anne had once done. Or that she would be able grimly to hold on to it, skilfully improving her status as Anne had done. But Jane did not need to. Her plain meekness was her advantage, emphasising her womanly attributes of demure subservience. She could rely on her family and friends to do the actual work, to tell her what to say to the King, and when and how to say it. The main weapon in the Seymour armoury was not Jane herself, it was the prolific family. That ability to breed, and rear, boys was what attracted Henry. It promised something none of his other women had been able to offer. Fecundity.

But it is not to be imagined that Mistress Seymour was entirely without personal ambition. That was not the case. Time was to prove that she could be, in her quiet way, just as ambitious as the rest of her family, and as prepared to use evil gossip as a lever to dislodge the Boleyns. She was to show herself to be surprisingly ruthless, willing to pour into Henry's ears tales of Anne's perfidy to undermine her position, perfectly well aware what the result was to be. She did not baulk at the idea of a horrifying public death for the woman she intended to supplant. She was well tutored by her family, and their friends, on the best ways to bring the King into their circle and give the impression of the innocent virgin.

They had already embarked on this course when Henry sent Jane a letter, with a purse full of money. Behaving entirely correctly, she knelt and kissed the letter, and refused the money, declaring that she could do nothing to taint her honour. She could, she claimed, only accept such a gift when 'God enabled her to make some honourable match.'[18] The Seymours, following Anne's own earlier example, knew that it did not look well to seem too eager, nor did it bode well to appear cheap. Jane's demure attitude was well suited to the pretence that she thought Henry would offer her a dowry when she found a husband, and it would also give him pause for thought.

The aim had to be marriage, not the temporary warming of the King's bed, despite the many surreptitious kisses and cuddles there had already been in corners between them, many of which had been remarked upon by courtiers, and some of which, unfortunately, the pregnant Anne had witnessed. They would have to be a lot more careful if Jane's reputation were not to be ruined by gossip, as Anne's had been. Yet, even while appearing circumspect, neither would it do for Jane to become too distant with Henry. He was absolutely desperate for a son, and could not afford to wait long, or to marry 'on spec' not knowing whether the lady could conceive. He would need proof of fertility before he could make so drastic a move. The Seymours would have to make Jane available to him, and yet guard her good name.

Due to her age, this seemed laughable to foreign observers, who had their own opinion of the chastity of English ladies. They frequently remarked on what they saw as great laxity among English women, far more free than their own. They were extremely reluctant to believe that any woman, even one who was plain of face, could still be a virgin at the English court at the age of 25.

Cromwell was to prove very useful, and made the ideal co-conspirator in the quest to please both the King with Jane's acquiescence and keep her good name intact. He was perfectly willing to give up his excellent rooms at Greenwich.[19] These were close to those of the King, and would enable Henry to visit her very privately 'by certain galleries, without being perceived' so he was playing the part of Jane's procurer, as well as her protector, for the King's benefit.[20]

He was also forging ahead with his other main project to please Henry, the Dissolution of the Monasteries. He was busy sending out commissioners whose task it was to find 'evidence' of wrongdoing in every religious house they entered. Sometimes, such 'evidence' was discussed and even written about long before they actually arrived at their destinations, where frightened and bewildered religious inhabitants would be harshly questioned. Whether the house was venal or not, the result was the same. It was not in their remit to find anyone innocent and able to retain their abbey. The vast majority were innocent but still the 'shocking discoveries' were claimed, such as the one that the Abbot of Fountains kept 'six women' and that the Prior had fathered several children.[21] Such accusations were widely known to be rubbish, merely forming the official excuse for takeover. What was far more important than any claims of immorality – and this was the usual form of accusation, not fraud or embezzlement, and it was always as salacious as possible – was that the abbeys and priories still owned vast wealth and extensive estates.

The Abbey of Jervaulx, in Wensleydale, so struck the commissioners by its beauty on their arrival that they remarked on it officially, describing the loveliness of its setting. They were particularly impressed by the famous and very profitable horse studs the Abbey owned, where the horses of the northern nobility had been bred for generations.[22] Even though they destroyed the beauty of the Abbey, and took away almost everything of value, even blowing up the church with gunpowder, they recommended to the King that the horse studs should be kept in operation, and that he should send his own best mares there. Even a relatively small abbey like Jervaulx had plenty of property to be stripped away for the benefit of the King – and of Cromwell. With part of his mind on this work, and part on formulating the plot to bring down the Queen, Cromwell must have been very busy in the early weeks of 1536.

Physically, Anne had recovered and her life had resumed its normal pattern. Katherine of Aragon's personal possessions had been inventoried, but the days of the many valuable belongings of that particular Queen were long over. Her remaining effects consisted mainly of old clothing and items connected with religion. Henry claimed for himself a set of red and white ivory chessmen, and a desk covered with black velvet. A crimson velvet covered coffer and two ivory stools went to Anne.[23] There were several ivory tablets of a religious nature, and none of those would have appealed to anyone but her daughter Mary. Katherine had intended her daughter also to have her furs, shabby though they may well have been by then, but Mary was unlikely to receive any newer ones while her exile lasted. Whether Mary ever actually received those items we cannot be sure.

Anne cannot have been comfortable during that time of whispers and averted eyes, aware that her relationship with Cromwell was now one of mutual, and open, dislike. Her uncle of Norfolk had long since stepped back, and her sister was not at court. Apart from the steadfast loyalty of her beloved brother, and the continuing reliability of their narrow circle of friends, her world was shrinking. She put on a brave face, giving freely to her charities and running her household on the correct principles as usual. She adored her small daughter, despite seeing less of her than she might have liked, but that was usual in noble households. We know that at that time Anne was still ordering new clothes, including many items for Elizabeth. She was concerned with trivia, making new caps for the child, keeping herself occupied, waiting on events.

She had, just prior to her miscarriage, sent for the measurements of the little Princess's head, so that new caps could be made for her. She also requested that 'the purple satin cap' should be sent to her, 'to mend it'.[24] By 19 February 1536 a new purple satin cap had been paid for, 'laid with a rich caul of gold, the work being of roundels of damask gold'. On 10 March a crimson fringe was also paid for, which went towards the decoration of the Princess's 'cradle head'. On 20 March another satin cap was ordered for Elizabeth to wear, this one in white, 'laid with a rich caul of gold' and costing the immense sum, for so small an item, of £4. Another, of crimson satin, ordered at the same time, cost £3 13*s*. 4*d*.[25]

During February Henry had left Anne at Greenwich, also Jane Seymour, although Jane was not left without messages. Anne was by then in the very uncomfortable position of knowing that Henry's attentions were elsewhere. Though recovered well from her miscarriage, she could not conceive another child if he gave her no opportunity. It began to seem as if the threat of 'no more sons' by him might prove a reality.

When the King returned to Greenwich, Anne was spared the sight of Jane basking in his approval as she still 'entertained him privily' in Cromwell's apartments. Henry was taking no chances, this time, of his sweetheart's good name being besmirched. In public he behaved with restraint, but there were still opportunities made for him to be with Jane, in secret. He could visit her unseen by creeping down the private galleries connecting the apartments. Any other hypothesis of their behaviour being entirely innocent at that time is simply naïve and unreasonable, the subject of romantic fiction.

This ability to meet privately meant more to the Seymours than the chance for Henry to get Jane with child. It gave them the ability to speak with him in a private capacity, along with those of their friends who were in on the secret. They took every opportunity to pour poison into Henry's ears regarding Anne and her brother. Henry was still hesitating regarding the final move. It must have been as busy and as anxious a time for the Seymours as it had once been for Anne. They regaled the King with rumours they said they had heard, in efforts to convince him that discarding Anne would be a safe and popular move for him to make. In the privacy of Jane's rooms they could speak freely. Jane was keen to drop venomous remarks against Anne. She assured Henry that 'your marriage to Anne is considered an abomination by all the people, and nobody considers it to be legitimate!'.[26]

That particular bombshell was dropped deliberately while the room was full of Imperial supporters, who immediately played their part by expressing their agreement, declaring that they 'swore on their allegiance' that Jane was speaking truth. Jane brazenly went so far as to discuss with the King, in the hearing of her family, what children she would have with him, when Anne was removed. It had started with a discussion about the Princess Mary, whom Jane always ostentatiously supported, the better to oppose Anne. Henry had remarked, 'You are a fool, you ought to think of the children we shall have together.' Jane's reply was, 'I was thinking about the repose and tranquility of Your Grace, as well as the children we shall have together.' One can almost picture the prim expression accompanying that reply.[27]

It was a promise for the future, that once Anne was removed, Jane would quickly fill the void in the nursery with healthy boys. But what it also was, spoken in the presence of the Imperial Ambassador Chapuys, whom we know to have encouraged Mistress Seymour and her brothers, was evidence that the plot against Anne was already well underway. Not only were the Seymours involved in it, but all those who had lost position, or the King's favour, while Anne and her family had been prominent. These of course included Chapuys, representing the Emperor, but also Princess Mary herself, who foolishly believed all of Anne's bad press, and remained convinced that if the woman were gone, she and her father would swiftly be on familiar terms. She would find out differently, but that was for a later time, when Anne could not possibly be blamed for the harsh treatment she would receive at the hands of her father.

Cromwell had his own axe to grind, but felt confident by then that he could bring down the Queen with little or no risk to himself. Nicholas Carewe and Francis Bryan were also active supporters. Neither of them had had any very great part to play while the Boleyns had been at the forefront of court life, and they looked forward to changes.

There would, for Anne, be one last moment when she felt that her position might yet be saved. On Easter Sunday Cromwell heard from Chapuys that he had just received instructions from the Emperor. Chapuys was obliged to request an official audience with the King to relay the important news.[28] Charles V wanted an alliance with England.

On Tuesday, 18 April 1536 Chapuys met with the King to discuss the matter. The political climate had so changed that the Emperor was inclined to overlook Henry's marriage to Anne Boleyn. In fact, Chapuys' instructions had been that he was to treat with the Queen as well as with the King. This was an absolute revelation, given the enmity between Spain and all Anne stood for, but it was an apparent lifesaver. The fact that the papers Chapuys carried contained a proviso was unknown to her. Charles V had actually stated that Chapuys could also treat with Queen Anne 'if King Henry had NOT already decided to take another Queen'.[29]

Anne and George Boleyn must have suddenly felt as though they were released from a dark and frightening prison, a narrow tunnel leading nowhere. To Anne it was the acknowledgment from Spain that she had dreamed of. With the Emperor's recognition of her position she could completely recover herself. George Boleyn had been hovering protectively around his sister since her miscarriage, trying to help and support her, though in the atmosphere of frigid disapproval there was little that he could actually do. Now the long wait was vindicated. If the Emperor would make public his new attitude towards Anne, it would boost her standing in

Europe enormously. The sudden relief and euphoria caused Anne and George, both quite unaware of his secret intentions, to treat him suddenly as a friend. George met him cordially at the gate, and Anne sent him a message that he was to 'come and kiss her cheek'. This was an honour reserved only for the most favoured people, which Chapuys had certainly never been, nor wanted to be with Anne. He did not, however, accept her invitation.

The formal meeting with Henry was intended to take place in the afternoon. At morning Mass, Anne looked out for Chapuys and, seeing him standing almost behind the door through which she had entered, turned towards him and made him a low curtsey. He bowed towards her in response. During the service itself, he handed a candle to her, which she took as another sign of renewed friendship and approval. After Mass, when leaving in the company of the King, to dine in her apartments with the other Ambassadors, Anne realised that Chapuys was not accompanying the party.

'Why does he not enter, like the other Ambassadors?' she asked Henry. Henry's mind was already on more important matters than Anne's comfort or security and he replied curtly, 'It is not without good reason!'

Anne immediately realised that Chapuys' exclusion from her gathering was a message to him, and to the Emperor he served. It made clear that there was no need for them to consider Anne's position or preferences in any new alliance made between England and Spain. The decision was already made and the secret instructions already put into effect. Henry had definitely decided to take another Queen.

Fortunately for Anne, when the two sides met terms could not be agreed. Chapuys was obliged to retreat without having achieved anything and Cromwell also allowed his extreme disappointment to show. It was hardly a triumph for Anne and George, merely a brief reprieve, but there was worse to come.

On St George's Day, 25 April 1536, there was a vacancy to be filled among the Knights of the Garter. It had been widely expected that George Boleyn was the natural candidate. If everything had gone as it should, with the Queen continuing her pregnancy, George would doubtless have been awarded the honour. He had almost received it in the previous year, only having to step down because it was to be given instead to the King of Scots. In 1536 his nomination had been made, and it seemed a foregone conclusion that he would have it. Unfortunately, the King chose to make his feelings plain for the occasion. The Garter went to Sir Nicholas Carewe, one of the Boleyns most active enemies, and a great supporter of the Seymours.

The Spanish Ambassador wrote a few days later, 'This has been a great heartbreak for Lord Rochford. But even more so for the Concubine [Anne] who did not have the influence to have the Order given to her brother.'[30] The letter continued, 'It would only need the said Squire to unhorse the said Concubine, for all that he is her cousin, and he does not cease to counsel Mistress Seymour, with other conspirators, to do her some ill.'[31]

All seemed to be set for Anne's imminent fall except for one thing holding Henry back from making the final move. Despite all the private meetings between Henry and Jane, there was still no sign of her having conceived a child.

It is inconceivable that Henry would have married her without hope in that direction. He was far too desperate to take on any lady with whom he had been sleeping (as he certainly was sleeping with Jane) who had after all that time shown no reassuring sign of fertility. Despite all the trotting down the 'secret corridors' between his rooms and what had once been Cromwell's apartments, Jane's condition was no different. For Henry, another infertile marriage was a risk far too great to take. Despite all the talk, the show of preferment for Seymour supporters and the disfavour shown to Anne and George Boleyn, Henry was still hesitating.

The impasse had to be broken so they could all move forward. As it was, the Seymours, and certainly Cromwell had staked far too much on the throw to be able to allow it to just fizzle out. They were far too exposed and needed it to move onto the next stage. There is absolutely no documentary evidence that Jane became pregnant at that time, or that she had a miscarriage in the ensuing weeks. Therefore, despite Henry's attentions, she had not conceived. This was the insuperable barrier for him, but the solution was a simple, if very dangerous one. Jane and her family would have to let Henry BELIEVE that she was with child.[32]

That would allow Henry to marry Jane, it would allow the plot to bring down Anne to go forward, and it would allow Jane a little more time hopefully to effect a natural conception. Of course, there was the difficulty of dates if she managed that, and also the confession about some 'mistake' if she didn't, but that was all for the future. It was certainly risky, and if Jane never proved with child at all it could be very risky indeed, but by then the Seymours and their party were probably desperate enough to decide to worry about that later. With their family record of generations of prolific breeding, they must have been confident enough to take the chance. Henry with his vagrant attentions, might turn to some other lady, if he were disappointed with Jane.

It would be a relatively simple thing for Jane demurely to tell the King that she was with child. Knowledge at that time centred largely on the 'quickening' which confirmed a pregnancy, and that might allow them the leeway they needed to start the ball rolling.

If they were successfully to bring the King to their side then it was essential for him to marry Jane, and he would not do that if he did not believe she could produce children. That Henry was to be duped by them, with Jane's active connivance, was a necessity. For him to be told that suddenly the miracle had happened, meant that all his hesitation was thrown aside. Jane would have to be legally married before her condition began to show, as the pretence of her innocence would need to be maintained.

All delay would be at an end, Jane would become Henry's wife before her condition could be expected to show. Cromwell had to find a way for it all to be achieved. There is no other logical explanation for the long delay from Anne's miscarriage in

January, to her sudden fall in May. That the plot against her had already begun is a fact, but it had not moved forward fully, and something was obviously needed to impel it to do so. Henry's belief in a pregnant Jane, who would need to be shielded and legitimately married, was just the spur he needed.

Suddenly Cromwell would have to bring a case against Anne, and also her nearest associates. It was necessary to bring down not only the Queen, but also her party, and the case made against them, which was ludicrous in its content and pathetic in its paucity of genuine evidence, was the result. It all gave clear signs of a sudden, panicked rush.

The stage was set for the final act.

Henry VIII in 1536, only 45 years old but grossly overweight and lame.

Chapter Seventeen

We'll never know what was said to Henry to persuade him that the marriage to Jane Seymour, over which he had already hesitated for three months, must suddenly go ahead with all speed. But he would have been informed that speed was suddenly of the essence if his sweetheart was to bring him a child, without the added shame of showing a big belly on her wedding day.

Cromwell had found the means of promoting the marriage, but he would also have to find the means of achieving it.[1] That was what he was there for and the scanty and contradictory claims, the paucity of basic forethought regarding Anne's movements at the times she was supposed to be with male courtiers betrayed the lack of time to polish his case against her. The desperate lack of preparation with which he had to achieve the job in hand was only too obvious.

The end result was the only thing that mattered. The years of Anne's queenship, the striving for respectability and the efforts made to establish a cultured and refined court and household then counted for nothing. It would all be dragged down to the lowest common denominator, and on that level alone would she be judged. Cromwell would use the public's general lack of affection for her, their belief that she had been Henry's mistress while Katherine was still his wife and their own still fresh grief over Katherine's demise to work a case against Anne in which correct procedure, or even sufficient evidence, mattered little.

All these ingredients would go into the mix where possible treason, adultery, anticipating the King's death, a whiff of scandalous incest and even a dash of witchcraft would all be vigorously stirred together by court jealousies and festering resentments. Few people would actually stop to think that the image they were presented with, of a sexually aggressive harpy, was totally at odds with the cultured Queen who encouraged learning. That the fairly prim young woman, who had held off from sleeping with her first love, Henry Percy (when it would surely have benefited her to do so), did not relate to a harlot. On the contrary, she had fought a long battle against the pre-conceived idea of her, in the face of her sister's laxity.

Few would care that the mother, patiently mending her daughter's small caps, was not the same person as the supposed trollop who lured men into her marriage bed. But they would be content to accept the image given to them, created by Cromwell for public consumption.

It would unfortunately be many years before the lack of evidence against her gave anyone pause for thought, or for the passing of time to give a different perspective to what had happened to her. That was intentional too. It was all designed to happen too swiftly, to be too scandalous, for anyone to stand back to consider the details. The very rush and confusion would serve to blur and disguise the gaps in the case brought against her.

For there were many gaps. In years to come, when Henry was besotted with a fifth wife (ironically Anne's young cousin, Catherine Howard) and he was informed that she had kept company with men of his household it was plain that the ladies who served the young Queen were well aware of their mistress's activities. It was perfectly obvious that, living such a public life, it was very rare, if not impossible, for a woman in that position to be able to commit such acts without the compliance of her ladies. It may well have made Cromwell sweat just a little, the thought that some ladies of high standing might spring to Anne's defence. He could reassure himself that the speed of the accusations and arrests, together with a very natural fear of being involved in anything so unsavoury, would prevent others from coming forward. On the other hand, neither did they come forward to receive the undoubted rewards offered for those prepared to speak against the Queen.

Henry's obvious, if unspoken wish, and the need to keep one's position for family's sake might well keep people silent, which was what Cromwell counted on. However, a distaste of the proceedings and a reluctance to bring a woman to her death through false testimony would also prevent him from gathering sufficient scandal.

This was what Cromwell was trying to work with. Having to make a viable case out of nothing but a few carelessly spoken words, must have been rather like having to make a fine court gown out of a pile of rags.[2] Except for two things. One was the King's wish, which meant that it was clear to all that to speak out, in anything except condemnation, would run counter to Henry's clear intentions, and would be desperately dangerous for the person recklessly becoming Anne's defender. The remembrance of the previous year's murders of Fisher and More should be quite enough to encourage people to keep their mouths shut, in order to keep their heads where God intended them to be.

The other was Cromwell's secret weapon. This was not the eager plotting, or the determined lying of the Seymours and their friends, or even the hope that Jane's belly might actually shelter the King's son, one day soon, if not immediately. It was something, and someone, else entirely. It was the wild card in the Boleyn pack, the estranged and embittered wife of George, Lord Rochford.[3]

How Cromwell ever came to hold this foolish woman in his hand we will never know. Her subsequent career at court showed that her dislike of, and distance from, her married family was complete.[4] She had entirely thrown in her lot with the King. Not, perhaps, with the Seymours themselves, they had hangers-on enough of their own, but certainly with Henry. It would be the King who would ultimately reward her, with financial security, with land, with a position at court of both respectability and responsibility, when her Boleyn in-laws were dead and gone. Such lavish recompense was in complete contravention of the usual custom, when generally the relict of an executed man would find herself in a poor way, and would probably have to seek a home with her own family again. Not so Jane, except for a short time in the immediate aftermath of the case she successfully supported and enhanced her position. She not only was to live in comfort, but with status, becoming the close confidante of Henry's fifth wife. Therefore we know that her contribution to the matter of her husband and sister-in-law was considered substantial. It must also have been voluntary. Evidence extracted under pressure would not have received such reward, nor would it have had anything like such value.

Did she actually approach Cromwell with her story? Or was she simply overheard speaking openly and recklessly, as she had done before, and been sent for by him? We are in the dark about such details, but through her Cromwell became the possessor of information that could easily be used. Not only to strengthen the case against Anne, but to create an atmosphere of such shock and disgust in any normal person that it would cause a repugnance that would make it far simpler for the rest of the case to be believed. Even that the Queen had plotted the death of the King, or that she had used witchcraft to achieve her aims. That Anne should plot the death of Henry is plainly ridiculous, given the abject fear of his loss had caused a miscarriage back in January.[5] There was certainly no reason for her to plan his removal. She had much to fear from him, but she had not yet plumbed the depths of what he was capable of doing to her. Her fear was of divorce and disgrace, probably not yet of death itself.

Jane Rochford's evidence would add another dimension to Cromwell's case, transforming the mutual affection of the Queen and her brother into something dirty and despicable, successfully turning the minds of others against them both. Whether Jane came up with the full accusation on her own, and presented it complete, or whether it was created over a little time, out of her willingness to make trouble for the family, is not known. But along with Cromwell's urgent need to find sufficient scandal, however unlikely, to pad out his case, it is clear that Jane's bitterness must have been extreme.[6] She would not even be required to speak against the Queen in open court, making her astounding accusation face to face. Her statement was taken in writing, to be read out in court on her behalf.[7]

She would not have to undergo the strain of being questioned in public, or face the people she accused with such a lie on her lips. It is possible that if she had met her victims face to face, she may not have been capable of recounting her tale. If so, Cromwell's most inflammatory, therefore most valuable, piece of information would have been lost.

But it might also have given him the idea that the rest of the case against the Queen would have to be dealt with similarly, using shock tactics to discredit her.

Treason it would certainly have to be, nothing else would serve so definitely to remove her with the maximum publicity and disgrace. However, the idea of Anne plotting the removal or death of the King was a difficult line to take. It was so obvious that with their already shrinking powerbase the Boleyns would have no reason to wish his demise. It would be far easier if the case against Anne was to rest almost solely on sexual matters.

It would not only disgrace her, but would seem a more logical case to bring, particularly if it could be made to seem that she was sleeping around in an attempt to fill the royal nursery. She was younger than Henry, and more healthy, so it would be clear (without having to say so) that she considered any lack in that direction to be more his fault than her own. In Henry's eyes no punishment would be severe enough for an unfaithful wife, and it had the added bonus of being able to bring in the entire Boleyn circle as possible paramours, which would clear the decks in one fell swoop.

Therefore, it is quite possible that Jane Rochford's nasty little tale had far more effect than merely adding a bit of spice and a well-bred shudder to Cromwell's case. It might have been the reminder that a sexual accusation was the easiest to bring against any woman, and the hardest to refute. Anne, on hearing the gist of the charges against her, may well have despaired, also knowing this. So much so, that she cried out in anguish that she could not show herself innocent of the touch of any man 'except I open my body!'.[8] It would be far easier than having to invent some more difficult 'death threat' against the King at short notice. It was perfect for the purpose.

By 23 April 1536 Cromwell was as ready as he was likely to be. He drew up a secret commission which would give Henry's leading nobles and the officers of the royal household the authority to look into a long list of treasonable acts 'by whomsoever committed'. Henry signed it and the following day Jane Rochford and Nan Cobham were two of the three of Anne's ladies known to have been questioned. If others had had anything useful to tell they would certainly have been used too and their statements recorded. We know that in the case against George Boleyn, and the other gentlemen who were dragged into the Boleyns' downfall with them, there was no evidence at all. There could be none. The case was built up entirely out of the statements of those few people who had an axe to grind, padded out by scurrilous gossip and wild conjecture. Cromwell's spies had already been given the task of watching Anne's household closely, and reporting anything and everything, while he put together the necessary paperwork.

By the middle of April 1536 the weather had turned hot. It was a very promising prospect for the usual May Day Tournament which was approaching, although Anne, already filled with foreboding, must have had little heart for festivities. We know that she sent for Matthew Parker, her chaplain, around that time, and asked him, in the event of anything happening to her, to take what care he could of the Princess Elizabeth. It was to be a responsibility he would fulfil honourably in the years ahead, even when as Queen Elizabeth's Archbishop of Canterbury he often found his position difficult.[9]

Cromwell's eager spies soon reported back to him all that was said in the Queen's chambers. Whatever her fears, Anne, as Queen, could not allow herself to sink. She had to maintain a cheerful countenance and carry on as if fear could not touch her. It would seem that at this point she was without any plan of action of her own, almost inert, quite different to her earlier years when she would have made a rapid and vigorous response to any eventuality. The household would continue its normal routine, and Anne could do little but go with the flow. She was certainly aware by then of strain and danger, but seemed unable to make any move.

On 23 April, the day on which Henry signed Cromwell's commission, the Queen was reported as having been seen talking to Sir Francis Weston. This man was a great favourite at court, an athlete and a seasoned courtier, though still young. Anne was overheard discussing with him Sir Henry Norris' love affair with Madge Shelton. Sir Henry was a widower who was attracted by Madge, but seemed to be hesitating in taking any further step in the romance. It was quite likely that Sir Henry's hesitation was due to the difficult position the Boleyns and their relatives then stood in, and that Sir Francis was well aware of it. However, he would not wish to make such an insulting detail clear to the Queen, so he simply attempted to sweeten the truth. Flatteringly, he remarked, 'Norris comes more to your chamber for Your Grace, than he does for Madge.' Anne responded by saying archly that Weston himself had been reported as 'not loving his wife' and asked if that meant that he was also in love with Madge. His reply was in accordance with the tradition of romantic banter that constituted the 'courts of love' and in which a gentleman would always seek a lady, usually of higher rank than himself, to flatter and pay attention to.[10] Weston said, 'I love one in your house better than them both' and when asked who, he gave the stock answer 'It is yourself!'

The Queen, sensing danger, immediately recoiled. The French tradition of gentlemanly devotion to a lady must suddenly have seemed empty, as well as perilous. Anne told Weston firmly that he was talking nonsense. However, it was already too late. His words of flattery, intended to please, would be repeated with embellishments, as part of the case Cromwell was preparing.

Sir Henry Norris, the widower who had been the subject of their talk, was rather older than Weston and was a well-known and well-respected member of the King's household.[11] A day or two after the incident had been reported, he was in Anne's presence chamber when she asked him openly why he did not go ahead with his courting of Madge Shelton.

Obviously embarrassed, he merely remarked that he intended to 'Tarry awhile' before making a final decision. Anne, probably aware that her present lack of influence at court was the cause of his diffidence with regard to her cousin, became slightly irritated by his evasion, and pretended to interpret it along the lines of some personal affection towards herself. 'Then you look for dead men's shoes' she replied sharply. 'If ought but good should come to the King, you would look to have me!' Norris, seeing the danger of such remarks, immediately backtracked, declaring firmly, 'If I had any such thought, I would my head were off!'

His horror at the idea of his intentions being so misconstrued must have reached through to Anne, when he told her that she should be careful about making such remarks, as there were rumours about and people were very fond of carrying tales.

Anne's remark was, in the circumstances, a very foolish one. She had never been fully able to keep control of her tongue when she was irritated and her temper was short. Very often her angry retorts meant nothing at all, but the knowledge of Norris' real reason for not wishing to commit himself with regard to Madge had made her reckless. However, on this occasion she controlled herself, and said merely that she was aware that people carried tales about her. People were accusing her of being disloyal to the King, she said, and then asked him to contradict any such rumours if he heard them. Suddenly pitying her, he promised that he would.[12]

Keeping his word, Norris did indeed attempt to speak on Anne's behalf. On Sunday, 30 April another snippet of conversation was reported to Cromwell. Norris had been overheard talking to Anne's almoner, when he said, 'he believed that the Queen was a good woman'. In view of his last words, it was a rather obvious effort at spreading a good word about her, but to other ears it must have sounded as though he was trying to cover his tracks, especially when placed with the gist of the earlier remarks. To Cromwell it probably seemed a very clumsy defence, and it would do nicely to add to his growing file of nothing, which had to be made into something.

Anne's nerves already seemed on edge and her behaviour very jumpy. On 29 April she was seen with Mark Smeaton, who was the young musician much favoured by the King. He was not a gentleman but his skills had placed him on the periphery of Anne's talented circle of friends. He certainly revered the Queen, and may even have harboured fantasies about her. He was dangerously eager to show his loyalty and devotion to the family who had helped to advance him at court, particularly in view of the threat posed by the seemingly ever-present Seymours. But despite his veneer of sophistication, he still retained a good deal of naivety, along with perhaps a little pique that his lesser status did not allow him to join in with the small acts of intimacy, such as a kiss on the cheek, which old friends enjoyed.

Anne was reported as asking him why he seemed 'sad' and his answer was that it did not matter.[13] Anne perhaps thought that he was sulking, and said, 'You must not look to have me speak to you as I would do to a nobleman, because you are an inferior person.'[14] The words were not intended to insult, as they would be construed in modern times, but merely stating the facts as understood by people of her own era. Smeaton, hastening to apologise for any assumed presumption on his part, said, 'Oh no, a look sufficeth me, and so fare you well.' It is another example of a few words taken out of context and written down with the intention of making them appear quite different to what they actually were.

Again, on Sunday, 30 April, Anne had decided to try to speak privately with Henry. There had been some plans made for her to visit Calais with him just after the May Day celebrations, but word had gone out that the trip was to be postponed, at least for a further week. No reason for the change of plan had been given, even to the Queen, who would otherwise expect to have been kept informed.[15] Anne also knew that a writ had been issued on 27 April that recalled Parliament, so there was obviously something important in the air. She was quite within her rights as Queen to want to know what was going on, apart from her position as Henry's wife, although she was presently being excluded from any close contact with him.

The extent of her disquiet is shown clearly by her intention to take the Princess Elizabeth with her when she confronted the King. Henry had recently shown affection for the child, and Anne was partly using the child as a shield between herself and Henry, and partly in the hope that his affection for the Princess would prevent him from being openly dismissive of her in the child's presence. She was wrong.

At Greenwich on that day was a distinguished visitor, the Scottish reformer 'Alesius', otherwise known as Alexander Aless. He was a man who had a good deal of admiration for Anne Boleyn, and it must have seemed to him to be a stroke of good luck to see the Queen, actually carrying the young Princess, approaching the King. He watched the meeting from the courtyard below the window at which Henry was then standing, and was the unfortunate witness to a distressing scene, which was far from being the touching family moment he expected.

He was, many years later, to recount the whole thing to Elizabeth, when she was Queen of England.[16]

> Alas, I shall never forget the sorrow I felt, when I saw the sainted Queen, your most religious Mother, carrying you while still a little baby, in her arms. Entreating from the most serene King, your Father, at Greenwich Palace, from the open window of which he was looking into the courtyard when she brought you to him. The faces and gestures of the speakers plainly showed that the King was angry, although he could conceal anger wonderfully well. Yet from the protracted conference of the Council, (for whom the crowd was waiting until it was quite dark, expecting that they would return to London) it was most obvious to everyone that some deep and difficult question was being discussed.

Henry knew that the plot against Anne was already in its final stages, and she would certainly have been the last person he wished to speak to at that moment. Did he feel no remorse at all, casting her off? She was still considered young and attractive, she held their small child in her arms, and she showed her fear and her humiliation at being rejected by him in front of an interested audience. Did Elizabeth later remember anything of that awkward moment? Children are apt to pick up quickly on the emotions of the adults they know well. Did the words of Alesius, so many years later, spark an unpleasant and distressing memory?

We know that the disfunctional family life of both Mary and Elizabeth had a definite effect on them. Due to Elizabeth's later reticence on the subject of her mother we are not privileged to know how much she actually remembered.[17] But her later determination never to marry, and entrust her life and liberty to the hands of any man, clearly tells its own story. She drew her royalty from her father, and was clearly proud of him in many ways. However, her relationships with those connected by blood to her mother's family and her wearing of a ring that had her mother's image inside as well as her own show that she was not so indifferent as she might have appeared.

What Anne did not know, on that Sunday at the end of April, was that Mark Smeaton had been taken for questioning at the home of Thomas Cromwell himself. Cromwell would later vehemently deny that his house held any of the 'instruments of torture', but one does not need to have thumbscrews or a rack installed to cause a person distress and pain. There are various versions of what might have happened to Smeaton on that day, none verified, but the *Cronico Del Rey Enrico Ottavo da Anglaterra* states that he was tortured by means of a knotted rope, which was wound and tightened around his head.[18] It is as reasonable an assumption as any other, and would have been frightening and painful enough to break the spirit of a terrified young man, and persuade him to say whatever was wanted.

Once he had 'confessed' and had signed whatever he was told to sign, his usefulness was over. He could hardly expect to be released after such a catastrophic betrayal of the Queen. Oddly enough, Alesius himself was later to state that on the same evening after he saw the Queen approach the King at Greenwich, he heard the firing of a cannon. This was the usual signal that a prisoner had just been taken into the Tower of London. It did not, at the time, raise any alarms concerning Smeaton, as nobody was aware that he was missing. Apart from which, the very tense atmosphere at court, the cancelled visit abroad and the sudden gathering of the Parliament would have given people enough to think and speculate about, without anyone wondering about the whereabouts of a musician, even if he was a Groom of the Privy Chamber.

Anne would have been distressed and humiliated enough at her failure to connect with Henry, and perhaps did not associate the eerie atmosphere around her with her conversation with Smeaton 24 anxious hours before. He was taken to the Tower by boat, under cover of darkness, to prevent any word leaking to the Queen and her family of what was about to happen.

The May Day celebrations were always much looked forward to. May is often one of the best months of the year, the epitome of springtime, and promises better weather and the approach of summer with its outdoor pleasures.

At Greenwich the usual tourney had been arranged, where jousting and tilting would be watched by an admiring crowd of ladies, and now also the King, who was taking a less active role. The specially constructed galleries were draped with tapestries and cloths of gold and silver. There was ample fine embroidery, many fluttering gold fringes, rich silks and velvets and the gold jewellery of the noble spectators glittering in sunlight; banners, the rich caparisons of the horses, the smells of perfume and trodden grass, cries of pleasure or disappointment, conversation and smiles. Did Anne sit beside Henry smiling bravely? Putting on the required public face. Was her heart thumping, waiting for her husband to do or say something, give her a clue as to his mood? Did she feel the edge of tension that was not a usual part of the proceedings? Her brother Lord Rochford was present, taking his part, along with Sir Henry Norris, Sir William Brereton and Sir Thomas Wyatt – all old friends, out to enjoy what was an essentially masculine occasion, despite the presence of, and deference towards, the ladies.

It was reported that the King did not sit glowering and ignoring the others. On the contrary, he appeared to be affable. He even lent Sir Henry Norris one of his own horses.

The jousts were completed and the ladies had begun to disperse when the King, with several other gentlemen, followed by the King's Yeoman of the Guard, left for London, apparently without any word of explanation to the Queen.[19]

Sir Henry Norris rode with the small party of gentlemen attendant on the King. All had seemed well and Norris, particularly in view of the King's amiable loan to him, had no reason to suppose that Henry had any designs on him at all. However, during the pleasant early summer evening ride, the King suddenly turned on him, showing a very different face. Henry demanded of Norris that he admit that he had committed adultery with the Queen. It was the most astonishing accusation to make after such a pleasant and innocent day. Norris must have been deeply shocked, but before he was able to make a suitable reply, Henry struck again. He claimed that he knew that Anne had committed adultery with 'several men' and demanded to know their names. Slyly he added that Norris' own involvement might be forgiven, and his freedom permitted, if he gave the King the names of all the others.

Despite his obvious shock and dismay, Norris managed to control himself sufficiently to deny absolutely any knowledge of wrongdoing on the part of the Queen. He declared that he was not involved in any way, and didn't know anyone who was. He insisted on the innocence of the Queen, and declared her clear of such an appalling charge. Norris' servant, George Constantine, who was present and was also later examined by Cromwell, reported that for the remainder of the ride into London the King kept pestering Norris to confess to a guilty association with Anne. Norris insisted that there was no truth at all in such wicked rumours, and that Anne was totally free from any guilt.

Norris must have been panicked by the time London was reached, but he was still stubborn and refused to give Henry any reason to think the Queen culpable. He even offered to 'prove' her innocence with his own body, offering himself as her champion in any trial by duel.

That was, of course, the very last thing that Henry wanted. That a well-respected man should offer himself for trial by duel to prove the Queen's innocence, with all the publicity it implied and all the excitement and interest it would provoke. Let alone the very real possibility that an experienced and capable Norris might actually win.

It was all for nothing, as even Norris must have known it would be. His earlier suspicions had proved correct, Anne had indeed been watched, and all her angry or merely petulant words recorded. They would be given a meaning never intended and would be used against her and against them all.

Norris, like the other gentlemen who should shortly find themselves in the same position, would continue to deny any adultery, either with the Queen, or on her part with anyone else. There was absolutely no case to answer, but of course it was futile. The Queen had to be made to seem culpable and so would they all be. By the following morning, after a fraught evening of questions and answers, Norris found himself confined in the Tower, where he would shortly be joined by two of the others, Sir Francis Weston and Sir William Brereton. Sir Thomas Wyatt would also be arrested, along with Sir Richard Page. Smeaton, of course, was already incarcerated and George, Lord Rochford, would not be far behind.

Anne was reputedly at dinner on the following morning when her uncle, the Duke of Norfolk, arrived. He had no sympathy for her and did not pretend to any. He spoke very bluntly to her, even roughly, without giving her any of the honours due to her position as Queen. Anne's reaction has been reported differently, some believing that she was then told of the charges against her. Others, more logically, owing to a remark made by Sir William Kingston, show that she did not really know why she had been arrested.

This was, unfortunately, the norm. Some unlucky prisoners in the system did not know the full charges against them until they appeared at trial.

Norfolk would have been happy enough to let her go on worrying, wondering what was happening and why. It was not in anyone's interest to give her much prior knowledge of what the future held, except for what she may have surmised during that terrifying, stomach-churning boat ride along the river to the Tower. She had not even been given time to change her clothes, or take anything with her, having just been bundled, protesting, into the barge. Anne was later to claim that she had been 'cruelly handled' at Greenwich by her uncle, and it is quite likely true. Norfolk's brutal streak would have come well to the fore at the idea of finally being able to frighten and punish the niece who had humiliated him. Not so much the proud Queen then, just a terrified woman, huddling in a barge, on her way to a dim, and probably short, future. He would have had little family feeling to spare for her, merely the knowledge that another enemy was brought low.

Anne did, however, show one last flash of pride and defiance and made one last effort to keep her dignity intact. 'The King', she said, was ordering this 'merely to prove her'.[20] It made no difference, and Norfolk was long past any admiration for her. His only interest in women had ever been dependent on what they might prove useful for, and Anne had long since outlived her usefulness to him. She was only a foolish proud woman who had rejected his good advice time after time, choosing to go her own way. His only concern was that their blood relationship might cause him to be affected by her fall, and he was determined to prove such a good servant to the King in the matter, that it could be discounted. He had more than once shown himself to be the kind of man who firmly believed that his womenfolk should be controlled.

When the barge finally halted at the court gate, Anne's tension caused her to fall to her knees on the steps. She then begged God to help her. Sir William Kingston helped her to her feet, realising that she was very much afraid. She managed to find her voice, asking him rather plaintively whether she would be 'put into a dungeon'. Two of the gentlemen present, Sir William Fitzwilliam and Sir William Paulet, showed clearly by their expressions that they disapproved of terrorising a gentlewoman, but Sir William Kingston answered her question kindly enough. 'No Madam. You go into your own lodging, where you lay at your Coronation.'

When Anne realised that the other gentlemen were on the point of leaving, she begged them to 'beseech the King's Grace to be good to her'. She was left in the care of Sir William Kingston and Sir Edmund Walsingham, who then became her jailors.[21]

Anne's own ladies-in-waiting had not been allowed to accompany her, and she then faced the four women who had been chosen to stay with her in the Tower. They would share her confinement up to a point, but they were there not only to serve, but also to spy. They were instructed to report on all that she said and did, and even to report her changes of mood. One of them was an aunt by marriage, the wife of her father's brother, Sir James Boleyn. But she could expect little family feeling from that particular Lady Boleyn. Mistress Coffin, the wife of Anne's own Master of Horse, was also there, along with Mistress Stoner, the wife of the King's Sergeant at Arms, and Lady Kingston, the wife of the Constable of the Tower, Sir William Kingston.

Anne attempted a protest, affirming that she considered it to be a 'great unkindness' on the part of the King, 'to set about me such as I have never loved, and I would fain have had mine own Privy Chamber, whom I favour most'. Kingston replied that the King 'took them to be honest and good women' but it was obvious that they were there to spy and that her own women would not be allowed entry. Kingston had been instructed to gather together all the information the women could provide, which he then passed on to Cromwell, in a series of six letters.[22]

Anne's nervousness made itself clear in her sudden garrulity, though her new companions had received instructions to tell her as little as possible. When she asked Kingston anxiously, 'Master Kingston, do you know wherefore I am here?' he lied to her, telling her he did not. Mind spinning, she requested that she might have the sacrament in her chamber, so that she might pray for mercy. Then her control snapped again, and she cried out, 'For I am as clear from the company of man as I am clear from you, and I am the King's true wedded wife!' It was obvious that she already had some idea of the way the case against her tended, and probably feared the foolish words already spoken, but she could not possibly have guessed all of it.

She was told nothing at all of the trial preparations, which were already speeding ahead nor, thankfully, had she any idea that the headsman from Calais had already been bespoken and his price agreed. She had no idea of the whereabouts of her father, brother or friends.

Cromwell, clever in his understanding of the reactions of people under stress, realised that the Queen would stand up defiantly to bullying tactics, but that her mind, whirling with questions, would be likely to break under silence and lack of information. Every word she was to utter, from her arrival in the Tower until her trial date was set, would be reported, sifted, evaluated and added to the growing pile of nonsense that was beginning to constitute the case against her. Anything would do to pad it out, make it seem more than it was. Because almost anything, taken out of its context, could be made to seem to be an admission.

'When saw you the King?' Anne asked. Again it was Kingston who answered her, saying, 'I saw him not, since I saw him in the Tiltyard.' Then again, 'Mr. Kingston, I pray you tell where my father is?' Kingston's reply to that was short and correct. 'I saw him afore dinner, in the court.'

And the final, anguished, cry 'Oh, where is my sweet brother?' 'I left him at York Place', Kingston replied. That was the cruellest lie of all, for Kingston knew very well that George Boleyn had already been taken into the Tower that same morning. He also knew that George was to be charged with incest with his sister – indeed his wife's lie was to be the only real charge against him, but that gem was hidden from Anne.

The whispers around her had penetrated her consciousness more than had been realised.

She suddenly cried, 'I hear tell I am to be accused with three men, and I can say no more than nay, without I should open my body!' Then, with her mind flitting homeward, she said sadly, 'Oh my mother, thou wilt die with sorrow!'

By the following day it was clear that Anne had been informed of the names of the three men she expected to be charged with. Norris, Weston and Smeaton. She went desperately over and over the conversations she had lately had with each of them, looking for clues to what words might be used against her. Looking for a loophole, trying to find some comfort in the idea that, without a case, there could be no case.[23]

Lady Kingston had by then been instructed to get Anne to talk as freely as possible, in the hope that she might implicate herself. Though aware there could be no real evidence, Anne still felt the weight of the situation she was in. She turned to Kingston and asked, 'Shall I die without justice?' He answered her gravely, saying, 'The poorest subject the King hath, hath justice.' Anne stared at him for a moment in astonishment, before bursting into disbelieving laughter.

That moment of stupefaction and surprise at his naivety showed that Anne was fully aware of the manner of man she was dealing with in Henry. Justice had no place in his justice system, and only absolute obedience to the King's declared will counted. Any who offended or disobeyed could expect to suffer, whether innocent of any real wrongdoing or not. The remark, and the strained ironic laughter it provoked, showed the real difference between Henry and Anne. She had a sharp tongue and a quick temper, which often got the better of her, but those were women's weapons, honed in a time when women generally had no real power at all. Henry, on the surface more genial, more pleasant, had behind his facade a very real ruthlessness that Anne lacked.

It was this callous ruthlessness that would eventually insist on a public humiliation for his daughter the Princess Mary, before she could be restored to his good graces. While Anne had already made clear that she would have accepted reconciliation with the Princess on easier terms, giving her own concessions in exchange.[24]

It was this streak of cruelty that was turned against Anne, nullifying all the years of his love for her and ignoring her reliance on him. But Henry was crafty as well as cruel. When Anne had gone into the Tower, he staged an affecting little scene with his illegitimate son, the Duke of Richmond. He claimed that Anne had plotted to kill both the boy and his half-sister, Princess Mary. This was said of a woman whose power, even in the days of her triumph, had been illusory at best, and who even then waited fearfully in the Tower to find out exactly what she was being accused of.[25]

The torture of Anne's mind continued throughout the Tuesday and Wednesday, and her frantic talk went on being recorded eagerly, despite its disjointed and erratic nature, simply because the accusers had little else to go on. Only Smeaton had said anything against her, under torture. The others all disdainfully refused to implicate her in anything. One Margery Houseman, one of Anne's ladies of whom Cromwell had entertained some hopes of gathering information, not only gave him no help at all, but instead proved her staunch loyalty to the Queen. The prosecutors seemed to have met with a dead end. Even with such charges as were seemingly impossible for a woman to defend herself from, they were getting nowhere. All they had to go on were the words of a spirit-broken musician and a vindictive sister-in-law.

By Wednesday Anne's own spirits had risen a little, possibly buoyed up with the belief that they would be unable to charge her with anything. Mistress Coffin and Lady Kingston reported that, 'She has been very merry, she made a great dinner, and yet soon after she called for her supper.' This was hardly earth-shattering information, but was an example of those fluctuating moods that Henry had once found so fascinating.

After supper she sent for Sir William Kingston, to ask why she had seen so little of him. 'Where have you been all day?' she asked him, to be told, 'I have been with the prisoners.' This prompted Anne to try to find out what was going on in the Tower, but without success. She then reverted to protesting about her treatment again, saying, 'To be a Queen and to be so cruelly handled was never seen, but I think the King does it but to prove me!' She laughed again, perhaps wryly, at the idea that Henry would go to such lengths as some form of test.

In fact, Cromwell was struggling to find enough evidence to make his case against Anne stick. Sir Edward Boynton wrote to Fitzwilliam:

> No-one will confess to anything. It would in my foolish conceit much touch the King's honour if it should no further appear. I cannot but believe that the other two are as culpable as he [Smeaton] but they keep each other's counsel. I think much of the communication which took place on the last occasion between the Queen and Master Norris ... I hear further that the Queen standeth stiffly to her opinion that she will not be convicted, which I think is the trust that she hath in the other two.[26]

Boynton makes it clear that he was prepared to accept the charges being prepared by Cromwell. However, it is interesting to note that he refers at that time only to Sir Henry Norris and Francis Weston (apart from Smeaton). He does admit that there was nowhere near enough evidence to achieve a conviction without causing a scandal of such proportions that it would only bring down shame on the King. However, Lord Rochford, Sir William Brereton, Sir Richard Page and Sir Thomas Wyatt were not mentioned by Boynton at all in his letter, although they had also been arrested by that time. Cromwell was still playing his cards very close to his chest while trying to pad out his case.

Kingston was also still busy collecting what details he could and remarked on Anne's changeable spirits, 'For one hour she is determined to die, and the next much to the contrary.' What did he expect? Grasping at the straws of frail hope, aided by the superstition of the times, and referring to the continuing hot weather, Anne had at one point said, 'There will be no rain until I am set free!' Another time she said, more sensibly:

> I would to God I had my Bishops, for they would all go to the King for me, for I think the most part of England prays for me, and if I die you will see the greatest punishment for me within these seven years, that ever came to England. And then I shall be in Heaven, for I have done many good deeds.

Anne had certainly done many good deeds, and had tried, particularly in the later part of her Queenship, to be a good Queen in the old traditional mould. She had become rightfully famed for her charities and the amounts she dispensed were truly substantial. Bishop Burnet (1643–1715) carefully studied that part of the reign of King Henry VIII for his book on the Reformation.[27]

He was not a writer who was entirely in Anne's favour, but he did make it clear that she had 'devoted herself to good works and that in her last nine months she distributed between £14,000 and £15,000 to the poor'. Also he stated that, shortly before her fall, she was still urging Henry to order a new English translation of the Bible. Burnet firmly believed that this side of Anne's nature was not incompatible with a certain freedom of manner, allied to 'an innocent lack of discretion'. But her freedom of manner had caused malicious gossip, which would long be remembered against her, while the generosity of her charity and her concern for the new religion were far more easily forgotten.

The one bishop of Anne's who should certainly have stood up for her, and who owed her the most, was the Archbishop of Canterbury, Thomas Cranmer. He had risen through the patronage of the Boleyns, but he did not speak in her defence when she most needed his support and when his intercession on her behalf might have been expected.

Cranmer received a 'summons' from Cromwell on 2 May, instructing him to return to London, as he was then in the country. Amazed and frightened at the turn of events, he wrote a confused, timid and grovelling excuse for a letter, in which he tried to refer obliquely to his previous good feeling for Anne, without committing himself to taking any part in defending her. As he finished the letter he had been called to see the Council, and on his return from that interview he added another, even more cringing line. He said, 'I am sorry such faults can be proved against the Queen as they report.' Of course, nothing could be 'proved' but he had been briefed by the Council and had taken his stance. He hadn't the slightest intention of questioning anything he was told, however little it may have fitted with the character of the woman he had known for so long.

Despite the instruction about Anne being told nothing, news was still seeping through to her. Eventually she said to Kingston, 'I hear that my Lord brother is here?' 'It is true', he answered. She pretended to be unconcerned, believing that there could be no possible charge to bring against George. 'I am very glad therefore, that we both be so nigh together.' It was at that point that she was informed that Weston and Brereton were also in the Tower. It is not clear whether she ever knew that Wyatt had been imprisoned, but he remained without any charge against him. His father had a long-standing friendship with Cromwell, which would eventually effect his release, but not before the anguish he suffered at the proceedings against the Boleyns had broken his spirit and his heart.[28]

The necessary widening of the investigation was due to there being so little to work with. This was a situation that could, in the wrong circumstances, quickly become a grave embarrassment to Cromwell and the Seymours. Once they had made their move, they had to be absolutely certain that they could carry it through, and be able to make it work out in their favour. For the case to have suffered a collapse at that point would have meant disaster for them all.

Henry was confident that all would go according to plan, despite the fevered and sometimes fruitless work behind the scenes. His was essentially a waiting role, and he should certainly by then have been playing the part of the shocked and grieving husband, aghast at the betrayal of his unfaithful wife. Unfortunately, he did not possess the patience to retire from the public gaze for even so short a time, and discretion was thrown out of the window. There were frequent reports of him riding on the river in his barge at night, in company with ladies and musicians, enjoying all kinds of merriment. It was hardly the sort of behaviour expected of a man who had just found out that his wife had betrayed him with several others. He was unable to see the inconsistency of it.

One evening, after dining with the Bishop of Carlisle, John Kite, he confided to the Bishop that he had 'long expected' some such outcome from his marriage to Anne, and proceeded to pull out a copy of a tragedy he had written on the subject. The dismayed Bishop, amazed at Henry's attitude, and quite likely even more concerned at its implication, refused to accept the copy.

The common people, seeing the air of festivity, which was so at odds with expected conduct in any genuine case, began to remark unfavourably on it. Public opinion actually began to swing round into Anne's favour, so great was the general disbelief and disgust of the outraged Londoners.

Even Eustace Chapuys, who was certainly glad enough of Anne's fall, in the hope that it would mean better prospects for the Princess Mary, showed his open repugnance at the situation unfolding before him.

He wrote to the Emperor Charles V reporting Henry's gaiety, the banquets and general merrymaking and the deplorable lack of any suitable comportment on the part of the King. He was forced to conclude that, in his opinion, even 'the Concubine' had deserved to be treated with a little more regard.[29]

Sir Thomas Cromwell, the plotter who brought down the Boleyns. He would face his own execution in 1540.

Chapter Eighteen

While the prisoners were incarcerated and the case still being built around them, there was the usual callous rush among the courtiers to acquire whatever they could of the estates and offices of the unfortunates who had so recently been respected figures at court. So certain were the authorities that the prisoners would not escape their 'justice' that it was generally assumed that if one was about to face a treason charge, then there would already be sufficient evidence to convict.

Even though the case against Anne and the majority of the gentlemen arrested was going ahead, there were still no charges brought against either Sir Thomas Wyatt or Sir Richard Page. There seems to have been a period where nobody who was not directly involved in preparing the case had any idea what was going on, and speculation at court was rife, sometimes even wild.

Finally, on Tuesday, 9 May, the King sent for twenty-two noblemen, along with twenty-seven gentlemen of the Privy Chamber, to discuss with them the case then in preparation. The official summons for the peers who would form the jury to try Anne's case was not sent out until 13 May, but was certainly discussed earlier, as Lord Latimer wrote to Cromwell on 12 May asking to be excused from it.

The actual legal proceedings against the Queen were not started until 10 May.[1] An assembly in Westminster Hall was informed that a true bill had been found against the accused and that the persons concerned were probably guilty and should therefore be tried for treason.[2]

A preference for a trial by jury might in the circumstances seem strange, but when the jury is carefully chosen and has been made fully aware of the King's will in the matter, then no problem regarding the conclusion need be expected.

On 11 May the Abbot of Cirencester wrote to Cromwell to inform him that he had already promised the Stewardship of the Abbey – until then in the keeping of Sir Henry Norris – to none other than Sir William Kingston. Kingston had certainly been quick off the mark, but he would not be the only one. Once it was known that the jury was chosen, and the trials going ahead, there would be a general baying of the hounds while everyone else fought at court for what could be grasped.

The one strange thing about this time was that the one man who might be expected to arouse the King's jealousy more than most had already been guaranteed his life. Sir Thomas Wyatt's attachment to the Queen was well known, as he had fallen in love with her on her return from France in the early 1520s.[3] He would therefore have seemed an ideal candidate to join that growing band of victims awaiting trial. But due to his father's friendship with Cromwell he was to escape the net almost completely.

His father, Sir Henry Wyatt, had written to Cromwell as soon as his son was arrested, begging for his release. Cromwell had answered the letter with reassurances that Sir Thomas would not be harmed, and a letter of relief and gratitude went back to Cromwell on 11 May. Wyatt would stay in the Tower until the trials and executions were over, but he would be released later that year. The other man similarly favoured, Sir Richard Page, would also be spared once the matter was completed.

So why were they arrested in the first place? Possibly merely to give an appearance of equality, to show that absolutely anyone, even the friends of Cromwell, could be gathered in. But they were never in any real danger, as the lack of charges against them show.[4]

Also on 11 May, Cromwell had visited the King at Hampton Court to finalise the arrangements. Anne's uncle, the Duke of Norfolk, was to preside over the hearings, although on that same day Sir William Paulet sent Cromwell a message that the Duke was still in the dark about 'whether the parties should proceed to trial or not'. Norfolk was still unaware how many Commissioners would be needed, or what rank they ought to be. He was behaving very cautiously indeed, doing absolutely nothing until he received full official instructions, and had said that he was naming none 'until he learned of the King's pleasure'.[5]

This not only shows that Norfolk needed to keep his head down and make sure he pleased the King, but that he, too, was uninformed about what was going on behind the scenes.

The letters from Kingston to Cromwell seemed to halt at around this time. It may have been because the hopes of getting Anne to make some damning confession had faded. They may also have felt that in view of the 'evidence' stacking up, the nature of the charges against the Queen and the carefully primed jury that they had enough with which to proceed.

It had been reported by Lancelot de Carles that some Lords of the Council had been to see Anne in the Tower in an attempt to extract a confession, but that the Queen, 'having no further hopes of the world' had refused to comply. Despite her situation Anne was holding onto her pride and he says, 'for all this, she would not give up her greatness but spoke to the Lords as a mistress, so that those who went to interrogate her were astonished'.[6]

The *Spanish Chronicle* makes the claim that the Councillors sent to question Anne were Cromwell, Cranmer, Norfolk and Audley. Cranmer had made haste to assure her that her situation greatly distressed him due to her 'bad conduct', and Anne supposedly rounded on him sharply. She made it clear that she knew the King had intentions towards Jane Seymour and ended her tirade with the words, 'he will get no more from me, and any confession that has been made is false!'.[7]

Chapuys at this time wrote to Charles V that Henry was 'determined on proceeding against the Queen, regardless of whether her guilt was proved …'.[8] That is a particularly damning statement to be made by a man who was always her enemy, but it shows the almost frantic way in which the case was being prepared and the fanatical attitude towards the victims.

The Councillors were reported to have seen Lord Rochford, who vehemently denied all the accusations against him. Further visits to Norris, Weston and Brereton met with the same response. After these failures it was then recorded that 'the King then ordered the trial to Westminster'.[9] Henry had no further time to waste, and there was no point in making further attempts to obtain confessions.

On Friday, 12 May the Duke of Norfolk was appointed High Steward of England. This was a transitory position that was generally used for the organising of great occasions, such as coronations, though now and then it involved presiding over important trials.

Norfolk was also at Westminster on that day to direct the special session of Oyer and Terminer, through which Norris, Weston, Brereton and Smeaton would be judged. This was due to their lower rank. They would then be tried by the Commissioners, who had officially brought the case against them. Anne and George, due to their higher status, would be dealt with separately at a slightly later date. Though in the present day it would be a matter of great concern that the first trial, of Anne's supposed lovers, would inevitably prejudice her own, this unsatisfactory situation was taken as a matter of course at the time, for the matter was largely considered to be pre-judged.

The judges of the King's Bench had been summoned to Westminster for the proceedings of 12 May, including a special jury of twelve knights, together with the men appointed on 24 April. There were also several Lords of the King's Council, including Sir William Fitzwilliam and, surprisingly to us, the Queen's own father, Lord Wiltshire. Chapuys was to state that Thomas Boleyn was 'ready to assist with the judgement', but it is likely that he had little choice if he were not to appear culpable in some way.[10] In either case, such an appearance must have been agony for him.

What appears even more despicable to the twenty-first-century mind is the fact that the judges very largely had a vested interest in arranging the deaths of the accused. Smeaton can be discounted, as he was considered of no importance and had served his purpose.

But for the others there were the complications of not only enemies but even debtors among the jury. The foreman of the jury, Edward Willoughby, was known to be in debt to William Brereton, and Brereton's death would, of course, free him from any need to repay. Impartiality was absent in other respects. Sir Gules Alington was a son-in-law of Thomas More, whose death was by many still laid at Anne's door. William Askew was a great friend of the Princess Mary and therefore Anne's enemy. Anthony Hungerford was actually related to Jane Seymour. Robert Dormer was an avid Catholic who opposed Anne's policies of religious reform, Richard Tempest was a friend of Cromwell's and Sir John Hampden was the father-in-law of William Paulet who was Controller of the Royal Household and unlikely to show any opinion contrary to the King's. William Sidney was a friend of the Duke of Suffolk, and already hostile towards Anne. Thomas Palmer was a client of Fitzwilliam and one of the King's favoured friends and gambling partners.[11]

There were a couple of others – for instance William Musgrave who had, in 1534, failed to secure the conviction of Lord Dacre and Walter Hungerford who in 1540 would be executed for buggery. Both men would have good reason to keep their heads down and do exactly as they were instructed, in order not to offend the King further.

Finding guilty the four accused at the first trial would not only make Anne's own trial a foregone conclusion, but due to the convictions of the accused they would then be prevented from saying anything in her defence. This was, of course, a moot point anyway, as none of them had any chance of escaping the verdicts.

There had been an astonishing turn of events in 1534 when Lord Dacre had been acquitted from a charge of treason and had escaped with his life. Henry had been extremely displeased with that verdict but the matter had been allowed to rest. However, the cases were not comparable. Not only was the Dacre verdict incredibly rare but it was highly unlikely to ever be repeated while Henry was King. There was far more than the usual interest in the present trials, from abroad as well as at home, and there could certainly be no leeway allowed for acquittal in those cases.[12]

On Friday, 12 May the four men were taken to Westminster Hall. They must have been dismayed to see the jury file in to be sworn, every man of them a potential enemy, with not a friend among them and not even the neutrals they may have hoped for. Under normal rules, the accused could challenge the jurors, in order to have them replaced with others who might be more favourably inclined. There is a suggestion that Anthony Hungerford was so challenged (due to being related to Jane Seymour) and even the ex-Lord Mayor, John Champneys, who was almost blind, but it was to no avail. William Sidney was put forward instead, and he was a friend of the Duke of Suffolk, so they were certainly no better off.

Smeaton pleaded guilty to adultery, but refused the other charges (i.e. against the person of the King). All the others declared most firmly that they were innocent of all the charges. As they had no prior warning of what would be said against them, and they had no defence counsel, they had to try to remember what was claimed against them in each case, and make some attempt to refute it. Naturally, the prosecutors were not only well prepared but also very hostile, so any opportunity of making any reasonable case for the accused against such antagonism was absolutely hopeless.

The verdicts were, in all cases, 'Guilty' and the sentences were read out. They were to be hanged, drawn and quartered, the full horror of the punishment for treason. The edge of the executioner's sword was then turned towards them, and they were led away, to await the arrangements for their executions at Tyburn.[13]

Anne and George Boleyn would have to wait over the weekend before they faced their own accusers. They would not have to travel to Westminster for their trials, for they were intended to take place within the Tower itself. Their waiting must have been excruciating, particularly as they would never be allowed to meet.

Anne did not know that on Saturday, 13 May her household was being disbanded, and that there was a list being drawn up detailing the assets of the condemned men. John Husee wrote to Lord Lisle confirming that all the normal business of government was then at a standstill until after the trial of the Queen. He wrote carelessly, 'if it be as some doth presume, it shall be all rid of by the end of this next week'.[14]

The list of Cromwell's 'remembrances' is interesting in that it gives some of the values of the condemned men's lands. Rochford's name is also on the list, although he had not yet been tried. This point is being reiterated because the modern mind shies away from the idea that a person's belongings and valuables can be divided up so blatantly, as if he were already dead, while the young man was still very much alive. The sheer injustice of the proceedings haunts – or should haunt – the reader of those lists, though in the sixteenth century people were cheerfully blasé about them, and saw nothing at all wrong in taking for granted that the owners would be dead within the week.

Lord George Rochford's lands were valued at £441 10*s*. 9*d*.
Sir William Brereton's were valued at £1,236 12*s*. 6*d*.
Sir Henry Norris's were valued at £1,327 15*s*. 7*d*.

Cromwell wrote to Stephen Gardiner, Bishop of Winchester, on Sunday, 14 May, to tell him that 'great suit is being made for the men's confiscated offices and goods'. He promised that Gardiner would receive back £200 worth, which was part of the life pensions that Wolsey in 1529 had made Gardiner pay out of his see to Rochford and Norris. The full amount was £300, so as he was not to receive back the full amount expended, it is very interesting to see that Cromwell had already taken his 'commission'.[15]

The reformer Robert Barnes asked to be given Rochford's Keepership of Bedlam Hospital, which was worth £40 per year. Husee had meanwhile already made out a list of those who had benefited which he sent to Lord Lisle in a letter. 'Sir Thomas Cheyney is now named Lord Warden of the Cinque Ports', which was an office held by George Boleyn since 1533. 'My Lord of Richmond is Chamberlain of Chester and North Wales and Mr. Harry Knyvett is Constable of Beaumaris', offices that had been held by Brereton. He also stated that 'Sir Francis Bryan is now Chief Gentleman of the Privy Chamber', taking the place of Henry Norris.

Husee was also concerned about the rumours flying around, some of which were of the possibility that 'none would die but the Queen and her brother'. But the talk had lately changed to 'those which shall suffer shall die when the Queen and her brother goeth to execution'.[16] He told Lord Lisle that the King had not yet assigned the office of Groom of the Stole, but that he intended to do so 'from time to time at his pleasure'.

There was a timely reminder at the end of his letter to Lord Lisle, 'I trust your Lordship will remember Mr. Secretary with wine and letters, and in like manner Mr. Heneage, so far as I can see they, or one of them, must strike the stroke.' And again, 'that your Lordship give credit to what Goodall shall tell you, and that to be kept a secret. Thus I pray God send to your Lordship his noble heart's desire.'

It is plain that not only was Husee telling Lord Lisle of the offices already assigned, but reminding him that if he wished to benefit, as others were doing, it would be necessary for him to send Cromwell not only 'letters' to keep his name in mind, but also 'wine'. The gifts would help Cromwell remember what it was Lord Lisle hoped for.

Many people had been touched by the condemnation of young Sir Francis Weston and although many believed he might yet escape, Weston's father Sir Richard had been quite unable to arrange either an audience with the King or a meeting with Cromwell. The family were desperate, and offered large sums of money in efforts to secure Sir Francis' freedom, but the King was not in a forgiving mood, even for hard cash.

His mind was entirely occupied at that time with Jane Seymour. On Sunday, 14 May she was moved from the house where she had been staying, in a small attempt at discretion while the arrests were completed. After that time Henry saw no further need to deprive himself of his sweetheart, so she was taken to Chelsea to the house that had once belonged to More, 'within a mile of York Place' for ease of visiting. There she was not only the recipient of many rich gifts from the King, but was treated in every way as if she were already Queen of England. The house itself was luxurious, having its own chapel, library and over 20 acres of gardens, orchards and parkland. She was accompanied by her parents, to keep up the pretence that she and Henry were being chaperoned. The whole party enjoyed their stay while they waited for the condemnation of the Queen, which Jane had been told to expect by mid-afternoon on Monday, 15 May.

Chapuys had become very friendly with the Seymours at that time, although the Emperor Charles V was evidently not at all convinced that Henry would actually marry Jane. He wrote on 15 May suggesting several possible ladies who would be suitable consorts for the King, once Anne was dead.[17]

There was, of course, no precedent in English law for the trial of an anointed queen. Even when King Edward III had needed to remove from power his mother, Queen Isabella, and her lover, Mortimer, the Queen, who was possibly involved in the murder of his father, Edward II, was merely forced into retirement from the court, though Mortimer was executed. Therefore, Cromwell was working in the dark with regard to procedure. However, in this case mere retirement from court was not the intended result of the case, so an open trial there had to be.

It was to be held in the King's Hall, which was the Great Hall of the Tower and stood close to the Royal Lodgings. The Constable of the Tower had provided 'a great scaffold' holding rows of benches to enable all the Lords and notables to be seated with a good view, but a great many ordinary spectators were also expected to attend. Chapuys mentioned there could be as many as 2,000 people in all, encouraged to watch the shame and disgrace of the Queen. Space was provided for the common people to stand in a cleared area behind barriers. Henry certainly intended as many people as possible, of all degrees, to hear the charges against the Queen. Hopefully, they would then return to their homes believing firmly in her guilt.

A canopy over the Chair of Estate was not for the use of the Queen, but for Norfolk, who in his capacity as High Steward would represent the King. Sadly, Anne may have had her strain added to by being able to see and hear something of the preparations for her trial during that difficult weekend.

On Monday, 15 May the Duke of Norfolk, the Earl of Surrey, his son, the Lord Chancellor Thomas Audley and the Duke of Suffolk were seated, followed by 'the greatest peers in the Realm' each in order of precedence.

Those present on the day were the Marquess of Exeter, the Earl of Northumberland, the Earls of Sussex, Worcester, Arundel, Oxford, Rutland, Westmorland, Huntingdon and Derby. Also present were the Lords LaWarr, Montagu, Morley, Cobham, Maltravers, Dacre of the South, Powys, Monteagle, Clinton, Sandys, Windsor, Wentworth, Burgh and Mordaunt.

Alesius would later claim that Lord Wiltshire had been ordered to attend the trial of his son and daughter, and the Harleian Mss actually stated that he was there. Chapuys also says that he had shown himself willing to attend, but the *Bag of Secrets* does not give his name as an attendee, though it is incomplete.[18]

The fact that Thomas Boleyn had certainly attended the previous trial on 12 May was bad enough. We cannot know what his feelings were then, being aware that the verdict would prejudice the trial of his offspring. The French Ambassador and other diplomats attended too, but, incredibly after so long and tense a battle between him and the woman he referred to as 'the Concubine', Chapuys was not there. His sudden fastidiousness regarding the way the proceedings were being handled may have prompted him to claim illness, but it meant that he was then reliant on other eyewitnesses for his reports.

The crowded hall, designed to intimidate, and also to give the appearance of legality, did not mean the case was less than an appalling abuse of power. Despite the preparations and the show, even Chapuys was forced to concede that there was no valid proof of Anne's guilt – so perhaps all the window-dressing was merely an attempt to cover over the many deficiencies.[19]

The Queen was taken into the court by Sir William Kingston and Sir Edmund Walsingham and was attended by Lady Kingston and Lady Boleyn, her aunt. Several eyewitnesses state that she was also attended by 'four young ladies' so these cannot refer to the mature ladies who were set to spy on her in the Tower. These 'young ladies' had appeared by her side for the trial, and were to stay with her during her final days and attend at her execution. It therefore seems that she was allowed to have with her some of the attendants she was accustomed to and had favoured before her arrest. If this is the case, it is likely to have been more for the sake of appearances and proper attendance in the eyes of the eagerly watching foreign observers than to please Anne. There has always been a tradition that Margaret Wyatt (Lady Lee) and Anne Savile were two of those who stayed with her until the end.

The full Indictment was then read out, a lengthy document that had already had an airing at the trial of the gentlemen two days previously. It made harrowing listening, but Anne, sitting with her hands still in her lap, managed to remain calm and to even appear unmoved by the shameful accusations. The gist of it is as follows.

That on 6 October 1533 she had procured Henry Norris to 'violate' her. Bear in mind that she had, at that time, only recently given birth to the Princess Elizabeth. She was then keeping to her chamber because she had still not been 'churched', i.e. cleansed following giving birth.

That on 3 December 1533 she procured William Brereton to have illicit intercourse with her, which he did on 8 December.

That on 12 April 1534 (and before or since) she had procured Mark Smeaton 'to violate her', whereby he did so at Westminster, on 26 April.

That on 8 May 1534 (and at other times) she had procured Francis Weston to have illicit intercourse with her, and again on 20 May.

That on 2 November 1535 (and at several other times) she procured and incited 'her natural brother' Lord Rochford 'to violate her' and that on 5 November 1535 he did 'violate and carnally know his own sister, the said Queen. Which he also did on divers days before and after, sometimes of his own procurement and sometimes that of the Queen'.

That on 27 November 1535 she gave gifts to 'inveigle' the gentlemen to her will, and that on 31 October 1535 and on various other times before or since, she had 'compassed and imagined' the King's death. That the Queen had also promised to marry one of the said gentlemen 'whenever the King should depart this life'.

These basic claims were padded out with salacious details of kissings and fondlings and also with dates and places, many of which Anne was easily able to refute, simply by remembering that the court was actually somewhere else at the time.

As Professor Eric Ives very sensibly said, 'Quadruple adultery and incest merely invites disbelief!' It is certainly amazing that none of Anne's many ladies or servants were aware of all the illicit activity going on in the Queen's apartments.[20]

Chapuys' later report concentrated less on the charges of having 'conspired the King's death' and more on the accusation that Anne and Norris had developed a serious relationship. As Norris, the widower, had been considering a match with Madge Shelton, Anne's cousin, it would suggest that they were certainly friendly, but it is hardly likely that he foolishly intended any other relationship with the Queen. Probably Cromwell, aware that the serious charge regarding the King's safety could not be proved, was prepared to emphasise the more titillating aspects in an attempt to produce disgust and abhorrence.

Alesius reported further details – that 'the Queen was accused of having danced in her rooms with the gentlemen of the Privy Chamber and of having kissed her brother Lord Rochford'. These seem innocuous enough. Certain letters were also produced which Anne had at an earlier time written to George Boleyn, in which she told him that she was pregnant. Again innocent enough in the circumstances, but these were twisted to imply that they meant that the coming child was actually fathered by George.

Chapuys' report also said that Anne was accused of 'having laughed at the King's dress, and made fun of his poems'. Seeing the already overweight King shambling around the court in his padded clothes may well have appeared risible, but it could hardly be considered a crime. But it suddenly was, and also constituted proof that the Queen was tired of him and preparing to replace him with another.[21] What a farrago of absolute nonsense!

Anne remained silent while listening to the accusations, but when she was allowed to speak she did so, putting up a firm and considered defence. She was regarded to have 'made so wise and discreet answers to all things laid against her, excusing herself with her words so clearly, as though she had never been guilty of the same!'. Sensible indeed.[22]

She took the opportunity to deny absolutely that she had ever been false to the King, and defended herself with such common sense and obvious innocence that the people in the packed hall began to have doubts that there was any case to answer at all. It was said that 'the Queen, sitting in her chair, having an excellent quick wit and being a ready speaker, did so answer to all the objections that, had the peers given their verdicts according to the expectations of the assembly, she would certainly have been acquitted!'.[23]

Later, on 20 May, Chapuys would write, 'no witnesses were produced against her, as it is usual to do, particularly when the accused denies the charge'.[24]

No doubt statements were read out, including the infamous one from Jane Rochford detailing Anne's liaison with her own brother, but the charges were plainly so ridiculous and so obviously contrived that Anne was easily able to dismiss them. All the accusations were that she had spent time alone with her brother and that they had exchanged the perfectly usual formal, or even affectionate, kisses. That she had written George letters and that she had danced with the gentlemen of the household were all such normal and usual matters and so very far from suggesting any kind of illicit relationship that they can indeed be dismissed.

There is, just for the record, the reminder that incest was not actually considered a crime in England until 1908, but that does not mean that Anne and George had taken advantage of any laxity in the law. The idea that an incestuous relationship can be made up out of the evidence provided, which showed nothing but the normal contact between members of the same family, is ludicrous.[25]

The Crown's case was then reduced to using hearsay as a weapon. Lady Wingfield, who was claimed to be 'just such another' as the promiscuous Queen, had died before 1534, so she was not available to defend either her own slandered reputation or Anne's. Therefore, any testimony supposedly given on her behalf, or in her words, was not only quite preposterous but also inadmissible.

George Wyatt was later to state, 'For the evidence, as I never could hear of any, small I believe it was. The accusers must have doubted whether their proofs would not prove only to be their reproofs!'

The Queen was not permitted to question anyone on her own behalf, or summon anyone to speak for her, nor could she have any legal counsel to conduct a defence. Yet she had done the very best she could, and it was good indeed. She successfully caused most of the audience, composed in the main part of people either hostile to her or enjoying the idea of a Queen on trial for her life due to sexual promiscuity, to think again and in many cases change the opinions they started with.

Despite the definite swing of the crowd in her favour it was to no avail.

The Lords pronounced their verdicts one by one, and they unanimously declared that she was guilty. It has since been described as 'a purely political verdict'.[26] It might equally correctly be described as sheer murder.

It was said that Anne was then 'degraded in all of her titles' and it is true that her lesser ones were taken from her. However, due to the technicality of the Act of Succession of 1534 she was actually Queen of England by statutory right, not merely by being the consort of the King.[27] Therefore, she would remain Queen of England while she lived and this was recognised by the fact that she continued to be served and referred to as 'Queen Anne'.

The Duke of Norfolk was then required to read out the sentence. It was 'that thou shalt be burnt here within the Tower of London on the Green, or else have thy head smitten off, as the King's pleasure shall be further known of the same'. Despite his estrangement from his niece, it was reported that the tears ran down his cheeks as he spoke.

Anne kept her composure. She was then given permission to speak briefly, when she declared firmly that she did not fear to die. She asserted that what grieved her the most was that the gentlemen accused with her, who were quite innocent of the charges, should have to suffer on her behalf. She clearly confirmed her own innocence and her loyalty to the King and begged all the people present to pray for her. She finally asked for a short while in which to prepare her conscience for death. The giddy or rash-tempered woman was suddenly gone. She was calm, she spoke in a cool and considered way, and she made her words count, knowing that they would not only stay in the memories of her listeners, but that they would also be reported. Anne was, at that moment, more of a Queen than she had ever been.[28]

That this was true was recognised by a very courageous and obviously heartfelt remark made after her trial by none other than the Lord Mayor of London, Sir Ralph Warren. He is reported to have said, 'I can see no evidence against her, except that they wanted an occasion to be rid of her!'

Even Chapuys was to admit that the woman he had long considered an enemy had, in fact, become a victim, not the person whom Cromwell had described, but someone who had been condemned 'without valid proof or any valid confession'.[29] From such a source it is a very telling and thought-provoking admission indeed.

The Queen was then taken back to her apartments by Kingston and Walsingham.

Jane Seymour, waiting at Chelsea with Sir Nicholas Carewe, was seen talking and smiling with him when the messenger arrived with news of the condemnation of the Queen, as Henry had promised.

Anne's place in the court was quickly taken by her brother, George Lord Rochford, but before the proceedings could begin Henry Percy, the Earl of Northumberland was taken ill and had to be removed from the hall. He was already ill and would not live very long after Anne, but whether or not he still had any affection for her, having to be present at her trial and see her condemned to die had certainly proved too much for him.

The court quickly resumed its business.

The same charges of having had an incestuous relationship with the Queen were read out to George Boleyn. Naturally, he firmly denied them all. He would have known by then that his sister was condemned as well as their friends. He answered all the charges against him competently, so much so that the people in the common part of the hall were betting that he would have to be released. There was no charge whatsoever to answer, and the accusations were so foolish and totally unable to be proved, but he seemed to have lost heart. It was in that reckless frame of mind that he threw away his chance of life. It was asserted that Anne had once told his estranged wife, Jane Rochford, that the King was no longer capable of producing children: '*ne virtu ne puissance*'. Cromwell did not wish so inflammatory and scandalous a statement to be read out in the court in front of the common people, avid for excitement. It was written on a piece of paper and shown to George that he might read it, and tell the court whether or not his sister had made such a claim. When it was given to him, he glanced at it, then carefully and deliberately read it aloud to the court.[30]

After a lengthy discussion, the peers again pronounced the guilt of the accused and George was allowed to say the customary few words. He spoke briefly, asking formally for mercy from the King, and for his outstanding debts to be paid from his fortune. He was then taken away. It was as if he had already done with life and was quite indifferent to the result of his action.

On 16 May Sir William Kingston begun to worry about whatever arrangements he would be expected to make with regard to the executions. He did not know whether the Queen was to be burned or beheaded, and wrote to Cromwell asking for his advice.

'What is the King's pleasure regarding the Queen? As for the preparation of scaffolds and other necessaries?' He may have been in the dark, but for the headsman from Calais to have been in London by the date of Anne's death on 19 May it is perfectly clear that he had been sent for in advance of the trial.

Cromwell was engaged with trying to erase Anne's marriage to Henry. He was not able to claim that the annulment of Henry's marriage to Katherine of Aragon had been in any way wrong, as that would automatically reinstate the Princess Mary as heir to the throne. What he needed was some way for both marriages to be invalid, and both children declared illegitimate. Thereby clearing the way for any child Jane Seymour was supposed to have.[31]

The assumed pre-contract with Henry Percy had already been gone over, but that had been dead in the water when his own wife had tried to use it to divorce him, and he had categorically denied that it had ever existed. Cranmer was summoned to try to convince Anne to admit that her marriage to the King had never been valid, but as he had married her and declared it to be perfectly legal, that put him in a very awkward and embarrassing position. Did he tell her that she would be spared the fire if she agreed to some loophole?

The 1534 Act of Supremacy had made papal dispensations void in England – was it possible that the 1528 Papal Bull which had been obtained to free Henry from the stain of consanguinity with Anne, due to his previous liaison with her sister Mary Carey, could be used? If that dispensation could be overturned, then the relationship between Anne and Henry, due to his affair with her sister, would again prevent their marriage from being valid. This could then be used to declare that their marriage was not only dissolved, but that it had never been legal. If Anne had believed that this sleight of hand might somehow save her life, then she was deluded, or deliberately tricked. It would make no difference at all. The marriage was declared invalid, Elizabeth was declared illegitimate and Anne must still die. Ridiculously, she would now be executed for adultery towards a man to whom she had never been officially married. It was a convoluted piece of chicanery well worthy of Cromwell's devious and disreputable imagination.

On Wednesday 17 May 1536 the gentlemen who were found guilty were to die.

For the others there had been a four-day respite since sentencing, but for Lord Rochford only 48 hours. The indecent haste is all the more obvious when one remembers that other victims, such as Fisher and More, waited for over a year between arrest and execution. Henry was certainly in a hurry and Cromwell was desperate to have the matter settled and done with before anyone could begin to think seriously about how the trials had been handled.

Chapuys stated that the gentlemen died on Tower Green but it is known that they actually died on Tower Hill, just outside the precinct. He also said that Anne was forced to watch the executions 'which cruelly aggravated her grief'. Although it is known that Thomas Wyatt did witness the executions from his prison in the Bell Tower, there is no evidence that Anne was taken to any other room to see her brother die. She would certainly not have been able to see anything from her rooms in the Royal Apartments, on the other side of the building close to the Privy Garden.

The bitter anguish of Wyatt's poem '*Circa Regna Tonat*' ('Around the Throne Thunder Rolls') is as clear to us now as it was when first written, and it can bring that day in May 1536 to life again.[32]

> These bloody days have broken my heart,
> My lust, my youth, did then depart,
> And blind desire and estate,
> Who seeks to climb seeks to revert,
> Of truth – *Circa Regna Tonat*.
>
> The Bell Tower showed me such a sight,
> That in my head sticks day and night,
> There I did lean out of a grate [grating],
> For all favour, glory and might,
> That yet – *Circa Regna Tonat*.
>
> By proof, I say, there did I learn,
> Wit helpeth not defence to yearne,
> Of innocence to plead or prate,
> Bear low, therefore, give God the stern,
> For sure, *Circa Regna Tonat*.

After taking communion for the last time, the gentlemen who were to die, Lord George Rochford, Sir Henry Norris, Sir William Brereton, Sir Francis Weston and Mark Smeaton, were taken together to Tower Hill, where they would all suffer the same death of beheading.

Lord Rochford suffered first, making a short speech in which he defended his religious opinions. All the prisoners were aware that it was customary for the King to confiscate the property of the condemned and they did not wish their families to be destitute or their debts to remain unpaid. George had been so concerned about this that Kingston had contacted Cromwell on the matter, saying, 'You must help my Lord of Rochford's conscience.' George asked forgiveness of all those he may have offended but made no direct mention of the King.[33]

The others in turn said very little, save for the usual admissions of generally having 'led a sinful life'. Weston said sadly, 'I had thought to live in abomination [sinfulness] these twenty or thirty years yet, and then to have made amends.' It could be the cry of disbelief for any of those men, still young enough to have hopes and dreams, who had to meet death far sooner than expected. He finished with the piteous words, 'I little thought that it would come to this!'

Due to his lesser rank, Smeaton went last, saying briefly, 'Masters I pray you all to pray for me, for I have deserved the death.' Whether he meant that he stuck by his forced confession, or whether he felt any guilt in helping to blacken Anne's name, we cannot know. It is always possible that he was well aware that the sentence of hanging, drawing and quartering still stood and that any retraction at that point might give him an even worse death than the one he faced.

Each man had taken his turn at the block swiftly and faced his death 'charitably'. The axeman briefly showed each head to the crowd, as the body was quickly removed. Then all the heads and bodies were taken back to the Tower in a wagon, to be buried at the Chapel of St Peter ad Vincula.[34] George Boleyn, as a peer, was buried inside the chapel, the others being laid to rest outside.

The attitude of the crowd was the most surprising thing, and to Cromwell the most worrying. There was no shouting or jeering at all, such as often accompanied executions. There was only a saddened and respectful silence. When it was all over the crowd dispersed quietly, without any show of gladness, or any remarks being made of the rightness of the verdicts. The knowledge of the way the world outside would react was grave enough to be of great concern to Cromwell. He wanted Anne's execution done with, before the stunned apathy of the crowd turned into something else, which might be far harder to control. He seemed to have already changed his mind about the wisdom of allowing so many 'strangers' to hear the 'able and eloquent defence' the Queen and George had made at their trials. He was anxious that the witnesses would, when back home, give very unfavourable accounts of the King's proceedings. He therefore gave orders that 'all foreigners' were to be kept out of the Tower.[35] Kingston's response to the order was the sensible one that if the time of the Queen's death was not announced, then it would prevent crowds from gathering outside.[36] So another small subterfuge was decided on, that everyone, including the Queen, would be led to believe that her execution would take place on the following day, 18 May, when it was in reality planned for Friday, 19 May. It was hoped that by then all the spectators, apart from those officially invited, would have lost interest and returned to their homes.

The Queen may initially have had some hope of escaping with her life, when her marriage was first made invalid, but if so all such hopes ended for her with the death of her beloved brother, the news of which must have been shattering. She would not long be kept in ignorance about her own death, nor would her natural grief be taken into consideration. Kingston merely informed her that she was to die the following day, on Thursday, 18 May.

Anne's resilience at this point was remarked on and was indeed unusual. Deep in grief she undoubtedly was, aware that trickery had played its part in the subsequent invalidation of her marriage she also was, but she could still rally at the awful news that her own death was imminent. She made some remark on the nature of the death to Kingston, and he assured her that death such as she would suffer, by the sword, was comparatively quick and easy, and also that the swordsman who would perform it was very skilled. Therefore she was unlikely to feel very much, and he described the pain as 'subtle'.

Anne's courage, in the face of catastrophic loss and genuine fear so disconcerted Kingston, that he wrote of it in amazement. 'I have seen many men, and also women, executed', he said, 'and they have been in great sorrow. To my knowledge, this lady hath much joy and pleasure in death.'[37]

What did he expect? Could he have imagined that she would wish to give Cromwell (who she knew was told everything) the satisfaction of knowing that his victim was incapacitated by grief and terror? There could also be another good reason for her apparent 'joy and relief' or at least ease of mind. That was the simple fact that when one has lost everything of real value, when one's good name is besmirched by disgusting and degrading accusations. When one has been reduced from the highest level to that of a helpless prisoner, when one's friends and loved ones have also suffered, then all quality of life has gone. With the years stretching ahead filled only with pain and regret, then life itself is the punishment, and death a blessed release.

This is probably the reason for Anne's cool acceptance of her fate. It would not be something Cromwell would be likely to understand. He could not emulate it when his own turn came in 1540, and he wrote desperate entreaties to Henry begging for 'mercy, mercy, mercy!'.[38]

The rest of that day was spent in prayer, or speaking quietly with her ladies. It has been said that her mind strayed towards the Princess Mary and that she openly regretted any earlier harshness towards Katherine's daughter.[39] If any such statement was made, it would be in the knowledge that it, like all her words, would be passed on and might even help to make things easier in the future for her own daughter, the Princess Elizabeth, the 2-year-old she was leaving behind.

In this way the hours passed, including those of her supposed execution day, 18 May. She would have slept very little, being anxious to spend as much time in prayer as possible, but it is reported that she did question Kingston about the delay, but was not until that evening told that she would actually die the following day.

On Friday, 19 May 1536 Kingston had again warned her to prepare for death, but this time it was in earnest. She had slept hardly at all for the past two nights, and must have been completely exhausted and with her nerves strung out. She was given a purse containing £20 to give as alms and had also given some thought to her dress. When she was ready she was wearing a long and full gown of grey damask, sometimes referred to as a 'bedgown' which was easy to remove. This was necessary because her outer garments were part of the fee of the headsman and would be taken from her. Under it she had a red petticoat. Was that also carefully thought out? Red is after all the Church's colour of martyrdom. Her long hair was tied up under a linen cap, with a normal headdress put on top. This, too, would have to be removed before death.

This simple recounting of the last hours could never have been so easy as it sounds. There was, we know, the taking of Communion for the last time, at which she cried out 'I am innocent, I am innocent!' both before and after taking the Sacrament. Such a declaration at that time was deliberate. It was intended to make perfectly clear to all hearing of it that she was free of guilt and was facing her maker cleanly, with no stain on her conscience. There would also have been the weeping ladies surrounding her, whose tears might have shaken her own resolve. The thoughts of her family left behind and particularly of her small daughter, whom she loved. She was anxious to remain calm and queenly, but there must still have been that basic human terror at the idea of the pain, and the knowledge that too much of it can thwart all good intentions. She was determined not to go to her death quaking with fear, but to appear composed, to give the lie to the foul accusations that had called her a whore.

She was taken outside, followed by the four young ladies who had stood with her at her trial and had kept her company since. It would seem that for this last public appearance the ladies set to spy on her, even her aunt Lady Boleyn and Lady Kingston, were not in attendance. As the young ladies who did escort her had known her for some time, in very different circumstances, they must by then have been in a pitiful state. Anne could not afford to allow herself to crumble, whatever the provocation, for she had to speak to those assembled to watch her die. A 'good death' was very important, and could confirm or deny one's claim to gentility and control. She would not be taken to die on Tower Green, but further inside, to what was then known as East Smithfield Green, a wide space at the north of the White Tower, though not far from St Peter ad Vincula.[40]

The scaffold was about 3–4ft high and draped with black, and already surrounded by a substantial number of people who had been invited and waited for her to appear. It is impossible to imagine the feelings of any condemned person at such a moment, but it is recorded that Anne remained calm.

Thomas Audley was there, the Duke of Suffolk, and the King's son, the Duke of Richmond (17 years old and also to die before long from that curse of teenaged Tudor boys, consumption). There were several other lords in attendance along with the Lord Mayor of London who had spoken well of her after her trial, with the Aldermen of the City, the Sheriffs and some of the leaders of the craft guilds.

Cromwell was also there, with his son, Gregory, now firmly allied to the Seymours. But the reactions of the common people were still causing concern, and they were not admitted. John Strype would later write of the Queen that it had been reported that she 'never looked more beautiful' and that she approached the scaffold 'with an untroubled countenance', which was confirmed by the Portuguese Ambassadors who were present.[41]

Once the Queen had been helped up the steps, she turned to face the watching officials, and spoke briefly, but clearly.

Good Christian people, I have come here to die, for according to the law I am judged to die, therefore I will speak nothing against it. I accuse no man, nor speak of that whereof I am accused and condemned, but pray God to save the King and send him long life to reign over you, for a gentler and more merciful prince was there never, and to me he ever was a good and gentle sovereign lord.

If that seemed to be an ironic statement, it must be remembered that it was the normal formula for such occasions, and that Anne was leaving behind her a small child, who would require the King's goodwill. She continued, 'If any person will meddle with my cause, I require them to judge the best. Thus I take my leave of the world, and of you all, and I heartily desire you all to pray for me.'[42]

Once her words were spoken, her headdress was removed. It is not known for sure whether the outer gown was taken from her at this point, or later, when she was dead. However, it seems logical that it should be removed beforehand, otherwise it would have been ruined by the bloodstains, and would be worthless. There is also a long standing tradition that it was at this point that the Queen gave to Margaret Wyatt, her old friend, a small prayer book which she had carried with her. There was no chaplain to say a prayer with her, or for her. There was also no block on which to rest her head, as victims about to be dispatched with the sword were required to remain kneeling upright to facilitate the stroke.

It is known that at this point she became very concerned about whether or not her clothes were decently covering her feet. She was anxious that her legs would not become exposed when her body fell and nervously looked behind her several times. Foreign observers seemed amazed that she was in no way restrained, as if they had expected her to be dragged to the scaffold struggling and screaming. There would certainly be nothing of that sort.

She prayed aloud, saying 'Jesu, receive my soul' and 'Oh, Lord God have pity on my soul!'. These were repeated several times, then the headsman stepped forward swinging the great sword, and her head was removed with one clean blow. It was reported that her lips continued to move for some little time afterwards, as if she continued to pray.

The general opinion was that the headsman had done his work well, and that it was all over 'before once could say a Paternoster!'.[43]

Whether or not Anne was dead as soon as her head hit the boards is another matter. Many experiments in France in the nineteenth century, carried out on criminals condemned to death, and designed to test whether or not the method was actually humane, concluded that the death was not instantaneous. In fact, unless knocked unconscious by the blow, some victims could not only move eyes and lips for some short time after decapitation, but could also apparently respond to speech and instructions. As Anne appeared to have been praying when her head fell, perhaps she was still aware of her surroundings. It would certainly seem so. The best one can hope for is that unconsciousness and freedom from pain came quickly.

Anne's ladies were obliged to wrap her body and head, separately, into white cloths, as was reported by the Portuguese witnesses. It must have been a very distressing as well as messy business. It was also disgraceful that the official witnesses then all calmly walked away, leaving the Queen's gently born ladies to handle her mutilated body without help.

It is said that she was laid into an elm chest, which had been intended for the carrying of bow staves, so not only had the Queen of England no chaplain with her to give her a final blessing, but she also had no coffin provided. Whether the box was already in place before Anne died or whether time was wasted on that hot day, with the body lying on the scaffold gathering flies while a receptacle was searched for, it is again not known.[44]

Once taken into the Chapel of St Peter ad Vincula (were the ladies expected to carry it themselves, dripping blood as it surely would be?), Anne's body was then buried in the chancel, not far from where her brother George had been laid two days previously.

Kingston, who had had no time to prepare a coffin or a decent burial for the Queen, still found time to write letters and told Cromwell, 'The Queen died boldly, God take her to his mercy.'[45]

John Husee told Lord Lisle that, 'Anne, the late Queen, suffered with sword this day upon a new scaffold, and died boldly.' He went on to say, 'The most part of the Queen's servants be set at liberty to seek service at their pleasure.'[46]

Anne's chaplain, Dr Matthew Parker, wrote on 19 May, 'There is no doubt that her soul is now in blessed facility with God!'

Even Cromwell unbent enough to 'greatly praise the intelligence, wit and courage of the Concubine and her brother', according to Chapuys.

Lancelot de Carles, also writing on 19 May about the Queen's death, said that 'her ladies were as sheep without a shepherd' but unlikely to be so for long, 'for already the King has taken a fancy to a choice lady. Other great things are also predicted, which the people are assured. If I see them take place, I will let you know, for never was there such news. People say that this is the year or marvels!'[47]

For many of the witnesses and the common people waiting outside the Tower for news, it must indeed have seemed to be an exciting time, with more to come as the King eagerly pushed forward into his new marriage with Jane Seymour. But there must have been many people, less easily excitable, who pondered on the happenings of early May 1536.

There must also have been, even in Henry's England, decent people who were shocked and dismayed at what had happened to the Queen, people who had heard not only of that farce of a trial, but also of the bravery and determination of the victims. Already Henry had raised comments and questions due to his conduct while Anne was in the Tower, condemned and alone. English people have always been concerned about fair play, about the underdog, about honesty and decency. These were all too obviously lacking, and it is not unreasonable to suppose that not everyone, even then, was either pleased at her death, or fully convinced by the evil tales told about her.

The Boleyns were broken and destroyed. They would not rise to position at court again until Elizabeth grew up and would favour the relatives of her mother's family. For Anne, fortunately, the long struggle was finally over.

Epilogue

It is almost impossible to know what words to use to describe what went on during the first half of May 1536. 'Miscarriage of justice' simply does not serve, as there was plainly no justice at all. The words of Sir Ralph Warren, the Lord Mayor of London, at that time, seem to satisfy the problem best, 'I can see no evidence against her, except that they wanted an occasion to be rid of her!'

The fixed resolve of the jury appointed to try the case, the antagonism of its members towards all the accused, the King's known wishes, which dare not be disobeyed, were all too blatant. That many – indeed most – of the jurors were in a position to benefit personally in some way from the death of one or other of the accused persons was simply disgraceful. The wild allegations, which were calmly refuted by most of the victims, and particularly by Queen Anne, regarding certain actions supposed to have taken place on certain days, were ridiculous. They were easily denied, simply by showing that she the Queen, and the court itself, was somewhere else at the time. The case shows extremely shoddy and poor work on the part of the accusers, yet these inaccuracies were still admissible as part of their evidence.

Yet in her own spirited and sensible defence Anne was totally ignored and the unsupported allegations preferred, including the 'hearsay' evidence of a woman already two years in her grave. All of this injustice causes feelings of anger and frustration in the extreme. In the present time, such a case would simply be inadmissible in court and immediately thrown out.

But that is also the point – it did not take place in the present time. It is the gravest possible mistake for any writer, or indeed reader, to attempt to judge any past time by the standards of their own. Anne knew her own time. She knew perfectly well that the King's will, however ludicrous, unfair or incompatible with honour, was paramount. Naturally, she wanted to live, naturally she feared to die, particularly by burning, which must be one of the most horrific ways for man to torture and destroy his fellow man. Even beheading was often a botched and agonising business.[1]

Anne knew that in the end she had failed, and that the price for such failure was death. She was aware of that, however vigorously and courageously she may have defended her life. In her case, unfortunately, her death also meant the destruction of her faction, involving the deaths of other innocent people and the tearing apart of their families too. But court life in the sixteenth century was always unstable, and it is no accident that the ultimate price of losing one's head would eventually become the mark, for the families down the ages, of one's ancient lineage and high status.

Therefore, it is also a mistake to give too much credence to the accusations made against Anne at her trial, or the trial of the other people involved. Ludicrous and insulting as the charges were, in one sense they did not matter at all. They were simply the means to an end, and most people living at that time would recognise that fact, hence the silent, respectful sympathy shown towards the gentlemen, both during and after their deaths on Tower Hill.

It is in later ages that this way of life becomes misunderstood. It is then that slandered reputations become fixed, by a misunderstanding of the status quo and an attempt to impose one's own criteria onto the enactments of others. This can be seen in the writings of the Victorians who often put quite a different slant on the way things were originally understood. Certainly matters of a sexual nature were then treated with more disgust and criticism than they were before, or since.

This is certainly not intended as any kind of attempt to excuse the behaviour of Henry VIII or those who grew rich and powerful in supporting him in his excesses. There is no doubt at all that the man was psychopathic, and that tyranny was endemic in his England. It would have been almost impossible at court to see others fall to ignominy and death and still to believe 'It can't happen to me!'. It did, in fact, happen all too easily to almost all of the people who had the misfortune to be in close contact with him. It happened to his wives, and Anne was not, of course, the last of those poor women to suffer death at his hands, or to fear that death might be close. It happened to his ministers, including Cromwell, who was not able to gather the same courage as so many of his victims, when his own turn came. It must have been a particularly delicate and fraught way of life, having to walk the tightrope of having much close contact with that most fickle and variable King, whose temper was so uncertain, particularly as he aged, and yet whose lightest word was law.

Even immediately after the death of Queen Anne Boleyn there were a few, even such as Chapuys, that surprising late supporter, who were able to state categorically their conviction that justice was absent at her trial. That did not, of course, mean that they did not see the need for such an outcome. For those people who delighted in the Queen's fall, in order that their own turn in the sunshine might come, they did well to remember that also on the scaffold their own turn might all too easily come.

Shortly after Jane Seymour's marriage to Henry he made it plain that he was not entirely happy. Had he by then realised that he had been duped, that the lady was not with child, and that he was, due to the deaths of his two previous queens in just over three months, not in a position to do anything about it? When the young maids-of-honour arrived at court to serve the new wife, he noticed that many of them were pretty. Glumly remarking on the contrast between these fresh young virgins and his own Queen, never a beauty even at her best, he said that he 'wished he had not ventured!'. It must also be remembered that Henry was not the sort of man who could ever admit himself in the wrong. Even if he took out his anger in private, on whatever unfortunate had raised his ire, he would not wish to appear to have made a wrong decision publicly. It would always have to be someone else's fault. Had Jane not become pregnant early in the following year, she would certainly have been discarded, and might even have found herself following in the footsteps of her predecessor.

Even during the early days, when romantic novelists like to imagine that all was sweetness and light, there was friction. When the Venetian Ambassadors arranged an audience with the new Queen, in order to briefly exchange compliments on her marriage, Henry did not feel that Jane was capable of dealing with the customary meeting, in which she would have to speak with the eminent gentlemen. Therefore, he made sure he was present, and spoke for her instead. The Venetians, proud of their Republic, 'La Serenissima', and always slightly contemptuous of kings, were astonished that the Queen was not able to manage so short and formal a meeting. Henry's interference gave a far worse impression than if he had left her to struggle on with it alone.[2]

The final honour of being interred with Henry at Windsor was not offered to Jane Seymour because of any love for her, it was given as recognition of her role as the mother of his son. Jane easily made good all her personal deficiencies by dying shortly after giving birth to the future Edward VI.[3] Even when she was on her deathbed, Henry was impatient to get away, having planned a hunting party at Esher. Despite the new mother's grave condition, he said clearly that he 'had no mind to tarry' and did not wish to wait to see whether or not she pulled through.[4] Hardly a declaration of affection, but he was probably incapable of anything better.

It was far easier to revere the woman when she was dead, than to live with any real woman in life, with normal human failings, which would irritate. Very shortly after her burial he was trying to arrange for a fourth bride, and was only thwarted in the attempts by the reluctance of France and Spain to offer him anybody suitable.

Cristina of Milan refused him boldly, saying that if she had a spare head she might venture, otherwise she would not. But she would never have dared to so insult the King if her masters in Spain had not allowed it. When Henry suggested to the French that they might send a selection of well-born ladies to Calais, where he might visit them and make his choice, the French Ambassador was openly sarcastic. He asked nastily whether Henry would prefer to try them all, one by one, before making his choice. When Henry demurred he was told firmly that 'it was not the way in which ladies were treated in France!'.[5]

A sudden apparent friendship between France and Spain panicked Cromwell into believing that England was due to be isolated. He then panicked Henry into making an alliance with the German princes, and a marriage with Anne of Cleves. The whole sorry episode betrays Cromwell's lack of skill. Wolsey would have remained calm, and would have ensured that Henry also remained calm, knowing that France and Spain would never be in each other's pockets for long. Sure enough, Henry was later offered other brides, but by then it was too late, he was committed. The poor Princess Anne, whose marriage was obsolete before she even arrived in England, then would have needed the beauty of Venus and the diplomatic skills of a veteran ambassador to have pleased the disappointed King.

Two further wives were to complete Henry's tally of queens. One of them was to be beheaded, young Catherine Howard, a cousin of Anne Boleyn. The other, Katherine Parr, was at one point to believe that she would not be long before meeting the headsman herself. It must have been the most exquisite relief when Henry died and she realised that she had managed to outlive him.[6]

After his death there was a period during which the country suffered several upheavals. His beloved son, Edward VI, did not reign for long, dying in 1553, and being replaced by another cousin, not directly in the line of succession, who had been slotted into place in an effort to prevent the Princess Mary from taking up her rightful inheritance. Lady Jane Grey, the nine-days' Queen, was another to face the headsman, but the Princess Mary, by then Queen Mary I was not able to build on her initial popularity.[7] Her ill-fated marriage to Philip of Spain lost her support and she died unhappily in 1558.[8]

She made way for Princess Elizabeth, Anne's daughter. Elizabeth was slowly to lift England from the bankruptcy of funds and pride into which it had fallen, restore its faith in itself and make it a force to be reckoned with in Europe, eventually even inflicting a humiliating defeat on Spain itself. Elizabeth was able to use the harsh and bitter lessons she had learned during her formative years to establish not only a country once again proud of itself but of good standing in the world. She forged a relationship with her people, which the rulers who followed her, who were not her equals, would have given anything for. She reigned for forty-five years and is still regarded as the pride and symbol of England.[9]

For Anne, too, there would be rehabilitation and recognition as the centuries changed and opinions changed with them. Once people were no longer afraid to challenge the pre-conceived misconceptions of tradition, it became clear that Anne's innocence shone through the shroud of infamy deliberately wound around her. Tudor propaganda became vilified, not fixed in stone, and Anne, as well as others, would benefit from the new appraisal. Her life could then be judged on a different level than merely the scandal of promiscuity into which Henry had dragged her down.

On that level she can be viewed as a normal woman, who though quick-tempered and sometimes rash, was also intelligent, kind and loyal to those she cared for. Though she sinned, as we all do, she certainly paid in full for any transgressions, and had been brutally sacrificed on the altar of Henry's all-encompassing desire for a male heir. It took Anne's daughter, Elizabeth, to prove that Henry's desperate quest, in the pursuit of which so many people had suffered, had not been necessary after all.

It seems only fitting, therefore, that 480 years after Anne Boleyn's death, she is still the most recognisable and interesting of Henry VIII's queens, with an admiring following who look back on her life from a world she cannot have imagined.

It is enough.

Notes

Chapter 1
1. Charles Fergusen, *Naked to Mine Enemies (The Life of Cardinal Wolsey)* (1958), quotes March of 1471 for Wolsey's birth. A.F. Pollard, *Wolsey* (1929), quotes 1472/3 for Wolsey's birth, although others refute this.
2. Fergusen, *Naked to Mine Enemies*, regarding the family's move from Coombe.
3. Fergusen, *Naked to Mine Enemies*, quotes Robert Wolsey's criminal activities and describes him as 'the worst offender before the leet'.
4. S.H. Burke, *Historical Portraits of the Tudor Dynasty, Vol. 1* (1893).
5. For fuller details of the allegation that King Edward IV's marriage to Elizabeth Woodville was bigamous due to his earlier pre-contract or marriage to Lady Eleanor Butler, see Michael K. Jones, *Bosworth 1485 – Psychology of a Battle* (2002).
6. S.C. Bindoff, *Tudor England* (1950).
7. Paul M. Kendall, *Richard III* (1955).
8. On the subject of the wealth of King Henry VII, he left his successor an absolutely unprecedented amount in hard cash, estimated at £1,800,000. Unfortunately, Henry VIII, unlike his father, preferred spending to saving, and he ran through this immense fortune in around twenty years.
9. Jasper Ridley, *Statesman and Saint. Cardinal Wolsey and Sir Thomas More and the Politics of Henry VIII* (1982), quotes Robert Wolsey's conditional bequest to his son.
10. Ridley, *Statesman and Saint*.
11. Peter Gwyn, *The King's Cardinal – The Rise and Fall of Thomas Wolsey* (1990).
12. Wolsey's daughter Dorothy was placed in the wealthy nunnery of Shaftesbury. His son, known as Thomas Winter, became 'the fortunate recipient of much wealth and church patronage', quoted by Gwyn, *The King's Cardinal*.
13. Ridley, *Statesman and Saint*, gives full details of Wolsey's career path and the competition between lay clergy.
14. Gwyn, *The King's Cardinal*, regarding Wolsey's attainments at Magdalen.
15. Gwyn, *The King's Cardinal*.
16. Fergusen, *Naked to Mine Enemies*, regarding Wolsey's continued use of the Limington revenues.
17. Fergusen, *Naked to Mine Enemies*.
18. David Starkey, *Henry, Virtuous Prince* (2008), regarding Henry VII's affection for, and training of, Prince Arthur, in preference to his siblings.
19. Garrett Mattingly, *Catherine of Aragon* (1944), regarding the possibility that Henry VII did not consider Princess Juana to be mad, but believed that Ferdinand of Aragon was using her behaviour as an excuse to confine her, so that he could maintain control over her extensive lands until her son came of age.
20. Fergusen, *Naked to Mine Enemies*.
21. Fergusen, *Naked to Mine Enemies*, regarding the extensive bequests made while Henry VII was dying. However, these bequests were not paid for by Henry's own funds, but were financed by the dissolution of several smaller religious foundations.

Chapter 2
1. Eric Ives, *Anne Boleyn* (1986), for his reasons for settling on the year 1501 as the date of Anne's birth.

2. Marie Louise Bruce, *Anne Boleyn* (1972).
3. Ives, *Anne Boleyn*, regarding Mary and Anne's court service and the minimum age for such service to begin.
4. This is where the later Boleyn claim to the Irish titles and lands came from. Margaret Butler had married a Sir Thomas Boleyn while her sister Anne married James St Leger. Margaret and Anne Butler were the daughters of Thomas Butler, Earl of Ormonde and his wife Anne Hankford. She was the daughter of Sir Richard Hankford and his wife Anne Montagu, daughter of the Earl of Salisbury. Margaret Boleyn was, incidentally, still alive until 1540. She was Queen Anne Boleyn's great-aunt.
5. Ives, *Anne Boleyn*, for full details of the Boleyn connections with members of the nobility, by both blood and marriage.
6. David Loades, *The Boleyns – Rise and Fall of a Tudor Family* (2012).
7. Ives, *Anne Boleyn*, regarding the court appointments of Piers Butler.
8. Starkey, *Henry, Virtuous Prince*.
9. Mattingly, *Catherine of Aragon*.
10. Mattingly, *Catherine of Aragon*, where he describes the ramifications of the death of Queen Isabella of Castile, with their effects on Katherine and Ferdinand of Aragon.
11. Mattingly, *Catherine of Aragon*, for description of the wedding of Katherine and Henry VIII in 1509 at the Church of the Franciscan Observant Friars at Greenwich.
12. Ives, *Anne Boleyn*, for details of Thomas Boleyn's early court appointments.
13. Margaret (daughter of the Emperor Maximilian I) had been married to the Infante Juan, only surviving son and heir to Isabella and Ferdinand of Spain. She married three times in all, but had no children. As widowed Duchess of Savoy she became Regent of the Netherlands on behalf of her paternal nephew Charles V. She was known as a very serious and also a very clever stateswoman.
14. Ives, *Anne Boleyn*, regarding the probable remodelling of the Palace of White Hall as a copy of the luxurious Palace of Mechelin where Anne stayed with the Archduchess Margaret. Also Sarah Morris and Natalie Grueninger, *In the Footsteps of Anne Boleyn* (2013), for details of Anne's whereabouts and description of the Palace of Mechelin, which still survives as the town's Courts of Justice.
15. Ives, *Anne Boleyn*, quoting Hugh Paget in BIHR 54 (1981) regarding the letter from Margaret of Austria to Thomas Boleyn about his daughter Anne.
16. David Starkey, *Six Wives –The Queens of Henry VIII* (2003), regarding the fiasco at San Sebastian and Ferdinand of Aragon's non-appearance.
17. Starkey, *Henry, Virtuous Prince*, for full details of the family of Henry VII and Elizabeth of York, with the dates of birth and death of their children.
18. Norah Lofts, *Queens of Britain* (1977). Two well-known cases of this stand out. One is that of Marie Antoinette, sent to France by its erstwhile enemy, Austria, at the age of 14. The other is that of Princess Vicky, daughter of Queen Victoria and Prince Albert. She was Crown Princess of Prussia for many years during which time she suffered from a good deal of animosity and anti-English prejudice.
19. Mattingly, *Catherine of Aragon*, for details of Henry VIII's outburst to the Venetian Ambassador Giustiniani, regarding the unreliability of all his allies.
20. Maria Perry, *Sisters to the King* (1998). Brandon had already flirted with the idea of marrying the widowed Archduchess Margaret, Regent of the Netherlands. But he had a previously tangled history with one Anne Browne. He had jilted this lady in order to marry her aunt, Dame Margaret Mortimer, but he then had the marriage annulled on the grounds of consanguinity. He then went back to Anne Browne, marrying her in 1508. He had two daughters by her and she died in 1510. He then acquired the wardship of Lady Elizabeth Grey, who was the Viscountess Lisle in her own right. He betrothed himself to her so that he could use her titles, lands and wealth. She was then 10 years old! He then encouraged

the Princess Mary Tudor in her infatuation with him, and finally married her in secret, to become Henry VIII's brother-in-law.
21. Perry, *Sisters to the King*. Jane Poppincourt had been having an affair with the Duke de Longueville, who was already married. When Louis XII became aware of it he refused absolutely (indeed vehemently) to allow her to attend on the Princess Mary, who was about to become Queen of France.
22. Morris and Grueninger, *In the Footsteps of Anne Boleyn*, regarding the lists of attendant ladies for Princess Mary at her marriage in France, and the fact that Anne Boleyn's name was not on the list at the time of the household's arrival in France. That she was resident with the Archduchess Margaret for almost a year and then transferred to the service of Princess Mary, as the start of several years at the French Court, is generally well recorded.

Chapter 3

1. Fergusen, *Naked to Mine Enemies*, regarding Wolsey's apparent acceptance of the match between Henry and Katherine of Aragon. However, it is doubtful whether, in those early days, he would have had any real authority to oppose it.
2. Fergusen, *Naked to Mine Enemies*, regarding the huge cash inheritance, later estimated at around £1,800,000 in coined money, which Henry VIII had from his late father. It would equate to billions in modern currency.
3. E.G. O'Donaghue, *Bridewell Hospital and Palace* (1923), for details of the property given to Wolsey in 1510.
4. Fergusen, *Naked to Mine Enemies*, for details of the family of Wolsey's mistress, Joan Larke.
5. Pollard, *Wolsey*.
6. Pollard, *Wolsey*, regarding Wolsey's letter to Richard Foxe.
7. George Cavendish, *Thomas Wolsey, Late Cardinal, His Life and Death*, ed. Roger Lockyer, Folio Society (1962).
8. Ernest Law, *England's First Great War Minister* (1916), regarding Wolsey's infinitely detailed arrangements.
9. Pollard, *Wolsey*. Pollard explains very clearly that it was not so much a matter of the Pope deciding that Wolsey was worthy of a hat, as of how much value it might eventually be to Rome if he were to be elevated to it.
10. Fergusen, *Naked to Mine Enemies*, regarding the Hunne case and its reverberations.
11. Fergusen, *Naked to Mine Enemies*, referring to the pressure put on the Pope both by Henry and Wolsey in order to reach a preferred settlement.
12. Cavendish, *Thomas Wolsey*.
13. Perry, *Sisters to the King*, for full details of Mary's wedding preparations and possessions.
14. Calendar State Papers, Venetian, Vol. III, for details of Mary's jewels and their estimated value.
15. Perry, *Sisters to the King*, regarding the wardrobe lists for Mary's wedding to Louis XII.
16. Perry, *Sisters to the King*, quoting Meyer's 'The Great Regent' for the remark made by Francis I of France at Fleuranges.
17. Ives, *Anne Boleyn*, regarding the omission of Anne's name from the list of female attendants for the Princess Mary's arrival in France.
18. W. Richardson, *Mary Tudor, the White Queen* (1970), regarding Mary's widowhood.
19. *Letters and Papers, Henry VIII*, ed. J.S. Brewer and J. Gairdner, Vol. II, regarding Suffolk's letter to the King.
20. S.J. Gunn, *Charles Brandon, Duke of Suffolk, 1484–1545* (1988), for details of the settlement (both the original and the revised versions) made between the newly wedded Suffolks and Henry VIII.
21. *Letters and Papers, Henry VIII*, Vol. II, for details of Sir William Sidney's document, after the re-marriage of the Suffolks.

22. Perry, *Sisters to the King*, regarding subsequent French attitudes towards Mary Tudor, after the removal of jewels belonging to the Crown. Francis I was known to have made several highly uncomplimentary remarks about Mary, and from then on considered her to be an evil woman, and little better than a thief.
23. Mattingly, *Catherine of Aragon*, regarding Bernadino De Mesa, Bishop of Elne in Roussillon, Dominican Friar and Ferdinand of Aragon's Ambassador.
24. Starkey, *Six Wives*, for Henry's use of certain of his friends, notably Carewe and Compton, as pimps and panders for their services of providing him with women (usually the wives of other courtiers) at their houses in London.

Chapter 4

1. King William of Orange was later to make it clear that he fully intended to demolish all the Tudor buildings there, and replace them with his own more 'modern' designs. As there are several buildings of that design remaining in England, and so heartbreakingly few of the real Tudor ones, that would have been an act of the greatest vandalism. It is perhaps a good thing (architecturally if not politically) that he met his nemesis with the 'little gentleman in black velvet' before he could complete his work of destruction. It might be almost said that Hampton Court Palace got its own back on him. It was there, on a hunting day, that his horse put its hoof into the molehill and this produced the fatal accident.
2. Dr Peter Gaunt, *Hampton Court Palace* (1988).
3. Fergusen, *Naked to Mine Enemies*.
4. Fergusen, *Naked to Mine Enemies*. George Legh was eventually to have a dispute over property with Sir John Stanley, one of the natural sons of the Bishop of Ely. During this dispute, Wolsey championed the cause of George, showing his continuing concern for Joan Larke and her family, and his staunch friendship over many years. She was certainly not casually cast aside.
5. Pollard, *Wolsey*, referring to Wolsey's obvious reluctance at being tracked down on business matters while 'at home' at Hampton Court, when he had retired there for some rest and recreation. It shows the dual purpose of the property in Wolsey's mind.
6. Fergusen, *Naked to Mine Enemies*, regarding the successes of Francis I in Italy in 1515.
7. J.S. Brewer. *The Reign of Henry VIII from the Accession to the Death of Wolsey*, Vol. II (1884).
8. Fergusen, *Naked to Mine Enemies*, regarding the Convocation to decide the rights of the clergy.
9. Fergusen, *Naked to Mine Enemies*, regarding the network of the law courts.
10. Cavendish, *Thomas Wolsey*.
11. Gwyn, *The King's Cardinal*, regarding the lords called to appear before the Court of Star Chamber, in which Wolsey prided himself in being egalitarian. However, the resentful courtiers merely believed he enjoyed humiliating them.
12. J.A. Guy, *The Cardinal's Court* (1977).
13. Starkey, *Six Wives*, regarding the May Day Riots.
14. Perry, *Sisters to the King*, regarding the necessity for Queen Katherine of Aragon and Cardinal Wolsey to make a show of pleading before Henry VIII on behalf of the rioters who were sentenced to death.
15. Edward Hall, *The Union of the Two Noble and Illustrious Families of York and Lancaster*, ed. H. Ellis (1809).
16. Mattingly, *Catherine of Aragon*, regarding Katherine's appearance on the day she pleaded for the lives of the rioters, particularly her undressed hair, which represented her as a supplicant.
17. Robert Hutchinson, *Young Henry, the Rise of Henry VIII* (2012), regarding the friends of Henry VIII who were dismissed from court for insolence.
18. Mattingly, *Catherine of Aragon*, regarding Pope Leo X's call to defend Europe against the inroads of the Turks, and his attempts to create a lasting peace between the European kings.

19. Mattingly, *Catherine of Aragon*, regarding the election to the title of Holy Roman Emperor after the death of Maximilian I.
20. Mattingly, *Catherine of Aragon*, regarding the meeting with Charles V at Canterbury.
21. Joycelyne Gledhill Russell, *The Field of the Cloth of Gold* (1969), regarding the expenses incurred in the meeting in France. This is full of wonderful details of the arrangements, expenses, extravagances and eventual results of the occasion.
22. Mattingly, *Catherine of Aragon*, regarding the behaviour of Henry VIII towards Francis I while his guest in France.
23. Russell, *The Field of the Cloth of Gold*, regarding Anne Boleyn's presumed attendance at the event in France, while she was still in the service of Queen Claude of France.
24. Russell, *The Field of the Cloth of Gold*, regarding the situation of Queen Claude of France and the dominance of the court by her mother-in-law and sister-in-law.

Chapter 5
1. Ridley, *Statesman and Saint*, for details of the ceremonial surrounding the first of the burnings of Luther's books, at St Paul's Cross, on 12 May 1521.
2. J. Grove, *The History of the Life and Times of Cardinal Wolsey* (1746), quoted by Fergusen in *Naked to Mine Enemies*.
3. Fergusen, *Naked to Mine Enemies*, for the Duke of Buckingham's character.
4. *Letters and Papers, Henry VIII*, Vol. IV, for the report that Buckingham 'shed the water in his shoes' when Wolsey dipped his hands into the basin. Wolsey was furious and declared that he would 'sit upon the skirts' of the Duke. When Buckingham next appeared before Wolsey he was wearing a short coat, which he said would 'disappoint the malice' of Wolsey.
5. Brewer, *The Reign of Henry VIII*, Vol. II.
6. Julia Fox, *Jane Boleyn, the Infamous Lady Rochford* (2007), in which she gives details of the early life at court of George Boleyn and the general rise to prominence of the family by the early 1520s.
7. Mattingly, *Catherine of Aragon*, regarding the Queen pleading for the life of Buckingham with whom she had been on friendly terms.
8. *Letters and Papers, Henry VIII*, Vol. IV, referring to the incidents of (supposedly) occult activities in which the Cardinal took part, by which it was hoped to keep the King's favour.
9. Fergusen, *Naked to Mine Enemies*, quoting Richardson, in which Wolsey attempted to 'introduce the same regularity in chamber audit as in the other departments of finance'.
10. Fergusen, *Naked to Mine Enemies*, quoting Karl Brandl, *The Emperor Charles V and the Growth of Destiny of a Man and a World Empire* (1939).
11. Fox, *Jane Boleyn*, regarding the Boleyn benefits from the confiscated estates of the Duke of Buckingham.
12. Pollard, *Wolsey*, often considered the definitive biography of Cardinal Wolsey. It is, however, unfortunate for later readers that Pollard seems to have created a character for the Cardinal quite different from the real and well-documented one. There are many examples extant of his making the facts fit a theory, rather than letting them speak for themselves.
13. D.S. Chambers, 'Cardinal Wolsey and the Papal Tiara', BIHR XXVIII (1965). This groundbreaking article by Chambers quite refutes the usual picture of Wolsey as a man dedicated to becoming Pope. It shows clearly through available evidence that the Cardinal never made the slightest attempt to form a support group, or to canvass voters, as would have been necessary in order to permit a foreign Cardinal to aspire to becoming Pope. In the case of Adrian VI it was undoubtedly the influence of the Emperor Charles V that enabled an absent and little-known Cardinal to receive an almost unanimous number of votes resulting in his election.
14. Michael Mallett, *The Borgias, The Rise and Fall of a Renaissance Dynasty* (1969). This is excellent regarding the actual running of the Vatican and the true position of the power struggles between various Popes and the College of Cardinals.

15. Richard Pace's letter to Wolsey, 25 September 1514, in *Original Letters Illustrative of English History*, ed. H. Ellis (1846).
16. Thomas Hannibal to Wolsey of 8 and 12 September 1522 in which Hannibal states, 'I wrote divers times touching the title of St. Cecilia, which should be and is better to Your Grace than you think, but I had never an answer from Your Grace.', British Museum, Cotton Ms. Vit B. v. F°.
17. *Letters and Papers, Henry VIII*, Vol. III, fragment of a letter referred to by Brewer, *The Reign of Henry VIII*, Vol. II, regarding Wolsey becoming the Abbot of St Albans.
18. *Letters and Papers, Henry VIII*, Vol. III. This reference was used by Philip W. Sergeant in his biography of Anne Boleyn dated 1924, *The Life of Anne Boleyn*. Also in *Anne Boleyn … A Study* (1934) by the same author.
19. Grove, *The History of the Life and Times of Cardinal Wolsey*.
20. H.A.L. Fisher, *The History of England from the Accession of Henry VII to the death of Henry VIII* (1934), regarding the strong opposition to the 'property tax' proposed as a money-raising ploy in order to finance the French war.
21. Grove, *The History of the Life and Times of Cardinal Wolsey*, regarding the amount of money that Henry VIII demanded. One wonders whether, over the years, one or two extra noughts have crept into this estimate. It certainly seems to be a fantastical sum of money to expect to be raised in 1523.
22. Ives, *Anne Boleyn*. Also Ives, *The Life and Death of Anne Boleyn*. Professor Ives provides what must be considered the definitive biography of Anne Boleyn's life and is regarded as her most scholarly and reliable biographer.
23. Cavendish, *Thomas Wolsey*, quotes the details of Henry Percy's defence of Anne Boleyn when berated by Wolsey at York Place.
24. Ives, *Anne Boleyn*, for details of the ill-fated and most unfortunate marriage of Henry Percy, later Earl of Northumberland, with Mary Talbot, daughter of the Earl of Shrewsbury, after he was forced to give up Anne Boleyn. Ives quotes from J.M.W. Bean, *Estates of the Percy Family 1416–1537* (1958), which gives details of the depredations to the estates.
25. Guy, *The Cardinal's Court*, gives details of the way in which Wolsey could still strike fear into the minds of the courtiers and that they would have hastened to do his bidding. Despite his increasing worries, the time of his fall had not yet come.
26. Pollard, *Wolsey*, for the Second Papal Election, in which he erroneously claims that Cardinal Wolsey 'did not get a single vote'. That this is quite untrue is demonstrated by the letter quoted in the text. Despite Wolsey's deliberately low profile in Rome it is evident that he did still have some support and actually did receive several votes before the election of Clement VII (Giulio de' Medici) in 1523.
27. *Letters and Papers, Henry VIII*, Vol. III, letter from Hannibal to Wolsey, 16 October 1523, followed by another of 24 October 1523 from Clerk, Pace and Hannibal together recording the proceedings and the opposition of Cardinal Colonna due to Wolsey's absence from Rome.
28. *Letters and Papers, Henry VIII*, Vol. III, letter to Clerk, Pace and Hannibal from Wolsey, January 1524. This is quoted in D.S. Chambers' article 'Cardinal Wolsey and the Papal Tiara', BIHR XXVIII (1965) in which he states 'There were similar sentiments in a letter of 6th Dec. 1523, which had been sent to the king'.

Chapter 6

1. Fox, *Jane Boleyn*, for Jane Parker's family background.
2. Fox, *Jane Boleyn*, for details of the marriage settlement for George Boleyn and Jane Parker.
3. Mattingly, *Catherine of Aragon*, for the full titles and honours of Henry Fitzroy awarded to him by Henry VIII in 1525. Also for the effect the child's investiture had upon Queen Katherine of Aragon.
4. What is usually conveniently forgotten in the general speculation on the subject of whether or not Henry Carey, the future Lord Hunsdon, was Henry VIII's son is that Mary Boleyn

was already a married woman when she became the King's mistress. Sir Thomas Boleyn is often blamed for profiting from his daughter's moral laxity, and even for encouraging it. However, at that time she would have been the responsibility of her husband, William Carey, not her father. It certainly seemed that Carey had no difficulty in turning a blind eye to his wife's association with the King.

5. *Letters and Papers, Henry VIII*, Vol. IV, regarding the rumours circulating at the time that Charles V could not afford to continue with the war.
6. Edward Hall, *Hall's Chronicle* (1809) for details of the courageous defence before Wolsey.
7. *Letters and Papers, Henry VIII*, Vol. IV. The official reply of the Pope to Henry VIII's request for money with which to pursue his dreams of invading France.
8. Thomas Wyatt's verses are a study in themselves. Certainly three of his works are attributable to that period when he was a close friend of the Boleyns, Anne and George, and when he was apparently attracted to Anne. That there was ever anything more sordid in their relationship is highly unlikely, given the conventions of 'courtly love' of the time. The poignant 'Whoso list to hunt ...' (Wyatt Poems VII) shows him backing off from a pursuit of her, once Henry VIII had shown his preference. It also, in its final lines, emphasises the point that Henry's rather obvious attentions were by then preventing Anne from forming any other, more normal, relationship. The full poem as follows:

> Whoso list to hunt, I know where is a hind,
> but as for me, alas, I may no more;
> the vain travail hath wearied me so sore,
> I am of them that farthest cometh behind.
> Yet may I by no means my wearied mind
> Draw from the deer, but as she fleeth afore
> Fainting I follow. I leave off therefore
> Sithins in a net I seek to hold the wind.
> Who list to hunt, I put him out of doubt,
> As well as I, may spend his time in vain,
> And graven in diamonds in letters plain,
> There is written her fair neck round about:
> 'Noli me tangere, for Caesar's I am,
> and wild for to hold, though I seem tame.'

9. Sergeant, *The Life of Anne Boleyn*. Letter to Anne Boleyn from Henry VIII. Most of these letters are undated, but this has confidently been placed early in the series of letters extant: 'but if it pleases you, to do the office of a true loyal mistress and friend, and to give yourself body and heart to me ... I do promise you that not only the name shall be yours, but also I will take you for my sole mistress, casting all others but you outside my thoughts, and will serve you alone.'
10. Joanna Denny, *Anne Boleyn* (2005), quoting Robert Johnson (*Full Well She Sang. Women's Music from the Middle Ages and Renaissance*, Toronto Consort (1993)):

> Defiled is my name full sore,
> through cruel spite and false report,
> that I may say for evermore,
> farewell, my joy, adieu comfort.
> For wrongfully ye judge of me,
> Unto my fame a mortal wound,
> Say what ye list, it will not be,
> Ye seek for that can not be found.

264   Tudor Victims

11. Ives, *Anne Boleyn*, for details of the reply sent by Henry VIII to Anne Boleyn's gift of a jewel showing a damsel adrift in a ship on stormy seas. The letter from Henry VIII is reproduced here in full:

> For so beautiful a gift, and so exceeding (taking it in all) I thank you right cordially. Not alone for the fair diamond and the ship in which the solitary damsel is tossed about, but chiefly for the good intent and too-humble submission vouchsafed in this by your kindness; considering well that by occasion to merit it would not a little perplex me, if I were not aided therein by your great benevolence and goodwill, for the which I have sought, do seek, and shall always seek by all services to me possible there to remain, in the which my hope hath set up his everlasting rest, saying aut ilic, aut nullibi [either here or nowhere].
>
> The proofs of your affection are such, the fine poesies of the letters so warmly couched, that they constrain me ever truly to honour, love and serve you, praying that you will continue in this same firm and constant purpose, ensuring you, for my part, that I will the rather go beyond than make reciproque [equivalent response], if loyalty or heart, the desire to do you pleasure, even with my whole heart root, may serve to advance it.

12. David Mathew, *The Courtiers of Henry VIII* (1970), for details of the life and career of Thomas Howard, Third Duke of Norfolk, brother of Anne's mother Elizabeth Howard. See also Robert Hutchinson, *House of Treason. The Rise and Fall of a Tudor Dynasty* (2009), for fuller details of the Howard family in general.
13. Lacey Baldwin Smith, *A Tudor Tragedy – the Life and Times of Katherine Howard* (1962), regarding the household of the Dowager Duchess of Norfolk (stepmother of the Third Duke) in which the young Catherine Howard (Henry VIII's fifth wife) was raised.
14. Mathew, *The Courtiers of Henry VIII*. The Third Duke of Norfolk's first wife was Anne Plantagenet, one of the daughters of King Edward IV. She was sister to Elizabeth of York, who was the wife of King Henry VII. This royal lady had had the misfortune to see all her children predecease her, therefore the Duke of Norfolk's heir, the Earl of Surrey, was the offspring of the second marriage, to Lady Elizabeth Stafford. Lady Elizabeth was 15 years old when she married the widower Thomas Howard in 1513. At the time of her marriage to him she wished to marry Ralph Neville, later the Earl of Westmorland, who returned her affection. However, her father (the Duke of Buckingham) and her husband Thomas Howard arranged the match between them, and Elizabeth was forced to comply. It is, perhaps, no surprise that the bride was unhappy and the marriage ill-fated. The bridegroom was actually five years older than the bride's father at the time of the marriage. See also Hutchinson, *House of Treason*.
15. John Harthan, *Books of Hours* (1977).
16. Fergusen, *Naked to Mine Enemies*, for details of Henry's continuing personal extravagance, in both gambling and gifts to favourites, and Wolsey's actions in attempting to control, at intervals, the rising expenditure.
17. F.A. Mumby, *The Youth of Henry VIII. A Narrative in Comtemporary Letters* (1913), regarding the orders given by Cardinal Wolsey at the time of attempts to reorganise the King's household.
18. Fox, *Jane Boleyn*, regarding the Privy Chamber reorganisation in 1526.
19. *Letters and Papers, Henry VIII*, Vol. IV, No. 1939, which shows that George Boleyn was quickly given a new post close to the King, when he had been dismissed from his privy chamber appointment during Wolsey's purge. His entitlement to lodgings at court at the King's expense is from the same source.
20. Fox, *Jane Boleyn*, for details of George Boleyn's court appointments.

Chapter 7

1. *Letters and Papers, Henry VIII*, Vol. IV.
2. Henry would later regret appearing so lukewarm in his support of the Pope. If he had been more active in the Pope's defence he might have been able to demand a swifter and more favourable response over the matter of the divorce. As it was, the Pope's pleas to Henry VIII fell on deaf ears. Likewise, when Henry needed the Pope's assistance, Clement had already decided that his only safe bet was to keep on the good side of Charles V. He had little choice, but a more positive attitude from Henry initially might have swung the balance a little more in his favour.
3. Colonna was the Cardinal who had previously opposed his election as Pope and was probably bribed to change his vote.
4. Originally the tomb of the Emperor Hadrian.
5. The sacrifice of the Swiss Guards in attempting to defend Clement VII on 6 May 1527 is commemorated each year in Rome, when the new Swiss Guard recruits are sworn in.
6. *Letters and Papers, Henry VIII*, Vol. IV, regarding his concern about the Pope's danger having a bad effect on Henry's plans.
7. Fergusen, *Naked to Mine Enemies*, quoting Brewer, *The Reign of Henry VIII*, Vol. II.
8. *Letters and Papers, Henry VIII*, Vol. IV. Also Cavendish, *Thomas Wolsey*.
9. *Letters and Papers, Henry VIII*, Vol. IV, regarding the Spanish Ambassador's report to Charles V and Spain's belief that Wolsey was the instigator of the proposed proceedings.
10. Giles Tremlett, *Catherine of Aragon, Henry's Spanish Queen* (2010), regarding the meeting at York Place where Henry first made it officially clear that he wanted a divorce from Katherine.
11. Calendar State Papers, Spanish, Vol. III, letter from Mendoza to Charles V of 18 May 1527 about the Tribunal the previous day at which Henry pretended to allow himself to be 'tried' for the charge of living in sin with Katherine.
12. Geoffrey de C. Parmiter, *The King's Great Matter, A Study of Anglo-Papal Relations 1527–1534* (1967).
13. *Letters and Papers, Henry VIII*, Vol. IV.
14. Cavendish, *Thomas Wolsey*, for description of Wolsey's journey to France in July of 1527, and the magnificence of his suite.
15. Princess Renée was the daughter of Louis XII and Anne of Brittany, sister to Queen Claude the wife of Francis I who had died in 1524. Through their mother they were co-heiresses to Brittany. Francis was suspected of keeping her unmarried in order to ensure that the full inheritance devolved upon his heirs. However, she did marry, her husband being Ercole II de'Este, Duke of Ferrara and Modena. He was the grandson of Pope Alexander VI through his mother Lucrezia Borgia, Duchess of Ferrara. Princess Renée would have five children of her own and would die in 1574 at the age of 63 years. However, born in 1510 she was only 17 years old when Wolsey saw her and her portrait by Jean Clouet shows her close resemblance to her sister Queen Claude. Interestingly, in the 1560s, in a conversation with Sir Nicholas Throckmorton, the Duchess Renée remarked that she had known Queen Elizabeth's mother, Anne Boleyn, quite well from the time when they were at the French court together. She said that she remembered Anne with 'great affection'.
16. Cavendish, *Thomas Wolsey*. Cavendish called the French courtiers 'slaves' displaying his Francophobia, which was not an unusual trait at that time.
17. Starkey, *Six Wives*, quoting *Letters and Papers, Henry VIII*, Vol. IV. Weary of the seemingly endless delays, Henry's impatience had got the better of his common sense. Knight was to ask Clement not only for permission to marry 'a woman whose sister had been his mistress', therefore placing her within the prohibited degree of consanguinity, but also for a dispensation to free Henry from all impediments to an immediate remarriage. This despite the fact that the marriage to Katherine of Aragon had not been dissolved. It would effectively allow him two wives at the same time, a quite preposterous proposal.

266   Tudor Victims

18. Letter from Wolsey to Henry VIII on 13 September 1527, *Letters and Papers, Henry VIII*, Vol. IV.
19. Calendar State Papers, Venetian, Vol. IV, Giustiniani to the Pope, letter dated 18 September 1527.
20. Brewer, *The Reign of Henry VIII*, Vol. II, quoting Gyangos (Calendar State Papers, Spanish, Vol. III) regarding Anne's remark in reply to Wolsey's request to see the King.
21. Starkey, *Six Wives*, regarding the reactions of Henry VIII and others to the outbreak of the sweating sickness in June of 1528.
22. Sergeant, *Anne Boleyn*, for the letter of Henry VIII to Anne Boleyn written from Hunsdon at the end of June 1528.
23. *Letters and Papers, Henry VIII*, Vol. V. Anne was granted the wardship of her sister's son after the death of Sir William Carey in 1528. This gave her the right to control Henry Carey's fortune and even to decide his marriage when the time came. However, Henry's granting of the wardship to Anne was not harsh, but actually an act of consideration. The boy would need an official guardian after losing his father, and far better for this control to come from Anne, his natural aunt, than from some stranger who might despoil the boy's estates. She was far more likely to have concern for his future wealth and happiness than a stranger, merely eager to get their hands on his property.
24. Sergeant, *Anne Boleyn*, regarding the appointment of Dame Isobel Jordan as Abbess of Wilton. Heneage wrote to Wolsey on 11 July, after he had moved to Ampthill in Bedfordshire. He confirmed the news of the King's displeasure that Wolsey had put his own preferred candidate into the post, rather than waiting for Henry to decide on the matter. Henry obviously feared Anne's annoyance over the otherwise minor election, and subsequently dealt with the business in a heavy-handed way which pleased nobody until Dame Isobel's appointment became fact. In reality, Anne was highly unlikely to have ever met the opposing candidate Dame Eleanor Carey, and knew nothing of her. She would have merely been doing a favour for the family, as a person in a position of influence was expected to do.

Chapter 8
1. Fergusen, *Naked to Mine Enemies*, for Campeggio's abortive talks with Wolsey on his arrival in England.
2. *Letters and Papers, Henry VIII*, Vol. IV, regarding the visit of the two Cardinals to Katherine of Aragon and her replies to them in which she asserted her intention to remain queen.
3. Ives, *Anne Boleyn*, for details of Anne's motto and badges. These were in use at different times in her career and tended to change as her situation changed. This particular one was short-lived but serves to show her annoyance with criticism and restrictions. It was embroidered on the livery jackets of her retainers in December 1530.
4. Ives, *Anne Boleyn*. Bridewell Palace is suggested by Professor Ives as the new residence of Anne Boleyn at that time. Wolsey had recently cleared a suite there and it may well have been so that Anne could move into it while the court was readying itself for the legal proceedings at nearby Blackfriars.
5. Hall, *Hall's Chronicle*. As stated, Campeggio was a widower when he took Holy Orders therefore his sons were legitimate. Katherine's agony of mind is apparent in the remark by Hall, but she doubtless expected to receive support from Campeggio. Perhaps she, too, had some suspicion that he had private instructions from the Pope.
6. Cavendish, *Thomas Wolsey*. He refers to Katherine as being a 'true, patient Griselda' who showed 'no spark or kind of grudge or displeasure' towards either Henry or Anne, although the strain was obvious. Equally obvious by then was the fact that Anne was proving to be more than a passing fancy of the king, of which he had had several, but which had been easy for Katherine to ignore, being in an unassailable position. Anne was now apparently a queen-in-waiting, which was a very different thing.

Tudor Victims 267

7. Fergusen, *Naked to Mine Enemies*, takes the firm line that the document referred to was a forgery, intended to skim over the problems of the first one and settle the matter fairly quickly. It failed to explode Henry's legal claims against the first such dispensation issued by Julius II because it was quickly disregarded.
8. Brewer, *The Reign of Henry VIII*, Vol. II. Brewer summarises the document sent to Katherine as being a trick to persuade her to have the new dispensation sent from Spain to Henry. The Emperor, warned in time, sent the document direct to the Pope, only allowing the English envoys time to examine it briefly while it was still in Spain.
9. Calendar State Papers, Spanish, Vol. III and *Letters and Papers, Henry VIII*, Vol. IV. Peter Gwyn, in *The King's Cardinal*, quotes both these sources as showing how dissatisfied Henry then was with the results so far in his quest for a divorce.
10. *Letters and Papers, Henry VIII*, Vol. IV, quoted by Ridley in *Statesman and Saint*, this refers to a memorandum regarding Wolsey dated June of 1529.
11. Carolly Erickson, *Great Harry. The Extravagant Life of Henry VIII* (2004).
12. Fergusen, *Naked to Mine Enemies*, refers to Stephen Gardiner's attempts to browbeat the Pope into admitting that the document sent from Spain by the Emperor was in fact a forgery.
13. Fergusen, *Naked to Mine Enemies*, quoting Mendoza (*Letters and Papers, Henry VIII*, Vol. II) regarding Henry's changing attitude towards Wolsey due to his perceived delays in getting the King what he wanted regarding Katherine. Henry frequently lost his temper with Wolsey during this period and was reported to have used 'bitter words' towards him on several occasions, which were overhead by others.
14. Erickson, *Great Harry*, gives many details of the costs of the establishment at court and the emphasis placed on amusements and extravagant shows of wealth.
15. Cavendish, *Thomas Wolsey*, for full description of the court at Blackfriars where the Legatine Court was held. Also full details of the lengthy speech given by Katherine to the King, which he ignored.
16. Cavendish, *Thomas Wolsey*, in which he describes Wolsey's admission to the Bishop that he had endured an unfortunate interview with Henry at Blackfriars.
17. Anne Boleyn's father, Thomas Lord Rochford, became Earl of Wiltshire and Ormonde in 1529 when the long-standing familial dispute between the Butler and Boleyn families was finally decided by the King, largely in favour of the Boleyns. At that time George Boleyn became Viscount Rochford and Anne was then known officially as the Lady Anne Rochford. After the fall of the Boleyns, the Ormonde title reverted to the Butlers in 1538.
18. Cavendish, *Thomas Wolsey*, for full details of Wolsey's angry tirade aimed at the Duke of Suffolk in response to his verbal attack on the Cardinals. This is also quoted in full by Fergusen, *Naked to Mine Enemies*.
19. Fergusen, *Naked to Mine Enemies*, for Wolsey's probable reasoning for his decision to cast in his lot with Rome, following the lead that Campeggio had given him.

Chapter 9

1. Lord Edward Herbert of Cherbury, *The Life and Reign of King Henry VIII* (1649), regarding having to travel to Hever to bring Anne back to the court after Blackfriars.
2. Hester W. Chapman, *Anne Boleyn* (1974), regarding the two peace treaties that were to marginalise Henry.
3. Ridley, *Statesman and Saint*, for the early career of Thomas More and his rise in the affections of Henry VIII.
4. Perry, *Sisters to the King*, regarding Margaret Tudor's divorce from her second husband, Archibald Douglas. Henry played the hypocrite with this. He criticised his sister for ending her unsatisfactory marriage while at the same time was exploring ways to end his own marriage to Katherine of Aragon.
5. Morris and Grueninger, *In the Footsteps of Anne Boleyn*, regarding the semi-derelict manor of Grafton which Henry had brought up to date, making it into a comfortable hunting lodge

with apartments which were referred to as 'The Queen's Chambers'. He and Anne were known to have been there together on at least four occasions in September 1529, September 1531, July 1532 and October 1534. Henry was eventually to add the suffix of 'Regis' to its name in honour of its royal associations. Elizabeth I also used the manor, but in 1628 King Charles I sold it to Sir Francis Crane who partly demolished it. An existing building is on the site, but this has none of the original fabric in its walls.

6. Cavendish, *Thomas Wolsey*, for full details of the disgraceful reception of the Cardinal at Grafton on 19 September 1529.
7. Cavendish, *Thomas Wolsey*, regarding the tirade Anne is supposed to have directed at Henry VIII when she heard that he had taken pity on Wolsey at Grafton and had talked with him privately, promising to speak with him further. Her anger was obvious to all at Grafton on that day and Cavendish said, 'I heard it reported that Mistress Anne was much offended with the King, as far as she durst, because he had so gently entertained my Lord.'
8. These seventeen letters are still in the Vatican Archives. All are undated. It will never be known which member of Anne's household passed them on to Cardinal Campeggio. It does show how much Anne was surrounded by spies, even among her own servants, despite her apparently favourable position.
9. *The Harleian Miscellany: Or a Collection of Scarce, Curious and Entertaining Pamphlets and Tracts*, ed. William Oldys and Thomas Park (1744), Vol. III, Letter no. 14, Henry VIII to Anne Boleyn. Henry had for some time been convinced that his personal business was being openly discussed by his inferiors. He blamed Anne's household and had already written to her about it. Security there cannot have improved if such personal property as the King's letters could be removed. Henry said, 'In my last letter to you, I said I trusted shortly to see you, which is now better known at London than with any that is about me. Whereof I not a little marvel. But lack of discreet handling must needs be the cause thereof'.
10. Esher, in Surrey, was one of the 220 properties in Wolsey's possession as Bishop of Winchester and Chancellor of England. It was built in the 1460s by William Waynflete and now only the beautiful gatehouse tower survives. This has been restored by Penny Rainbow, who charts its renovation in her book *The Tower of Esher*. It would certainly not have been an uncomfortable residence in Wolsey's day, it was more his exile from the court that upset him than his household conveniences.
11. Mattingly, *Catherine of Aragon*, shows Cromwell's rapid abandonment of his master when misfortune overtook him.
12. Calendar State Papers, Spanish, Vol. IV, Pt I, taken from Chapuys' account of the quarrel collected from various informants.
13. Calendar State Papers, Spanish, Vol. IV, Pt I. Henry's quarrels with both Katherine and Anne on the same day are well recorded. It must be remembered that nobody of any status lived privately and therefore conversations and particularly quarrels would be heard by many people, eager to pass on the details. Chapuys and other ambassadors could find rich pickings from the members of the households of prominent persons.
14. Cavendish, *Thomas Wolsey*, also quoted by Hester W. Chapman in *Anne Boleyn*, regarding the conversation with Dr Butts during which gifts and kind words were given to the doctor to pass on to Wolsey in order to reassure him of Henry's favour. The illness so reported must have been entirely psychosomatic as it improved dramatically as soon as Henry's reassurances reached Wolsey.
15. *Letters and Papers, Henry VIII*, Vol. IV, regarding the instructions from Henry VIII to Cranmer to put his mind to work over the divorce question. From this stems his attachment to the Boleyns, and his rise at court, after the Fellows of Oxford and Cambridge gave their opinions in Henry's favour.
16. Calendar State Papers, Venetian, Vol. IV. Even Suffolk was to be made to realise that Henry's determination to have his own way would not allow anyone, even him, to criticise his choice.

Although the Princess Mary, Suffolk's wife, was to keep away from court from this time, her husband managed to fit back in well enough, being unwilling to lose his place due to his wife's dislike of Anne.
17. Cavendish, *Thomas Wolsey*. The double-dealing of this suggestion rightly angered Henry who had learned not to trust either Clement VII or Charles V.
18. Calendar State Papers, Spanish, Vol. IV, Pt I. It was obvious that by this time the strain was telling on all the parties involved, not just on Anne who had borne the brunt of the problem for so long.
19. *Letters and Papers, Henry VIII*, Vol. IV. It is not surprising that Anne had given way to panic realising that Wolsey was not only close by in London itself, but actually in conference with her own uncle. That Anne still greatly feared Wolsey is equally obvious, knowing his previous level of power and influence. To have such a man as an open enemy was no light matter and although she was courageous and determined, her nerves were shot by all the stress she had undergone.
20. Henry Ellis (ed.), *Original Letters*, Series II, Vol. II, letter from Henry VIII asking for assistance for Wolsey from the local noblemen.
21. Until the recent past the manor of Scrooby (which stands on the site of the moated manor house of medieval times) boasted a mulberry tree reputed to have been planted by Wolsey while he stayed there in September of 1530. Henry VIII also visited Scrooby in 1541.
22. *Letters and Papers, Henry VIII*, Vol. IV, regarding the verbal abuse from one Vesey towards the Cardinal after he had been caught poaching the livestock of Wolsey's tenants. This item also records the problems of the colleges with the tenants. Wolsey could do little or nothing at that time but worried constantly about his college foundations.
23. *Letters and Papers, Henry VIII*, Vol. IV. Anne was naturally very worried about the lingering affection that she feared Henry still had for Wolsey. As his replacements were not suitable, it was a ready fear that Henry VIII would return him to court.
24. Fergusen, *Naked to Mine Enemies*. It is sad to think of magnificent Wolsey being reduced to delaying his Installation because he needed his rents to come in to pay for the feast that went with it.
25. Cavendish, *Thomas Wolsey*. Despite Wolsey's plans for the future he appeared to have felt a sudden sense of foreboding at this point. He was not at that time ill. There is no other ailment to account for the sudden illness and death that was to overcome him.
26. Fergusen, *Naked to Mine Enemies*. Why would Wolsey send back so urgently for a bag of hair shirts? They would certainly be available elsewhere if he felt that he could use more. Wolsey was no fool and had no intention of being made a show of by the King.
27. *Henry VIII*, Vol. IV, Chapuys to Charles V, report on the examination of Dr Agostini when he confirmed (under firm questioning) all that was required for a case to be made against Wolsey as a traitor.
28. Cavendish, *Thomas Wolsey*. Despite all the lies told to try to convince Wolsey of his safety, he was not fooled. He knew perfectly well what to expect from Henry if he was taken to London and he did not intend to go along with it.
29. Cavendish, *Thomas Wolsey*. The full account of Wolsey's last days comes from his man Cavendish who was with him. He reported as carefully as possible, but his book was not put together until several years later.
30. Calendar State Papers, Venetian, Vol. IV, Fol. 641, letter from Sebastiano Giustiniani to the Doge and Signory, dated 14 December 1530. Also, letter from Chapuys to Charles V, dated 4 December 1530.
31. Ridley, *Statesman and Saint*. It is assumed in this work that obtaining poison would be extremely difficult or impossible, but that is not the case. Wolsey could easily have had a supply already, which is borne out by the fact that he sent back for a particular bag, which he considered important to him but later appeared to have nothing in it worthy of the

extra journey. As the bag had been taken to him 'secretly' he could easily have removed any substance that he intended for later use. The argument that Wolsey, as a Catholic, would not be able to commit suicide, as he would consider it a mortal sin, is also unreasonable. At that time almost everyone in the country was a Catholic, and that did not prevent people from taking their own way out of impossible situations, nor does it today in Catholic countries. Ridley actually seems to be suggesting that once life became intolerable for Wolsey, he somehow 'willed' himself to death (p. 237). The only logical answer is that Wolsey, like many other people, was forced to decide to either take his own life, or have it snuffed out at the behest of his enemies. He made that choice for himself, in order to avoid a situation that had become unendurable for him.

32. Sandra Hempel, *The Inheritor's Powder* (2013), gives useful details of the early use and availability of poisons, including arsenic, the symptoms of which are consistent with the illness that finally took Wolsey's life.

Chapter 10

1. Sergeant, *Anne Boleyn*, Chapuys' letter to Charles V, dated 1 January 1531. Chapuys wrote indignantly to the Emperor, attempting to inflame him on behalf of Queen Katherine. But the Emperor had other, more pressing, concerns and did not intend to become embroiled in the English divorce, although a little posturing from time to time was useful as a brake on Henry's more extravagant attitudes.
2. Letter from Chapuys to the Emperor, dated 2 April 1531, which described in detail the developments in England, Sergeant, *Anne Boleyn*.
3. Nicholas Sander, *The Rise and Growth of the Anglican Schism*, ed. D. Lewis (1877). This was followed by Henry Clifford in his *Life of Jane Dormer* (1887). Both these authors were violently anti-Boleyn in their opinions and this is reflected in their work. Gilbert Burnet, after much research, discounted the accusations made against Anne as being quite without foundation. He also stated that they had not, in fact, been levelled against her at that time, except for a letter that Chapuys had written to Charles V, in a general way, in which he blamed all the recent ills in England on 'the Lady and her father'.
4. Letter from Cranmer to Lord Wiltshire, 13 June 1531. 'The King his Grace, my lady your wife, my lady Anne your daughter, all be in good health, whereof thanks be to God. The King and my Lady Anne rode yesterday to Windsor and this night they are looked for at Hampton Court, God be their guide!' The letter tells us two things – one is that Cranmer was still working as a Boleyn family chaplain, keeping Thomas Boleyn informed of the family's movements. The other is that Lady Wiltshire, Anne's mother, was with the hunting party, so Anne was presumably correctly chaperoned.
5. Calendar State Papers, Venetian, Vol. IV, letter dated 14 November 1531.
6. Sergeant, *Anne Boleyn*.
7. *Letters and Papers, Henry VIII*, Vol. V, letter from Ortiz to the Emperor, dated 25 January 1532.
8. Letter from Chapuys to Charles V, dated 29 May 1532 (Vienna Archives). In this letter Chapuys claimed that 'the Lady's father and uncle' were then working against her marriage to King Henry. It seems a strange idea, but Chapuys tended to blow back and forth with every breeze. It was typical of his gossipy nature to expand a family argument into a full-scale treachery against Anne.
9. *Letters and Papers, Henry VIII*, Vol. V. Also Vienna Archives. Chapuys to the Emperor, 22 July 1532, and also Northumberland's letter to Cromwell (when the matter was raised again at Anne's fall from favour), dated 13 May 1536.
10. Henry was obliged to face this again in the future, when he was married to Catherine Howard and became aware of her sexual peccadilloes. Was she, or was she not, actually contracted to Francis Dereham? Catherine fervently denied it, perhaps not wishing to admit that she

had never actually been Queen, but Dereham insisted that they were troth-plighted. Their exchange of vows had been followed by several incidents of sexual activity, which were well attested to by their friends. These had apparently taken place in the general dormitory of the ladies of the Dowager Duchess of Norfolk, Catherine's step-grandmother. It was customary for the ladies to share beds, and evidence shows that on at least one occasion Catherine and Dereham were in bed together while her lady companion was also still in it. That being the case, it would certainly seem that Catherine Howard, unlike Anne Boleyn, had been technically precontracted to another man at the time of her marriage to Henry. Thus, she had never really been married to him at all, by the law at the time.

11. H.F.M. Prescott, *Mary Tudor – the Spanish Tudor* (2003). King Henry, despite from time to time attempting to see his daughter, was well aware that she had espoused her mother's cause. Every insult suffered by Katherine was to estrange their daughter from him and force her to withdraw further. A very painful situation for them both which was to negate all their previous affection for, and pride in, each other.
12. Bruce, *Anne Boleyn*. Anne's quarrels with Henry became famous, but the 'sunshine and shadow' of Anne's mercurial temperament was one of the facets that had originally attracted the King. Her changeable character probably helped to keep an otherwise rather claustrophobic relationship fresh.
13. Parmiter, *The King's Great Matter*. William Warham's firmness of mind against the King's proposed divorce had increased during the last months of his life. It posed a serious problem for Henry, who was literally waiting for him to die so that he could replace him with someone more amenable. The obvious choice was Thomas Cranmer. Warham died of natural causes in August of 1532, leaving the way clear.
14. Ives, *Anne Boleyn*. The second wife of King Francis I of France was the sister of the Emperor Charles V so there was never any possibility of Anne being welcomed by Katherine's niece. Several other ladies of rank were suggested, but they were either unwilling or plainly unsuitable, therefore it was decided that Henry VIII would meet with Francis in Boulogne, without ladies being in attendance at all. He would then take him to meet with Anne within the bounds of Calais, where the problem of her reception would not arise.
15. Ives, *Anne Boleyn*. Anne tended to be blamed for this, as she was for most things pertaining to Katherine. The jewels held by Queen Katherine of Aragon were those of the Queen of England, therefore Henry's contention that she was not, and never had been Queen of England, meant that she had no right to hold on to them. He therefore wanted Anne to have them, as she was intended to be the next (in his opinion only) wife and Queen, and therefore entitled to them due to her rank. It was, in his opinion, quite appropriate that Anne should be given the jewels to boost her standing (by what they represented) when she went to France as his future wife.
16. Calendar State Papers, Spanish, Vol. IV.
17. The eldest daughter of King Francis was the Princess Madeleine (sometimes referred to as Magdalen). She was young and supposedly very lovely, but she was also frail. She married James V of Scotland but there were genuine concerns for her health both regarding the journey to Scotland and the weather she would experience in her new country. These fears proved to be justified, as she unfortunately died very shortly after her marriage.
18. Starkey, *Six Wives*. The Venetian Ambassador reported that not only was Anne most magnificently dressed, with her long train supported by Mary Howard, her first cousin, but that she was 'completely covered with the most costly jewels'.
19. Ives, *Anne Boleyn*, gives full details of Anne's investiture as Lady Marquis of Pembroke at Windsor on Sunday, 1 September 1532.
20. Edward Hall, *The Triumphant Reign of King Henry VIII*, ed. C. Whibley, T.C. Jack and E.C. Jack (1904).
21. Calendar State Papers, Spanish, Vol. IV. The Spanish papers give full details of the ladies attending Anne at the banquet. Their costumes, their escorts and their dancing were alike

272 Tudor Victims

all fully recorded, together with the fact that Henry and Anne indulged in a long private talk with King Francis.
22. Hall, *Hall's Chronicle*, gave details of the scattering of the ships of the royal party when they attempted to reach England ahead of the gales.
23. H.M. Colvin, *The History of the King's Works* (1963–82). This work gives many fascinating details about the comforts and conveniences of the Exchequer in Calais when Henry VIII and Anne Boleyn stayed there at the end of 1532.
24. Ives, *Anne Boleyn*. Ives argues that Henry and Anne first became intimate at Calais. *Hall's Chronicle* states a firm date of 14 November 1532 for a marriage between Henry and Anne. This was later generally accepted by Protestant writers, because its early date saved the reputation of Elizabeth I, preventing her from appearing to be illegitimate. However, Hall was probably actually giving the date when the relationship was consummated, which would have been well known by the people who were in close attendance upon the pair at that time. Their vows to each other, often repeated publicly (i.e. that they fully intended to marry) followed by sexual union would actually form a canonically valid marriage by the rules of the time. This was particularly so in view of Henry's contention that his earlier marriage to Katherine was, and always had been, invalid. Therefore his marriage to Anne would be his first. For those people who agreed with the King, this meant that his formal union with Anne would indeed date from 14 November 1532. See Note 10 of Chapter 10.

Chapter 11

1. Hall, *Hall's Chronicle*, Diarmid McCullough, *Cranmer – Thomas Cranmer, a Life* (1996), Ives, *Anne Boleyn* and Starkey, *Six Wives*. All have written of the apparent significance of this date, which must have been talked, and written, of as having some special meaning to the people who were present at that time, as part of the suite attending upon Henry and Anne.
2. *Letters and Papers, Henry VIII*, Vol. V, Calendar State Papers, Venetian, Vol. IV and Calendar State Papers, Spanish, Vol. IV, regarding the rumours around Henry's refurbishment of the Tower of London.
3. Starkey, *Six Wives*.
4. Parmiter, *The King's Great Matter*. How naïve, or was it arrogant, did people have to be to assume that any man, let alone one like Henry, could wait for ever for them to deliberate? With the years passing, fertility and virility waning, and the chance to rear any young prince to manhood in his own lifetime – even if he should have one – lessening day by day, it should have been obvious that Henry was not only determined, but also desperate.
5. McCullough, *Cranmer*, for details of Henry's impatience for the return of his new Archbishop elect and his having to send out officials to find him and bring him home as speedily as possible.
6. *Letters and Papers, Henry VIII*, Vol. VI.
7. *Letters and Papers, Henry VIII*, Vol. VI, warrant, dated 11 February 1533.
8. Parmiter, *The King's Great Matter*. Parmiter also refers to Wilkins' 'Concilia' (*Letters and Papers, Henry VIII*, Vol. VI) and John Strype's *Memorials of Thos Cranmer, Archbishop of Canterbury* (1694, Oxford Ecclesiastical Society, 1848–54). Also to be considered is Jasper Ridley's *Cranmer* (1962) – in which Ridley appears to condone Cranmer's actions on the grounds that he considered that his first Christian duty was the strengthening of Henry VIII's power. Surely that would be a duty for his ministers, not his clergy? Cranmer acknowledged that he was accepting the position of Primate 'only of the King and of none other' which makes it difficult, if not impossible, to refute any accusation of perjury on his part. His vows were therefore naturally accompanied by double-dealing, which leads one to agree with Parmiter that there was very little difference between Cranmer's 'principle' and simple time-serving.

9. *Letters and Papers, Henry VIII*, Vol. VI, letter of Chapuys to Charles V, dated 15 March 1533. 'Yesterday and today it was proposed in Parliament to make a statute declaring the Pope had no authority in this kingdom, which many people have found to be very strange.'
10. *Letters and Papers, Henry VIII*, Vol. VI, letter from Chapuys to Charles V, dated 31 March 1533. 'The King was waiting for the Bulls of the Archbishopric of Canterbury in order to proceed to the decision of the marriage. Which having arrived these five days to the great regret of everybody the King was extremely urgent with the synod here, for the determination of his said affair, so that those present could hardly eat and drink, using such terms to them that no one dared open his mouth to contradict, except the good Bishop of Rochester! But his single voice cannot avail against the majority …'.
11. Parmiter, *The King's Great Matter*. Henry did not seem to realise that the incongruity of telling the people of the marriage and its immediate result detracted from his otherwise sensible remarks in asking for their assistance in achieving the matter. His common sense only appeared to stretch so far, after which his impatience would take over. He would blurt out his private business to all and sundry, usually oblivious to the fact that others did not, and would not, see things the same way he did. It is a particularly childish trait that he could not control his tongue and would spectacularly spoil his own case by making it clear that he had already jumped the gun.
12. Edmund Bapst, *Two Gentlemen Poets at the Court of Henry VIII. George Boleyn and Henry Howard*, ed. C. Ridgeway (2013) This was quoted by Edmund Bapst. The letter referred to is in the *Letters and Papers, Henry VIII*, Vol. VI following the instructions given to George, Lord Rochford.
13. *Letters and Papers, Henry VIII*, Vol.VI, Cranmer to Henry VIII, dated 11 April 1533. There are actually two letters from Cranmer on this matter, very similar but not identical. Apparently Cranmer's first letter was not written in a suitably humble and meek manner to please the King, who intended to show that he held the authority, even though Cranmer was invested with the title, of head of the English Church.
14. Starkey, *Six Wives*, regarding the isolated venue chosen for the Dunstable Court which may well have had a bearing on the people supposed to be there who were actually unable to attend. It may also have been a deliberate ploy with the intention of holding the court almost in camera.
15. Ives, *Anne Boleyn*, regarding the expenses for those taking part in the celebrations for Anne's Coronation. Henry was not prepared to pay for everything and it was made plain to those chosen to attend that they were expected to provide suitable clothing and horses for their own attendants.
16. Ives, *Anne Boleyn*. Professor Ives quotes from Wynkyn de Worde's *The Noble and Tryumphant Coronacyon of Quene Anne* (1533), included in A.F. Pollard's *Tudor Tracts* (1903), and also from other authorities such as *Hall's Chronicle*, *Letters and Papers, Henry VIII*, Vol. V (1531–2) and Calendar State Papers, Venetian, Vol. IV. Also from *Ordinances for the Household* for the delightfully full details of Anne's Coronation and its attendant festivities.
17. *Letters and Papers, Henry VIII*, Vol. VI, for details of the water procession accompanying Anne's barge from Greenwich Palace into London itself on Thursday, 29 May 1533. Incidentally, Chapuys reported, and this was picked up by other writers, that Henry had been angry with Anne for using the 'royal' barge which had been Katherine's. There is no evidence that there was any disagreement between them over this matter. The barge was Katherine's only in the same sense as the jewels were hers – as Queen of England. Once she was no longer regarded as such then all the items associated with the Queen became the possessions of the new Queen, i.e. Anne Boleyn. It would appear that it was merely another example of the gossip spread by Chapuys and his chagrin that he was no longer considered to be quite at the centre of affairs, after he had been warned off. He tended to write whatever he believed would please the Emperor, rather than what was actually the truth.

274   Tudor Victims

18. De Worde, *The Noble and Tryumphant Coronacyon of Quene Anne*, for details of the elevations, on Friday, 30 May 1533.
19. Richard Marius, *Thomas More* (1984).
20. The *Cronico del Rey Enrico Ottavo da Inglaterra*, ed. M.A.S. Hume (1889) from the Marquis de Molins (1874). The *Cronico del Rey Enrico Ottavo da Inglaterra* is attributed to Antonio de Guaras. It is often known as the *Spanish Chronicle* and was edited by M.A.S. Hume in 1889.
21. *Letters and Papers, Henry VIII*, Vol. V (1531–2); Calendar State Papers, Venetian, Vol. IV.
22. Ives, *Anne Boleyn*, for details of Anne's Coronation day on Sunday, 1 June 1533.
23. There was some suggestion, made at the end of Anne's life, that the use of the actual St Edward's Crown at her Coronation had, technically, given her some unique power almost equal to Henry's own. This was to cause some consternation when she was to be executed and was perhaps the real reason (apart from Henry's always chronic lack of money) that he chose not to crown any future wife at all. Certainly Anne, at her Coronation, received several marks of special and unusual favour, which were only normally offered to the Sovereign and not merely to the Consort being crowned. This appeared to create a slight difficulty in assessing her exact status as the marriage ended.
24. *Letters and Papers, Henry VIII*, Vol. VI, for the letter written to France, to George Boleyn, Lord Rochford, from the court in England, which detailed the continuing merriment and festivity taking place in Anne's chambers during the month of June 1533 after she had been crowned Queen.
25. Calendar State Papers, Venetian, Vol. IV and Calendar State Papers, Spanish, Vol. IV, Pt II. Both refer to the expensive gift that Anne received from Francis I, sent via her brother George, consisting of a litter in which she could ride, along with three mules to carry it. Anne would have been especially delighted with the gift, showing the friendship between England and France at that time. Anne usually rode her own horses, but due to her pregnancy would be expected to refrain from riding for the duration.
26. Norah Lofts, *Anne Boleyn* (1979), for Henry VIII's use of, and presumably belief in, astrologers and fortune tellers who assured him that the expected child was certain to be a boy.

Chapter 12

1. *Letters and Papers, Henry VIII*, Vol. VI, regarding the Pope's reaction to Henry's marriage to Anne, which should have been expected once he had approved the elevation of Cranmer to the Archbishopric of Canterbury.
2. Calendar State Papers, Spanish, Vol. IV. Katherine had continued to be obdurate towards Henry which rather took the gloss of his achievements so far. He still believed that the birth of a son would prove that all his actions were right and were vindicated by God.
3. Calendar State Papers, Spanish, Vol. IV.
4. *Letters and Papers, Henry VIII*, Vol. VI, for the official record of the birth of the Princess Elizabeth.
5. Lancelot de Carles, 'L'Opinion', *De la royne d'Angleterre*, in G. Ascoli, *La Grande-Bretagne devant l'Opinion Française* (1927) and Charles Wriothesley, *A Chronicle of England in the Reigns of the Tudors, 1485–1559*, ed. W. Douglas Hamilton (1875–7) also contradict Chapuys' gloomy reports. Full details are given in Ives, *Anne Boleyn*.
6. Mattingly, *Catherine of Aragon*, regarding Katherine's regular pregnancies which must certainly have sapped her strength. Had she been allowed time to recover her health properly after each miscarriage or stillbirth she would certainly have had a greater chance of producing a healthy full-term child. Or perhaps the too-regular miscarriages simply showed that there was something wrong with each foetus, which might point to the fault lying with Henry anyway. Katherine certainly had no problem at all in conceiving.
7. Lynda Porter, *Katherine the Queen, The Remarkable Life of Katherine Parr* (2010). Katherine Parr, in her subsequent marriage to Thomas Seymour after Henry's death, died shortly after

bearing her first child at the age of 36. Henry's own mother, Queen Elizabeth of York, had died at the age of 37, after giving birth to a daughter, even though she had successfully produced several children already.

8. Paul Friedmann, *Anne Boleyn – A Chapter of English History, 1527–1536*, 2 vols (1884).
9. Calendar State Papers, Spanish, letter of Chapuys to Charles V, dated 3 November 1533, now in the Vienna Archives, P.C. 228.
10. *Letters and Papers, Henry VIII*, Vol. VI, for Henry's instructions to his ambassadors in France, appealing against the Pope's suggestions for conditions of a final judgement of his divorce from Katherine, 6 November 1533.
11. Cyfuentes to Charles V, dated 9 November 1533, British Museum, Add. Mss 28586, Fol. 62, as quoted by Friedmann, *Anne Boleyn*, Vol. I.
12. Bonner to Henry VIII, 13 November 1533, *Burnet Collectanea*, Pt 3, Book 11/23.
13. Report of Jean de Dinteville, November 1533. Paris Biblio. Nat. Mss Dupuis, Vol. 547, Fol. 321.
14. Princess Mary Tudor to Henry VIII, dated 2 October 1533.
15. Privy Purse Expenses of the Household of the Lady Elizabeth, regarding the extra expenses incurred by the governors of Elizabeth's household when Mary refused to dine or live as part of the household. The extra expense referred to of 10*s.* per week was incurred due to the Lady Mary demanding to take her meals in her room. Quoted by Friedmann, *Anne Boleyn*, Vol. I.
16. Friedmann, *Anne Boleyn*, Vol. I. Henry used the fear engendered by the Act of Attainder to silence any apparent opposition, thereby creating an atmosphere of oppression, which allowed him to push through his Bills of Succession.
17. Richard Rex, 'The Execution of the Holy Maid of Kent', Institute of Historical Research, Vol. 64 (1991). Also details taken from Wriothesley's *A Chronicle of England*, which states: 'This year the 20th day of April, being a Monday, 1534. The Holy Maid of Kent, being a nun of Canterbury; two monks of Canterbury Christ Church, one of them called Dr. Bocking, two Grey Friars Observant, and a priest, were drawn from the Tower of London to Tyburn, and there hanged and after cut down, and their heads smitten off. Two of their heads set on London Bridge and the other four at diverse gates of the City.'
18. Ives, *Anne Boleyn*.
19. Ives, *Anne Boleyn* and *Letters and Papers, Henry VIII*, Vol. VII (1534) and Calendar State Papers, Spanish, Vol. V, Pt I. Ives argues that it was not a stillbirth as there had been no attempt made by Queen Anne at 'taking her chamber' which would have been the case when a child was actually due.
20. Denny, *Anne Boleyn* and Lofts, *Anne Boleyn*, regarding reports of the killing of Anne's pet dog while she was pregnant with her second child. Also the report of Chapuys' making a malicious joke about it, which suggested that it was not an accident, but an act designed to hurt and upset the Queen.
21. Latimer's 'Treatyse'. Latimer's evidence that in the latter months of her life, Anne kept a copy of Coverdale's Bible in her suite for the general reading of her household. Anne's copy of Tyndale's 1534 edition of the New Testament is still extant, which came from Antwerp along with other religious works of the same year.
22. A.G. Dickens, *The English Reformation* (1964).
23. J. Shakespeare and M. Dowling, 'Religion and Politics in mid-Tudor England', Institute of Historical Research, Vol. 55 (1982).
24. Ives, *Anne Boleyn*, regarding Anne's desire to expand the knowledge of the new religion within her household and of her search for religious books, which could be sent to her from abroad.
25. Alison Weir, *Mary Boleyn, the Great and Infamous Whore* (2011), for the full text of Mary Boleyn's rather grovelling letter to Cromwell, in the usual style of the period, in which she begs his help in recovering the favour and approval of Henry and Anne.

276   Tudor Victims

26. Calendar State Papers, Spanish, Vol. V, Pt I and *Letters and Papers, Henry VIII*, Vol. VII (1534), Chapuys to Charles V. The letter informs the Emperor that Mary Boleyn had been banished from court due to her secret marriage and its apparent result. The child she is reputed to have been carrying at that time must have died young, or been miscarried, as the only offspring of Mary Boleyn to carry on into the next generation are Katherine and Henry Carey, the children of her first husband.

Chapter 13
1. Tremlett, *Catherine of Aragon*, regarding the Act of Succession and the 'official' bastardy of the Princess Mary.
2. Vienna Archives, P.C. 229, Chapuys to Charles V, dated July 1534, regarding Katherine's opinions after the sentence had been finally passed in her favour by Pope Clement VII.
3. Anne Somerset, *Elizabeth I* (1991).
4. Tremlett, *Catherine of Aragon*, regarding Chapuys famous difficulties with Henry VIII. It describes his lack of common ground with such a temperamental and incomprehensible individual as Henry, famous for changing his mind and also instilling wariness in those who had the misfortune to have to deal with him on a personal level.
5. Eamon Duffy, *Saints and Sinners – a History of the Popes* (1997).
6. Matthew Bunson, *The Pope Encyclopedia, An A to Z of the Holy See* (1995).
7. As part of the strong Counter-Reformation led by Pope Paul III, he would in 1540 issue the Bull that confirmed the founding of the Society of Jesus (the Jesuits), which would become the spearhead of the new resurgence of the Church in Europe. The Society had been formed earlier, but Pope Paul gave them their official standing and also encouraged them firmly in their work.
8. Michael Walsh, *History of the Popes* (1980), regarding the early life of the Farnese Pope, Paul III. Also the way in which this man changed to become a firm upholder of the rights of the Church.
9. J.E.B. Mayor, *English Works* (1876), quoted in Mathew, *The Courtiers of Henry VIII*. This showed clearly the difference between the single-minded Bishop John Fisher and many of the other clerics of the time, who were confused and frightened, having lost a sense of their true function as leaders and guides. The new world created at that time by the King must have been a very frightening place to be. Few men are capable of standing in the front line and offering themselves as a sacrifice for what they believe in. Nobody knows how he would behave in a similar situation, so it is not possible to make firm judgements whether other people should have martyred themselves or not, but Bishop Fisher and those others who died had no such fears. They were courageous enough, and perhaps already marginalised enough, to consider the sacrifice worth making on a point of honour.
10. He was fortunately able to prove that he had sent a letter to Elizabeth Barton in which he warned her against making any pronouncements relating to the King's business. He had already retired from political life due to his inability to agree with Henry VIII's changes and could see that the nun was putting herself into danger by her foolish and increasingly offensive remarks.
11. *Letters and Papers, Henry VIII*, Vol. VII. The Princess Mary had isolated herself as far as she could from the mainstream of her half-sister's household. Whenever the Princess Elizabeth's household was visited by Queen Anne she absented herself and refused to leave her chamber until her stepmother and her suite had left. This may have been construed as an insult to the new Queen, but I am certain that Anne had no more desire for Mary's company than Mary had for hers. A stubborn teenaged stepdaughter is an uncomfortable appendage at the best of times. However, the visiting back and forth by members of the new Queen's suite can only be put down to people wishing to keep a foot in both camps in case of changes in the future, and its certain that Anne, never a fool, also saw it as such.
12. Friedmann, *Anne Boleyn*, Vol. 2.

13. J.A. Froude, *The Divorce of Katherine of Aragon* (1891). The remarks made about the character and abilities of Chapuys are certainly not flattering. Although the man was loyal to Spain, also to Katherine and her daughter, he allowed his personal feelings of dislike against the Boleyns to blind him to the fact that much of what he wrote was rubbish. Unfortunately, this has robbed future generations of a wonderful opportunity to understand those difficult times at first hand, from the point of view of a foreigner in England, therefore not under restraint as an Englishman would be, as so much of what he reported was simply untrue.
14. *Letters and Papers, Henry VIII*, Vol. VIII, regarding Anne's conversation with Gontier at the court entertainment on 1 December 1534. When Henry VIII was distracted from his intention to find the Treasurer, by meeting a new young lady who caught his eye, Anne's reaction may have seemed extreme. However, she was in a position of great insecurity, which would get worse as the following year progressed, and must have been always on her guard for just such an eventuality, when she might have been replaced. This incident has been reported, with relish, by many novelists and therefore might be considered to be apocryphal. However, as it was reported by the French Ambassador its veracity is verified.
15. Calendar State Papers, Spanish, Vol. V, Pt I and Vienna Archives, P.C. 229, Chapuys to Charles V, regarding the rumours spread by Chapuys about the supposed ill-treatment of Katherine of Aragon and the Princess Mary.

Chapter 14

1. Cotton Mss Nero B.III, Fol. 105. The instructions to the Ambassadors to France for this occasion are in the British Museum. Unfortunately, the first part of the document has been lost.
2. Vienna Archives, P.C. 229, letter from Chapuys to Charles V, dated 14 May 1534, regarding the praise the King gave his envoys on their return.
3. Bapst, *Two gentlemen Poets at the Court of Henry VIII*, regarding George Boleyn's appointments in June 1534 as reward for his work in France.
4. *Letters and Papers, Henry VIII*, Vol. VII, regarding George Boleyn's return from France when the royal visit was called off due to Anne's miscarriage, end of the summer of 1534. The instructions of George Boleyn were dated 10 July of that year.
5. Bapst, *Two gentlemen Poets at the Court of Henry VIII*. George Boleyn's visit to France on this occasion was very short and he returned by the end of July. He had succeeded in persuading Francis to agree to a meeting between the two kings set for April 1535.
6. Vienna Archives, P.C. 229, Chapuys to Charles V, dated 19 December 1534. It is to be noted that Chapuys' reports back to the Emperor were rather behind events, as usual.
7. *Letters and Papers, Henry VIII*, Vol. VII, excerpts of a letter from George Boleyn to the Duke of Norfolk, 11 November 1534, in which he explained the reason for the delay in conducting the newly arrived Admiral Chabot to the King. The full letter appears in Bapst, *Two gentlemen Poets at the Court of Henry VIII*.
8. The Dauphin of France was to die, still unmarried, on 19 August 1536. He was aged only 18.
9. Francis' third son, the Duc d'Angoulême would also die young, in September of 1545, at the age of 23.
10. The Infanta Maria was at that time 6 years old. She would eventually be married to her cousin, who became the Emperor Maximilian II. The details of this convoluted negotiation are to be found in a memoir written by the Imperial Chancellor Granvelle in approximately mid-November 1534.
11. *Letters and Papers, Henry VIII*, Vol. VII, regarding Henry's counter proposal to Francis I in the marriage of Princess Elizabeth to the Duke d'Angoulême.
12. Letter from Palamede Gontier to Admiral Chabot, dated 5 February 1535. This refers to Francis I's further conditions and his great desire to be relieved of the burden of the pensions paid to England.

13. Princess Madeleine was to marry King James V of Scotland and died very early in that marriage. Princess Marguerite married Duke Philibert-Emmanuel of Savoy in 1559.
14. Letter from Palamede Gontier to Admiral Chabot, dated 5 February 1535. This refers to Henry VIII's continued reluctance to discount the pension payments. It also records Henry's suspicion and general mistrust of the French King's loyalty towards himself.
15. Letter from Henry VIII to Chabot, dated end of February or early March 1535. It is to be noted that the Duke of Norfolk, despite being blood kin to the Boleyns, was already beginning to dissociate himself from their affairs.
16. Weir, *Mary Boleyn*.
17. Weir, *Mary Boleyn*.
18. Lofts, *Anne Boleyn*, quoted as an example of the impossibility of stopping the progress of reform once it had begun to gather pace.
19. Weir, *Mary Boleyn*, regarding details of the pension still being paid to Mary after the deaths of her siblings.
20. Susan Brigdon, *New Worlds, Lost Worlds. The Rule of the Tudors, 1485–1503* (2000), refers to the use of the impediment between Henry and Anne due to his affair with Mary Boleyn. This was something he was, of course, fully aware of at the time of his marriage with Anne, having already used a similar argument to divorce himself from Katherine of Aragon. He chose to ignore it at the time, but was happy to remember and reuse it when he wished to be rid of Anne in her turn, and to have an excuse to bastardise their daughter Elizabeth.
21. Ives, *Anne Boleyn*, regarding the complicated relationship between Anne and Henry at this time. The tensions both within it and outside of it, created by the political and religious upheavals then in full swing, were instrumental in taking the gloss off their personal life. It did not, however, actually mean that Henry was in a position to divorce Anne at that time, nor did it seem that he wished to, as they were still living fully as man and wife.
22. *Letters and Papers, Henry VIII*, Vol. VII, remarks of the Abbot of Whitby quoted by Ives in *Anne Boleyn*.
23. *Letters and Papers, Henry VIII*, Vol. VII, regarding Cromwell's efficient spy system which was so well organised that it could pick up and record details of speeches made against the King almost anywhere. It was intended to monitor all sources of discontent within the Kingdom and stamp them out before they had an opportunity to burst into flame.
24. Mattingly, *Catherine of Aragon* and also Vienna Archives, P.C. 229. These refer to Henry's very real fears of an uprising in favour of Katherine and/or Mary, which would have been supported by Spain. Even after Katherine's death in 1536 Henry feared that the Emperor would intervene on behalf of his kinswoman.
25. Anne had persuaded Henry to agree to the match between his son the Duke of Richmond and her cousin Mary Howard. This was achieved without the Duke of Norfolk being obliged to make the large payment of dowry to the King, which would normally have been expected. Even this valuable concession and the position of daughter-in-law to the King for his daughter were not enough for the Duke of Norfolk's feelings of resentment to be assuaged. He remained resentful of what he considered to be Anne's lack of family respect and obedience, and also concerned about the rise of Thomas Cromwell who had swiftly insinuated himself into a central position at court, and one of influence with the King.
26. Hanart to Granvelle, 14 January 1535, British Museum Additional Mss 28587, Fol. 207.
27. Friedmann, *Anne Boleyn*, Vol. II.
28. Palamede Gontier to Admiral Chabot de Brion, reported 5 February 1535.
29. Friedmann, *Anne Boleyn*, Vol. II, regarding the negotiations with France and the request from Francis to Henry that the next available Garter should be given to the gentleman of his choice – which was Sir Nicholas Carewe.
30. Letter from Chapuys to Charles V, dated 25 February 1535, regarding the Princess Mary's illness and her attendance by Dr Butts and the physician of Katherine of Aragon.

31. Chapuys to Charles V, dated 25 April 1535, Vienna Archives, P.C. 229, ½ Fol. 74, regarding the fact that Henry VIII seemed oblivious to the ease with which Charles V could, if he so wished, make himself 'master of England'.
32. Letters from Chapuys to Charles V, dated 1 January, 25 February and 23 March 1535, regarding proposals to get Princess Mary out of England and to safety under the protection of the Emperor, of which Cromwell was fully aware.
33. Friedmann, *Anne Boleyn*, Vol. II, regarding Cromwell's illness and incapacity which gave new impetus to the hopes of the followers of Katherine and Mary.
34. Chapuys to Charles V, letter dated 17 April 1535, Vienna Archives, P.C. 229, ½ Fol. 68.

Chapter 15
1. Denny, *Anne Boleyn*, showing that Henry's even-handedness in his approach to executions was dictated by his desire to embrace a middle line controlled only by himself.
2. Casale to Cromwell, 1 June 1535, Calendar State Papers, Spanish, Vol. VII. Also, Bishop of Mâcon to Francis I, 29 May 1535, Paris Biblio. Nat. Mss Dupuis, Vol. 265.
3. More had remarked of Sir Richard Rich that he was 'always reputed to be light of tongue, a great dicer, and gamester, and not of any commendable fame'. Rich was to prove the decisive witness against both Fisher and More, on his word only. He became Chancellor of the Court of Augmentations in 1536.
4. Ridley, *Statesman and Saint*.
5. *Letters and Papers, Henry VIII*, Vol. VIII (January–July 1535), Chapuys to Charles V, 16 June 1535.
6. *Letters and Papers, Henry VIII*, Vol. VIII. Also, Calendar State Papers, Spanish, Vol. V, a report of August 1535 giving details of Richard Rich's verbal evidence against More at his trial.
7. Calendar State Papers, Spanish, Vol. V, report of August 1535. Also, W. Roper, *The Life of Sir Thomas More, Knight* (1935), T. Stapleton, *The Life and Illustrious Martyrdom of Sir Thomas More* (1928) and N. Harpsfield, *The Life and Death of Thomas More, Knight* (1932).
8. Calendar State Papers, Spanish, Vol. IV, Pt II.
9. Calendar State Papers, Spanish, Vol. V. Also, *Letters and Papers, Henry VIII*, Vol. VIII.
10. Edward Seymour would become Duke of Somerset during the reign of Edward VI.
11. Denny, *Anne Boleyn*.
12. *Letters and Papers, Henry VIII*, Vol. IX. This would actually have been Anne's fourth pregnancy in three years, so there was no apparent lack of fertility at that time. The difficulty, as with Katherine of Aragon, was one of carrying the child to term, which may possibly suggest some defect in the foetus, caused perhaps by the father of the children conceived by both the women concerned.
13. Friedmann, *Anne Boleyn*, Vol. II, regarding the disgust and outrage in Europe at the deaths of Fisher and More. Also, the suggestion that Henry should somehow be deposed in favour of his daughter the Princess Mary.
14. Friedmann, *Anne Boleyn*, Vol. II, regarding Henry's own claim to kindness and piety as his defence against the open abhorrence towards his actions.
15. Letter of Anne de Montmorency to Cardinal du Bellay, 28 September 1535, Paris Biblio. Nat. Mss Fr. 19,577, regarding Francis' warning to Henry.
16. Francis I to Jean de Dinteville, 29 August 1535, Paris Biblio. Nat. Mss Dupuis, Vol. 547.
17. Chapuys to Charles V, 13 October 1535, Vienna Archives, P.C. 229 ½ Fol. 130.
18. Memorandum of the French Ambassadors, Paris Biblio. Nat. Mss Dupuis, Vol. 547, Fol. 200.
19. Memorandum of the French Ambassadors, Paris Biblio. Nat. Mss Dupuis, Vol. 547, Fol. 200, regarding Henry's inability to be able to rely even on his own servants.
20. Memorandum of the French Ambassadors, Paris Biblio. Nat. Mss Dupuis, Vol. 547, Fol. 200.
21. Chapuys to Charles V, 11 July 1535, Vienna Archives, P.C. 229 ½ Fol. 105.

280   Tudor Victims

22. *Letters and Papers, Henry VIII*, Vol. VIII (January–July 1535), Chapuys to Granvelle, 11 July 1535. Also, *Letters and Papers, Henry VIII*, Vol. IX (August–December 1535), Chapuys to Charles V, 13 October 1535, regarding the amicable talk Eustace Chapuys had with Jean de Dinteville before the French Ambassador left England to report to Francis I. This showed that the Ambassadors were less taken in by the subterfuge than the English had hoped.

Chapter 16
1. 15 October 1535, Katherine of Aragon to Pope Paul III, Mattingly, *Catherine of Aragon*.
2. Mattingly, *Catherine of Aragon*.
3. Maria de Salinas was Katherine's lady-in-waiting and close friend. She had married Lord Willoughby d'Eresby. Their daughter, Catherine, was briefly considered as a possible wife by Henry VIII, before he married Katherine Parr. She eventually married his friend, Charles Brandon, Duke of Suffolk instead, the widower of Henry's sister Princess Mary, one-time Queen of France.
4. Mattingly, *Katherine of Aragon*, for full text of letter from Katherine to Henry VIII written just prior to Katherine's death.
5. Katherine's desire to be buried at a House of the Observant Friars, an Order she particularly favoured, could not be met. They had already been dissolved.
6. Calendar State Papers, Spanish, Vol. V, Chapuys' disgusted report of the joy shown at Katherine's death.
7. *Letters and Papers, Henry VIII*, Vol. IX.
8. Calendar State Papers, Venetian, Vol. V, from Giustiniani. Also, Calendar State Papers, Spanish, Vol. V, regarding Henry being 'unconscious for two hours'. Henry was obviously 'out' long enough for his condition to have caused grave concern.
9. Retha Warnicke, *The Rise and Fall of Anne Boleyn* (1987). This author claims that Anne's final child was deformed, which in her opinion is why Henry was so eager to accredit her with 'many lovers' so that the child could not be attributed to him. It is also claimed that this was the reason for the 'witchcraft' accusation, based on the child's supposed condition. This wild assertion can be easily discounted. There is no record at all of any child of Anne's having been disabled or deformed at birth in any way. Anne's many enemies would have been delighted to have had such material to work with, and Chapuys would have jumped at the chance to discredit her with such a story, had he been able to do so.
10. Lancelot de Carles in Ascoli, *Le Grande Bretagne devant L'Opinion Francaise*, regarding the description of the lost child as 'a beautiful boy'.
11. *Letters and Papers, Henry VIII*, Vol. X.
12. Nicholas Sander, *The Rise and Growth of the Anglican Schism*, ed. D. Lewis (1877). Sander was an inveterate enemy of Anne Boleyn and this needs to be taken into account when reading his work.
13. Ives, *Anne Boleyn*.
14. Denny, *Anne Boleyn*.
15. *Letters and Papers, Henry VIII*, Vol. X, this entry testifies to Anne's weakness after the final miscarriage which would have prevented her leaving Greenwich with Henry.
16. Robert Hutchinson, *Thomas Cromwell, the Rise and Fall of Henry VIII's Most Notorious Minister*, for the letter from Wolsey to Cromwell of July 1530. (Also in B.L. Cotton Mss, Appendix XLVIII, Fol. 25.)
17. Hutchinson, *Thomas Cromwell*. Also, Neville Williams, *The Cardinal and the Secretary* (1975) and Roger Merriman, *The Life and Letters of Thomas Cromwell* (1902), for the letter from Cromwell to Wolsey threatening him to make no fuss about the loss of his colleges, which had caused Wolsey great grief.
18. Starkey, *Six Wives*. Jane's family had obviously learned from Anne's earlier example that Jane's maidenly demeanour was one of her attractions for Henry.

19. Hutchinson, *Thomas Cromwell*, referring to the change of rooms that Cromwell agreed to in order to allow Jane to live nearer the King, to facilitate private meetings, while continuing the pretence that she was still virginal.
20. It is a pity that Cromwell did not think to use Anne's example of life in other ways. In her early years with Henry and secure in his affection she had doubtless felt the same. She was brave enough to challenge anyone, even Queen Katherine. At that stage of his career, Cromwell must also have felt the euphoria of invincibility, believing that the King's need of his services would guarantee his security. He should have remembered Henry's casual discarding of Wolsey, Katherine and then Anne, who had also been highly favoured by him in the past. Cromwell did not remember it, or heed the warning. Henry never personally liked him enough to support him indefinitely. Even in his 'successful' days, Henry was often impatient with him, and berated him openly, which showed his complete disregard for his minister's dignity. He would dispose of him easily when he failed to please.
21. Denny, *Anne Boleyn*. The accusations listed against the religious houses were often discussed, and even written out, by the commissioners, as fact, before arrival. The extensive lands and still considerable wealth of Fountains Abbey, for instance, was the irresistible lure, rather than any supposed 'sins'. It is ridiculous to believe that every single religious house in the country was a den of iniquity, or rife with sexual shenanigans. Many of the religious were devout and many were actually elderly, as the religious fervour of earlier years had slackened off. The aged and undoubtedly scholarly Abbot of Jervaulx was entirely innocent of the charges brought against him, but all evidence in his defence was discounted, and he was hanged. It is a great mistake to allow basic common sense or basic justice to be subjugated to personal bias.
22. There is a strong local belief that Richard III's destrier 'White Surrey' was bred at Jervaulx. The lovely Abbey was famous for its white horses, and the superb quality of its stud farms. These were a magnet for all the aristocratic youths in the area. It is very close to Middleham Castle and it is known that Richard often visited there. It is perfectly likely that he and his friends would have obtained their horses at the Abbey where they spent so much time.
23. *Letters and Papers, Henry VIII*, Vol. X, showed the pitiful remains of what had been Katherine of Aragon's possessions as Queen.
24. Bruce, *Anne Boleyn*. Also, *Letters and Papers, Henry VIII*, Vol. X. Anne Boleyn's household accounts show the order on 18 January 1536 for Elizabeth's measurements to be taken to London. The messenger was to be sent in a hired boat from Greenwich for the purpose.
25. *Letters and Papers, Henry VIII*, Vol. X.
26. Friedmann, *Anne Boleyn*, Vol. 2. No doubt Jane had been primed in her response to Henry, but she performed her part willingly, though she was aware of what the result of her mistress's downfall would be. Chapuys saw them primarily as a way of returning Princess Mary to favour.
27. Calendar State Papers, Spanish, Vol. V, also Friedmann, *Anne Boleyn*, Vol. II. Chapuys' support of the plot was crucial in convincing Henry that everyone approved of the changes. He believed that the position of the Princess Mary and the friendship of Spain itself could easily be restored once Anne was removed. There has been speculation among historians about Mary's involvement in the plot against Anne. It is certain that she still looked on Anne as the cause of all her grief, and believed that once she was gone all would be well. When Anne was removed Mary was to find to her dismay that it was not the case, and Henry swiftly disabused her of any notion that he would take her back into favour on her own terms. She eventually realised that it was not only Anne who had ruined her life, and she would be obliged to suffer appalling humiliation before being restored to her father's approval again.
28. Calendar State Papers, Spanish, Vol. V.
29. Friedmann, *Anne Boleyn*, Vol. V.
30. Chapuys to Emperor Charles V, 29 April 1536, Vienna Archives, P.C. 230, Fol. 78.

31. Bapst, *Two Gentleman Poets at the Court of Henry VIII*, refers to the thickening plot around Anne, Carewe's support (and subsequent tutoring of) Jane Seymour in her behaviour with Henry and also Eustace Chapuys' awareness of the danger then surrounding the Boleyns.
32. There is no other logical explanation that so fully accounts for the sudden rush to bring down the Boleyn faction, after Henry had wasted the whole springtime in hesitation. It is difficult to accept the 'assurances' of the Seymours that Jane and Henry were never alone together. That assertion was obviously merely to protect her reputation, which would have been fouled if she had openly been associating with the King. It was very much in the interests of the Seymours that Jane became pregnant by Henry, as it was the only sure way to effect the necessary marriage. Nor is it believable that Henry would have been tempted into the marriage if, after several months of intimacy, Jane still did not appear to have become pregnant. As he had been seeing her privately for some time, it is clear that he was waiting for her to prove with child, before he was prepared to make his final move. Henry's fickle nature was such that there was always the danger that he might be attracted by a different lady altogether, which would leave the Seymours, and incidentally Cromwell, who was then maritally allied to them, high and dry. To circumvent this possibility, it was necessary to 'pretend' that Jane had conceived, obviously with her connivance, in order to prod the King into action on her behalf. That the so-called pregnancy was indeed pretence is shown by the fact that there was no evidence of either a pregnancy for Jane at that time, or any subsequent miscarriage after her marriage to the King. Also the King's irritation with Jane, on more than one occasion, only a short time after their marriage, suggests that he had realised that he had been duped. Due to the deaths of Katherine of Aragon and Anne Boleyn within four months of each other, he was not in a position, immediately, to do more than hope the situation would right itself. Fortunately for the Seymours, it eventually did, with the birth of Prince Edward in late 1537.

Chapter 17

1. Bruce, *Anne Boleyn*. It is known that the supposed pre-contract of Anne and Henry Percy had first been considered as an expedient, but the Countess of Northumberland had tried it, and the Earl had denied ever having had any such contract. Cromwell must have been desperate to find a 'hook' on which to hang the case. It would certainly be considered treason for Anne to have slept with her own brother, thereby betraying not only her husband, but any possible succession.
2. The evidence provided was so shaky with regard to dates and places that at her trial Anne would be easily able to refute, from her own memory, many of the times when she was supposed to have been illicitly with men, simply by showing that her household was elsewhere. Some of the accusations were downright silly, in claiming for instance that she had done so while still pregnant, or had just delivered a child.
3. Fox, *Jane Boleyn*. There has been latterly some effort made to defend Jane Rochford and to rehabilitate her reputation, with a biography favourable to her. Unfortunately, it fails in its object. It ignores the important points rather than deals with them, as if in the hope that they would fade away. They will not. The facts are that she reported an 'unsuitable' relationship between Anne and George Boleyn, there was some salacious detail of them having been seen kissing in an intimate fashion, and they were duly accused of incest on the strength of it. Jane Rochford was not required to speak in court, or face the people she accused, merely signing a statement. She was then given preference by the King, recovered her place at court quite quickly, and when later executed with Queen Catherine Howard six years later, she admitted that she had lied.
4. Jane Rochford had already once been arrested with that disaffected member of the Howard clan Lady Mary. This could be taken as an indication that she was foolishly prepared to stick her neck out in order to embarrass her husband and his family, as well as to make her dislike plain.

5. This was the very fear that Anne claimed had caused her to miscarry. Certainly in the earliest part of the pregnancy all seemed to be proceeding normally and Anne was reported to have been 'well and merry'.
6. It is well recorded that Cromwell was still trying to build up the case against Anne when she was already in the Tower.
7. Why was that? Why was it considered that she would not be a satisfactory witness? Did they expect her to break down when faced with her victims, or change her mind if confronted? It is possible that Cromwell did not feel entirely secure with her evidence, although she was well rewarded for it. Her involvement in Catherine Howard and Thomas Culpeper's relationship may well show that she was unstable and could explain why she failed to 'fit in' with her married family.
8. This was Anne's anguished cry to Kingston when informed of the likely charges against her. But she obviously knew already that it was the one accusation almost impossible for any woman to refute successfully, especially for one whose reputation had already been spoiled (however unjustly) and when her prosecutors were not willing to accept her statements.
9. John Strype, *Life of Matthew Parker*, 3 vols (1821). W.P.M. Kennedy, *Archbishop Parker* (2008). He was devoted to Elizabeth for her mother's sake, but often found her difficult to work with, particularly in view of her dislike of married clergy. He was, however, a moderate, sensible and responsible man, and a good choice on Anne's part.
10. Douglas Boyd, *April Queen, Eleanor of Aquitaine* (2011). The courts of love were a tradition from the days of Queen Eleanor in which it was fashionable to pretend adoration and knightly loyalty to some other woman, usually one of higher rank. Poetry, small gifts and ardent signs of devotion were common, but it was never expected that the relationship should become intimate. It was probably an emotional release from the often loveless arranged marriages then common, but the declarations of undying affection had to be kept within bounds on both sides.
11. *Letters and Papers, Henry VIII*, Vol. X. Sir Henry Norris had been a close and trusted servant of Henry's since his youth. He was then Principal Gentleman of the Bedchamber and had the privilege of sleeping in Henry's room. He was also Keeper of the Privy Purse and the Groom of the Stole.
12. *Letters and Papers, Henry VIII*, Vol. X. Norris may have felt sorry for Anne at that time. He had been a loyal and close friend to her and to George, and had probably seen her in every mood, but by then she was like an animal at bay, angry, defensive and afraid. He little realised that he, and the other gentlemen, would be dragged down with the Boleyns.
13. 'Sad' often meant as serious or thoughtful. He may merely have been deep in thought.
14. The remark 'inferior person' would appear very offensive to any modern ear. In Anne's own time it was merely a mark of queenly courtesy that she should attempt to explain to him why she could not allow him the small favours (such as kissing her cheek) which the other gentlemen were allowed. In the sixteenth century the lines between the ranks were very firmly and clearly drawn, and Smeaton, though favoured in the Royal household, was still not of sufficient status to be allowed intimacies.
15. *Letters and Papers, Henry VIII*, Vol. X. That the proposed visit was cancelled without any explanation having been given to the Queen was an insult, and she was very concerned by it. So much so, that she attempted to speak with Henry privately.
16. John Foxe, *The Actes and Monuments of John Foxe*, ed. G. Townsend and S. Cattley (1975 edn). Also, *Letters and Papers, Henry VIII*, Vol. X. Also quoted in full in Denny, *Anne Boleyn*, Alexander Aless' report to Queen Elizabeth regarding his witnessing of Anne, carrying Elizabeth, attempting to reason with Henry VIII on Sunday, 30 April 1536. Henry rejected Anne's pleas angrily and we know now that the plot against her was already prepared. Henry, never liking to be placed in an embarrassing situation, would not have wished to speak with her when her future was already planned.

284 Tudor Victims

17. Elizabeth's reluctance to discuss her mother's death did not mean that she had no feeling for her. We know that she wore a ring containing enamelled portraits of Anne and herself, she used Anne's personal falcon badge as a device and Anne's black and white jousting colours were the tournament livery for Elizabeth's Champion. She frequently also used the symbolic phoenix device, both pictorially and in goldwork, representing herself as the phoenix rising from the ashes of her mother's death. There is extant a gold pendant showing Elizabeth, the phoenix and on the reverse the initials AB. Though drawing her queenship from her father, she often proudly referred to herself as 'pure English' due to her mother's descent.
18. The *Cronico del Rey Enrico Ottavo da Inglaterra* claims that a knotted rope was used to torture Mark Smeaton. George Constantine, one of Sir Henry Norris' servants, reported, 'the saying is that he was first grievously racked, which I could never know of as a truth' (G. Constantine, 'Memorial of Thomas Lord Cromwell', *Archaeologia*, ed. Thomas Amyot (1831)). The truth of how much torture was used to persuade Smeaton to speak against Anne is not known. The other accused, being gentlemen, were not tortured, and refused to say anything against her.
19. Hall, *The Triumphant Reign of King Henry VIII*, for the report that a bewildered Anne had asked why Henry had left so suddenly.
20. Hall, *The Triumphant Reign of King Henry VIII*.
21. *Letters and Papers, Henry VIII*, Vol. X, for Anne's recorded words on entering the Tower as a prisoner.
22. Cavendish, *Thomas Wolsey*, for the system whereby Anne's words and attitude would be reported back in detail to Cromwell.
23. Cavendish, *Thomas Wolsey*, for Anne's nervous talk on the Tuesday night in the Tower, when the ladies in attendance encouraged her to speak, in the hope she would implicate herself.
24. Bruce, *Anne Boleyn*, for the letter from Anne Boleyn to Lady Shelton regarding the intransigence of the Princess Mary.
25. Friedmann, *Anne Boleyn*, Vol. II.
26. Sergeant, *Anne Boleyn*, for Boynton's letter to Fitzwilliam.
27. Bishop Gilbert Burnet, *History of the Reformation of the Church of England*, 7 vols, ed. N. Pocock (1865). Also, Lord Herbert of Cherbury confirmed Burnet's findings regarding Anne's expenditure on her charities.
28. Sergeant, *The Life of Anne Boleyn*, regarding the letter from Sir Henry Wyatt to Cromwell, and that Thomas Wyatt's name (like that of Sir Richard Page another gentleman of the Privy Chamber) was entirely absent from the Indictments.
29. Friedmann, *Anne Boleyn*, Vol. II, Letter from Chapuys to Charles V, 19 May 1536.

Chapter 18
1. *Letters and Papers, Henry VIII*, Vol. X. Also quoted by Alison Weir, *Lady in the Tower, the Fall of Anne Boleyn* (2009), regarding the discussion of the case with the proposed jury.
2. Quoted by Weir, *Lady in the Tower* from the *Bag of Secrets* now in The National Archives. Translated by Glen Lucas, the *Bag of Secrets* gives full details of the twenty-one offences cited. The *Bag of Secrets* (1499–1537) are the indictments and documents relating to State trials (TNA KB/2).
3. Sir Thomas Wyatt's grandson, Henry, was always convinced that his grandfather carried a torch for Queen Anne. Thomas Wyatt had married young, as was expected, and his wife was Elizabeth Brooke, the daughter of Lord Cobham. They had produced four sons. They had long been separated due to the alleged adultery of Elizabeth Brooke and Sir Thomas was left relatively free to pursue his own life at court. Although the King had made his interest in the young Anne Boleyn plain, and Thomas Wyatt had very wisely retreated, a bond had remained.
4. *Lisle Letters*, ed. Muriel St Clair Byrne (1936), Vol. III, No. 694, 12 May 1536, John Husee to Lord Lisle. 'Mr Page and Mr. Wyatt are in the Tower, it is said without danger of death,

but Mr. Page is banished the King's presence at court.' *Lisle Letters*, Vol. 3, No. 695, 13 May 1536, John Husee to Lord Lisle. 'Some say that Wyatt and Page are as like to suffer as the others … in any case if any do escape it shall be young Weston for whose life there is importunate suit made …'. Certainly, Weston's distraught mother and wife, Anne Pickering, had tried to persuade Cromwell and the King to accept a money payment for his life, but it was rejected. Francis Weston and Anne Pickering had a young son.

5. *Letters and Papers, Henry VIII*, Vol. X.
6. Lancelot de Carles, Paris Biblio. Nat., Mss Fr. 1742 and 2370, letter containing the criminal trial of Queen Anne Boleyn of England, 1536.
7. *Cronico del Rey Enrico Ottavo da Inglaterra*, or *Spanish Chronicle*, ed. Hume (1889).
8. Calendar State Papers, Spanish, Vol. V, Chapuys to Charles V.
9. Lancelot de Carles, Paris Biblio. Nat., Mss Fr. 1742 and 2370.
10. *Letters and Papers, Henry VIII*, Vol. X (January–June 1536). To modern eyes it seems unnecessarily cruel for Thomas Boleyn to be made to take part in the proceedings against his son and daughter. In the sixteenth century his presence would be required to show not only that he was personally innocent of any involvement, but that he deplored the conduct of his relatives. Whether he believed the charges against them, or even whether he had much paternal affection for them, the appearance cannot have been other than extremely painful for him.
11. Friedmann, *Anne Boleyn*, Vol. II. The list of the jury members showed a frightening example of the case being prejudiced before the accused before it even started.
12. Ives, *Anne Boleyn*, and also Francis Hackett, *Henry the Eighth* (1929). Lord Dacre had fallen into dispute with the Earl of Northumberland in 1534. He was tried for treason by his peers, but they had the courage to acquit him. Although the King was very displeased at the way the matter had gone, he was hardly likely to have been as personally involved as he later was with the case against his wife.
13. Ives, *Anne Boleyn*, for description of the trial of the gentlemen on 12 May 1536.
14. *Lisle Letters*, Vol. III, No. 695, 13 May 1536, John Husee to Lord Lisle.
15. *Letters and Papers, Henry VIII*, Vol. X, regarding the provisions made for dividing the estates of the victims, 14 May 1536.
16. *Lisle Letters*, Vol. III, No. 695, 13 May 1536, John Husee to Lord Lisle.
17. Calendar State Papers, Spanish, Vol. V, Charles V to Chapuys, 15 May 1536.
18. Friedmann, *Anne Boleyn*, Vol. II.
19. Friedmann, Vol. II. The surviving trial documents, which are incomplete, are in the *Bag of Secrets*, Pouch 9, in The National Archives.
20. Ives, *The Life and Death of Anne Boleyn*.
21. *Letters and Papers, Henry VIII*, Vol. X.
22. Wriothesley, *A Chronicle of England*.
23. Harleian Mss, British Library.
24. *Letters and Papers, Henry VIII*, Vol. X. No doubt the prosecutors were already disconcerted by the response of the audience to Anne's clear and sensible refutation of the charges and decided that the sooner the matter was concluded the better.
25. Weir, *Lady in the Tower*.
26. David Loades, *Henry VIII and his Queens* (1994).
27. *Letters and Papers, Henry VIII*, Vol. X. The Act of Succession of March 1534 had made Anne Boleyn Queen by statutory right, so that although her lesser titles were taken from her, and she was divorced from Henry, she was still technically Queen until her death. This was one of the reasons why she had to die – he could not have two ladies legally referred to as Queen of England.
28. Friedmann, *Anne Boleyn*, Vol. II, letter of 19 May 1536, Chapuys to Charles V.
29. Friedmann, *Anne Boleyn*, Vol. II, letter of 19 May 1536, Chapuys to Charles V.
30. Friedmann, *Anne Boleyn*, Vol. II.

286   Tudor Victims

31. In actual fact, the subsequent illegitimacy of both the Princesses Mary and Elizabeth would actually put the King's son, Henry Fitzroy (Duke of Richmond), ahead of them both in the succession. He had been illegitimate all along, but then had the benefit of being male, which gave him precedence.
32. Excerpt from Thomas Wyatt's poem '*Circa Regna Tonat*' ('Around the Throne Thunder Rolls'). This makes clear that he watched from the Bell Tower while Lord Rochford and the others went to their deaths on Tower Hill.
33. *Chronicle of Calais in the Reigns of Henry VII and Henry VIII to 1540*, ed. J.G. Nichols, Camden Society (1846).
34. *Lisle Letters*, Vol. III, No. 698, 19 May 1536, John Husee to Lord Lisle.
35. Friedmann, *Anne Boleyn*, Vol. II.
36. *Letters and Papers, Henry VIII*, Vol. X (January–June 1536), Sir William Kingston to Cromwell, 18 May 1536. The timing of this letter shows that although Anne was told that she would die on 18 May, it had not actually been intended that she should do so. Cromwell probably hoped that if the crowds gathered on the wrong day, they would become discouraged and leave before the execution of the Queen took place.
37. Sir William Kingston to Cromwell, 18 May 1536.
38. Robert Hutchinson, *Thomas Cromwell, The Rise and Fall of Henry VIII's Most Notorious Minister* (2008).
39. This may be apocryphal, along with the story that she asked Lady Kingston to visit the Princess Mary to beg her forgiveness on Anne's behalf after her death.
40. Ives, *Anne Boleyn*, regarding the area known as East Smithfield Green being the actual place of Queen Anne's execution.
41. John Strype, *Ecclesiastical Memoirs* (1820–40). His remarks about Queen Anne on 19 May were certainly made much later, when her story had become a romance rather than a tragedy. However, Lancelot de Carles had said at the time of her death that 'her face and complexion had never looked more beautiful' and the Portuguese witnesses at her death also said, 'Never had the Queen looked more beautiful!', *Excerpta Historica*, ed. Bentley and Nichols (1831).
42. Ives, *Anne Boleyn*.
43. John Spelman, *The Reports of John Spelman*, ed. J.H. Baker (1976–7).
44. *Letters and Papers, Henry VIII*, Vol. X. Also Anthony Anthony and the Imperial accounts say that the box in which Anne's body was eventually laid was not present at the scaffold when she arrived, as it had been intended to go to Ireland. On the other hand, an Italian account states that it was waiting and ready for her execution.
45. *Letters and Papers, Henry VIII*, Vol. X.
46. *Lisle Letters*, Vol. III, No. 698, 19 May 1536, John Husee to Lord Lisle.
47. Quoted by Weir, *Lady in the Tower*.

Epilogue
1. Hutchinson, *Thomas Cromwell*, regarding the death by beheading suffered by Cromwell on 28 July 1540. Gurrea the Headsman is said to have botched the execution and had to chop several times at the neck before succeeding in beheading the victim.
2. Calendar State Papers, Venetian, Vol. V.
3. On 12 October 1537 Jane Seymour died. She probably suffered from puerperal fever, which is an infection common at the time, when hygiene was less regarded and the woman in childbirth very often a victim.
4. Chris Skidmore, *Edward VI, The Lost King of England* (2008).
5. Henry's difficulties in finding a fourth bride are well known and well documented. It is only due to a friendship between France and Spain that he found himself obliged to settle for a marriage with the Princess Anne of Cleves, which was a miserable failure within six months.
6. The King died on 28 January 1547.

7. Perry, *Sisters to the King*, regarding the brief reign of Lady Jane Grey who was the granddaughter of Henry VIII's sister Mary, one-time Queen of France.
8. Prescott, *Mary Tudor*.
9. Somerset, *Elizabeth I*, for details of the difficult youth and triumphant reign of Anne's daughter, who proved to be one of the greatest of England's rulers.

Select Bibliography

Manuscript Sources
British Museum:
Additional Mss 28587, Fol. 207
Calendar State Papers of Queen Elizabeth I
Calendar State Papers, Spanish, Vols III to V (1527–38)
Calendar State Papers, Venetian, Vols III to V (1520–36)
Cotton Mss Nero B.III, Fol. 105
Cotton Mss Appendix XLVIII, Fol. 25

Letters and Papers, Henry VIII, ed. J.S. Brewer and J. Gairdner: Vol. II (1515–18); Vol. III (1519–23); Vol. IV (1524–30); Vol. V (1531–2); Vol. VI (1533); Vol. VII (1534); Vol. VIII (January–July 1535); Vol. IX (August–December 1535); Vol. X (January–June 1536)

Paris Biblio. Nat.:
Mss Fr. 1742, 2370, 19,577
Mss Dupuis, Vol. 265
Mss Dupuis, Vol. 547, Fol. 200
Mss Dupuis, Vol. 547, Fol. 321
The National Archives, *Bag of Secrets*, Pouch 9
Vienna Archives, P.C. 228, 229, ½ Fol. 74, ½ Fol. 105, ½ Fol. 130, ½ Fol. 230

Primary Sources
Burnet Collectanea, Part 3, Book 11/23
Cavendish, George. *Thomas Wolsey, Late Cardinal, His Life and Death*, ed. Roger Lockyer, Folio Society (1962)
Chronicle of Calais in the Reigns of Henry VII and Henry VIII to 1540, ed. J.G. Nichols, Camden Society (1846)
Cronico del Rey Enrico Ottavo da Anglaterra, ed. M.A.S. Hume (1889) from the Marquis de Molins (1874)
Excerpta Historica, ed. S. Bentley and H. Nicolas (1831)
Foxe, John. *The Actes and Monuments of John Foxe*, ed. G. Townsend and S. Cattley (1975 edn)
Giustiniani, Francesco Sebastiano. *Four Years at the Court of Henry VIII*, trans. R.L. Brown (1854 rev. edn 1970)
Hall, Edward. *The Triumphant Reign of King Henry VIII*, ed. C. Whibley, T.C. Jack and E.C. Jack (1904)
Hall, Edward. *The Union of the Two Noble and Illustrious Families of York and Lancaster*, ed. H. Ellis. (1809)
The Harleian Miscellany: Or a Collection of Scarce, Curious and Entertaining Pamphlets and Tracts, ed. William Oldys and Thomas Park (1744), Vol. III
Herbert, Edward (Lord Herbert of Cherbury). *The Life and Reign of King Henry VIII* (1649)
Household Expenses of the Princess Elizabeth at Hatfield, ed. Viscount Strangford, Camden Miscellany (1853)
Letters of King Henry VIII, ed. Muriel St Clair Byrne (1936)
Letters of Royal and Illustrious Ladies of Great Britain, ed. M.A.E. Wood, 3 vols (1846)
Lisle Letters, ed. Muriel St Clair Byrne, 6 vols (1981), Vol. III

Love Letters of Henry VIII, ed. Jasper Ridley (1988)
Original Letters Illustrative of English History, ed. H. Ellis (1846)
Paston Letters, ed. James Gairdner (repr. 1986)
Sander, Nicholas. *The Rise and Growth of the Anglican Schism*, ed. D. Lewis (1877)
Spelman, Sir John. *Reports of Sir John Spelman*, ed. J.H. Baker, Seldon Society (1976–7)
Strype, John. *Ecclesiastical Memoirs* (1820–40)
Strype, John. *Historical and Biographical Works* (1812–28)
Strype, John. *Life of Matthew Parker*, 3 vols (1821)
Strype, John. *Memorials of Thos Cranmer, Archbishop of Canterbury* (1694), Oxford Ecclesiastical Society (1848–54)
Vergil, Polydore. *Anglia Historia 1485–1537*, trans. D. Hay, Camden Series, RHS (1950)
Worde, Wynkyn de. *The Noble and Tryumphant Coronacyon of Quene Anne* (1533)
Wriothesley, Charles. *A chronicle of England in the Reigns of the Tudors, 1485–1559*, ed. W. Douglas Hamilton, Camden Society (1875–7)
Wyatt, George. 'Extracts from the Life of the Virtuoius, Christian and Renowned Queen Anne Boleigne', *in George Cavendish*, Life of Wolsey, ed. S.W. Singer (1825)
Wyatt, George. *Papers of George Wyatt Esquire*, ed. David Loades, RHS (1968)
Wyatt, Sir Thomas. *Collected Poems of Sir Thomas Wyatt*, ed. J. Daalder (1975), excerpts of 'Whoso List to Hunt' and '*Cirga Regna Tonat*'

Secondary Sources
Bapst, Edmond. *Two Gentlemen at the Court of Henry VIII. George Boleyn and Henry Howard* ed. C. Ridgeway (2013)
Bindoff, S.C. *Tudor England* (1950)
Boyd, Douglas. *April Queen, Eleanor of Aquitaine* (2011)
Brandl, Karl. *The Emperor Charles V and the Growth of Destiny of a Man and a World Empire* (1939)
Brewer, J.S. *The Reign of Henry VIII from his Accession to the Death of Wolsey*, 2 vols (1884), Vol. II
Brigdon, Susan. *New Worlds, Lost Worlds. The Rule of the Tudors (1485–1503)* (2000)
Bruce, Marie Louise. *Anne Boleyn* (1972)
Burke, S.H. *Historical Portraits of the Tudor Dynasty Vol. I* (1893)
Burnet, Bishop Gilbert. *History of the Reformation of the Church of England* 7 vols, ed. N. Pocock (1865)
Chamberlin, Frederick. *The Private Character of Henry VIII* (1932)
Chambers' Biographical Dictionary
Chambers, D.S. 'Cardinal Wolsey and the Papal Tiara', BIHR XXVIII (1965)
Chapman, Hester W. *Anne Boleyn* (1974)
Chapman, Hester W. *The Last Tudor King, Study of Edward VI* (1958)
Colvin, H.M. *The History of the King's Works, 1485–1660 (Part I)* (1963–82)
De Lisle, Leanda. *The Sisters Who Would be Queen* (2009)
Denny, Joanna. *Anne Boleyn* (2005)
Denny, Joanna. *Katherine Howard* (2008)
Dent, John. *The Quest for Nonsuch* (1981)
Dickens, A.G. *The English Reformation* (1964)
Duffy, Eamon. *Saints and Sinners – a History of the Popes* (1997)
Erickson, Carolly. *Anne Boleyn* (1984)
Erickson, Carolly. *Great Harry, the Extravagant Life of Henry VIII* (2004)
Evans, Victoria Sylvia. *Ladies in Waiting: the Women Who Served the Tudor Court* (2014)
Fergusen, Charles. *Naked to Mine Enemies, The Life of Cardinal Wolsey* (1958)
Fisher, H.A.L. *The History of England from the Accession of Henry VII to the Death of Henry VIII* (1934)

Fox, Julia. *Jane Boleyn, the Infamous Lady Rochford* (2007)
Fraser, Antonia. *Six Wives of Henry VIII* (1992)
Friedmann, Paul. *Anne Boleyn – A Chapter of English History (1527–1536)*, 2 vols (1884)
Froude, J.A. *The Divorce of Katherine of Aragon* (1891)
Gasquet, Cardinal Francis Aidan. *The Eve of the Reformation* (1900)
Gasquet, Cardinal Francis Aidan. *Henry VIII and the English Monasteries* (1925)
Gaunt, Dr Peter. *Hampton Court Palace* (1988)
Grove, J. *The History of the Life and Times of Cardinal Wolsey* (1746)
Gunn, S.J. *Charles Brandon, Duke of Suffolk 1484–1545* (1988)
Guy, J.A. *The Cardinal's Court* (1977)
Gwyn, Peter. *The King's Cardinal – The Rise and Fall of Thomas Wolsey* (1990)
Hackett, Francis. *Henry the Eighth* (1929)
Hall, Edward. *Hall's Chronicle* (1809)
Harpsfield, N. *The Life and Death of Thomas More, Knight*, Early English Text Society (1932)
Harthan, John. *Books of Hours* (1977)
Hempel, Sandra. *The Inheritor's Powder* (2013)
Hutchinson, Robert. *House of Treason. The Rise and Fall of a Tudor Dynasty* (2009)
Hutchinson, Robert. *The Last Days of Henry VIII* (2006)
Hutchinson, Robert. *Thomas Cromwell, the Rise and Fall of Henry VIII's Most Notorious Minister* (2008)
Hutchinson, Robert. *Young Henry, the Rise of Henry VIII* (2012)
Ives, E.W. *Anne Boleyn* (1986)
Ives, E.W. *Life and Death of Anne Boleyn, the Most Happy* (2004)
Jones, Michael K. *Bosworth 1485 – Psychology of a Battle* (2002)
Kendall, Paul M. *Richard III* (1955)
Kennedy, W.P.M. *Archbishop Parker* (2008)
Knowles, D. 'The Matter of Wilton in 1528', IHR, XXXI (1958)
Law, Ernest. *England's First Great War Minister* (1916)
Loades, David. *The Boleyns – Rise and Fall of a Tudor Family* (2012)
Loades, David. *Catherine Howard* (2012)
Loades, David. *The Chronicle of the Tudor Queens of England* (2009)
Loades, David. *Henry VIII* (2011)
Loades, David. *Henry VIII and his Queens* (1994)
Loades, David. *Six Wives of Henry VIII* (1996)
Lofts, Norah. *Anne Boleyn* (1979)
Lofts, Norah. *Queens of Britain* (1977)
McCullough, Diarmid. *Cranmer – Thomas Cranmer, a Life* (1996)
Marius, Richard. *Thomas More* (1984)
Mathew, David. *The Courtiers of Henry VIII* (1970)
Mattingly, Garrett. *Catherine of Aragon* (1944)
Merriman, Roger. *The Life and Letters of Thomas Cromwell* (1902)
Morris, Sarah and Grueninger, Natalie. *In the Footsteps of Anne Boleyn* (2013)
Mumby, F.A. *The Youth of Henry VIII. A Narrative in Comtemporary Letters* (1913)
Murphy, Beverley A. *Bastard Prince, Henry VIII's Lost Son* (2001)
O'Donaghue, E.G. *Bridewell Hospital and Palace* (1923)
Parmiter, Geoffrey de. C. *The King's Great Matter* (1967)
Paul, J.E. *Catherine of Aragon and her Friends* (1966)
Perry, Maria. *Sisters to the King* (1998)
Plowden, Alison. *The House of Tudor* (1998)
Pollard, A.F. *Henry VIII* (1951)
Pollard, A.F. *Wolsey* (1929)

Porter, Linda. *Katherine the Queen, The Remarkable Life of Katherine Parr* (2010)
Porter, Linda. *Mary Tudor* (2007)
Prescott, H.F.M. *Mary Tudor – the Spanish Tudor* (2003)
Rex, Richard. 'The Execution of the Holy Maid of Kent', IHR, Vol. 64 (1991)
Richardson, W. *Mary Tudor, the White Queen* (1970)
Ridley, Jasper. *Cranmer* (1962)
Ridley, Jasper. *Statesman and Saint. Cardinal Wolsey and Sir Thomas More and the Politics of Henry VIII* (1982)
Ridley, Jasper. *Thomas Cromwell* (1962)
Russell, Joycelyne Gledhill. *The Field of the Cloth of Gold* (1969)
Scarisbrick, J.J. *Henry VIII* (1968)
Sergeant, Philip W. *Anne Boleyn – A Study* (1934)
Sergeant, Philip W. *The Life of Anne Boleyn* (1924)
Shakespeare, J. and Dowling, M. 'Religion and Politics in mid-Tudor England', IHR, Vol. 55 (1982)
Skidmore, Chris. *Edward VI, the Lost King of England* (2008)
Smith, Lacey Baldwin. *A Tudor Tragedy – the Life and Times of Catherine Howard* (1962)
Somerset, Anne. *Elizabeth I* (1991)
Stapleton, T. *The Life and Illustrious Martyrdom of Sir Thomas More* (1928)
Starkey, David. *Henry, Virtuous Prince* (2008)
Starkey, David. *The Reign of Henry VIII, Personalities and Politics* (1985)
Starkey, David. *Six Wives – The Queens of Henry VIII* (2003)
Tremlett, Giles. *Catherine of Aragon, Henry's Spanish Queen* (2010)
Walsh, Michael. *History of the Popes* (1980)
Warnicke, Retha. *The Rise and Fall of Anne Boleyn* (1987)
Weir, Alison. *Henry VIII, King and Court* (2001)
Weir, Alison. *The Lady in the Tower, the Fall of Anne Boleyn* (2009)
Weir, Alison. *Mary Boleyn, the Great and Infamous Whore* (2011)
Weir, Alison. *Six Wives of Henry VIII* (1991)
Wilkinson, Josephine. *Anne Boleyn, the Young Queen-to-be* (2011)
Wilkinson, Josephine. *Mary Boleyn, the True Story of Henry VIII's Favourite Mistress* (2009)
Williams, Neville. *The Cardinal and the Secretary* (1975)
Youings, Joyce. *The Dissolution of the Monasteries* (1971)

Index

Locators in **bold** indicate pictures

A supplication for beggars (Fish), 94
Abbess of St Edith
  and the Abbess of St Edith appointment, 87
  condenders for post as, 85–7
Abbey of Jervaulx, 212
Abbot of Cirencester, 235
Abbot of St Albans, 58
Abbot of Winchcombe, 40
Abell, Thomas, 93
Abergavenny, Lord, 34
Act in Restraint of Appeals, 140
Act of Attainder, 161, 191
  victims of, 160
Act of Succession, 166, 172–3, 177, *see also* Oath to the Succession
Act of Supremacy, 245
Adrian VI (pope), 58, 61
Agostini, Dr, 111–12, 115
  testimony of, 116
Alen, Sir Thomas, 38
Aless, Alexander, 225
Alexander VI (pope), 172
Amicable Loan, 67–8
Anglo-Irish Earl of Ormonde, 14
Anne of Britanny, 30
Anne of Cleves, Princess, 182, 255
apprentices, riots, 42
Archbishop of Canterbury, 5, 7
Archbishop of York, 37
Arthur, Prince, 7, 15, 17
assets list, of condemned, 239
Audley, Thomas, 128, 241, 249

Bag of Secrets, 241
Bainbridge, Christopher, 26–8, 56
Barnes, Robert, 197, 239
Barton, Elizabeth, 157, 166
  High Treason claims against, 160–1
Battle of Bosworth, 72
Battle of Flodden, 20–1
Battle of Stoke, 4
Beal, Dr, 42
Beaufort, Eleanor, 66
Beaufort, Lady Margaret, 2, 63, 153, 172
Becket, Thomas à, 40
Belknap, Sir Edward, 47
Bell, Dr John, 86
Bellay, Cardinal du, 106, 109, 190
Benet, Thomas, 86, 125–6, 139
Bergavenny, Lord, 41
Bills of Succession, 160
Bishop of Lincoln, 27

Bishop of Lydda, 5
Bishop of Tournai, 27
Bishop of Winchester, 10
Blackfriars Court, 142
Blackfriars Stairs, 97
Blakeney, Robert, 182
Blount, Elizabeth, 21, 24–5, 36, 46, 64, 69
Bocking, Dr Edward, 161
Boleyn, Anne, 49–50, 122
  accusations against, 123–4
  assumed role as queen, 141–2
  and Blackfriars trial, 101
  coronation of, 143–50
  education at court, 33
  and Harry Percy, 59–60, 128–9
  and Henry VIII, 69, 84
    physical relationship with, 134–5
  Henry VIII (king) and divorce, 91
  illness of, 85–6
  love letters of, 106
  marriage proposal and, 56
  power of, 110
  pregnancy of, 139–40, 143
  and Princess Mary, 32–3
  return to England, 58
  and Thomas Wolsey, 60, 94–6, 101–3, 105–6, 111–14
  title given to, 132–3
Boleyn, Anne (queen), **12**, 13–14, 16, 22–3
  accusations against, 221–2, 227
  arrest/imprisonment, 228–31
  confinement, 153–4
  divorce and, 183
  education at court, 18–19
  execution of, 250–1
  letter to Princess Mary, 206
  marital problems, 206–7
  marriage of, 159
  plots against, 209, 216–20
  pregnancy of, 160, 188, 206–8
  as queen, 162–5, 208–9
  as a reformer, 181
  religion of, 181
  and Sir Thomas More, 193–4
  trial of, 235, 241–4
  views about, 161–2, 183–4, 256
Boleyn, Edmund, 13
Boleyn, Elizabeth, 17
Boleyn, Geoffrey, 14
Boleyn, George (Lord Rochford), 13–14, 16, 53, 55, 65, 76, 102, 155, 177–8, 180–1, 219–21
  charges against, 245

children and, 73
  illness of, 85–6
  marriage of, 63
Boleyn, James, 142
Boleyn, Lady Elizabeth, 13
Boleyn, Mary, 13–14, 22, 32, 36, 66, 163–4, 182
  children of, 66, 156
  and Princess Mary, 33
Boleyn, Sir James, 229
Boleyn, Sir Thomas, 13
Boleyn, Thomas, 14–15, 17–19, 22, 63
  as Ambassador, 18
  bestowal of honours on, 65
  and Princess Mary, 35
  and Thomas Wolsey, 97–8
Boleyn, Thomas (brother), 13
Boleyn, Thomas (Earl of Wiltshire and Ormonde), 13
Boleyn/Butler inheritance, 13
Boleyn family, 13–15
  accusations against, 222
Bonner, Dr, 115, 159
Bosworth Field, 3
Bourbon, Nicholas, 181
Boynton, Sir Edward, 142
Bradgate Park, Leicester, 4
Brandon, Charles (Duke of Suffolk), 22, 32–3, 110, 177
Bray, Reginald, 5, 10
Brereton, Sir William, 41, 76, 155, 226–7
Brewer, J.S., 58
Bryan, Sir Francis, 36, 43, 65, 162, 178, 214, 239
Bucer, Martin, 125
Bude, 48
Bull of Excommunication and Deprivation, 200
Bull of Julius II, 80
Bulmer, Sir William, 41
Burgh, Lord, 142
Burgundian ducal court, 18
Burnet, Bishop, 232
Bursar of Magdalen, 4
Butler, James, 59, 128
Butler, Margaret, 14
Butler, Piers, 16, 56
Butts, Dr, 109, 119, 181, 186

Calais, Governor of, 7–8
Calais Conference, 18, 54–5, 58
Calvin, John, 182
Campeggio, Cardinal, 61, 84–5, 87, 89–90, 92–3, 104–5
  Legatine Court, 98
Capon, William, 114
Cardinal Bainbridge, 27
Cardinal's Hat, 27, 37
Carewe, Nicholas, 36, 43, 66, 185–6, 214
Carey, Dame Eleanor, 86–7
Carey, George (2nd Lord Hunsdon), 13
Carey, Henry, 181
Carey, Katherine, 182
Carey, Mary (née Boleyn), 13, 86, 133, 156, 245,
  see also Boleyn, Mary
Carey, William, 65–6, 76, 85, 181

Carles, Lancelot de, 208, 251
Carthusian Priors, 173
  execution of, 191, 198
Casale, Sir Gregory, 121, 125, 190–1
Castile, 9
Castile, Isabella of, 69
Castillon, de, 159
Cavendish, George, 26, 29, 79, 81, 98, 105–7, 115–16
celibacy, 6
Cellini, Benvenuto, 48
Ceri, Renzo de, 78
Chabot, Admiral, 175, 178–9, 185
Chancellor of England, 5
Chapuys, Eustace, 107, 110–11, 114, 116, 120, 122–3, 126, 139, 164
  and Anne Boleyn, 124, 208–9
  concerns, 233
  criticisms of, 174–5
  and Henry VIII, 168–9
  popularity of, 200
  warning given to, 142–3
Charles (Archduke), 10, 22
Charles V (emperor), 9, 18, 44, 51, 54, 58, 61, 66–8, 74, 78, 107, 110, 120, 130, 178, 202, 204
  and Henry VIII, relationship between, 195, 214–15
  and Henry VIII's divorce, 112
  marriage proposal and, 55
  and the Papacy, 170
  report on Katherine's death, 205
  visit to England, 59
Charles of Castile, 32
Cheyney, Sir Thomas, 239
Christian, Duke, 197
Christian of Schleswick-Holstein, 196
Church, the, 5–6, 40
Church of England, 173, 179, 192–3
Claude (princess), 30
Claude (queen), 14, 33–4, 48–50, 74
Clement VII (Pope), 61–2, 79, 92, 110, 170–1
  acceptance of, 77–8
  and of Henry VIII, 84
  and Henry VIII's divorce, 112, 122, 125–6, 137, 158–9
  illness of, 94
clergy, the, papal decree and, 40
Clerk, John, 78–9
Clifford, Henry, 124
Cobham, Lord, 154
Cobham, Nan, 222
Coffin, Mistress, 229
Coffin, Sir William, 43, 142
Colet, John, 39–40
College of Cardinals, 57–8
  Italianisation of, 58
College of St Mary Magdalen, 2
Colonna, Cardinal Pompeo, 78
comet, appearance of, 1
Compton, 36
Compton, Sir William, 41, 65, 86
Constable, Sir Robert, 41
Constantine, George, arrest/imprisonment, 227

Convocation, 115
Convocation of Canterbury, 115, 122–3
Counter-Reformation, 172
Countess of Northumberland, 128–9
court, career at, 15–16
court access, 15
Court of Star Chamber, 41
Cranmer, Thomas, 102, 107, 109–10, 121, 131, 134–7, 158, 232
Cristina of Milan, 255
Cromwell, Geoffrey, 209
Cromwell, Thomas, 25, 103, 107, 114, 121–3, 128, 137, 155, 183–4, **234**, 235, 255
　alliance to Seymour family, 209–10
　spy system, 183, 186, 222
Cronico Del Rey Enrico Ottavo da Anglaterra, 226
Curwen, Dr Richard, 127
Cyfuentes, 167

Dacre, Lord Thomas, 41, 238
d'Albret, Henry, 54
d'Angoulême, Duke, 178
de Carles, 19
De la Sa, Dr, 203
de' Medici, Giulio, 61, 77
De Mesa, Bishop of Elne, 35, 39
Dean of Divinity, 6
Dean of Lincoln, 10
Dean of Windsor, 31
Deane, Henry (Archbishop), 7
Decretal Commission, 84
Defender of the Faith, 51
Denmark, relationship with, 197–9
Denonville, Charles de, 190
Dering, John, 161
determiner, 3
Dinteville, de, 159, 197–8
Dissolution of the Monasteries, 210–11
divorce
　and Henry VIII (king), 78–80
　and legitimacy of children, 90–1
Docwra, Sir Thomas, 31
Doge and Signory of Venice, 125
Doge of Venice, 46
Dormer, Jane, 208
Douglas, Archibald, 104
Douglas, Lady Margaret, 91, 104
Dowager Countess of Willoughby, 204
du Bellay, Jean, 14
Duchess of Norfolk, 35
Dudley, John, 154
Dudley, Robert, 182
Duke of Angoulême, 187
Duke of Buckingham, 41
Duke of Norfolk, 53, 128, 159, 176, 184, 228
Duke of Richmond, 184, 230, 249
Duke of Suffolk, 155, 204
Dunstable Court, 142
Duprat, Cardinal, 157

Earl of Northumberland, 41, 115
Earl of Ormonde, 13, 15

Earl of Ossory, 16
Earl of Shrewsbury, 38, 116, 128
Earl of Surrey, 61
Earl of Wiltshire, 140–1
Earl of Worcester, 31
East Smithfield Green, 249
Edward II (king), 240
Edward IV (king), 1–2, 35
　illegitimate children of, 134
Edward VI (king), 254, 256
Eleanora of Austria, 74
Elizabeth (queen), 13, 164, 182
Elizabeth, Princess, 159–60, 175, 177, 194, 206, 256
　christening of, 155
　marriage proposal and, 168–9, 175, 186
Elizabeth of York, 21
Elizabeth of York (queen), 7, 10, 15
　Chamberlain to, 16
Empson, Richard, 25
England and France, relationship between, 34–5
England and Spain, relationship between, 35
English Commissioners, 187
England-France meeting, preparations for, 46–50
'English mare', 14
Executory Brief, 203–4

false pregnancy, 188
Farnese, Alessandro, 171
Farnese, Luigi, 200
Faversham, 7
Featherstone, Richard, 168
Fellow of Magdalen, 3
Ferdinand (king), 7, 9, 21, 26, 35, 63
Ferdinand of Aragon, 19–20
Field of the Cloth of Gold, 18, 46–7, 49–50, 132
Fish, Simon, *A supplication for beggars*, 94
Fisher, Bishop John, **96**, 97, 140–1, 157, 161, 172–3
　arrest/imprisonment, 188–9
　elevation of, 190
　execution of, 192
　risks to, 190–1
Fisher, Dr, 123, *see also* Fisher, Bishop
Fitzwilliam, Sir William, 110, 177, 180, 228
foreigners, in London, 42
Fox, Edward, 84
Foxe, Bishop of Exeter, 5
Foxe, Richard (Bishop of Winchester), 9–10, 24, 84
France, war with, 19–20, 58
Francis I, the Pope and, 77
Francis I (king), 14, 33, 39, 51, 54, 66–7, 121, 155, 177–8
　freedom of, 74
　and Henry VIII, relationship between, 44, 130, 134, 159, 185
　and Italy, 39
　and Mary Boleyn, 66
Francis of Angoulême, 21, 30, 32
　as king, 32–3
French pensions, 46
Friars Observant, arrest of, 167

Index

Gage, Sir John, 113
Gainsford, Anne, 142
Gardiner, Stephen, 82–3, 107, 110, 124, 133, 173, 195, 239
German Reformers, 197
Ghinucci, 125
Gigli, Sylvester de, 27, 28
Gilbert, Robert, 52–3
Giustiniani, Sebastiano, 19, 46, 57, 120
Gold, Henry, 161
Gontier, Palamede, 175, 180, 185, 187
Gravelines, 18
Great Seal, 106
Gregory VII (Pope), 6
Greville, Sir Richard, 195
Grey, Lady Jane, 256
Grey, Sir Henry, 41
Grey, Thomas (Marquess of Dorset), 4
Greyfriars, Warden of the, 40
Griffith, Master, 96
Grynee, Simon, 125
Guildford, Lady Jane, 31
Gwyn, Peter, *The King's Cardinal*, 2

Hadrian, Cardinal, 27
Hallingbury Morley, 63
Hampton Court Palace, 37–8, 43, 64, 112
Hankford family, 15
Hannibal, Thomas, 57, 61
Hastings, Brian, 41, 114
Hayes, Cornelius, 161
Heneage, Mr, 239
Henri, Prince), 158
Henry V (king), 26
Henry VII (king), 3–4, 8–10
Henry VIII (king), 3–4, 11, 14–16, 21, 28, 32, 56, 77, 85, **218**
   and Anne Boleyn, 66–72
   annulment wishes, 92
   and the Boleyn-Parker marriage, 63
   and Charles V (emperor), relationship between, 184, 195
   and Charles Brandon, 33–4
   and the Church of England, 123, 158, 179
   divorce and, 84–5, 121–2
      disapproval for, 126–7
      public reaction to, 89
   excommunication of, 152, 157
   financial needs of, 67–8
   and France, 19, 24–6
   and Francis I (king), 54
      relationship between, 44
   and Hampton Court Palace, 64
   health of, 207
   and the Holy League, 77
   illegitimate children of, 21, 46–7, 64–5, 182
   international relationships and, 196–9
   and Jane Seymour, 208–12
   and Katherine (queen), 124–5
      marriage annulment of, 142–3
   and the Legatine Court, 95–7
   and London rioters, 42–3
   and Louis XII, 21
   Manor of Grafton, 104
   mistresses of, 36
   Papal Bull against, 115
   Paul III (Pope) disapproval of, 197
   petition to the Pope, 110–11
   plans to dethrone, 195–7
   and the Pope, 158–9, 171
   proposed divorce of, 78–9
   and Protestants, 196
   succession concerns of, 64–5, 69, 108, 136
   threats of beheadings, 160
   visit to France, 133
Henry, Prince, 8
Henry Fitzroy, 66
   bestowal of honours on, 65
Henry of Richmond, 156
heresy, 51
Hervey, Sir Nicholas, 181
Hervey, Thomas, 181
Hever in Kent, 15
High Treason, claims of, 160
Hill, Richard, 161
History of the Reformation (Burnet), 124
Holbein, Hans, 12
Holinshed, 46
Holland, Elizabeth, 73, 142
Holy League, 26, 77
Holy Maid of Kent, 172
Holy Roman Emperor, 51
Hone, Galyon, 48
Hoo, Thomas Lord, 14
Hoo, William, 14
Howard, Catherine, 255
Howard, Lady Elizabeth, 13–14, 132
Howard, Lady William, marriage proposal and, 199
Howard, Lord Edmund, 41–2
Howard, Mary, 132, 184
Howard, Thomas, 26, 42, 72–3, 128, 184
Hundred Years War, 2
Hungerford, Walter, 238
Hunne, Richard, 27–8, 40
Husee, John, 41, 238–40, 251, 161, 181

Infante Juan, 18
Innocent VIII (Pope), 57
Ipswich butcher, 1
Ipswich Grammar School, 2
Isabella (queen), 7, 9, 21, 153, 240
Italy, Francis I and war against, 39
Ives, Professor, 14

James (king), 20
James IV (king), 15
Jewellers Row, 31
John (Lord Hussey), 155
John Paul II (Pope), 58
Jordan, Dame Isobel, 86–7
Juana, 9
Julius II (Pope), 27, 93, 121, 172

Katherine of Aragon (Princess), 7–9, 10, 15, 16–18, 32, 35–6, 53, 69, 79
   and Francis I (king), 44–5
   and Henry VIII, 20
   marriage of, 25
Katherine of Aragon (queen), 19–20, 26–7, 42–3, 58, 64–5, 74, **88**
   accusations against, 157
   death of, 206
   deputation to, 124, 141
   divorce and, 78–80, 93, 107–8, 165
   exiled, 129, 141
   final years, 201, 203–6
   and the Legatine Court, 95–6
   letter to Henry VII, 204–5
   pregnancies and, 17–18, 20–1
   support for, 89–90, 93, 130, 167–8
King's Privy Chamber, 65, 76
Kingston, Lady, 229, 249
Kingston, Sir William, 116–19, 120, 228–9, 235, 241
Kite, John, 233
Knights Hospitallers, 37
Knollys, Letttice, 182
Knollys, Sir Francis, 182
Knyvett, Harry, 239

Larke, Joan, 5, 25, 38
Larke, Peter, 25
Larke, Thomas, 25
Latimer, William, 163
Lawrence, Friar, 156–7
League of Peace, 81
Lee, Dr, 124
Legate Latere, 28
Legatine Court, 92, 94–5, 101, 107, 120, 137
   adjournment of, 98–9
Legh, George, 25, 38
Leo X (Pope), 27–9, 44, 51, 54, 56, 62
Life of Jane Dormer (Clifford), 207
Lisle, Lord, 238
Lok, William, 163
London, riots in, 42
Lord Chamberlain, 47
Lord Chancellor, 40–1
Lord Darcy of Templehurst, 9
Lord Mayor, 14
Loredano, Leonardo, 46
Louis XII (king), 13, 21–2, 30, 34
   death of, 32
   and Henry VIII, 21
   marriage of, 30–1
Louise of Savoy, 50
Lovel, Alice, 63
Lovell, Sir Thomas, 9
Low Countries, 148, 163, 198
Luther, Martin, 51
Lydd in Kent, 10

Magdalen, Wolsey's resignation from, 6–7
Magdalen Tower, 5
Marchioness of Exeter, 157

Margaret (Archduchess), 10, 13
Margaret (Princess), 15
Margaret of Angoulême, 50
Margaret of Austria, 18–19, 21–3, 32, 45, 55
Margaret of Savoy, 9
Margaret of Scotland, 91
   divorce and, 104
Marguerite of Navarre (queen), 180
Marlborough, 5
Marquess of Dorset, 4, 6–7, 41
Marquess of Exeter, 155, 160, 241
Mary (queen), 182
Mary, Princess, 10, 21, 30–2, 44–5, 69, 75, 123 159–60, 166–8, 174–80, 195, 199, 205
   birth of, 35–6
   effect of parents' divorce on, 90, 129–30
   escape plan for, 186
   legitimacy of, 97, 109
   marriage proposal and, 55, 199
   marriage to Charles Brandon, 32–4
Mary I (queen), 256, *see also* Mary (princess)
Mary of Suffolk, 48
Mary Tudor, 13, 23, 110
Mass money, 4–5
Master, Richard, 161
Mastership of the School, 6
Maximilian I (emperor), 20, 22, 26, 44
Mechelin, 18, 22
Medici, Alessandro de,' 171
Medici, Cardinal Giulio de,' 52
Medici, Catherine de', 141, 158, 171, 177
Medici, Lorenzo de', 170
Mendoza, Diego Hurtado de, 79, 93–4
Mesa De, Bishop of Elne, 39
Milan question, the, 203–4
Mirror of Naples, 31, 34, 48
Misprision of Treason, 173
monks, 6
   execution of, 187, 191, 198
More, Sir Thomas, 107, 110, 122, 173, **194**
   accusations against, 157
   arrest/imprisonment, 81, 103–4, 161, 188–9, 192–3
   execution of, 193
   resignation of, 127–8
Morton, John (Archbishop), 5
Morton, John (cardinal), 10
Mountjoy, Lord, 21, 152
Musgrave, William, 238

Nanfan, Sir Richard, 7, 9
Netherlands, 9–10, 13
Neville, Edward, 43
Neville, Sir William, 53
Nicander of Colophon, 120
Norfolk, 14, 110, 121, 126
Norris, Henry, 43, 65, 76, 235
   accusations against and arrest, 227
Norris, Sir Henry, 107, 181, 223, 226–7
Northern Alliance, 196
Northumberland, Earl of, 41
Norwich, 5

Index

Oath of Supremacy, 127
Oath to the Succession, 161, *see also* Act of Succession
Observant Friars, as spies, 156
Oratory of the Franciscan Observant Friars at Greenwich, 17
Ormonde fortune, 14
Ortiz, Dr, 125
Oxford, 2, 4

Page, Sir Richard, 235
  arrest/imprisonment, 227
Paget, Sir William, 174
Palace of Richmond, 10
Palmer, Thomas, 237
Papacy, 61
  Wolsey and, 56–8
Papal Legate 'Natus', 28, 51
Papa Nuncio, 140
Parish of St Nicholas, 3
Parker, Jane, 63–4
  children and, 73
Parker, Matthew, 222
Parker, Sir Henry, 63
Parr, Katherine, 255
Parr, Sir Thomas, 35
Pasqualigo, Lorenzo, 31
Passetto di Borgo, 78
Pate, Richard, 200
Paul III (Pope), 171–3, 189–90, 197, 200
Paulet, Sir William, 175, 228
peace treaties, 102, 104
Penizzoni, Girolamo, 159
Percy, Harry, 59–60, 69, 72, 219, 245
  and Anne Boleyn, 128–9
Peto, Friars, 156
Peto, William, 127
Philip of Spain, 256
Philip the Fair of the Netherlands, 9
Plantagenet, Arthur, 133
Plantagenet, Catherine, 35
Plantagenet dynasty, 3
Pole, Arthur, 43
Pole, Lady Margaret, 29, 35
Pollard, A.F., 56
Pommeraye, Giles de la, 125
Poppincourt, Jane, 22
Praemunire, 40, 122–3, 127, 140
Priest, Hugh, 161
Prior of the London Charterhouse, 173
Privy Council, 9
Protestants, 27
Pygot, Thomas, 41

Queen Mother of France, 47
Queen of Naples, 9
Queen of Navarre, 177

Reformation, 232
Regent Margaret, 18
Renée (Princess), 81
Rice, Richard, 123

Rich, Sir Richard, 191–2, **191**
Richard III (king), 2–3, 15, 68, 140
  opposition to, 3
rioters, pardon of, 42–3
Risby, Richard, 161
Rochford, George, 121
Rochford, Lady Jane, 133, 162, 174, 222, 245
Rochford, Lord George, 185
Rochford's Keepership of Bedlam Hospital, 239
Roist, Kaspar, 78
Roper, Margaret, 192–3
Rosemary Lane, 2
Royal Almoner, 10
Royal Supremacy, 173

Sack of Rome, 79–80, 170
St John, Sir John, 63
St Peter's Basilica, 78
St Thomas Aquinas, feast day of, 1
St Thomas of Canterbury, 131
Salic law, 21
Salisbury, Lady Margaret, 65
Sampson, Dr, 124
San Sebastian, 19
Sander, Nicholas, 208
Sands, Sir William, 47
Savage, Anne, 142
Savagnano, 112
Savile, Anne, 142
Schwaben, 197
Scotland, 21
  attack on England, 20
Sechaverell, Sir Richard, 41
secular priests, celibacy and, 6
Seymour, Edward, 195
Seymour, Elizabeth, 209
Seymour, Jane, 142, 201, 208–14, 244
  children and, 254
  pregnancy of, 216
Seymour, Sir John, 195
Sforza II, Francesco Maria, 77, 203–4
Sheffield, Sir Robert, 41
Shelford, Elizabeth, 85
Shelton, Margaret (Madge), 160, 162, 180, 223, 226
Shelton, Sir John, 186
Sidney, Sir William, 34
Sieur de Marigny, 31
Simnel, Lambert, 4
Skelton, John, 38
Smeaton, Mark, 225, 228, 230
  torture of, 224–6, 231
Somers, Will, 194
Spanish Chronicle, 236
Stafford, Edward, 43
Stafford, George (Duke of Buckingham), 52–3, 55
Stafford, Lady Elizabeth, 73
Stafford, Sir Humphrey, 164
Stafford, William, 163, 181–2
Standish, Dr Henry, 40
Stanhope, Anne, 195
Statute of Praemunire, 140

Stewardship of the Abbey, 235
Stokesley, John, 121
Stoner, Mistress, 229
sweating sickness, 85–6
Swiss Guards, 78

Tailboys, Gilbert, 46
Talbot, Gilbert, 26
Talbot, Mary, 59–60, 128
taxation, 61, 67–8, 200–1
Taylor, George, 142
Tempest, Sir Richard, 114
The King's Cardinal (Gwyn), 2
Tilney, Agnes, 73
Torregiano, 10
Tower of London, 116, 136, 167, 192, 226, 244
Trastamaras, 24
treason charges, 52–3
Treaty of Alliance, 125
Treaty of London, 54
Treaty of Madrid, 77
Tudor, Jasper, 132–3
Tunstall, 173
Turks, 44

University of Oxford, registrar of, 5
Uvedale, John, 142

Vasa, Gustavus, 198
Vatican, the, 62, 78
Vaughan, Stephen, 137
Vaux, Sir Nicholas, 47
Vendôme, Duchess de, 131
Venetian Ambassador, 22
Vere, Frances, 126
Vergil, Polydore, 27, 57
Vesey, 114

Walsh, Walter, 115–16
Walsingham, Sir Edmund, 229, 241
Warham, Archbishop William, 25, 28, 39, 130–1
Warren, Sir Ralph, 253
Waynflete, Bishop William, 2
Westminster Hall, 42
Weston, Sir Francis, 76, 223
　arrest/imprisonment, 227
White Hall, 18
Willoughby, Sir Christopher, 41
Wiltshire, Lord, 241
Windsor, Dean of, 31
Windsor, Sir Andrew, 41
Wolman, Richard, 80–1
Wolsey, Jane (née Daundy), 1
Wolsey, Robert, 1–3
　will of, 4–5

Wolsey, Thomas, 1–3, **118**
　accusations against, 5
　and Anne Boleyn, 87, 109, 112–13
　arrest of, 115–16
　bishoprics and, 27, 46
　campaign against, 101–2
　career path of, 7–8, 11
　children of, 5
　the Church and, 5
　claim against, 53–4
　colleges of, 114
　as Dean of Lincoln, 10
　death of, 119
　as determiner, 3
　disrespect shown to, 105
　and divorce of Henry VIII, 78–81, 93–4
　as Fellow of Magdalen, 3
　friendships of, 10
　and Henry VIII, 17, 20–1, 26–30, 42–4, 68, 74–5, 87, 109
　and his work, 40–2
　holy orders and, 4–5
　illness of, 116–19
　as Junior Bursar, 5
　Legatine Court, 99–100
　as Lord Chancellor, 40–1
　loss of power, 106–7, 111–12
　as mentor, 24–6
　and the Papacy, 56–8
　as Papal Legate, 51, 99, 112
　positions wanted by, 27–9
　as Prebendary of York Minster, 26
　and Princess Mary, 35
　as Rector of Limington in Somerset, 6–7, 10
　reforms of, 184
　religious duties and, 113–14
　request for powers, 84
　as Royal Almoner, 11, 25–6
　schools attended by
　　Ipswich Grammar School, 2
　　Oxford, 2
　siding with Rome, 99–100
　and Thomas Boleyn, 18, 97–8
　visit to Scotland, 9
　visit to the Netherlands, 9, 10
　Writ of Praemunire and, 106
'Wolsey's War', 26
Woodville, Elizabeth, 104
wool trade, 3
Worcester, Earl of, 31
Writ of Praemunire, 106
Wyatt, Sir Thomas, 69–70, 235
　arrest/imprisonment, 227

York Place, 38